Health Psychology

The new edition of *Health Psychology* is the perfect introduction to this rapidly developing field. Throughout the book, the psychological processes that shape health-related behaviors and affect core functions, such as the immune and cardiovascular systems, are clearly explained. These relationships provide the foundation for psychological interventions that can change cognition, perception and behavior, thereby improving health.

The book is split into five sections and builds to provide a comprehensive overview of the field:

- the biological bases of health and illness;
- stress and health;
- coping resources: social support and individual differences;
- motivation and behavior;
- relating to patients.

Extensively revised to include new material on behavioral change, the role of stress, resilience and social support, recovery from work and the care of people with chronic disease, the book also includes a range of features that highlight key issues and engage readers in applying what we have learned from research.

This is essential reading for any undergraduates studying this exciting field for the first time and the perfect primer for those embarking on postgraduate study.

Charles Abraham is Professor of Psychology Applied to Health at the University of Exeter Medical School.

Mark Conner is Professor of Applied Social Psychology at the University of Leeds.

Fiona Jones is Visiting Senior Research Fellow in the Institute of Psychological Sciences, University of Leeds.

Daryl O'Connor is Professor of Psychology at the University of Leeds.

Topics in Applied Psychology

Series Editor: Graham Davey, Professor of Psychology at the University of Sussex, UK, and former president of the British Psychological Society.

Topics in Applied Psychology is a series of accessible, integrated textbooks ideal for courses in applied psychology. Written by leading figures in their field, the books provide a comprehensive academic and professional overview of the subject area, bringing the topics to life through a range of features, including personal stories, case studies, ethical debates and learner activities. Each book addresses a broad range of cutting-edge topics, providing students with both theoretical foundations and real-life applications.

Clinical Psychology
Second Edition
Graham Davey

Educational Psychology
Second Edition
Tony Cline, Anthea Gulliford and Susan Birch

Work and Organizational Psychology
Second Edition
Ian Rothmann and Cary Cooper

Sport and Exercise Psychology
Second Edition
Andy Lane

Health Psychology
Second Edition
Charles Abraham, Mark Conner, Fiona Jones and Daryl O'Conner

Criminal Psychology
Second Edition
David Canter

Health Psychology

Second edition

Charles Abraham, Mark Conner, Fiona Jones and Daryl O'Connor

Routledge
Taylor & Francis Group

LONDON AND NEW YORK

Second edition published 2016
by Routledge
2 Park Square, Milton Park, Abingdon, Oxon OX14 4RN

and by Routledge
711 Third Avenue, New York, NY 10017

Routledge is an imprint of the Taylor & Francis Group, an informa business

First edition published 2008 by Hodder.

British Library Cataloguing in Publication Data
A catalogue record for this book is available from the British Library

Library of Congress Cataloging in Publication Data
Names: Abraham, Charles. | Conner, Mark, 1962– | Jones, Fiona (Psychologist) |
O'Connor, Daryl (Daryl Brian)
Title: Health psychology/Charles Abraham, Mark Conner, Fiona Jones &
Daryl O'Connor.
Description: 2 [2nd edition]. | Abingdon, Oxon; New York, NY :
Routledge, 2016. | Previous edition: Health psychology: topics in applied psychology
(London: Hodder Education, 2008). | Includes bibliographical references and index.
Identifiers: LCCN 2015047068| ISBN 9781138023390 (hardback: alk. paper) |
ISBN 9781138023406 (pbk.: alk. paper) | ISBN 9781315776453 (e-book)
Subjects: LCSH: Clinical health psychology.
Classification: LCC R726.7 .H44 2016 | DDC 616.001/9 – dc23
LC record available at http://lccn.loc.gov/2015047068

ISBN: 978-1-138-02339-0 (hbk)
ISBN: 978-1-138-02340-6 (pbk)
ISBN: 978-1-315-77645-3 (ebk)

Typeset in Bembo and Univers
by Florence Production Ltd, Stoodleigh, Devon, UK

Printed and bound by CPI Group (UK) Ltd, Croydon, CR0 4YY

Contents

Series preface

Psychology is still one of the most popular subjects for study at undergraduate degree level. As well as providing the student with a range of academic and applied skills that are valued by a broad range of employers, a psychology degree also serves as the basis for subsequent training and a career in professional psychology. A substantial proportion of students entering a degree programme in psychology do so with a subsequent career in applied psychology firmly in mind, and as a result the number of applied psychology courses available at undergraduate level has significantly increased over recent years. In some cases these courses supplement core academic areas and in others they provide the student with a flavour of what they might experience as a professional psychologist.

The original series of *Topics in Applied Psychology* consisted of six textbooks designed to provide a comprehensive academic and professional insight into specific areas of professional psychology. The texts covered the areas of *Clinical Psychology*, *Criminal Psychology*, *Educational Psychology*, *Health Psychology*, *Sports and Exercise Psychology* and *Work and Organizational Psychology* and each text was written and edited by the foremost professional and academic figures in each of these areas.

These texts were so successful that we are now able to provide you with a second edition of this series. All texts have been updated with details of recent professional developments as well as relevant research and we have responded to the requests of teachers and reviewers to include new material and new approaches to this material. Perhaps most significantly, all texts in the series will now have back-up web resources.

Just as in the first series, each textbook is based on a similar academic formula that combines a comprehensive review of cutting-edge research and professional knowledge with accessible teaching and learning features. The books are also structured so they can be used as an integrated teaching support for a one-term or one-semester course in each of their relevant areas of applied psychology. Given the increasing importance of applying psychological knowledge across a growing range of areas of practice, we feel this series is timely and comprehensive. We hope you find each book in the series readable, enlightening, accessible and instructive.

Graham Davey
University of Sussex, Brighton, UK
August 2014

Preface

Health psychology is an area of applied psychological research and a profession. Psychological research has established how perceptions, cognitions and behaviour patterns affect physiological processes such as those constituting the cardiovascular, endocrine and immune systems. These physiological processes, in turn, determine symptomatology, morbidity and mortality. Our perceptions, cognitions and behaviour patterns are strongly influenced by our social interactions. Consequently health psychology research is inherently biopsychosocial.

Health psychology research examines the determinants and consequences of physical rather than mental health and illness (which, in the UK, is the focus of clinical psychology). This area of research is becoming increasingly important since it is clear that (1) health behaviour patterns are critical to health; and (2) without effective promotion of health-preserving lifestyles it will become impossible to fund the treatment of those with ill health and chronic illness. Comprehensive and widely accessible health services depend on the population being engaged in protecting and maintaining good health. In addition, health psychology brings useful methodological tools to outcome and process evaluations of interventions to change perceptions, cognitions and health behaviour patterns. Consequently, there is an increasing need to provide health care professionals with health-psychology-based skills (e.g. in relation to stress reduction and health-behaviour change) and to employ health psychologists in health care services.

Health psychology is now making an important contribution to undergraduate degree programmes (at all levels) and a substantial proportion of undergraduate students (in psychology and applied health) study health psychology. The purpose of this book is to introduce undergraduate students to health psychology research and to illustrate the links between such research and health psychology practice (e.g. in relation to health behaviour change). The book will prepare students for final examinations in health psychology at undergraduate level and provide a solid foundation for students wishing to pursue graduate studies in health psychology. The book has a UK and European perspective but is relevant to any health care system. It is divided into five sections: (1) the biological bases of health and illness; (2) stress and health; (3) coping resources: social support and individual differences; (4) motivation and behaviour; and (5) relating to patients. Throughout the book, we discuss health-related perceptions and behaviours and explain how psychological processes (e.g. emotional responses) shape health-related behaviours and affect physiological systems such as the immune and cardiovascular systems. These relationships provide the foundation for psychological interventions, which can change cognition, perception and behaviour and thereby improve health.

As with all the books in the *Topics in Applied Psychology* series, this text is written as a support for a one-term or one-semester course. *Health Psychology* contains a range of teaching and learning features such as focus boxes, research methods boxes, activity boxes (supporting students to engage actively with presented material), as well as consideration of issues of contemporary interest (including developments within the UK National Health Service (NHS), the National Institute for Health and Clinical Excellence (NICE) and the Health and Safety Executive (HSE)). Each chapter also ends with support for further reading, including relevant journal articles and books, which will enable the interested student to engage with key topics in more depth.

The aim of this book is to provide the undergraduate student with a concise, readable, structured introduction to health psychology. We have focused on core topics that define the sub-discipline and linked these together so that the text can be read as a continuous course. All of the authors teach health psychology to undergraduates and postgraduates and we hope that, like us, readers will be inspired by the findings of health psychology research and the impact of health psychology practice. The second edition of the book provides an update on the exciting and growing area of health psychology.

Charles Abraham, Mark Conner, Fiona Jones and Daryl O'Connor
October 2015

1 Introduction

This book provides a concise, one-term course covering core topics in health psychology suitable for undergraduate or masters study in psychology or specialist health programmes. We discuss the origins and definition of the sub-discipline as well as considering evidence identifying processes that affect psychological well-being, physiological functioning, health behaviour patterns, behaviour change, usage of health services and responses to health services, such as following medical advice.

CHAPTER PLAN

In this chapter we discuss definitions of health psychology as an academic discipline and as a profession. We also consider other academic traditions that have contributed to the development of health psychology illustrating the rich mix of theories, methodologies and practice, which make health psychology what it is today. In addition, we offer guidance on using the book and studying health psychology generally, including introducing the structure and topic order used in this book.

   This chapter has four sections: (1) what is health psychology?; (2) foundations of health psychology; (3) using this book effectively; and (4) the structure and content of this book.

LEARNING OUTCOMES

When you have completed this chapter you should be able to:

1 Define and describe the discipline and profession of health psychology.
2 Identify psychological sub-disciplines that contribute to health psychology research and practice.
3 Explain what is meant by the biopsychosocial model of health and illness.
4 Understand how this book is structured and how to study it effectively.

WHAT IS HEALTH PSYCHOLOGY?

The World Health Organization (1948) defines health as 'a state of complete physical, mental and social well-being and not merely the absence of disease or infirmity'. This definition, which has not been amended since 1948, challenges psychologists to define and assess the determinants of 'physical, mental and social well being'. Within UK psychology there has been a division between health psychology, which focuses on physical health, and clinical psychology, which focuses on mental health. The two sub-disciplines overlap because psychological processes that affect physical health are also important to mental health. For example, anxiety and stress responses have important consequences for both physical and mental health and the broader social well-being of an individual.

The following broad definition of health psychology was provided by Matarazzo (1980: 118):

> Health psychology is an aggregate of the educational, scientific and professional contributions of the discipline of psychology to the promotion and maintenance of health, the prevention and treatment of illness, the identification of etiologic and diagnostic correlates of health, illness and related dysfunction and the improvement of the health care system and health policy formation.

This much-cited definition is usefully inclusive and highlights (1) the overarching aims of the sub-discipline, namely, promoting health and preventing illness; (2) the scientific focus of research in health psychology, that is, understanding etiologic and diagnostic correlates of health; and (3) key priorities of professional practice in health psychology, that is, improving health care by focusing on delivery systems and policy.

Health psychologists seek to understand the processes that link individual perceptions, beliefs and behaviours to biological processes, which, in turn, result in physical health problems and the processes by which they can be ameliorated or cured. For example, how a person perceives work demands and copes with them will determine his/her stress levels (see Chapter 3), which, in turn, may affect the functioning of the cardiovascular and immune systems (see Chapter 2). Health psychologists also study social processes including the effect of wider social structure (such as socio-economic status) and face-to-face interactions with others (e.g. work colleagues) because these social processes shape perceptions, beliefs and behaviour (see Chapter 4). In addition, health psychologists explore individual processes that shape health outcomes and health behaviour patterns (see Chapters 6 and 7) and social processes, which influence the effectiveness of health care delivery. For example, the way health care professionals communicate with their patients influences patient behaviour, including patients' willingness to take medication and adopt health-enhancing behaviours (see Chapters 8 and 10). Since most health and medical interventions depend both on the behaviour of health care professionals and, critically, on the behaviour of patients, behaviour change processes determine the potential of health service delivery.

When research allows us to develop good models of underlying causal processes this establishes the evidence base for the design of interventions capable of changing psychological functioning (see Chapter 8) and behaviour patterns (see Chapter 9). This enables us to provide guidance that can enhance the effectiveness and cost–effectiveness of health care services. Professional health psychologists use research findings to assess individuals and design and evaluate interventions that change perceptions, beliefs, behaviours and social relationships, which affect health-related behaviour patterns, quality of life and physical health. These interventions operate at different levels ranging from those focusing on the individual to those designed to change society, i.e. targeting, on the one hand, individual health and, on the other, public health (see Chapter 9).

We will examine the determinants of health behaviours, highlight the impact they have on health and health care delivery and consider how we can change such behaviour. Health behaviours have a crucial impact on individual and public health. The Alameda County study, which followed nearly 7,000 people over 10 years, revealed that sleep, exercise, drinking alcohol and eating habits predict mortality (Belloc and Breslow, 1972). Moreover, the leading causes of death in the US in 2000 were tobacco use (18.1 per cent), poor diet and physical inactivity (16.6 per cent) and alcohol consumption (3.5 per cent) accounting collectively for almost 40 per cent of all deaths (Mokdad et al., 2004). Similar findings emerge from other population studies. For example, in the UK, Khaw et al. (2008) measured four key health behaviours among people with no known cardiovascular disease or cancer. These behaviours were (1) not smoking; (2) being physically active; (3) only drinking alcohol moderately; and (4) plasma vitamins indicating consumption of five portions of fruit and vegetables a day. Eleven years later more than 20,000 people were followed up. Results showed that, controlling for age, gender, body mass index and socio-economic status, those engaging in none of the four behaviours were more than four times more likely to have died than those engaging in all four. The researchers note that this effect is equivalent to those who engaged in four behaviours having the health of someone 14 years younger than those who engaged in none! Health behaviours are not just relevant to our early and middle years but to older people as well. Yates et al. (2008) studied a sample of 2,357 healthy men aged 70 and examined the predictors of mortality over the next 20 years. A healthy 70-year-old had a 54 per cent chance of living to be 90 but this reduced to 44 per cent if he had a sedentary lifestyle, 36 per cent if he had hypertension, 26 per cent if he was obese and only 22 per cent if he smoked. The percentage living to be 90 dropped to only 14 per cent if three of these factors were present. So promoting health behaviours among 70-year-olds is important because of the years of life that can be gained.

It is not surprising, therefore, that a review of the UK National Health Service concluded that its long-term effectiveness and economic viability depended on more successful disease prevention strategies and high levels of public engagement in health care and maintenance (Wanless, 2002). The economic implications of promoting preventive health behaviours, minimising demands on health services and supporting people coping with chronic illness are substantial (e.g. see Chapters 8 and 10). For example, in 2014, it was reported that more than 130 million days a year are lost to sickness absence in Great Britain, which has a substantial impact on workers, employers and taxpayers (Department of Work and Pensions, 2015). Consequently, research-based interventions to prevent illness, enhance coping with chronic illness and reduce health service demand have the potential to make a substantial difference to public health and the efficiency of health services (Friedman et al., 1995).

Psychological processes can have direct and indirect effects on health and illness. The indirect effects are frequently referred to as behavioural pathways because they provide an explanation as to how psychological factors such as stress can indirectly influence health by producing positive or negative changes in health behaviours (e.g. exercise, diet, smoking). Direct effects are often referred to as psychophysiological pathways because they help us understand how psychological factors can directly impact on the body's physical systems such as the immune or cardiovascular systems (see Chapter 2). Feeling anxious or stressed changes physiological processes and cumulatively these effects can damage physical systems and so compromise health. A number of studies have found that people who frequently have relatively large physiological responses to stress are more likely to develop serious illnesses in the future. For example, the Kuopio Heart Study, which has been following over 2,500 men for the last 25 years in Finland, found that men who had large increases in blood pressure or heart rate when they felt stressed at the beginning of the study were more likely to have had a stroke or to have developed hypertension many years later (Everson *et al.*, 1996a; Everson *et al.*, 2001). These researchers suggested that the experience of frequent daily stressors over time lead to excessive wear and tear of the cardiovascular system and ultimately to poorer health and earlier death of these 'reactive' individuals. Psychological processes can also initiate healing processes. These explain what are referred to as placebo effects and a better understanding of these processes could enable health care professionals to harness patients' own, internal healing processes.

FOUNDATIONS OF HEALTH PSYCHOLOGY

Hippocrates is credited with the establishment of the medical professional and the Hippocratic Oath. He was born around 460 BC on the Greek island of Kos and sought to understand the processes that cause a variety of illnesses. While this search for causal processes seems self-evident to us it was a formative step in the development of scientific medicine. Hippocrates also linked behaviour, including diet, to health and emphasized the healing power of the doctor–patient relationship. These topics remain key areas of health psychology research today.

More than half a millenium later, in the second century AD, the Greek leader Diogenes commissioned a wall etched with core messages taken from the teachings of the philosopher Epicurus in the city of Oenoanda in Lycia. The wall included 25,000 words written over 260 square metres and emphasized the importance of quality of life, self-reflection and self-regulation (see Chapter 9). This wall can be viewed as one of the first public health campaigns designed to enhance the lifestyle and quality of life of the general population. Nearly 2,000 years later, we are still designing and evaluating such interventions (see Chapters 8 and 9), although we have more accessible and interactive media now, including websites, podcasts and smartphones! Thus the questions and concerns that define health psychology are millennia old and intricately interwoven into the development of medicine.

Modern medicine is founded on basic research, which revealed the biological processes that constitute health and illness. Painstaking studies of human physiology over many centuries together with key scientific breakthroughs have provided the foundation for understanding how the body's systems work. Breakthroughs included understanding the nature of respiration, clarifying that specific bacteria cause particular illnesses, discovering compounds that kill bacteria and showing how vaccination works. Such research continues today but we already have good models of how physiological systems (such as the immune and cardiovascular system) operate. It is these models that allow effective medical intervention through diagnosis and treatment. The science of health psychology has important contributions to make because we now know that psychological processes and behaviour patterns affect the operation of these bodily systems and are important determinants of health and illness. Thus a key strand of health psychology research focuses on clarifying how psychological responses and behaviour impact on the body's physiological systems (see Chapters 2 and 10).

Health psychology also has its origins in early cognitive and social psychology as well as behaviourism. Wundt established the first experimental psychological laboratory at the University of Leipzig in 1879 and he is credited with establishing psychology as a research discipline. In the early part of the twentieth century, learning theorists including Pavlov, Watson and Skinner established the behaviourist school of psychology, which focused on observable behaviour and on learning (e.g. through classical and operant conditioning; Skinner, 1974). The success of behaviourism in explaining behaviour and providing tools with which to change behaviour was critical to the recognition that professional psychology had an important contribution to make to the management of behaviour relevant to mental and physical health. The role of learning theory in health behaviour change interventions is still under investigation by health psychologists today (e.g. Hegel et al., 1992; and see Chapter 9).

Wundt had studied internal individual processes including attention and use of imagery. Later work clarified that even when explaining how rats learn to run mazes we require a psychology of internal representation. Tolman (1948) found that rats learned mazes even when the behaviour was not reinforced and concluded that they had developed internal cognitive maps. This was an important development in what we now think of as cognitive psychology, which seeks to understand the kind of representations of reality that are necessary to explain people's behaviour and how we process information (cf. Neisser, 1967). Developing models of how people perceive and understand their reality and in particular their health and illnesses, is central to health psychology research (see Chapters 7, 8 and 10).

The sub-discipline of social psychology became established when researchers focused on the effects of others on our behaviour (e.g. Triplett, 1898). Social psychologists applied experimental methods to understanding how we perceive and represent others, how others influence us and how our position in wider society shapes our beliefs, attitudes and behaviour (cf. Allport, 1924; Sherif, 1936). These processes are important to health psychologists because health-relevant perceptions and behaviours are affected by others. For example, interactions with work colleagues may cause stress and interactions with health care professionals may change beliefs and motivations relevant to taking medication (see Chapters 4 and 10).

Thus health psychology draws upon the methods and theories of a range of sub-disciplines within psychology including learning theory, psychobiology, cognitive psychology and social psychology. More recently collaboration between psychologists and neuroscientists has generated new insights. For example, researchers have developed a standardized way of assessing the extent to which features in a video (such as an advertisement) arouse and engage attention referred to as 'message sensation value'(Seelig *et al.*, 2014). Health psychology research applies these various theories and methods in order to better understand how our perceptions, beliefs and behaviour can maintain health or cause illness. The recognition that health (or illness) results from the interaction of biological characteristics and processes (including genetic predispositions and physiological mechanisms), psychological processes (including perceptions, beliefs and behaviours) and social processes and contexts (including social structure, cultural influences and interpersonal relationships) is what is meant by adopting a *biopsychosocial model* (Schwartz, 1980) of health and illness. This biopsychosocial perspective is central to current health psychology research and practice.

The profession of health psychology was institutionalized in 1978 when the Division of Health Psychology of the American Psychology Association (APA) was established. The European Health Psychology Society (EHPS) was established in 1986 in Tilberg and, in the UK, the Division of Health Psychology of the British Psychology Society (BPS) first met in January 1998. The establishment of these organisational structures recognized the profession of health psychology and allowed research-based training courses to be set up to train professional health psychologists worldwide (see Chapter 11). These organizations also provided a focus for research by arranging conferences and sponsoring academic journals. For example, the journal *Health Psychology* is published by the APA, *Psychology and Health* and *Health Psychology Review* are published by the EHPS and the *British Journal of Health Psychology* is published by the BPS. Other journals publishing health psychology research include: *Journal of Behavioral Medicine, Preventive Medicine, Social Science and Medicine, Journal of Health Psychology, Health Education Research, Patient Education and Counselling, Annals of Behavioral Medicine* and *Psychology and Health and Medicine.*

USING THIS BOOK EFFECTIVELY

In each chapter of this book we have included brief chapter plans, learning outcomes, lists of terms introduced, individual and/or group exercises and short lists of recommended additional readings. These are designed to help you actively learn as you proceed through the course. In Chapter 8, we note that lasting cognitive change depends on systematic processing of incoming messages involving active engagement with the content. This includes linking content to prior knowledge and, critically, evaluating it in terms of pre-existing standards and principles. In building your expertise in health psychology you are managing your own cognitive development. So how can you facilitate systematic processing of the material in this book?

It is important to read the chapter plans and learning outcomes before reading the chapters to develop an overview of the material. Then at the end of each chapter check that you understand the terms introduced and that you can now do whatever is specified in the learning objectives. Testing yourself by checking through previous learning objectives and planning essays is also important. Research has found that testing improves retention compared to just studying and that this is true even if the test is never marked (Roediger and Karpicke, 2006)! Testing is a central part of learning. It is not just an assessment tool. Testing can also work well when students work together in a study groups.

You should read papers from our additional reading lists and make your own notes on these papers and the chapters in this book. Research has shown that making notes enhances learning and the transfer of learning from one topic to another (e.g. Wittrock and Alesandrini, 1990). Your notes are not just useful for revision. Making them will enhance your learning even if you do not consult them later.

When reading empirical papers it may be helpful to think of them as boxes that contain things you want rather than stories that need to be read from beginning to end. You might try reading the abstract first and then the first couple of paragraphs of the discussion to get a good overview of the paper before you decide what else you need to know about it. When reading a paper reporting an empirical study it is useful to check that you can answer the questions highlighted in Activity 1.1.

ACTIVITY 1.1

Reading empirical papers

Try reading an empirical paper and answering the questions below. For example you could try reading the following paper, which is highlighted as an additional reading in Chapter 9.

> Luszczynska, A., Sobczyk, A. and Abraham, C., (2007). Planning to lose weight: RCT of an implementation intention prompt to enhance weight reduction among overweight and obese women. *Health Psychology*, 26, 507–512.

What kind of study is reported? For example is it an experiment, a correlational study (cross-sectional or longitudinal), a qualitative analysis of text or interview data, or a review (narrative, systematic or meta-analysis)?

What are the independent variables and which are the dependent variables (or outcome measures)? Are there any mediating or moderating variables (see Research methods 3.1)?

How do the measures used relate to measures of these (or similar) constructs in other studies? Are the measures reliable? Do they have good construct and predictive validity?

Are there any confounding variables? Have these been controlled for?

What population is studied? How does this relate to other populations studied in this area?

What are the key findings?

Is the sample size adequate? Is the sample representative? Can we generalize from these findings? If so, what are the limits to this generalization?

Does the study suggest any new theoretical development/s? What further research should be undertaken to explore questions arising from the results or problems with the study's methodology?

Does the study have practice and/or policy implications?

Does the study need to be replicated?

Planning and writing essays are also effective ways to test and develop your understanding of a topic. You may have a well-developed approach to writing essays but it may be useful to revise the points in Focus 1.1 when thinking about your next health psychology essay.

FOCUS 1.1

Essay writing

First make sure you understand the question. The question will direct you towards particular readings and research and perhaps ask you to treat these in a particular way – e.g. 'discuss', 'contrast', etc. Make sure you have good plan, which sets out a clear structure for your essay that corresponds to what the question asks. Also try to ensure that you know how your arguments link together (e.g. using a diagram).

In the opening sections ensure your title makes sense to the reader by providing any necessary definitions and explanations. Also outline and explain your objectives in writing the essay – what do you intend to argue and achieve in the essay – how is this linked to previous research? Use appropriate references to anchor your essay to previous research findings.

The main body of your essay will convey your core arguments, which have been outlined in the introduction. Think about the following points.

You should be able to summarize your essay as a series of core arguments or points. It is often helpful to state these explicitly early on in the relevant paragraph. For example, 'I will highlight one strength and two weaknesses in this theory. First . . .' Then for each of these (three) arguments, consider what evidence and illustrations you need.

Be precise about theoretical distinctions and definitions and avoid lapsing into lay psychology.

Know the data you are discussing. Be specific about measures and methods used and illustrate measures where this clarifies a construct or a methodological critique. Support your arguments with data (e.g. means, correlations or effect sizes). This can emphasize the strength or weakness of an association or the effect of an intervention and, thereby, strengthen an argument or critique. However, it is uninformative to provide 'p' values alone without references to statistics that convey size of associations, differences or effects.

Note too that, sometimes, an anecdote or case study can illustrate a point in a concrete way.

Reference claims you make about previous findings using author names and dates. Your essay is about research findings so avoid unsupported claims. Use American Psychological Association (APA) referencing rules unless told otherwise by your tutor.

Link your arguments. Each paragraph should lead onto the next and the introduction should link clearly to the conclusion. You may want to make this explicit, e.g. 'The study by Brown (2003) outlined above also emphasizes . . .'

Make links across the reading you have completed for the course.

Provide a short conclusion at the end of the essay. This should summarize your main points and highlight connections between them. In many essays this will also be the opportunity to succinctly state what you think needs to be done next, in terms of further research, intervention, adoption or policy changes (including implications for health care practice and social policy).

You may have been told correctly that your psychology essays are not about your opinion but about research findings. However, a good essay will involve a personal synthesis of research, including your evaluations of findings and your evidence-based conclusions (e.g. the weight of the evidence suggests . . .). Do not be afraid to draw your own conclusions – it's your essay.

Finally, make sure you provide a complete set of references (i.e. all papers, books, etc. that you have referred to in your text in APA format).

THE STRUCTURE AND CONTENT OF THIS BOOK

The book is divided into five sections: (1) biological bases of health and illness; (2) stress and illness; (3) coping resources: social support and individual differences; (4) motivation and behaviour; and, finally (5) relating to and caring for patients.

Chapter 2 deals with the body's physical systems such as the central nervous system, the endocrine system and the immune system. We then consider how these basic biological processes may be influenced by psychological factors such as stress. A brief overview of the role of psychological processes in the experience of pain is also provided. This chapter finishes by introducing important developments linking psychological factors to immune function.

In Chapters 3 and 4 we review and critically appraise research into the nature of stress. We introduce key theories and methodologies used in researching stress and examine its impacts on health. In Chapter 3 we introduce theories that viewed stress primarily as a physiological phenomenon, before moving on to more contemporary approaches examining the impact of major life events and day-to-day hassles on health. We also consider possible pathways for links between stress and disease. In Chapter 4 we focus on specific environmental or contextual factors that have been prominent in stress research and have been shown to affect health, in particular, social inequality and employment factors. Models of work stress are discussed and evidence relating work stress to disease is considered. We conclude by examining the role of organizational change and worksite interventions in reducing stress, foreshadowing our focus on behaviour change in Chapter 9.

In Chapters 5 and 6 we focus on key individual differences between people that affect the way in which environmental factors (such as stress or social inequality) impact on health. These factors are said to 'moderate' the relationships between the environment and an outcome such as stress. In Chapter 5 the focus is on individual differences in the ways that people cope and in the types of social support they receive. We first consider types of coping strategies that individuals use and whether these are consistent across situations (i.e. whether people have their own coping style). We review the effect that such styles have on health. We then consider different types of social support and their value for preventing illness. In Chapter 6 we review work on how personality factors influence health. Much of this research focuses on the Big Five dimensions of personality: openness, conscientiousness, extraversion, agreeableness and neuroticism. Several of these personality dimensions have important consequences for health including how long we can expect to live. A key issue addressed in this chapter is the nature of mechanisms by which personality factors affect health outcomes. So, for example, the personality trait of conscientiousness appears to exert effects on health outcomes by influencing the extent to which individuals will engage in health behaviours.

In Chapters 7–9 we focus on motivation and behaviour. In Chapter 7 we examine models that identify beliefs, attitudes and intentions (that is *cognitions*), which predict individual behaviour. We note the success of these models in predicting behaviour using prospective surveys and objective measures. These models identify potentially modifiable determinants of behaviour patterns (including, e.g. attitudes), which, if changed, would lead to changes in health behaviour patterns. In Chapter 8 we discuss methods used to change these cognitions, including use of information provision and social influence and note some of the pitfalls that health educators must avoid in using these methods. We highlight how best to change attitudes using persuasive methods and also discuss how self-efficacy can be enhanced. This leads directly into approaches to behaviour change and we consider how behaviour change interventions need to be carefully planned, implemented and evaluated if they are to contribute to health promotion. We identify key features of behaviour change interventions and highlight a range of change techniques that may be employed in such interventions.

In Chapter 10 we focus on interactions between health care professionals and patients, examining the processes that prompt medical help seeking and the reasons why some patients follow advice given by health care professionals, while others do not. We consider consultation management in some detail and discuss the particular needs of people with long-term illness. We explore the role of complementary therapies in health care and explain why people may show health benefit even when they have only received a placebo treatment such as a sugar pill. Research in these areas clearly highlights the importance of consultation management to patients' satisfaction, adherence and health. Cognitive and emotional care affects health-related behaviour and health over and above the pharmacological effects of medication. Psychological interventions are especially important to patients with long-term illnesses and have been shown to be effective in pain management.

We draw to a close in Chapter 11 by reflecting on current and future developments in health psychology research, the professional roles health psychologists may occupy and the competencies required to practise in those roles.

KEY CONCEPTS AND TERMS

- American Psychology Association
- Behaviour change
- Biopsychosocial model
- British Psychology Society
- Classical and operant conditioning
- Cognitive maps
- Direct and indirect effects on health

- Essay writing
- Etiologic
- European Health Psychology Society
- Health behaviours
- Hippocrates
- Making notes
- Professional practice
- Promoting health and preventing illness etiologic and diagnostic correlates of health

- Psychophysiological pathways
- Public health campaigns
- Social influence
- Systematic processing
- Testing
- World Health Organization

SUMMARY

Health psychology aims to promote health and prevent illness through scientific research that elucidates psychological processes linked to health. Evidence-based causal models provide the basis for effective interventions that may enhance health by changing psychological processes. Interventions designed to change demand for health services can have substantial effects on the cost-effectiveness of services. Emotional responses and health behaviours have been shown to have important measurable effects on morbidity and mortality. Behavioural effects are referred to as indirect effects whereas psychological processes, which affect health through psychophysiological pathways, are referred to as direct effects.

The origins of health psychology research can be seen in the teaching of ancient Greek philosophers and more recently in the application of learning theory, cognitive theories and social psychological theories to health and health behaviour. The biopsychosocial model incorporates biological, psychological and social processes.

You will learn more effectively if you (1) read chapter plans and learning outcomes before reading chapters; and (2) check that you understand terms introduced and that you can do what is specified in the learning objectives at the end of each chapter. Taking notes, reading recommended additional readings and writing essays will also consolidate your learning.

FIGURE 1.1 Structured learning makes studying easier.

Source: Copyright Lucky Business/Shutterstock.com.

SAMPLE ESSAY TITLE

• Discuss the main theoretical concepts that underpin research and practice in health psychology today.

FURTHER READING

Journal articles

Adler, N. and Matthews, K. (1994). Health psychology: Why do some people get sick and some stay well? *Annual Review of Psychology*, 45, 229–259.

Schwartz, G.E. (1980). Testing the biopsychosocial model: The ultimate challenge facing behavioural medicine? *Journal of Consulting and Clinical Psychology*, 50, 1040–1053.

1 | Biological bases of health and illness

2 Biopsychosocial pathways to health and illness

CHAPTER PLAN

In Chapter 1, we introduced health psychology as a discipline, the biopsychosocial model of health and illness, the context in which health psychology research takes place and areas studied. In this chapter we consider the main psychophysiological pathways through which psychological factors impact on physical health and illness.

We discuss the body's physical systems including the central nervous system, the endocrine system, the cardiovascular system and the immune system. We then consider how these basic biological processes may be influenced by psychological factors such as stress. In particular, we will describe how activation of the hypothalamic–pituitary–adrenal (HPA) axis and the sympathetic adrenal medullary (SAM) system are linked to increased cardiovascular disease. Next, we present a brief overview of the role of psychological factors in the experience of pain and gate-control theory. Finally, we introduce important developments in the area of psychoneuroimmunology and discuss how psychological factors can affect the immune system within the context of susceptibility to upper respiratory illness and the speed of wound healing.

The chapter is composed of five sections: (1) basic features of the nervous system; (2) the stress response; (3) biopsychosocial aspects of pain; (4) psychoneuroimmunology; and (5) stress and the immune system.

LEARNING OUTCOMES

When you have completed this chapter you should be able to:

1 Describe the basic features of the central nervous system.
2 Explain how activation of the hypothalamic–pituitary–adrenal (HPA) axis and the sympathetic adrenal medullary (SAM) system links to stress and health.
3 Understand the role of psychological factors in the experience of pain.
4 Discuss how psychoneuroimmunology (PNI) plays a role in illness processes.
5 Design an experiment to examine the effects of psychological stress on health outcomes within a laboratory setting.

WHAT IS THE BIOPSYCHOSOCIAL PERSPECTIVE ON HEALTH AND ILLNESS?

As outlined in Chapter 1, the biopsychosocial model postulates that health and illness are influenced by psychological factors (e.g. cognition, emotion, personality), social factors (e.g. people in your social world, social class, ethnicity) and biological factors (e.g. viruses, lesions, bacteria). Within this context, there is increasing evidence that psychological factors such as stress affect health directly, through autonomic and neuro-endocrine responses (e.g. blood pressure and hormonal changes), but also indirectly, through changes to health behaviours (e.g. exercise, diet, smoking). The direct effects of stress on health are often referred to as psychophysiological pathways because they help us understand how psychological factors can directly impact on physiological disease-related processes. The indirect effects are frequently referred to as the behavioural pathways as they provide an explanation as to how psychological factors can indirectly influence disease-related processes by producing negative changes in health behaviours. This chapter describes the main psychophysiological pathways that may influence health and illness, while the key behavioural pathways are considered in Chapter 3. Before the direct effects are considered in more detail, we introduce you to the basic features of the nervous system. It is paramount that you understand some of the basic biological processes constituting the human body in order to gain a good understanding of the psychophysiology of health and illness. Throughout this book we use activity boxes to consolidate your learning and there is one just beyond the next section so read carefully!

BASIC FEATURES OF THE NERVOUS SYSTEM

The role of the nervous system is to allow us to adapt to changes within our body and environment by using our five senses (touch, sight, smell, taste, sound) to understand, interpret and respond to internal and external changes quickly and appropriately. The nervous system consists of the brain, the spinal cord and the nerves (bundles of fibres that transmit information in and out of the nervous system). The brain is the central part of the nervous system and it helps control our behaviour. It receives and sends messages for the rest of the body through the spinal cord. The brain has three major anatomic components: the forebrain, the midbrain and the hindbrain.

The anatomy of the brain

The forebrain consists of dense, elaborate masses of tissue and has two main subdivisions:

1   The *telencephalon*, which is composed of the cerebrum and limbic system.
2   The *diencephalon*, which comprises the thalamus and hypothalamus.

The cerebrum is the largest part of the human brain and is divided into the two halves – the left and right cerebral hemispheres – that are connected in the middle by a bundle of nerve fibres called the corpus callosum. The upper part of the cerebrum is the cerebral cortex (its outermost area). This is subdivided into the frontal, parietal, occipital and temporal lobes and controls higher processes such as speaking, reasoning, memory, etc. (see Figure 2.1). More specifically, the frontal lobe (located towards the front of the cerebrum) is involved in speech, thought and emotion. Behind this is the parietal lobe, which perceives and interprets sensations like touch, temperature and pain. The occipital lobe is at the centre back of the cerebrum and detects and interprets visual images. Finally, the temporal lobes located on either side are involved in hearing and aspects of memory storage. The limbic system is evolutionarily older than other parts of the brain and consists of the amygdala and hippocampus among other structures (not shown below). This system interacts with the endocrine system (a network of glands that secrete hormones throughout the body, described later) and the autonomic nervous system (ANS) and plays an important role in motivational and emotional aspects of behaviours such as sex, eating, drinking and aggression. It is also involved in aspects of memory processes.

The second major division of the forebrain is the diencephalon. Its two most important structures are the thalamus and the hypothalamus (see Figure 2.1). The thalamus is thought to have multiple functions and plays an important role in regulating states of sleep, arousal and consciousness. The hypothalamus is located below the thalamus and although it is a relatively small structure it is very important as it regulates

Median section of the brain

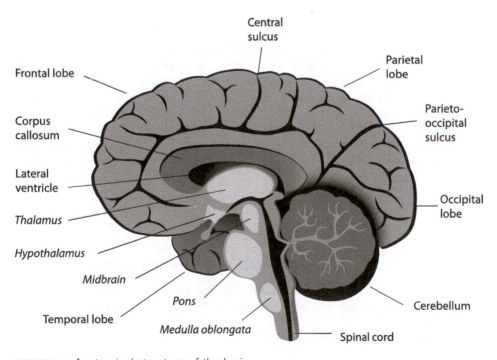

FIGURE 2.1 Anatomical structure of the brain.

Source: Copyright Tefi/Shutterstock.com.

the ANS and the endocrine system and, as we will see later in this chapter, it controls how individuals respond to stressful encounters. In short, it oversees the basic behaviours associated with the survival of the species: fighting, feeding, fleeing and mating, often referred to as the four Fs!

The midbrain consists of two major parts: the tectum and the tegmentum.

Broadly speaking, the midbrain, including the brain stem, regulates critical bodily functions such as breathing, swallowing, posture, movement and the rate at which the body metabolizes foods.

The hindbrain has two major divisions: the metencephalon and the myelencephalon. The former comprises the cerebellum and the pons and the latter contains one major structure, the medulla oblongata (usually referred to simply as the medulla). The cerebellum is involved in coordinating the body's movements and the pons has been implicated in sleep and arousal. The medulla controls vital functions linked to the regulation of the cardiovascular system and respiration.

ACTIVITY 2.1

You have just read that the brain has three major anatomical components and each has a number of subdivisions. Can you list them? If not, it might be useful as a revision aid to draw a diagram of each component and its subdivisions.

The spinal cord and nerve cells

The spinal cord is a long, delicate structure that begins at the end of the brain stem and continues down to the bottom of the spine. It carries incoming and outgoing messages between the brain and the rest of the body. The brain communicates with much of the body through nerves that run up and down the spinal cord. As you will see later, the spinal cord plays an important role in responding to pain stimuli. The nervous system contains 100 billion or more nerve cells that run throughout the body. A nerve cell, called a neuron, is made up of a large cell body and a single, elongated extension (axon) for sending messages. Neurons usually have many branches (dendrites) for receiving messages. Nerves transmit messages electrically from the axon of one neuron to the dendrite of another (at the synapse) by secreting tiny amounts of chemicals called neurotransmitters. These substances trigger the receptors on the next neuron's dendrite to start up a new electrical impulse.

Central nervous system and peripheral nervous system

The nervous system is classified into various different subsystems and subdivisions but these different components are all part of an integrated system and do not operate independently.

The nervous system has two distinct parts:

1 the *central* nervous system; and
2 the *peripheral* nervous system.

The central nervous system (CNS) comprises the brain and spinal cord and is protected by bone. The brain is encased in the cranial subcavity within the skull and the spinal cord is enclosed in the spinal cavity and protected by the vertebrae. Both the brain and the spinal cord do not come into direct contact with the skull or the vertebrae as they are further enclosed by a three-layered set of membranes called the meninges. Instead, they float in a clear liquid called cerebrospinal fluid.

The peripheral nervous system (PNS) is a network of nerves that connects the brain and spinal cord to the rest of the body. The PNS is further subdivided, according to its function, into the

1   *somatic* nervous system (SNS); and
2   *autonomic* nervous system (ANS).

The SNS is concerned with coordinating the 'voluntary' body movements controlled by the skeletal muscles. The ANS regulates internal body processes that require no conscious awareness, for example, the rate of heart contractions and breathing and the speed at which food passes through the digestive tract.

The ANS is subdivided into the

1   *sympathetic* division; and
2   *parasympathetic* division.

As shown in Figure 2.2, the sympathetic division mobilizes the body by increasing heart rate and blood pressure among other physiological changes, whereas the parasympathetic division generally restores the body's energy by reducing heart rate and respiration while increasing the rate of digestion. The changes in each of the divisions occur when the ANS triggers the endocrine system to react in the face of stress.

Endocrine system

The endocrine system is an integrated system of small glands that work closely with the ANS and are extremely important for everything we do! In particular, endocrine glands, which secrete their chemicals into the bloodstream to be carried to their point of use, are most important here. Similar to the nervous system, the endocrine system communicates with many different parts of the body, however, it uses a different 'signalling system'. Whereas the nervous system uses nerves to send electrical and chemical messages, the endocrine system only uses blood vessels to send chemical messages. In particular, each of the endocrine glands, once activated, secretes chemical substances called hormones into the bloodstream, which carry messages to different parts of the body. There are a number of endocrine glands located throughout the human body such as the adrenal glands, gonads, pancreas, thyroid, thymus and pituitary gland (see Figure 2.2). Within the context of understanding the influence of psychological factors, such as stress, on the development of disease, the most important glands to consider are the adrenal and pituitary glands. Moreover, the endocrine system is linked to the nervous system by connections between the hypothalamus and the pituitary gland, the latter of which is discussed next.

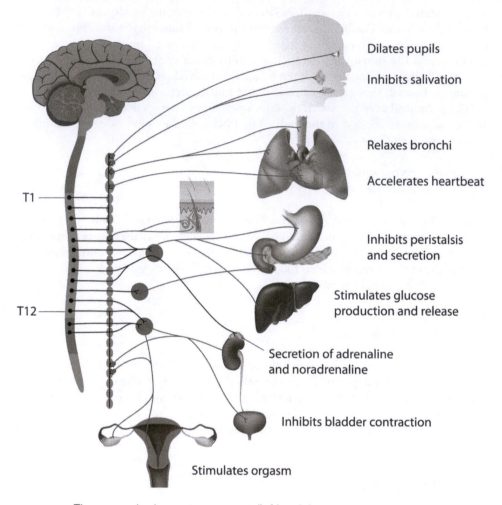

Dilates pupils

Inhibits salivation

Relaxes bronchi

Accelerates heartbeat

Inhibits peristalsis and secretion

Stimulates glucose production and release

Secretion of adrenaline and noradrenaline

Inhibits bladder contraction

Stimulates orgasm

T1

T12

FIGURE 2.2 The sympathetic nervous system *(left)* and the parasympathetic nervous system *(right)*.

Source: Copyright Alila Medical Media/Shutterstock.com.

The pituitary gland

The pituitary gland is located just below the hypothalamus and is considered the 'master' gland because it regulates the endocrine gland secretions. It has two parts: the anterior pituitary and the posterior pituitary. The former secretes growth hormone (GH), adrenocorticotrophic hormone (ACTH), thyroid stimulating hormone (TSH), follicle stimulating hormone (FSH) and luteinizing hormone (LH). The latter component releases oxytocin and vasopressin. Overall the pituitary gland plays an important role in the regulation of the growth of body tissues (through release of GH), the development of the gonads, ovum and sperm (through the release of FSH and

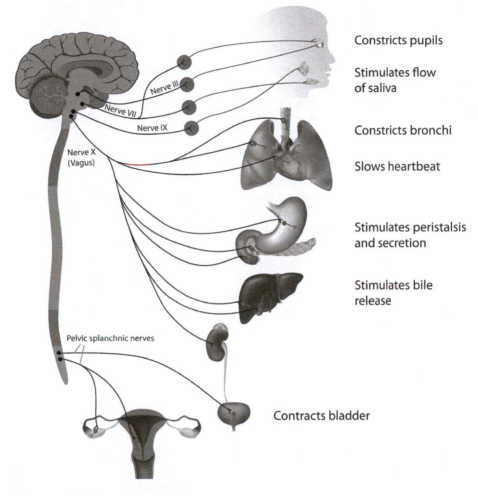

Constricts pupils

Stimulates flow of saliva

Constricts bronchi

Slows heartbeat

Stimulates peristalsis and secretion

Stimulates bile release

Contracts bladder

FIGURE 2.2 Continued

LH) as well as stimulating lactation (through the release of oxytocin) and maintaining blood pressure (through the release of vasopressin). However, it also releases ACTH (after stimulation by the hypothalamus), which stimulates the adrenal cortex – this is known as the hypothalamic–pituitary–adrenal (HPA) axis response. This is a most important response system, which we consider in some detail shortly.

The adrenal glands

There are two adrenal glands located on the top of each kidney (see Figure 2.2). The adrenal glands are best considered as being two glands within one. Each has a central core, called the adrenal medulla, which secretes the hormones adrenaline and noradrenaline (also known as epinephrine and norepinephrine), which act on the visceral organs in the same way as neurons in the nervous system. In other words, they increase heart rate and mobilize glucose into the blood among other things. Collectively, adrenaline and noradrenaline (and dopamine) are known as catecholamines. The outer portion of the adrenal gland, called the adrenal cortex, produces mineralocorticoids and glucocorticoids. The former hormones act on the kidneys to conserve salt and water by returning them to the blood during urine formation. The latter are secreted when we encounter stressors in order to help the body respond appropriately. One of the most important glucocorticoids is cortisol (corticosterone in rodents) and as such it is frequently referred to as the 'stress hormone' and measured in studies of psychological stress.

Cardiovascular system

The central function of the cardiovascular system is to ensure that oxygen (with other nutrients) is transported to all the organs of the body and that carbon dioxide (as well as other waste products) is removed from each of the body's cells. The blood is the vehicle that transports the oxygen with the heart and blood vessels allowing the blood to be carried around the body. The heart, the centre of the cardiovascular system, is made of muscle and 'beats' or 'pumps' approximately 100,000 times per day. The main muscular outer part of the heart, which contains the cardiac veins and arteries, is called the myocardium. The heart has four chambers: the two upper chambers are known as atriums and the two lower ones are called ventricles. In the cardiovascular system, veins carry blood to the heart and myocardium and the arteries carry blood from the heart and myocardium.

We can follow the journey of blood flow by considering where it enters the heart. Blood enters the right atrium deficient of oxygen and full of waste products (carbon dioxide) and is bluish in colour. Once the atrium is full, the blood is pushed into the right ventricle, which then contracts, thus pumping the blood from the heart towards the lungs, where it becomes oxygenated (and red in colour). Once oxygenated, the blood travels to the left atrium in the heart and is passed into the left ventricle before it is pumped into the general circulation via the aorta (a large artery). Before returning to the heart, some of the blood is cleansed of waste products by passing through the kidneys (where the waste products are filtered out and excreted in urine) and the liver (where nutrients, e.g. simple sugars, are stored and harmful bacteria are removed).

The cardiovascular system is a closed system and therefore it always contains some pressure. Blood pressure is the force exerted by the blood on the artery walls and has two components:

1 *Diastolic* blood pressure is the resting level in the arteries in between contractions.
2 *Systolic* blood pressure is the maximum pressure in the arteries when the heart pumps.

An individual's blood pressure is described using two numbers representing both the systolic and diastolic components and is expressed in units known as millimetres of mercury (mmHg; e.g. 126 over 70 or 126/70 mmHg). A number of factors increase blood pressure including temperature, weight, posture and food intake. Psychological factors, such as chronic stress, have also been found to be associated with the development of high blood pressure (or hypertension), which is known to damage the heart and the arteries. We will consider the links between stress, blood pressure and cardiovascular disease in more detail later.

THE STRESS RESPONSE

What happens when you experience stress? Two systems are activated. The first and easiest to activate is the sympathetic adrenal medullary (SAM) system; the second is the hypothalamic–pituitary–adrenal (HPA) axis. To borrow an analogy from Clow (2001: 53) activating the SAM system.

> can be likened to lighting a match whereas activating the HPA axis is like lighting a fire. Lighting a match is easy, has an instant effect and the effect does not last long, whereas lighting a fire takes a lot more effort and its effects last much longer. The HPA axis is only activated in extreme circumstances.

Each of these systems is considered in more detail in the following sections. In addition, later we consider how researchers induce the stress response in the laboratory using the Trier Social Stress Test (see Research methods 2.1).

The sympathetic adrenal medullary (SAM) response system

When an individual is suddenly under threat or frightened, their brain instantly sends a message to the adrenal glands, which quickly release noradrenaline that in turn activates the internal organs. This is the basic ANS sympathetic division response to threat. However, at the same time, the adrenal medulla releases adrenaline, which is rapidly transported through the bloodstream in order to further prepare the body for its response. This system is known as the sympathetic adrenal medullary (SAM) system (see Figure 2.3). Within moments adrenaline and noradrenaline have the entire body on alert, a response sometimes called the fight or flight response. As outlined earlier, as a result breathing quickens, the heart beats more rapidly and powerfully, the eyes dilate to allow more light in and the activity of the digestive system decreases to permit more blood to go to the muscles. This effect is both rapid and intense.

The hypothalamic–pituitary–adrenal (HPA) axis response system

In addition to the SAM response, when an individual experiences an unpleasant event in their environment that they perceive as stressful, the hypothalamus (the H in HPA) releases a chemical messenger called corticotrophin releasing factor (CRF). Once released, CRF is transported in the blood supply to the pituitary gland (the P) where it stimulates the release of adrenocorticotrophic hormone (ACTH). Subsequently, the latter hormone travels through the circulatory system to the adrenal (the A) cortex where it stimulates production of the glucocorticoid cortisol – known as the 'stress hormone' (see Figure 2.3).

Why is cortisol released in response to stress? One of the central functions of cortisol is to increase access to energy stores, increase protein and fat mobilization and decrease inflammation. Therefore, when an individual experiences stress, the release of cortisol triggers excess energy stored in the muscle and liver as glycogen to be liberated and broken down into glucose ready for utilization by the muscles and brain.

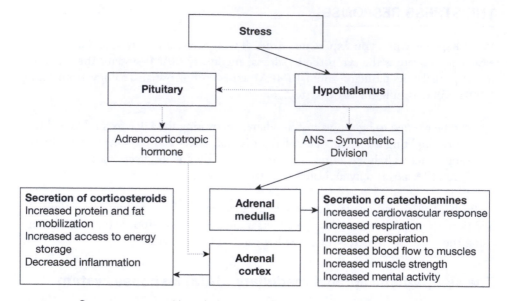

FIGURE 2.3 Stress response. Hypothalamic–pituitary–adrenal (HPA) axis response system (dashed line) and the sympathetic adrenal medullary system (SAM) response system (solid line).

The stress response and cardiovascular disease

In evolutionary terms, these stress response processes are adaptive and help ensure survival. Nevertheless, they are only adaptive in so much as they are short-lived and the body's systems swiftly return to normal. Our ancestors may well have encountered acute stressors in the form of wild animals while hunting, which made such 'flight or fight' responses adaptive. The SAM and HPA response systems would prepare the body appropriately. However, the stress of modern-day life rarely affords such infrequent, acute, life-threatening stressful encounters. Instead, we are exposed to frequent daily hassles as well as long-lasting, chronic stressors. As a result, the stress response system is repeatedly activated and the cardiovascular system is potentially exposed to excessive wear and tear. Over time, such repetitive activation may contribute to future ill health by increasing cardiovascular disease risk (see Steptoe and Kivimaki, 2013).

This may result in the development of atherosclerosis, that is, the build-up of fatty plaques in the inner lining of the blood vessels, which leads to the occlusion (narrowing) of the arteries. The increase in blood pressure as a result of the repeated activation of the SAM system may cause damage to the lining of the blood vessels, thus allowing access to fatty acids and glucose. At the same time, activation of the HPA axis leads to the release of cortisol, which increases the liberation of glucose from glycogen stores. These processes taken together increase the likelihood that chronic stress may lead to a build-up of plaque. The development of plaque can have serious health consequences. The first symptom of a narrowing artery may be pain or cramps at times when the blood flow cannot keep up with the body's demands for oxygen. During exercise, an individual may feel chest pain (angina) because of the lack of oxygen reaching the heart. In addition, this person may experience leg cramps because of lack of oxygen to the legs. However, more seriously, if the coronary arteries supplying the heart become 'blocked', which may happen if increased blood pressure in a narrowed artery sheers off a section of plaque, this can lead to a myocardial infarction (or heart attack) where part of the heart muscle (deprived of oxygen) dies. If blood flow to the brain is obstructed, this can result in a stroke where part of the brain dies.

We will consider evidence linking stress with cardiovascular disease in more detail in Chapter 3. Research has found that acute (i.e. short-lived) and chronic (long-lasting) stress are both associated with the development of cardiovascular disease. For example, Matthews and Gump (2002) examined the impact of different work stressors and marital breakdown (a major stressor in its own right) on coronary heart disease mortality during a 9-year follow-up period. These researchers found that an increasing number of different work stressors and being divorced were associated with an increased risk of cardiovascular-related deaths during the study. Another study investigating the impact of an acute stressor found that admissions to hospitals in England increased on the day following England losing to Argentina in a penalty shoot-out in the 1998 Football World Cup (Carroll *et al.*, 2002). The authors argue that their results suggest myocardial infarction can be triggered by emotional upset, such as watching your football team lose an important match! More recently, a meta-analysis of five studies showed that the risk of having a cardiac event was increased 2.5 times if preceded by a period of emotional stress (Steptoe and Kivimaki, 2013). Another study by Mostofsky and colleagues (2012) reported that the risk of having an acute myocardial infarction increased 21-fold following the death of a significant person in one's life.

RESEARCH METHODS 2.1

How to induce stress in the laboratory: the Trier Social Stress Test (TSST)

The Trier Social Stress Test (TSST) was developed in 1993 by Kirschbaum, Pirke and Helhammer at the University of Trier. The aim was to develop a stress paradigm that would reliably stimulate the HPA axis. Previous techniques had yielded inconsistent results, therefore a standardized protocol was deemed necessary.

After arriving in the laboratory (room A), participants rest for between 10 and 30 minutes depending on whether hormones are being measured in saliva (using salivettes) or in blood (using an intravenous catheter). Participants are then taken to a different room (room B) where they are introduced to three individuals sitting in a panel and asked to stand by a microphone. Next the investigator explains that the participant is to take the role of a job applicant who will be interviewed by the panel. As part of the interview process, the participants are given 10 minutes to prepare a 5-minute free speech in which they must convince the interview panel that they are the perfect applicant for the vacant position. The participant is informed that the presentation will be video-taped and evaluated for non-verbal behaviour and voice frequency and that a video analysis of the participant's performance will also be conducted. The anticipation of giving such a presentation is the stressor that stimulates the HPA axis. Following receipt of the instructions, participants return to room A to prepare a speech with the aid of paper and a pen. After 10 minutes, the participant returns to room B to deliver the speech in front of the panel. If the speech falls short of 5 minutes, the participant is told 'You still have some time left. Please continue'. After 15 minutes, the panel asks the participant to start to serially subtract the number 13 from 1022 as quickly and accurately as possible. If an error is made, one of the panel requests that the participant start again at 1022. After 20 minutes, the task is ended and the participant returns to room A to rest and be debriefed about the nature of the experiment and be informed that no voice and video analysis of their performance will be conducted. The rest period may last between 30 and 70 minutes depending on which hormones are being monitored.

The TSST has been widely used by health psychologists because it is simple to administer and researchers can easily monitor changes in a wide range of cardiovascular (e.g. heart rate, blood pressure) and neuroendocrine (e.g. cortisol, ACTH) parameters during the paradigm. Changes in salivary and serum (in the blood) cortisol levels have probably received the most attention in the literature. A typical cortisol profile (using salivettes) in response to the TSST is shown in Figure 2.4. Two characteristics of the profile are worth noting: the extent to which cortisol increases in response to the stressor (i.e. stress reactivity); and the length of time it takes for cortisol levels to return to baseline (stress recovery). Stress reactivity and stress recovery are discussed further in Chapter 3.

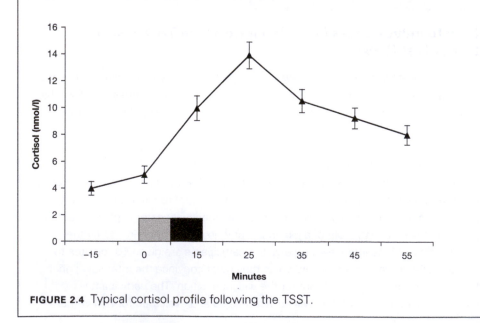

FIGURE 2.4 Typical cortisol profile following the TSST.

BIOPSYCHOSOCIAL ASPECTS OF PAIN

Psychological factors have been found to affect many different biological processes too numerous to describe here. However, one area in which psychology has made a substantial impact is in understanding the experience of pain and the management of pain.

Early theories of pain did not incorporate a role for psychological factors in explaining how we experience pain. This is surprising given that we can all think of episodes when someone's perception of pain has been influenced by cognitive, emotional or social factors. For example, we are less likely to experience pain when we are distracted by the demands of taking part in a competitive sporting event.

The role of meaning in pain

The meaning an individual attributes to pain has been found to affect their experience of it. Beecher (1956) provided striking evidence of the important role of the meaning of pain during World War II. As a physician he treated many soldiers who had been badly wounded and found that 49 per cent reported being in 'moderate' or 'severe' pain with only 32 per cent requesting medication when it was offered. However, several years later when he was treating civilians with similar if not less severe wounds after having undergone surgery, he found that 75 per cent of the civilians reported being in 'moderate' or 'severe' pain with 83 per cent requesting medication. Beecher accounted for these stark differences in terms of the meaning the injuries had for the soldiers compared to the civilian surgical patients. For the soldiers, their injuries represented the end of their war and they could look forward to resuming their lives away from the dangerous battleground. In contrast, for the civilians, the surgery represented the beginning of a long and challenging disruption to their lives.

Two of the early dominant theories of pain perception are specificity theory and pattern theory. The former theory takes a very mechanistic view and assumes that we have a separate sensory system for perceiving pain similar to hearing and vision. Moreover, specificity theory posits that the 'pain system' has its own set of special pain receptors for detecting pain stimuli and its own peripheral nerves, which communicates via a separate pathway to a designated area in the brain for the processing of pain signals.

Pattern theory offers a competing view. It suggests that a separate sensory system does not exist but instead receptors for pain are shared with the other senses. Central to this view is the notion that an individual will only experience pain when a certain pattern of neural activity reaches a critical level in the brain. Moreover, given that mild and strong pain stimulation uses the same sense modality, this theory suggests that only intense stimulation will produce a pattern of neural activity that will result in pain.

Nevertheless, as outlined above, none of these early theories can explain the role of psychological factors in pain perception. For example, they cannot account for how cognitive, emotional and social factors such as the meaning of pain can influence the experience of pain.

Gate-control theory of pain

In 1965, Melzack and Wall introduced the gate-control theory of pain perception. This theory was innovative as it incorporated important aspects of earlier theories but

FIGURE 2.5 Anxiety and worry can open the gate leading
to the experience of greater pain.

at the same time provided a detailed description of the physiological mechanisms through which psychological factors could influence an individual's experience of pain. In a nutshell, gate-control theory proposes that a neural gate in the spinal cord can modulate incoming pain signals and that a number of factors influence the opening and closing of the gate. Broadly speaking, these are

1   the amount of activity in pain fibres;
2   the amount of activity in other peripheral fibres; and
3   messages that descend from the brain (or central nervous system).

When the neural gate receives information from each of these sources it decides whether to open or close the gate. When the gate is open, pain is experienced.

The theory postulates that the gating mechanism is located in the substantia gelatinosa (i.e. the grey matter that extends along the length of the spinal cord) of the dorsal horns in the spinal cord. When we are exposed to a painful stimulus the gating mechanism receives signals from pain fibres (A-delta and C-fibres) located at the site of the injury, other peripheral fibres (A-beta fibres), which transmit information about harmless stimuli and the brain (or central nervous system) to open the gate. The pain fibres then release a neurotransmitter called substance P that passes through the gating mechanism (substantia gelatinosa) and stimulates transmission cells that in turn transmit impulses to specific locations in the brain (e.g. thalamus, limbic system, hypothalamus).

When the activity of the transmission cells reaches a critical threshold level we experience pain with greater pain intensity associated with greater activity. Once the pain centres in the brain have been activated, we are able to respond quickly to remove ourselves from danger. It is worth noting that the brain produces its own pain-relieving chemicals in the form of endorphins (i.e. a chemical similar to opiates), which inhibits the pain fibres from releasing substance P, which subsequently reduces the experience of pain. This is why endorphins are often described as being associated with a 'jogger's high'.

Moreover, pain sensations from the injury site are transmitted to the gating mechanism by pain fibres (or nerves) known as nociceptors. This is known as an afferent pathway because it indicates information is travelling towards the CNS. As outlined above, in addition to A-beta fibres two other key fibre types have been identified:

- *A-delta fibres (types I and II)*:

  - transmit information about sharp, brief pain;
  - wrapped in layers of 'fatty' cell membranes (i.e. myelinated) which increases the speed of action.

- *C-fibres*:

  - transmit information about dull, throbbing pain;
  - not wrapped in 'fatty' cell membranes, therefore they have a slower speed of action.

Each of the three types of nociceptors is important as stated by Melzack and Wall (1965: 972) 'The degree to which the gate increases or decreases sensory transmission is determined by the relative activity in large diameter (A-beta) and small diameter (A-delta and C) fibres and by descending influences from the brain.' The other group of nerves that transmit information to the gating mechanism are the other peripheral fibres. In particular, A-beta fibres carry information about harmless stimulation or mild irritation, such as gentle touch or stroking or lightly scratching the skin, to the spinal cord. When A-beta fibres are stimulated the gate is likely to close and pain perception is inhibited, explaining why people experience a reduction in pain during a gentle massage or when heat is applied to aching limbs.

The final factor that influences the opening and closing of the gate is the impact of messages descending from the brain. Neurons in different parts of the brain send impulses, via what are known as efferent pathways (i.e. indicating they lead away from the CNS or are descending from the brain), to the spinal cord. Various brain processes such as anxiety, distraction, hypnosis and excitement have the capacity to influence this neural activity by releasing chemicals such as endorphins and therefore the opening and closing of the gate. From a biopsychosocial point of view, this is the most important component of gate-control theory as it provides a clear route through which cognitive, emotional and social factors can influence pain perception. Focus 2.1 provides an overview of various conditions that individuals may experience that may open and close the gate. Since the introduction of this theory, researchers have been inspired to investigate the efficacy of psychological and behavioural approaches to pain management. We will consider these approaches in Chapter 10.

FOCUS 2.1

Conditions that can open and close the pain gate

Conditions that open the gate

- *Physical conditions*:

  - extent of the injury;
  - inappropriate activity level.

- *Emotional conditions*:

  - anxiety or worry;
  - tension;
  - depression.

- *Mental conditions*:

  - focusing on the pain;
  - boredom, little involvement in life activities.

Conditions that close the gate

- *Physical conditions*:

  - medication;
  - counterstimulation (e.g. heat or massage).

- *Emotional conditions*:

  - positive emotions (e.g. happiness or optimism);
  - relaxation;
  - rest.

- *Mental conditions*:

  - intense concentration or distraction;
  - involvement and interest in life activities.

Source: Adapted from Sarafino (2008); based on material by Karol *et al.*, cited in Turk, Meichenbaum and Genest (1983).

Neuromatrix theory of pain

Melzack (1999) extended his gate-control theory of pain during the 1980s and 1990s. The primary reason for this was the original theory's inability to explain the phenomenon known as phantom limb pain (i.e. experiencing pain in a limb that no longer exists). This new model has suggested a stronger and more dominant role for the brain. The central tenets of the theory are:

1   The areas of the brain linked to particular parts of the body continue to be active and receive inputs even if a body part no longer exists.
2   We can still experience the qualities of the human condition, including pain, without receiving input from the body, indicating that the origins of the patterns of activation that bring about these qualities of experience must be located in neural networks in the brain.
3   Conscious awareness of 'body' and 'self' is generated in the brain via patterns of input that can be modified by different perceptual inputs.
4   A network of neurons, known as the neuromatrix, is distributed throughout the brain to process all incoming sensory information including pain signals (known as the body–self neuromatrix). This neural network consists of cyclical, feedback loops between three of the brain's main neural circuits: the thalamus, limbic system and the cortex. The neuromatrix can process 'experiences' such as pain without receiving direct input from the body.
5   When the neuromatrix receives sensory inputs, they are processed (synthesized) and become imprinted on the matrix creating what is known as a neurosignature. The neurosignature is projected to areas of the brain – the sentient neural hub – where the flow of nerve impulses is transformed into a constantly changing stream of awareness.
6   An action neuromatrix is then activated to signal appropriate movements when pain is experienced (e.g. remove hand from hot iron).
7   The neuromatrix is genetically determined, however, it is modified through sensory inputs such as pain experiences.

As you will have gathered, this is a complicated theory and further work is required before researchers fully understand phantom limb pain. For example, recent advances of the theory have suggested that exploration of how the stress response systems interact and provide additional inputs into the neuromatrix is required. Nevertheless, the developments presented by Melzack's neuromatrix theory of pain have provided valuable insights into the mechanisms underlying this phenomenon (Giummarra *et al.*, 2007; Jensen and Turk, 2014).

PSYCHONEUROIMMUNOLOGY

Have you ever wondered why a relatively large number of students report having the common cold around the time of important examinations? Is this simply bad luck, all in the mind, or is there a biological explanation? A growing body of evidence indicates that there is a link between social and psychological factors and susceptibility to respiratory infectious illness. This is noteworthy given that historically these two realms were considered quite distinct (i.e. the mind versus body debate).

The term psychoneuroimmunology or PNI was coined by Robert Ader and Nicholas Cohen of the University of Rochester in the USA, to describe this new area of science that explored the interaction between psychological processes and the nervous and immune systems. Ader and Cohen were at the forefront of this area and demonstrated the link between the brain and the immune system early on (Ader and Cohen, 1975). Using a paradigm called conditioned immunosuppression, based upon Pavlov's classical conditioning, they discovered that the immune system of rats could be conditioned to respond to external stimuli unrelated to immune function. They found that after an artificially flavoured drink was paired with an immune suppressive drug in rats, the presentation of the drink alone was sufficient to suppress immune functioning. Studies such as this one have provided the starting point for researchers to examine the effects of various psychological factors on human immunity. Over the last 25 years or so, a large amount of research effort has concentrated on exploring the extent to which psychological stress may influence different aspects of the immune system. Two areas that have received particular attention are respiratory infectious illness and wound healing (cf., Kiecolt-Glaser *et al.*, 1998; Cohen, 2005). However, in order to understand the link between stress, the common cold and wound healing, we need to appreciate how the immune system works. Therefore, the next section provides a basic introduction to the immune system.

The immune system

The function of the immune system is to defend the body against invaders. Microbes (germs or microorganisms), cancer cells and transplanted tissues or organs are all interpreted by the immune system as 'non-self' against which the body must be defended. Although the immune system is incredibly complex, its basic strategy is straightforward: to recognize the enemy, mobilize forces and attack. Amazingly, the immune system can distinguish between 'self' and 'non-self' and learns to remember the distinctive cellular features of invaders. Moreover, it is able to form an immunological memory of infectious agents and so mount a more effective response the next time the invader attacks. It is this process that is exploited when a person is vaccinated with a mild dose of an infectious agent – the body becomes primed for a real invasion.

What are the basic features of the immune system? Broadly speaking, the human body has the capacity to mount two types of immune defence:

1   *cell-mediated* immunity; and
2   *antibody-mediated* immunity.

In both cases, the basic immune response is brought about by the actions of two types of white blood cells known as lymphocytes and monocytes. Importantly, there are two types of lymphocytes with different functions: T (for thymus) cells and B (for bone) cells. Both types are formed in the bone marrow, but the T cells migrate to the thymus to mature while the B cells remain in the marrow. B cells produce antibodies (i.e. large proteins that will recognize and bind to invading infectious agents), whereas

TABLE 2.1 Comparison of the roles of T and B cells

Cell-mediated immunity: T cells	*Antibody-mediated immunity: B cells*
Work directly at cell level	Work via the bloodstream
A type of lymphocyte (white blood cell)	A type of lymphocyte (white blood cell)
Formed in the bone marrow, but matured in thymus (T)	Formed and matured in the bone (B) marrow
Attack and destroy infectious agents by triggering release of cytotoxic killer cells	Attack and destroy infectious agents by stimulating the release of antibodies

T cells do not. It is also worth noting that there are a number of different kinds of T cells including T helper cells, natural killer cells, T suppressor cells and cytotoxic killer cells.

T and B cells operate very differently when attacking infectious agents. The former bring about cell-mediated immunity while the latter bring about antibody-mediated immunity (see Table 2.1 for an overview of the roles of T and B cells). In the former case, when an infectious agent enters the body, it is recognized by a type of monocyte called a macrophage, which presents the infectious agent to a T helper cell and releases interleukin-1 (IL-1; a type of cytokine released from cells to influence the activity of other cells), this in turn stimulates T-helper cell activity. As a result, the T helper cells then release interleukin-2 (another cytokine), which triggers the proliferation of T cells and eventually the release of cytotoxic killer cells which attack and destroy the infectious agent.

In antibody-mediated immunity, the initial stages are similar, such that there is collaboration between macrophages and T helper cells. However, in this case, the T helper cells stimulate the proliferation of B cells leading to the secretion of antibodies, which identify and bind to specific features of the infectious agent. The antibodies then immobilize and destroy the pathogen.

STRESS AND THE IMMUNE SYSTEM

Can stress alter immune functioning? There is evidence to show that stress can suppress cell-mediated immunity, although the data relating to the antibody response and B cell function in particular are less clear (cf., Rabin, 1999; Cohen, Miller and Rabin, 2001). For example, many studies have shown that increased secretion of stress hormones such as cortisol can alter the production of cytokines. As we already know, cytokines are important in the activation of T cells as well as in mediating the pro-inflammatory response (this process is explained further later in this chapter). Therefore, stress-induced changes in the production of cytokines may represent an important mechanism through which stress compromises the body's response to infectious illness. An important study by Kunz-Ebrecht *et al.*(2003) showed that cortisol responses to psychological stress were inversely associated with the production of two cytokines (IL-6 and IL-1ra), indicating that psychological factors can influence important components of immune functioning. Moreover, there is emerging evidence to suggest that psychological stress, suffered as a result of adverse early experiences, is likely to increase people's vulnerability to immune dysregulation in adulthood (Fagundes, Glaser and Kiecolt-Glaser, 2013; Miller, Chen and Parker, 2011).

Stress and respiratory infectious illness

Over the last 25 years, Sheldon Cohen, a psychologist at Carnegie Mellon University in the USA, has explored the extent to which psychological and social factors influence susceptibility to infectious illnesses such as the common cold (see Cohen, 2005, for a review). As part of this work, Cohen and his colleagues have developed a unique prospective study design in which healthy participants are exposed to a virus that causes the common cold. Participants are then monitored following exposure in order to determine who develops a respiratory illness and reports cold-like symptoms. At baseline, participants also normally complete a range of psychological measures to assess their current level of perceived stress, their mood and any recent stressful life events.

In 1991, Cohen and his colleagues published a seminal paper, in the prestigious journal, *The New England Journal of Medicine*, in which they demonstrated for the first time that increases in psychological stress are associated with increases in risk for developing a cold after exposure to a cold virus. If this is not impressive enough, they also demonstrated that this association was independent of the participants' baseline levels of specific antibody, age, sex, education, allergic status and body mass index and the season of the year. In addition, they also explored whether the increased susceptibility was related to changes in stress-related health behaviours such as smoking, exercise and diet. None of these variables explained the relationship.

In a subsequent study, Cohen and colleagues (1998) concentrated on identifying the types of stressful life events that were most predictive of increased susceptibility to infectious illness. In order to do this, these researchers conducted detailed interviews with each of the participants who took part in their standard prospective design and found two types of stressful life events were most strongly related to susceptibility. The first type of event was enduring (1 month or longer) interpersonal problems with family and friends. The second type was enduring problems associated with work (such as under- or unemployment). They also found that the longer the stressful event had lasted, the greater was the risk of developing an infectious illness.

Similar to their earlier study, the authors again examined which psychological and biological factors may be mediating the effects of psychological stress on increased susceptibility (see Focus 5.2). Interestingly, they found that regular exercise, non-smoking and greater sleep efficacy (per cent of time in bed sleeping) were associated with lower susceptibility to developing a common cold. In addition, they also found that higher levels of adrenaline and noradrenaline (in the urine in the past 24 hours) were related to greater susceptibility. However, surprisingly, the effects of these factors were independent of the relationship between psychological stress and risk of developing a cold.

In the last 15 years, research has turned its attention to exploring the role of pro-inflammatory cytokine regulation in explaining the mediating pathways between psychological stress and the common cold. You will recall from earlier that cytokines are produced in response to infection. They are also believed to trigger symptoms associated with upper respiratory infections such as the common cold and the influenza virus (Cohen, 2005). Therefore, using a more complex study design, Cohen, Doyle and Skoner (1999) investigated whether psychological stress influenced cytokine production in participants after receiving an influenza virus. Specifically, they tested whether stress had the capacity to interfere with the body's ability to regulate cytokine production. Normally, when a virus is detected, the body produces enough cytokines to remove the virus. However, Cohen *et al.* 1999 found that stress short-circuited the body's ability to switch off the cytokine response. Individuals who had previously experienced high stress prior to receiving the virus were found to have higher IL-6 (cytokine) levels and greater symptom scores in response to the viral challenge. In a subsequent study, these researchers replicated their findings and demonstrated that prolonged stress influences susceptibility to infectious illness by decreasing cortisol's effectiveness in regulating the pro-inflammatory cytokine response, leading to increased production of IL-6 and greater illness expression (Miller, Cohen and Ritchey , 2002). Taken together, these findings bring us to a surprising conclusion: psychological stress does not influence upper respiratory illness by suppressing the immune system. On the contrary, stress experienced over an extended period of time results in the immune system over-responding, which in turn activates and extends the symptoms of upper respiratory infections.

There have been a number of exciting new developments in the area of stress and the common cold. Of particular note is the investigation of the relationship between telomeres and the development of upper respiratory infections (Cohen *et al.*, 2013a, 2013b). Telomeres are 'caps' at the end of chromosomes, which get shorter as we get older and it has been suggested that these are biomarkers (or indicators) of good or bad aging. For example, shorter telomeres have been linked with the development of diseases such as cardiovascular disease and cancer. Moreover, a recent study has shown that people with shorter telomeres were at greater risk of developing an upper respiratory infection after receiving the common cold virus in the laboratory (Cohen *et al.*, 2013a). In addition, in a related investigation, these authors also found that participants from lower socio-economic backgrounds were also more likely to be infected by the cold virus and that this was explained, in part, by having shorter telomeres (Cohen *et al.*, 2013b).

Stress and wound healing

In 1995, Janice Kiecolt-Glaser and colleagues from Ohio State University published a seminal study that provided evidence, for the first time, that psychological stress slowed wound healing. Similar to Cohen and his co-investigators, Kiecolt-Glaser and her colleagues developed an unusual research design to investigate the links between stress and immune functioning. Using a punch biopsy, a 3.5 mm full thickness wound was created on the non-dominant forearm, approximately 4 cm below the elbow, in each of the study participants. Levels of perceived stress were then measured using questionnaires and the wound was photographed every day until it completely healed. A wound was considered fully healed when it no longer foamed after hydrogen peroxide was applied! In this study the researchers were interested in the effects of chronic stress on immune function and wound healing. Therefore, participants who were caring for a relative with Alzheimer's disease (high stress group) were compared to control participants (low stress group) matched for age and family income.

The results of the study showed that complete wound healing took an average of 9 days or 24 per cent longer in the caregiver group compared to the controls. They also found differences between the groups in the production of an important cytokine (interleukin-1ß) suggesting this as one of the immunological mechanisms underlying the observed effects.

Next this research group investigated whether a relatively minor, commonplace stressful event such as an examination had the potential to similarly influence wound healing. In this study, Marucha, Kiecolt-Glaser and Favagehi (1998) placed a 3.5 mm punch biopsy wound in the mouths (i.e. on the hard palate) of a sample of dental students, once during the summer vacation and again 3 days before a major examination. This repeated measures design allowed the participants to act as their own controls. Again, two independent methods assessed wound healing (daily photographs and a foaming response to hydrogen peroxide). Surprisingly, all students took longer to heal in the examination conditions compared to control conditions with complete healing taking an average of 3 days (or 40 per cent) longer in the examination condition. These data suggest that even short-lived, predictable and relatively benign stressors can have significant consequences for wound healing. More importantly, these findings have important implications for understanding recovery from surgery. Evidence suggests that a more negative psychological response to surgery is associated with a slower and more complicated post-operative recovery, greater pain, longer hospital stay and worse treatment adherence (for more detailed discussion see Kiecolt-Glaser et al., 1998). Moreover, these results indicate that if patients are psychologically better prepared for surgery they are likely to experience significant health benefits. This is consistent with a recent investigation of recovery from total knee replacement surgery that showed that higher levels of anxiety and depression pre-operatively were associated with poorer recovery one year later (Hanusch et al., 2014).

Psychological influences on recovery from surgery

Using this work as a starting point, Kiecolt-Glaser and colleagues (1998: 1209) have developed a model of psychological influences on surgical recovery. They suggest that psychological factors can impact wound healing, a key variable in short-term post surgical recovery, via three key pathways:

1 Emotions have direct effects on 'stress' hormones and they can modulate immune function.
2 The patient's emotional response to surgery can influence the type and amount of anaesthetic and anaesthetics vary in their effects on the immune and endocrine system.
3 Individuals who are more anxious are also more likely to experience greater post-surgical pain and pain can suppress immune functioning.

SUMMARY

In this chapter we have considered several of the key psychophysiological pathways through which psychological factors (and particularly stress) may influence health and illness processes. Chapter 3 describes the key theoretical approaches to stress and evaluates the research evidence concerning the links between stressors and illness and between stressors and health behaviour. Psychological factors such as stress can affect health directly, through autonomic and neuroendocrine changes but also indirectly, through changes in health behaviours. The direct effects of stress on health outcomes are known as psychophysiological pathways, while the indirect effects are known as behavioural pathways.

The role of the nervous system is to allow us to adapt to changes both within our body and our environment. It consists of the brain, the spinal cord and billions of nerves. The brain is the central part of the nervous system and consists of three major components: the forebrain, the midbrain and the hindbrain. The forebrain is divided into two main subdivisions: 1) the telencephalon, which comprises the cerebrum and the limbic system; and 2) the diencephalon, which is composed of the thalamus and hypothalamus. The midbrain consists of two major parts: the tectum and the tegmentum. Similarly, the hindbrain has two major divisions: the metencephalon and the myelencephalon.

The nervous system is divided into the central nervous system (CNS) and the peripheral nervous system (PNS). The CNS comprises the brain and spinal cord whereas the PNS is a network of nerves that connects the brain and spinal cord to the rest of the body. An important part of the PNS is the autonomic nervous system (ANS) that has a sympathetic division and a parasympathetic division. The former mobilizes bodily processes (e.g. increases heart rate), whereas the latter restores the body's energy resources.

Two response systems are activated when we experience stress. The first and easiest to activate is the sympathetic adrenal medullary (SAM) system; the second is the hypothalamic–pituitary–adrenal (HPA) axis response system. The SAM system leads to the release of the adrenaline and noradrenaline that put the body on alert; the HPA axis response system leads to the release of the stress hormone, cortisol. The stress response has been found to impact negatively on a number of health outcomes such as cardiovascular disease. Excessive wear and tear of the cardiovascular system through repeated activation of the stress response may increase the development of athero-sclerosis and increase the likelihood of myocardial infarction and stroke.

Psychological factors can play a role in the perception of pain. Early theories of pain were mechanistic and did not account for the influence of cognitive, emotional and social factors. Gate-control theory, introduced by Melzack and Wall (1965), proposes that a neural gate in the spinal cord receives signals from pain fibres at the site of injury, other peripheral fibres and messages descending from the brain. The degree to which the gate opens (leading to experience of pain) is determined by the combined effects of these three factors. Gate-control theory was extended by Melzack and is known as the neuromatrix theory of pain. This theory contends that the pain experience is governed by the body–self neuromatrix.

The human body has the capacity to mount two types of defence known as cell-mediated immunity and antibody-mediated immunity. Psychological factors such as stress have been found to influence these immune functions. A number of researchers have shown stress to be associated with increased susceptibility to infectious illnesses and the slowing down of wound healing.

KEY CONCEPTS AND TERMS

- Antibody-mediated immunity
- Autonomic nervous system
- Cardiovascular system
- Cell-mediated immunity
- Central nervous system
- Endocrine system
- Gate-control theory

- Hypothalamic–pituitary–adrenal (HPA) axis response system
- Limbic system
- Neuromatrix theory of pain
- Parasympathetic nervous system
- Peripheral nervous system
- Psychoneuro-immunology

- Psychophysiological pathways
- Somatic nervous system
- Sympathetic adrenal medullary (SAM) response system
- Sympathetic nervous system
- Trier Social Stress Test

SAMPLE ESSAY TITLES

- To what extent can psychological factors influence health and illness processes?
- Cognitive, emotional and social factors affect pain. Discuss this statement with reference to recent psychological theory.
- Social and psychological factors are linked to susceptibility and respiratory infectious illness. Discuss.
- What are the pathways through which stress can alter immune functioning?

FURTHER READING

Books

Contrada, R.J., and Baum, A. (2011). *Handbook of Stress Science: Psychology, Biology and Health.* New York: Springer.

Flor, H. and Turk, D.C. (2011). *Chronic Pain: An Integrated Biobehavioral Perspective.* Seattle, WA: IASP Press.

Kalat, J.W. (2009). *Biological Psychology.* New York: Thomson Wadsworth.

Vedhara, K. and Irwin, M. (2005). *Human Psychoneuroimmunology.* Oxford: Oxford University Press.

Journal articles

Cohen, S. (2005). The Pittsburgh common cold studies: Psychosocial predictors of susceptibility to respiratory infectious illness. *International Journal of Behavioral Medicine*, 12, 123–131.

Fagundes, C.P., Glaser, R. and Kiecolt-Glaser, J.K. (2013). Stressful early life experiences and immune dysregulation across the lifespan. *Brain, Behavior and Immunity*, 27, 8–12.

Jensen, M.P. and Turk, D.C. (2014). Contributions of psychology to the understanding and treatment of people with chronic pain: Why it matters to ALL psychologists. *American Psychologist*, 69, 105–118.

Miller, G.E., Chen, E. and Parker, K.J. (2011). Psychological stress in childhood and susceptibility to the chronic diseases of aging: Moving towards a model of behavioural and biological mechanisms. *Psychological. Bulletin*, 137, 959–997.

Steptoe, A., Hamer, M. and Chida, Y. (2007). The effects of acute psychological stress on circulating inflammatory factors in humans: A review and meta-analysis. *Brain Behavior and Immunity*, 21, 901–912.

2 | Stress and health

3 Stress theory and research

CHAPTER PLAN

Stress is widespread and media coverage suggests that it causes illness. In this chapter we will examine how stress is studied and how it is linked to disease. We will consider evolutionary perspectives on stress in preparing humans for fight or flight as well as more contemporary views. Building on Chapter 2, we discuss a model of physiological responses to stress leading to the long-term health impact of stress, known as allostatic load. We then explore different measures of stress including life events such as marriage, divorce or bereavement and daily hassles such as losing one's keys. We discuss these in terms of Lazarus' transactional theory of stress (1966, 1999, Lazarus and Folkman, 1984). Finally, we discuss conservation of resources theory (Hobfoll, 1989, 2001).

We highlight the pathways by which stress impacts on health. Stress affects health through biological processes (e.g. blood pressure, release of stress hormones, immune functioning) and (indirectly) through health behaviours (e.g. exercise, diet, smoking). We consider evidence for both pathways when discussing the impact of life events and daily stressors on health outcomes. In the final section of this chapter we consider why some people become ill in response to stressful situations and others do not.

The chapter has five sections: (1) what is stress?; (2) early approaches to stress; (3) contemporary approaches to stress – allostatic load and health; (4) contemporary psychological approaches; and (5) why do some people get ill in response to stressors and others do not?

LEARNING OUTCOMES

When you have completed this chapter you should be able to:

1 Describe what is meant by stress. Discuss whether stress is a growing problem.
2 Describe and evaluate key theoretical approaches to stress.
3 Describe and evaluate key ways in which stress has been measured.
4 Discuss and evaluate research evidence concerning the links between stressors and a) illness; and b) health behaviour.
5 Describe the impact of individual differences in responses to stressors.

WHAT IS STRESS?

The increase in press and television coverage of stress over the last few decades has corresponded to a growth in research and public awareness. Indeed, stress is now the most common cause of long-term sick leave and is frequently shown to be a very important factor accounting for nearly 10 million working days lost per annum in the UK (HSE, 2015). In 2014/2015, stress accounted for 35 per cent of all cases of work-related illnesses in the UK (i.e. 440,000 cases). In the United States, the impact of stress is also far reaching, with 66 per cent of Americans reporting that stress is impacting on their physical health and 63 per cent believing the same for their mental health (American Psychological Association, 2012).

We can all empathize with feeling stressed. However, it is not always clear what we mean by 'stress' (Segerstrom and O'Connor, 2012). Over centuries, 'stress' has come to mean pressure or strain (e.g. Cooper and Dewe, 2004). Scientific interest dates back to the early part of the twentieth century. For example, World War I concerns about industrial efficiency led to studies of fatigue in wartime munitions factories and the war focused attention on 'shellshock', which was subsequently acknowledged as a manifestation of post-traumatic stress disorder (Lazarus, 1999).

There have been three different approaches to the study of stress: the stimulus-based or engineering approach; the response-based or medico-physiological approach; and the psychological 'interactional-appraisal' approach (Cox, 1978). The engineering approach views stress as a demand on an individual from their environment, which produces a strain reaction: the greater the strain, the larger the reaction. This approach assumes that undemanding situations are not stressful. However, monotonous undemanding work environments very often are stressful. The engineering analogy is also problematic because it makes the assumption that individuals function both uncon- sciously and automatically; no consideration is given to the mediating psychological processes (e.g. cognitive appraisal) but such processes are very important. The response- based approach mainly considers stress in terms of the general physiological reaction to noxious events in a person's environment such as changes in blood pressure, heart rate and stress hormones. Again this approach does not account for individual psychological processes. More recent work has adopted an interactional-appraisal (or transactional) approach in order to explain the stress process. Such theories have contributed to our understanding of the variation in responses to similar noxious (or stressful) stimuli by emphasizing the importance of the intervening psychological processes.

The development of the transactional approach owes much to the work of Richard Lazarus and his colleague Susan Folkman (Lazarus, 1966; Lazarus and Folkman, 1984). They define stress as 'a particular relationship between the person and the environment that is appraised by the person as taxing or exceeding his or her resources and endangering his or her well-being' (Lazarus and Folkman, 1984: 19). This means that researchers need to look at the environment, the individual's reaction to the environ- ment and the outcome (which might be in terms of physiological or psychological well-being). Perhaps because of the breadth of issues encompassed within this concept of stress, Lazarus also suggested that the most useful approach would be to regard stress not as a single variable but as a 'rubric consisting of many variables and processes' (Lazarus and Folkman, 1984: 12). Thus stress may be viewed as an umbrella term covering a general field of study. Within this field there are many diverse areas of research, which look at relationships between objective or perceived antecedents (or stressors) and a range of physiological, psychological or behavioural outcomes (often referred to as strains). The latter may include the kind of physiological measures (e.g. cortisol, blood pressure) discussed in Chapter 2, as well as illness outcomes (like the occurrence of cancer or heart disease), measures of work performance or health behaviours or, perhaps most frequently, self-ratings of satisfaction or anxiety.

Perhaps because of the vagueness of the concept there is sometimes disagreement about basic issues such as whether a certain amount of stress is good for you. This clearly depends on the definition you use. For example, taking a stimulus–based approach, up to a certain point, stimuli such as work pressures may certainly be motivating and beneficial. However, using Lazarus' popular definition given above, which views stress in terms of a process involving threats to our well-being, it is harder to see how this can be construed as beneficial! A number of different approaches to stress are considered in the following sections.

ACTIVITY 3.1

Is stress increasing?

There is a widespread view often reflected in the media that the amount of stress in society, both within the family and the workplace, has increased greatly in recent decades. This has been attributed to the breakdown of the nuclear family, the loosening of extended family bonds caused by the widespread mobility in the community and the rapid changes in the workplace. What do you think? Is life really much more stressful than it was 50 years ago? Discuss this topic in groups, taking into account the increased public awareness of psychological responses to stressors and changes in people's expectations.

Consider also what variables you would need to consider in making an assessment of whether stress had increased. This could include increases in stressors such as wars, poverty, unemployment or work stressors. It could also include increases in outcomes such as psychiatric illness or stress-related disease.

EARLY APPROACHES TO STRESS

Two theorists who had a great influence in terms of popularizing the concept of stress were both physiologists: Walter Cannon and Hans Selye. Cannon (1932) wrote about the 'fight-or-flight' reaction to describe the human response to threats. Cannon believed that when faced with danger, such as a predator, the human being feels the emotions of fear or anger, the former being linked to an instinct to run away and the latter with the urge to fight. These reactions served to prepare the body for action as outlined in Chapter 2.

Hans Selye (1956) built on Cannon's work and described a reaction pattern called the general adaptation syndrome (GAS). Selye wrote that 'Adaptability and resistance to stress are fundamental prerequisites for life and every vital organ participates in them' (1950: 1383). He believed that the basic physiological reaction was always the same regardless of the stressor and that an understanding of this phenomenon depended on many branches of physiology, biochemistry and medicine. He even stated that the phenomenon would never be really understood 'since the complete comprehension of life is beyond the limits of the human mind' (Selye, 1950: 1383). It is difficult to do justice to this complex theory in a brief paragraph! However, in essence it comprises three stages:

- *Alarm*: the immediate reaction whereby stress hormones are released to prepare the body for action (fight or flight).
- *Resistance*: if stress is prolonged, levels of stress hormones remain high. However, during this period the individual seems superficially to adapt to the stressor but will still have heightened susceptibility to disease.
- *Exhaustion*: if the stress continues long enough the body's defensive resources are used up leading to illness and, ultimately, death.

In summary, according to Selye, prolonged exposure to a strong stressor will increase an individual's risk of developing health problems, which he described as diseases of adaptation (e.g. ulcers, high blood pressure). Moreover, he suggested that repeated and long-term exposure to stress will lead to dysfunction of a number of the body's basic systems such as the immune and metabolic systems.

Selye's early approach focused on stress as a physiological reaction and his theory influenced many subsequent researchers. However, Mason (1971) questioned the generality of this approach, arguing that some noxious (stressful) physical conditions do not produce the predicted three-stage alarm, resistance and ultimately exhaustion responses (e.g. exercise, fasting, heat). More recent approaches have tended to emphasize psychological process and impacts and have recognized that individuals may respond differently to the same stressful events.

RESEARCH METHODS 3.1

How is stress measured?

There are three main types of measures used to study stress: (1) generic measures of perceived stress; (2) event measures; and (3) cognitive appraisal measures. These are not mutually exclusive. Generic measures of perceived stress aim to capture appraisals of non-event-specific perceptions of stress over the recent past. Event measures examine the experience of major life events, hassles and single acutely stressful events. Cognitive appraisal measures assess primary (the extent to which an event is appraised as threatening, challenging or likely to lead to loss) and secondary appraisals (e.g. the extent to which an event is appraised as controllable).

Generic measures of perceived stress

The most popular global measure of stress is the Perceived Stress Scale (PSS) developed by Cohen, Kamarck and Mermelstein (1983). This measure was designed to evaluate the degree to which situations in general in one's life are appraised as being stressful. This scale asks participants to report about their feelings and thoughts during the *last month* in relation to non-specific events. For example, in the last month, 'how often have you been upset because of something that happened unexpectedly' and 'how often have you been able to control irritations in your life?' Other generic measures of stress have been developed such as the Stress Arousal Checklist (SACL; Cox and Mackay, 1985) and more recently the Trier Inventory of Chronic Stress has been introduced (TICS) (Schulz, Schlotz and Becker, 2011).

Event measures of stress

These types of measures aim to capture participants' responses to significant life events (e.g. divorce), a single acutely stressful event (e.g. examination) and daily hassles (e.g. being late for a meeting). This may be achieved by the use of a questionnaire or by a structured interview. These may be generic life events as in the original Holmes and Rahe (1967) work (described later) or developed to focus on specific groups such as children. Event measures also include assessments of 'hassles', minor daily stressful events or annoyances as conceptualized by the original Hassles Scale (Kanner *et al.*, 1981).

Cognitive appraisal measures of stress

Appraisal measures of stress are informed by the transactional model of stress (Lazarus and Folkman, 1984). As outlined earlier, cognitive stress appraisals are the interpretations of events in terms of their benefit or harm for the individual and the theory posits two dimensions: primary and secondary appraisals (Lazarus and Folkman, 1984). For example, the Appraisal of Life Events (ALE) (Ferguson, Matthews and Cox, 1999) scale consists of three primary appraisal scales: Threat, Challenge and Loss. The 'Threat' scale assesses how threatening and anxiety-provoking the situation is; 'Challenge' assesses the potential for growth and learning from the situation and 'Loss' how sad and depressing the situation is.

Gartland, O'Connor and Lawton (2012) have recently developed a new Stressor Appraisal Scale (SAS) that can be used to assess stressor appraisals in relation to the most stressful hassle in the past 7 days and it can be used in a daily diary format (see Gartland *et al.*, 2014b). This new scale comprises 10 items tapping primary appraisal and secondary appraisal.

CONTEMPORARY PHYSIOLOGICAL APPROACHES TO STRESS – ALLOSTATIC LOAD AND HEALTH

Building on the work of Selye is an important contemporary approach to stress, introduced by McEwen and Stellar (1993), which helps us understand how stress can cause illness over a lifetime. This approach attempts to provide a complete physiological account of the various bodily systems that may be affected by stress and how different stressful situations may impact on health. McEwen (1998) proposed that the long-term impact of stress, known as allostatic load–affects the body at cardiovascular, metabolic, neural, behavioural and cellular levels. Similar to basic homeostatic systems such as body temperature, the HPA axis, the autonomic nervous system and the cardiovascular, metabolic and immune systems protect the body by adapting to internal and external stress. This is known as allostasis. However, if the activation of these systems is repeated and prolonged, allostatic load will be experienced in the form of increased release of stress hormones, immune cells, brain activity and cardiovascular response. It is suggested that if a person experiences allostatic load for a long time, they are at increased risk of developing disease because the bodily systems will stop working as effectively (for a full account see McEwen, 1998, 2007). Indeed, this has been confirmed by a number of recent studies. For example, a large-scale prospective study, using a comprehensive measure of allostatic load, found that participants with higher allostatic load scores had a greater risk of having died 10 years later (Hwang et al., 2014).

In terms of allostasis, when we encounter a psychological or physical stressor (e.g. giving a speech or encountering an infection or a physical threat), our body has a twofold response. First, it initiates an allostatic response that activates the stress response (as described in Chapter 2). Second, when the stressor has passed, the allostatic response is terminated. As you already know, activation of these systems leads to the release of several stress hormones including cortisol and changes in blood pressure and heart rate, which normally return to baseline levels when the stressful encounter has ended. However, if the allostatic response is not shut off but is maintained over time, due to inadequate coping, this will result in allostatic load, thus placing excessive pressure on our bodily systems.

McEwen has suggested that four situations are associated with allostatic load. Each situation differs in terms of how often we encounter stressful situations and whether we can cope with them:

1   repeated 'hits' from multiple stressors;
2   lack of adaptation;
3   prolonged response; and
4   inadequate response.

As shown in Figure 3.1, the first situation is when we experience frequent stressors. If these are sustained over long periods of time they can trigger repeated elevations in blood pressure, thereby increasing the risk of having a heart attack or speeding up the early stages of heart disease. The second is where we are unable to cope with or to adapt to the same type of stressor and as a result our body is exposed to stress hormones for a long period of time. The third condition is when our bodily systems are exposed to the stress response over an extended episode due to a delayed shutdown of the body's

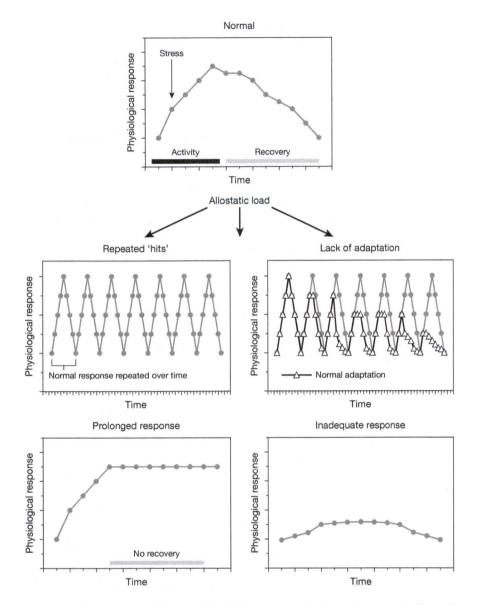

FIGURE 3.1 Four types of allostatic load. The top graph shows the normal allostatic response in which a response is initiated by a stressor, sustained for an appropriate interval and then turned off. The other four panels illustrate four conditions that lead to allostatic load: repeated 'hits' from multiple stressors; lack of adaptation; prolonged response due to delayed shutdown; and inadequate response that leads to compensatory hyperactivity of other mediators (e.g. inadequate secretion of glucocorticoids, resulting in increased concentrations of cytokines that are normally counter-regulated by glucocorticoids.

Source: From McEwen (1998). Copyright © 1998 Massachusetts Medical Society. Reprinted with permission from Massachusetts Medical Society.

response. The fourth is when an inadequate stress response causes the body to release extra, unnecessary hormones and other chemical messengers, which may be harmful to health. As you can see, this approach deals primarily with the physiological changes that accompany stress. Contemporary psychological approaches are considered in the next section.

CONTEMPORARY PSYCHOLOGICAL APPROACHES TO STRESS

In parallel with the development of physiological explanations of the stress process, psychologists have focused on stress as a predominantly psychological phenomenon and produced definitions and theories which concentrate on the psychological precursors and processes. The three approaches described in this section have all been influential but approach the conceptualization and study of stress in different ways. For each approach the evidence linking them to disease is considered.

Life events

The study of major life events is perhaps the earliest, as well as most enduring, approach to measuring stressors. The idea that emotionally distressing events might be associated with disease and particularly cancer goes back at least as far as the nineteenth century where many anecdotal reports of links between negative events such as bereavement and cancer can be found in the medical literature (LeShan, 1959). The first statistical study of this association is attributed to Snow (1893) who studied 250 cancer patients in London and found that in over 60 per cent of them there had been some problem before the onset of the disease. Frequently this was the death of a close relative.

More formal measurement approaches to studying life events originated in the 1960s when Holmes and Rahe (1967) published a checklist of life events called the Social Readjustment Rating Scale, which is reproduced in Table 3.1. The idea of a change being stressful and requiring adaptation is central to the approach. Thus life events were changes rather than persistent states. Furthermore, they were objectively verifiable events.

In the initial research to establish this measure, Holmes and Rahe drew on their clinical experience to list 43 events. A sample of 394 people were asked to rate these for the degree of 'social readjustment' they required. Marriage was given an arbitrary value (50 in the final scale) and they were asked to assign numeric values to all the other events based on how much more (or less) adjustment the event required than marriage. The sum of ratings for events that an individual experiences in the last year is known as their life change unit (LCU) score. Holmes and Masuda (1974) described an LCU score of over 150 in one year as a life crisis (150–199 is a mild crisis; 200–299 a moderate crisis; and over 300 a major crisis). They also reported an early study, which indicated that life crises were linked to deterioration in health. For example, 37 per cent of those whose scores indicated they had experienced a minor crisis and 79 per cent of those with a major crisis, reported changes in health. Further studies in the 1970s by Rahe and colleagues suggested that high LCU scores were linked with heart disease (Rahe and Paasikivi, 1971; Theorell and Rahe, 1971). However, as the methodology has improved and more longitudinal studies have been conducted, results have tended to be less consistent.

TABLE 3.1 Social readjustment rating scale

Rank	Life events	LCU* score
1	Death of spouse	100
2	Divorce	173
3	Marital separation	165
4	Jail term	163
5	Death of close family member	163
6	Personal illness or injury	153
7	Marriage	150
8	Fired at work	147
9	Marital reconciliation	145
10	Retirement	145
11	Change in health of a family member	144
12	Pregnancy	140
13	Sex difficulties	139
14	Gain of a new family member	139
15	Business readjustment	139
16	Change in financial state	138
17	Death of a close friend	137
18	Change to a different line of work	136
19	Change in number of arguments with spouse	135
20	Mortgage over $10,000	131
21	Foreclosure of mortgage or loan	130
22	Change in responsibilities at work	129
23	Son or daughter leaving home	129
24	Trouble with in-laws	129
25	Outstanding personal achievement	128
26	Wife begin or stop work	126
27	Begin or end school	126
28	Change in living conditions	125
29	Revision of personal habits	124
30	Trouble with boss	123
31	Change in work hours or conditions	120
32	Change in residence	120
33	Change in schools	120
34	Change in recreation	119
35	Change in church activities	119
36	Change in social activities	118
37	Mortgage or loan less than $10,000	117
38	Change in sleeping habits	116
39	Change in number of family get-togethers	115
40	Change in eating habits	115
41	Vacation	113
42	Christmas	112
43	Minor violations of the law	111

Source: Reprinted from Holmes and Rahe (1967), with permission from Elsevier.

Note: * LCU = Life change unit.

ACTIVITY 3.2

Look at Table 3.1 and work out your own LCU score for the past year. Do you think this is a reasonable indication of the stress you have experienced in the last year? Before you read on, write down any problems you can see with this approach to measuring stress.

There have been a number of criticisms of the life events approach highlighting limitations that may account for the large number of positive findings in the early literature. Some critics have commented on the fact that where two people both have the same score their subjective experience may actually be very different. In one study, researchers interviewed people about their responses and found that, for some people, the death of a close friend involved the death of a childhood friend who they had not seen for a long time whereas for others it was a much more significant loss (Dohrenwend et al., 1990). This has been labelled the problem of 'intracategory variability' (Dohrenwend, 2006).

A further criticism, which you may have identified, is that the Social Readjustment Rating Scale does not discriminate between positive and negative events (Jones and Kinman, 2001). However, most people would assume that only negative events would be harmful for health, while positive events might even be beneficial. Because of this criticism many more recent approaches to life events measurement also take into account people's appraisals of each event.

Research on life events has also been criticized for the reliability and validity of measures (that is, do people produce the same scores if asked to complete the questionnaire after a time interval and do the measures actually measure what they are intended to measure?). In the 1970s and 1980s researchers considered reliability over time (usually called test–retest reliability). One study found that, when people repeated the measure after 1–2 weeks, there was only 70 per cent agreement (Steele, Henderson and Duncan-Jones, 1980) and other research has indicated that reliability declines dramatically over longer periods (Dohrenwend, 2006). Related to this, there are concerns that retrospective reports may not be valid when, as is often the case, they are reported by people who are already diagnosed with a disease. In these circumstances people may be inclined to want to find an explanation for their illness, leading them to report more life events than those who have no illness (Brown, 1974). This factor may account for some of the positive relationships found in the early studies. Nowadays limited credence is given to studies unless they use longitudinal approaches, which assess life events prior to the development (or at least the diagnosis) of disease.

Over the years there have been improvements to life events methodology and many different measures of stressful life events have been developed. Some have been established that are relevant to particular subgroups. For example, there are a range of scales specifically for use with children and adolescents (Grant et al., 2004). Others have tried to overcome the methodological limitations of the checklist approach by using the much more time-consuming method of semi-structured interviews where people describe events, which are then rated by trained individuals. The most well-known example of this is the Life Events and Difficulties Schedule (LEDS) developed by Brown and Harris (1978). This was used in an important study of life events, social support and depression, which is described in more detail in Chapter 5 (Brown and Harris, 1978).

Over the past 50 years researchers have studied the relationship between life events and disease. Yet there is still controversy concerning whether major life events do cause disease. The early studies showed strong links but have been subject to criticism. Literature on breast cancer provides a good example of how some well-publicized studies find links between life events and cancer (e.g. Geyer, 1991; Chen *et al.*, 1995) but other research fails to support the findings (e.g. Greer and Morris, 1975; Protheroe *et al.*, 1999). Many studies have used what is known as a 'limited prospective design'. For example, Chen *et al.* (1995) studied 119 women who were referred for biopsies for suspected breast cancer. They were interviewed and their experience of life events was assessed before they received a definitive diagnosis. The researchers found that 19 out of 41 women who were subsequently diagnosed with cancer had experienced threatening life events during the 5 years before diagnosis compared with 15 out of the 78 controls. While isolated studies such as this often get media publicity and strengthen public perceptions that there is a link, literature reviews and meta-analyses of the overall associations tend to conclude that there is little evidence to link life events and breast cancer incidence (e.g. Nielsen and Brønbæk, 2006), though it is still unclear whether stress may affect progression of the disease.

Stressful life events may be more strongly linked to psychological outcomes. Research into life events in extreme situations such as wars and natural disasters suggests that exposure to such events is likely to lead to serious psychopathology (Dohrenwend, 2000). There is also convincing evidence that stressful life events are linked to an increase in depression (Kessler, 1997; Mazure, 1998). However, it is clear that there are considerable individual differences in people's susceptibility. The idea that some people are genetically more susceptible to stressors is known as the stress diathesis model (the term 'diathesis' meaning a predisposition to illness). A number of studies have suggested that some people are indeed more genetically vulnerable to stressful life events than others (e.g. Kendler *et al.*, 1995). Advances in genetics have now enabled researchers to explore specific genes that may be associated with this susceptibility. For example, Lessard and Holman (2014) provide evidence that long-term health impacts of exposure to child abuse and stressful life events in adulthood are moderated by hypothalamic–pituitary–adrenal axis polymorphism genotypes.

Overall, despite the many criticisms of life events research, it seems to be an approach that is here to stay with the number of studies increasing dramatically decade by decade (Dohrenwend, 2006). Furthermore, modifications in methodology have helped to improve reliability and validity of measurement.

Transactional theory and the daily hassles and uplifts approach

One of the most influential critics of life events research was Richard Lazarus who suggested that the focus on major life changes, which are comparatively rare, ignores the fact that a great deal of stress stems from recurrent day-to-day problems or chronic conditions, which he describes as daily hassles. He also suggested that many of the other limitations of the approach (which are discussed above) stem from the fact that it is essentially atheoretical (Lazarus, 1990).

Lazarus (1966; Lazarus and Folkman, 1984) suggested a new approach to stress based on his own transactional theory of stress. Central to this theory and to his definition of stress (see above) is the notion of appraisal. Lazarus takes the view that stress is not a property of the environment (as suggested by the life events approach), nor is it a property of the individual (as implied by research into physiological markers discussed in Chapter 2), rather it is a transaction between the individual and the environment (Lazarus, 1990). The focus is therefore on the process of appraisal and coping. In any potentially stressful transaction or encounter, a person may appraise the situation as involving harm or threat of harm, or alternatively they may see it in a positive, optimistic light and view it as a challenge. The type of appraisal will then determine the person's coping processes, which will in turn determine subsequent appraisals (see Chapter 5 for further discussion of the role of coping in this theory). Lazarus is therefore describing a constantly changing relationship between the person and the environment. Furthermore, he suggests that stress is a complex phenomenon that involves many variables in terms of inputs, outputs and mediating factors associated with appraisal and coping.

This approach clearly has implications for the way stress is measured. In particular, Lazarus (1990) suggests that the search for a single satisfactory measure is 'doomed to failure'. He argues that stress needs to be assessed by a series of different measures, which each capture different aspects of the stress process. Relevant measures therefore might include environmental inputs (e.g. daily stressors as well as life events), measures of individual differences, coping, and physiological and psychological responses. A critical feature of this approach is that, because stress is a process, assessments should be repeated over time. This theory led to the development of a measure of daily stressors known as the Hassles Scale (e.g. Kanner *et al.*, 1981) and subsequently a shorter Hassles and Uplifts Scale (DeLongis *et al.*, 1982). In this measure 53 items are listed, for example, 'your children', 'your fellow workers', 'your health' and respondents are asked to rate separately the extent to which each item is a hassle or an uplift. A number of studies have examined the extent to which both daily hassles and major life events predict ill health and these have tended to suggest that hassles are more predictive (e.g. Kanner *et al.*, 1981; DeLongis *et al.*, 1982). Research based on the transactional theory has been associated with a growth in daily assessment to tap the stress process. This typically uses 'daily diaries', which contain rating scales, such as the Hassles and Uplifts Scale. In addition, they may also offer scope to provide qualitative descriptions of daily events (see Research methods 3.2).

Inevitably, Lazarus' approach has not been without critics. Criticisms have primarily focused upon the notion that by including appraisal of the stressful nature of transactions within measures of hassles, items may be inadvertently measuring psychological distress. If correct, this would inevitably lead to positive correlations between stressors and strains (Dohrenwend *et al.*, 1984; Dohrenwend and Shrout, 1985). Dohrenwend *et al.* (1984) suggested that while life events measures may also sometimes include items that are symptoms rather than causes of distress, this is much more of a problem for Lazarus' measures. Here the mere instruction to rate the severity of hassles implies a level of distress. Thus all items are potentially confounded with psychological distress. Dohrenwend and Shrout (1985: 782) argue that environmental events should be

RESEARCH METHODS 3.2

Using diaries in health psychology research

Approaches to studying stress differ in their focus. For example, compare the life events approach with the transactional approach. The life events approach has been criticized on methodological grounds and stress research, like other areas in health, social and clinical psychology, has been criticized for over-reliance on cross-sectional, 'snap-shot' methodologies (see Affleck *et al.*, 1999; Nezlek, 2001 for further discussion). For example, research into the impact of stress on eating behaviour has tended to use laboratory-based methods, which employ single measures of stress (e.g. life events over the previous year) or one-off retrospective measurements of stress in the short term (e.g. perceptions of stress over the past two weeks). Such research ignores the substantial evidence showing that changes in within-person stressful daily hassles are important in understanding stress-outcome processes (see Bolger, Davis and Rafaeli, 2003; Bolger and Laurenceau, 2013).

We are often interested in investigating causal relationships between study variables and/or determining whether a particular psychological variable influences a later health outcome, e.g. on the following day or week (known as a lagged effect). Imagine we wanted to find out if negative mood was associated with the onset of pain episodes in arthritis patients or whether in psoriasis patients, stressful events on one day could trigger 'flare ups' the next day. Conventional cross-sectional or longitudinal study designs would not be very useful here because they miss the detailed daily variation driving the causal processes we are interested in. In these cases and others in health psychology research, the dependent variable under investigation is a daily process, that is, it changes from day to day and/or frequently within days. Therefore, in order to assess it we need to measure it repeatedly during and over several days. A diary approach is ideally suited to such research.

What are the advantages of using diary designs and measuring daily processes? Affleck *et al.* (1999: 747) argue that daily diary studies allow researchers to

- capture as closely as possible the 'real-time' occurrences or moments of change (in study variables);
- reduce recall bias;
- mitigate some forms of confounding by using participants as their own controls; and
- establish temporal precedence to strengthen causal inferences.

In addition, using daily diaries permits researchers to use sophisticated statistical techniques (e.g. hierarchical linear modelling) to examine day-to-day within-person effects together with the impact of between-person factors such as personality or gender.

There are important procedural differences in the way daily diary studies are conducted. If we were designing a study, we would have to consider how frequently our participants completed their diaries. Three main methods exist:

1 *Interval-contingent*: the participant completes diary at regular intervals (e.g. before going to bed).
2 *Event-contingent*: the participant completes diary each time a specific event happens (e.g. every time they experience a daily hassle).
3 *Signal-contingent*: the patient completes diary in response to random 'alarms' or 'beeps' from a palmtop computer or similar device.

Researchers also have to consider how participants actually record their responses. Typically researchers use either paper and pencil diaries or handheld computers. In fact, the issue of which method is best has recently sparked a lively debate within the research methods literature (see Stone *et al.*, 2002; Green *et al.*, 2006; Tennen *et al.*, 2006; Bolger and Laurenceau, 2013). Both methods have their pros and cons. For example, using paper and pencil methods, the researcher cannot be certain that the participant has completed their diary when they claimed to have done so (this is known as 'compliance'), whereas a computer will date and time stamp all diary entries. However, handheld computers are relatively expensive and they can malfunction resulting in loss of important data. Nevertheless, a study that compared paper and pencil with electronic techniques showed that both methods found a similar pattern of findings and yielded equivalent data (Green *et al.*, 2006). In either case it is critical that the researcher designs the entry system so participants can easily and efficiently record the particular events under investigation.

measured 'uncontaminated by perceptions, appraisals or reactions'. While self-report measures are arguably always likely to be influenced by the individual's appraisal, the implication of this argument is that researchers should use items that ask about the existence of stressors (e.g. whether or not a particular event happened) rather than items that ask people to rate stress or hassles associated with the event. This more objective approach to stressors is commonly found in the work-stress literature (see Chapter 4), where researchers (and employers) are primarily concerned with identifying the negative effects of work irrespective of individuals' idiosyncratic appraisal.

Within the current literature you may spot both relatively objective measures of stressors and measures that include elements of appraisal of distress. In your reading of research it is important to look out for instances where there is overlap between stressors and strains. It is likely to be a particular problem where, for example, individuals' ratings of hassles are correlated with a rating of anxiety or depression. The findings may not be very meaningful if both measures are essentially measuring anxiety! However, subjective ratings may not be a problem if ratings of hassles are correlated with a more objective outcome such as a physiological measure or a rating of health behaviour (see Research methods 3.3)

RESEARCH METHODS 3.3

Daily hassles and eating behaviour (O'Connor *et al.*, 2008a)

Background

When under pressure we may be more likely to skip exercise sessions and replace nourishing meals with quick fast food snacks or indulge in comfort eating of sweets and other high fat foods. Such negative health behaviours may be one of the ways in which stress indirectly contributes to both cardiovascular disease and cancer risk. This study set out to explore the complex relationship between stress (assessed as daily hassles) and eating behaviour in a sample of employed men and women in a naturalistic setting using a multi-level prospective diary design.

The study also aimed to explore the different types of stressors that may affect changes in eating behaviour. A number of researchers have previously found that particular types of stress had different effects on eating. For example, in the laboratory, Heatherton and colleagues (1991, 1992) found stressors of an ego-threatening nature (e.g. where there is a fear of failure) were associated with an increase in eating whereas physical threats (e.g. fear of an electric shock) led to a decrease in eating. Therefore, the study described here looked at the effect of a range of different daily hassles, namely ego-threatening, interpersonal, physical and work-related stressors.

A final aim of the study was to investigate the influence of individual difference variables on the relationship between hassles and eating. Individual difference models of stress hypothesize that certain groups of individuals will show different responses to stress (e.g. the obese and non-obese; women and men; and those with certain eating styles such as emotional eating). In addition, few previous studies have explored multiple individual differences variables, therefore not allowing conclusions to be drawn about the relative importance of these different variables (e.g. Conner, Fitter and Fletcher, 1999; O'Connor and O'Connor, 2004).

Design and methods

A total of 422 employees completed daily diaries over 4 weeks in which they recorded daily hassles and provided free response reports of between-meal snacking, fruit and vegetable consumption and perceived variations in daily food intake. Eating styles were assessed using the Dutch Eating Behaviour Questionnaire and the Three Factor Eating Questionnaire. Each of the hassles reported was coded by independent raters as to whether or not it was ego-threatening (e.g. job interview, public talk, criticism); interpersonal (e.g. argument with partner, family problems, visiting relatives); work-related (e.g. difficult work task, late for meeting, deadline); or physical in nature (e.g. anxious/frightened, feeling ill). The data were analysed using a technique known as hierarchical linear modelling, which allowed the researchers to examine the day-to-day changes (in hassles and eating) together with the eating style variables.

Results

The results showed daily hassles were associated with increased consumption of high fat/sugar snacks and with a reduction in main meals and vegetable consumption. Ego-threatening, interpersonal and work-related hassles were associated with increased snacking, whereas physical stressors were associated with decreased snacking. In addition, an emotional eating style was found to be the most important moderator of the hassles–snacking relationship, such that individuals who had higher levels of emotional eating consumed more snacks in response to daily stressors.

Conclusion

Daily hassles were associated with an increase in unhealthy eating behaviour, with most marked effects for those who were emotional eaters. These results highlight an important indirect pathway through which stress influences health risk. More recently, O'Connor, Armitage and Ferguson (2015) have developed a stress management support tool to help reduce stress-related unhealthy snacking and to promote stress-related healthy snacking.

Compared to life events research, less work has examined the relationship between hassles and health despite the fact that there are strong arguments in favour of examining the effect of day-to-day events and hassles in order to fully understand stress-outcome processes. Over 30 years ago, Kanner *et al.* (1981: 3) argued that it is 'day-to-day events that ultimately have proximal significance for health outcomes and whose accumulative impact . . . should be assessed'. Nevertheless, of the existing studies, a number have demonstrated that daily hassles can have a substantial cumulative effect on health and well-being (e.g. Zautra, 2003; Almeida, 2005; Kaplan and Stone, 2013). The outcomes that are measured in this research are rather different to those in the life events literature. Thus, while researchers looking at major life events have looked at long-term effects on the likelihood of contracting serious diseases such as cancer, those looking at daily events have focused on much shorter time scales and linked hassles to much more proximal changes in physiological markers of stress, or the occurrence of minor diseases such as colds. This focus has also enabled them to shed more light on processes whereby stress may impact on disease.

Nowadays, a range of different types of approach to measuring hassles and other daily stressors are used. For example, the study described in Research methods 3.3 asked people to describe their own hassles, which were then categorized by independent raters. There have also been significant advances in the technologies available to collect and assess daily stressors, together with other health–related and psychological variables. For example, mobile phones, tablets, sensors and other ambulatory monitors are now widely used (Kaplan and Stone, 2013). Mobile technologies represent an exciting way forward to 'bring the laboratory and clinic to the community' (Kaplan and Stone, 2013).

Researchers have found that hassles transmit their harmful effects directly through psychophysiological pathways as well as indirectly via changes in health behaviours. In a 2-year longitudinal study, Twisk *et al.* (1999) explored the effects of changes in daily hassles and life events on a number of biological and lifestyle variables associated with coronary heart disease risk. The main findings of this study showed that daily hassles were more important than life events and they predicted changes in lipoproteins (a combination of fats and proteins found in the blood), daily physical activity and smoking behaviour. In another study conducted by Newman, O'Connor and Conner (2007), daily hassles were associated with increased (high fat) snack intake over a 2-week period. However, these effects were only observed in women who had previously been identified as high cortisol reactors following a laboratory stressor and not in low cortisol reactors. These findings are noteworthy because they suggest that the impact of daily hassles on eating behaviour is moderated by individual differences in cortisol reactivity.

More recently, other studies have demonstrated that daily hassles have the capacity to activate the HPA axis, as evidenced by increases in cortisol levels (e.g. Smyth *et al.*, 1998; Hanson *et al.*, 2000). In fact, hassles that produce negative emotional responses have been found to be most likely to activate the stress response. Jacobs *et al.* (2007) found daily hassles were associated with increased negative affect, decreased positive affect, agitation and raised cortisol levels. However, only negative affect accounted for the effects of daily hassles on cortisol. As you will recall from Chapter 2, frequent and excessive cortisol secretions over a prolonged period can cause wear and tear to the body's cardiovascular and immune systems leading to physical illness. In a 28-day study of daily experience and cortisol, low cortisol levels in the morning were related to anxiety, exhaustion, sleepiness at awakening and poor health the day before; while high levels of cortisol in the evening were related to stress and poor health (Dahlgren *et al.*, 2009). In addition, it has been suggested that increased cortisol secretion caused by daily hassles may contribute to several common psychological disorders such as depression (Sher, 2004). In other words, repeated minor daily hassles akin to having an argument with your partner or boss may lead to depression in vulnerable individuals.

Daily hassles have also been found to make some chronic illness conditions worse. In a study of irritable bowel syndrome sufferers, daily stress was shown to be associated with greater symptomatology (Dancey, Taghavi and Fox, 1998). In another study, Fifield *et al.* (2004) showed that rheumatoid arthritis sufferers who worked in high strain jobs (high demands/low control) experienced greater pain on days when they reported a high number of stressors. Daily hassles can also impact on important self-care behaviours in people with chronic conditions. For example, Riazi, Pickup and Bradley (2004) found that daily hassles disrupted glycaemic control (i.e. regulation of blood glucose levels) in patients with type I diabetes who were prone to respond to stress. More recently, a study of women with current bulimia nervosa showed that daily hassles frequently precede episodes of bulimia and they seem to play a role in maintaining these behaviours (Goldschmidt *et al.*, 2014). Similarly, another recent investigation demonstrated that yesterday's daily stressors influence the amount of cortisol that is released the following morning and these (lower) levels of cortisol are associated with a greater frequency of physical symptoms on the same day (Gartland *et al.*, 2014a).

Taken together, these studies indicate that daily hassles are able to influence health and illness processes by disrupting habitual health behaviours, increasing the release of stress hormones as well as exacerbating symptomatology and disrupting self-care behaviours in a number of chronic illness conditions. Moreover, this work suggests that stress management programmes may prove to be very beneficial for longer-term well-being (see Chapter 4 for more detail on approaches to stress management).

WHERE IS STRESS LOCATED?

Recent theorizing by Segerstrom and O'Connor (2012) has built upon each of the approaches outlined and suggested that identifying where stress is located is important to improve its conceptualization and assessment. Specifically, in keeping with Lazarus and Folkman (1984), it is argued that stress can be located in the environment, in appraisal or in response (i.e. emotions or physiology), however, in order to fully understand the stress process, there is a need to investigate how each of these locales interact. For example, the experience of a major life event, such as unemployment or divorce, is likely to have a knock-on effect on the frequency and intensity of minor daily stressors such as being late for a meeting or having an argument with your partner, and conversely, minor daily stressors may reduce the ability to cope with a major life event; thus the system is reciprocal (Segerstrom and O'Connor, 2012). Both types of stressor are located in the environment; however, the relationship between these events is dynamic, bi-directional and will change frequently over time.

Therefore, a major challenge for stress research is to 'appropriately and explicitly locate stress and to understand the effects on other stress *locations*' (Segerstrom and O'Connor, 2012: 131). In order to do this, it is imperative that researchers adopt an integrated approach to measurement and ensure that the different locations of stress are assessed using a variety of longitudinal, panel, multi-level and daily research designs. For example, a major life stressor such as unemployment is likely to lead to an increased number of minor daily stressors (e.g. financial stressors), which are likely to influence appraisals of threat, challenge and loss, which may generalize to other situations and stressors, thereby resulting in increased levels of psychological distress. However, importantly, such a cascade will also depend on personality (see Ferguson, 2013). For example, losing one's job may result in reduced stress (assuming all else is equal in terms of financial constraints) in people who tend to be cautious, methodical and emotionally stable.

Conservation of resources theory – a resource-based model of stress

An approach to stress, which poses a challenge to the transactional model, is the conservation of resources model (COR) (Hobfoll, 1989, 2001). This represents a shift away from the emphasis placed on appraisal in the transactional model back towards a more objective approach. This model suggests that resources (not demands) are the key variables of importance and that people strive to 'retain, protect and build resources' (Hobfoll, 1989: 516). Stress is defined as a reaction to loss, a threatened loss, or a failure to gain resources following an investment of resources. This may include personal resources (such as a sense of mastery) and social resources (such as social support), which have been well studied outside of the context of this theory (see

Chapter 5). However, they also include a range of other factors such as financial/material resources. The model predicts that when faced with stress people will seek to minimize the potential loss of resources. In the absence of stress, Hobfoll suggests they will seek to build resources as a hedge against future stressors. He argues that the association of social resources with positive well-being is an example of the benefits of resource building (e.g. Cohen and Wills, 1985).

A central principle of the theory is that 'resource loss is disproportionally more salient than resource gain' (Hobfoll, 2001: 343), so that in circumstances of equal resource loss and gain, the loss will have greater impact. Hobfoll suggests that this emphasis on resources differentiates this theory from transactional theory, which emphasizes appraisals. In the COR approach, although stress processes may be assessed via people's appraisals, most are resources that are objectively observable. The model is also distinct from the transactional theory in its idea of building resources for prevention of, or protection against, future stressors. Thus it highlights the importance of proactive coping (see Chapter 5). It also introduced the notion of 'resource caravans'. This is the idea that resources cluster together in groups so that if you have one major resource such as self-efficacy this is likely to be linked to a range of others such as social support and other positive coping styles. Over time these caravans travel with us such that resources at one time period tend to carry over into future times (Hobfoll, 2001). Hobfoll further suggests the notion of loss or gain spirals whereby initial resource gain leads to future gain and loss leads to future loss. These principles seem intuitively sensible and Hobfoll supports them with examples, frequently drawing on studies of stress and coping in disaster areas.

The model is underpinned by its own questionnaire, the Conservation of Resources Evaluation (COR-E) (Hobfoll, 2007). This consists of a list of 74 resources ranging from 'adequate income', 'support from coworkers' to 'adequate home furnishings' and 'positive feelings about myself'. Currently, there is little research using this model to predict major physical health outcomes, however, resource loss has been linked to depression and other psychological strains. For example, Ennis, Hobfoll and Schröder (2000) report that lack of resources such as low income or poor education was almost unrelated to depressed mood whereas loss of material resources (e.g. deterioration in finances) was highly related.

More recently, Hobfall has suggested that resources are an important predictor of resilience in the face of disasters (Hobfall, 2011). Research based on data from the 11 September 2001 terrorist attack in New York, supports this theory. The presence of resources (such as social support) predicted resilience, whereas those who experienced resource loss (in terms of income decline) were less than half as likely to be resilient as participants who did not experience this loss. Resilience was defined in terms of low levels of depression, substance abuse and post-traumatic stress disorder (Bonanno et al., 2007; for more on resilience see Chapter 5).

The model has produced a certain amount of controversy, particularly as it can be seen as a challenge to Lazarus' highly influential theory. It was hotly debated in a series of articles in *Applied Psychology: An International Review* (2001). Here Hobfoll describes the theory and a number of other experts, including Lazarus himself, debate the issues in a series of subsequent articles. Lazarus (2001) attacks the theory in no uncertain terms and states that all the elements of the COR theory can already be found in his transactional theory. For example, there are plenty of references to resources within his theory and resource loss is central to the idea of loss appraisal, for example in the grief process (e.g. Lazarus and Folkman, 1984; Lazarus, 1999). His view is therefore that the COR approach is 'fundamentally unsound and fails to advance us beyond what we know' (Lazarus, 2001: 381). Others take a more moderate view. For example, Schwarzer (2001) suggests that Hobfoll's and Lazarus' views differ in emphasis rather than in fundamental principles. He argues that the difference lies in the centrality of either objective or subjective resources. Thus Lazarus takes the view that objective resources are simply antecedents, which lead to appraisals (subjective resources) that are the direct precursors of perceptions of stress. In contrast, Hobfoll examines both objective and subjective resources but emphasizes the former. Schwarzer (2001) further suggests that the inclusion of the notion of resource investment and proactive coping introduces a forward time perspective, which opens up new research questions. Thus, he suggests that this theory represents an advance on the earlier theories rather than a major paradigm shift.

WHY DO SOME PEOPLE GET ILL IN RESPONSE TO STRESS AND OTHERS DO NOT?

It is often claimed that stress can cause all sorts of diseases including cancer. In fact consideration of the life events literature suggests that the evidence linking stress and many diseases is far from clear. Evidence is much clearer that experiencing certain stressors can have negative impacts in terms of increasing risk of coronary heart disease and can impact on immune functioning and day-to-day deterioration in health outcomes (e.g. Everson *et al.*, 1996a, 2001; Cohen, 2005). However, not everyone who feels stressed becomes ill, distressed or experiences stress-related disruptions to their normal health behaviours. In fact, researchers now believe that certain individuals are more vulnerable to the effects of stress due to differences in their psychological as well as biological make-up. As you will see in Chapter 5, the effects of stress can be buffered by having a good social support network of friends and family and being well equipped to cope with different stressful situations. Personality also plays an important role in the stress process and will be covered in detail in Chapter 6. A number of personality traits have been found to predispose people to respond negatively to stress (e.g. type A personality, neuroticism, perfectionism). This is another example of the stress-diathesis paradigm. For example, individuals who have perfectionistic tendencies are more likely to experience serious psychological distress after each stressful encounter as it represents a chance for them to fail to meet their high standards (see O'Connor, O'Connor and Marshall, 2007). Therefore, as you can imagine, people who are perfectionistic may be more vulnerable to suffering from the negative effects of stress in the future.

As well as psychological differences, researchers have identified biological differences in the way people respond to and recover from stressful situations. It has been proposed that certain individuals generally may have a large physiological response to stress (this process is known as stress reactivity), while for others the body may take much longer to return to normal once the stressor has passed (this process is known as stress recovery). In both cases, over time, the body is likely to experience greater wear and tear. If such differences exist, then they may explain why some people are more likely to become ill as a result of stress and others do not. These exciting developments are considered in the next section.

Stress reactivity

The central idea linked to the 'stress reactivity hypothesis' is that individuals who have large emotional and physiological responses to stress may be more likely to develop health problems in the future (Kamarck and Lovallo, 2003). In particular, people who are prone to having dramatic increases in heart rate and/or blood pressure after stressful situations may be at greater risk of developing high blood pressure and cardiovascular disease. Over the last 25 years, evidence has accumulated in support of this hypothesis from animal as well as human studies. In a sample of monkeys, Manuck, Kaplan and Clarkson (1983) found greater evidence of heart disease in monkeys who were previously identified as being high reactors to stress compared to the low reactors. The high reactors were also found to be more aggressive than the low reactors. In a human study, the results from the Kuopio Heart Study in Finland showed that men who had a greater cardiovascular response to stress were more likely to develop hypertension (i.e. high blood pressure) and stroke (Everson *et al.*, 1996a, 2001). In another longitudinal study known as the Coronary Artery Risk Development in Young Adults (CARDIA) study, Matthews *et al.* (2004) found that cardiovascular reactivity to stress at the beginning of the study was associated with higher blood pressure levels 13 years later!

However, not all studies have been supportive with several researchers suggesting that the mixed findings may be associated with methodological inconsistencies (e.g. using different laboratory stress challenges; time of testing, Nebel *et al.*, 1996; Linden, Rutledge and Con, 1998; Kamarck and Lovallo, 2003) and with individual differences (e.g. cynical hostility (see Chapter 6), morningness–eveningness; Kamarck and Lovallo, 2003; Willis, O'Connor and Smith, 2005) which may obscure the effects. For example, Willis *et al.* (2005) found that stress reactivity levels were moderated by morningness–eveningness (i.e. the extent to which you are a 'lark', who prefers doing tasks in the morning, or an 'owl' who prefers the evening). They found that 'owls' had higher heart rate generally and in response to stress in the afternoon compared to the morning. Therefore, it seems that the research into the impact of stress reactivity is far from clear-cut. In addition, a number of researchers have begun to argue that low or blunted reactivity (and not just high!) may also be associated with negative health outcomes (Phillips, Ginty and Hughes, 2013). These authors have suggested that departures from the norm in either direction may indicate that the bodily systems are 'operating in a biased state' (Phillips *et al.*, 2013: 4). Overall, it seems that there is fairly strong evidence showing that people who have large or small responses to stress may be at greater risk of becoming ill following the long-term effects of stress.

Stress recovery

More recently, researchers have turned their attention to exploring the impact on health outcomes of the amount of time it takes the body to return to normal after stress. This is known as stress recovery and it is proposed that people who take longer to recover may be more vulnerable to future ill health (e.g. Schuler and O'Brien, 1997; Schneider *et al.*, 2003). For example, in a study by Steptoe and Marmot (2005) in which the effects of stress reactivity and post-stress recovery on blood pressure 3 years later were investigated, they showed that increases in blood pressure levels 3 years later were most strongly associated with longer post-stress recovery. More impressively, these effects were independent of all the other risk factors measured (e.g. age, gender, body mass index, socio-economic status, smoking status, hypertension medication, etc.). Steptoe and Marmot (2005) also suggested that post-stress recovery may become more important as we get older. When we are young our recovery from stress tends to be swift and efficient, whereas, as we age, it may become less well controlled. One reason for this may be linked to McEwen's concept of allostatic load – longer post-stress recovery may develop as a result of wear and tear to the cardiovascular system caused by the body having to frequently respond to stress over several decades. This area of research is relatively new, therefore we cannot draw firm conclusions about the importance of stress recovery; however, the initial findings are promising.

PERSEVERATIVE COGNITION

Recent developments in stress theory have highlighted the importance of worry, rumination and repetitive thought in improving our understanding of stress-disease relationships. Brosschot, Gerin and Thayer (2006), in their perseverative cognition hypothesis (PCH), have suggested that worry or repetitive thinking may lead to disease by prolonging stress-related physiological activation by amplifying short-term responses, delaying recovery or reactivating responses after a stressor has been experienced. There is a growing body of evidence that has demonstrated that perseverative cognition is associated with somatic outcomes cross-sectionally and prospectively (see Verkuil *et al.*, 2010 for a review). For example, Brosschot and van der Doef (2006), in a worry intervention study, showed that reduction in worry was associated with a decrease in somatic complaints. In a more sophisticated design using electronic diaries, Verkuil and colleagues (2012) clearly demonstrated that worry intensity was predictive of the frequency of somatic complaints and intensity mediated the effect of stressful events on these complaints. Building upon this work, another recent investigation found that stress-related thinking (triggered by the disclosure of traumatic thoughts) was associated with higher cortisol levels and upper respiratory infection symptoms at follow-up (O'Connor *et al.*, 2013). Similar to stress recovery, research exploring the effects of perseverative cognition on health is still in its infancy, however, it represents an exciting avenue for future work.

CONCLUSIONS

We have presented a range of perspectives on stress and its relationship with health. These have included research that has sought to establish links between the existence of objective stressors (such as measures of major life events) and physical health outcomes, research that has focused on the appraisal of stress (e.g. drawing on transactional theory) and research that has shed light on physiological processes. Across this research gradually stronger links are emerging between stressors, the processes whereby stressors lead to disease (e.g. impaired immune functioning) and actual disease outcomes. However, we are still a long way from knowing for sure the extent to which stress is implicated in most diseases.

At the start of this chapter we asked you to consider whether stress has increased in recent years. It is of course not possible to give a definitive answer to this question. Clearly the types of stressors we experience have changed over the last 50 years. For most in Western society, standards of living, working conditions, life expectancy and health have improved. Thus it might seem we have little to complain about. However, the pace of life seems to be ever increasing and the rate of change in technology and employment (for example) imposes new stressors. It is certainly the case that people are more aware of stress due to the work of psychologists and social scientists and the publicity that this has generated. Some have even suggested that stress is produced, or at least exacerbated by the increased awareness and expectation of stress in society (e.g. Pollock, 1988). While this may be a negative impact of our increased knowledge of stress, information about the impacts of psychological (as well as physiological) processes is essential for improving individual health and well-being.

SUMMARY

References to 'stress' are widespread in society but the term is used in different ways in different contexts. Lazarus suggested that stress is best regarded as a rubric or umbrella term, which covers a wide range of variables (including stressors such as life events or hassles and strain outcomes, such as physical symptoms or depression). Historically, stress has been variously viewed as a stimulus, a response or in terms of an interaction between the two. Selye's influential work on the general adaptation syndrome focused particularly on the physiological response. More recent approaches to research on allostatic load, which build on Selye's work, have helped to explain the ways in which stressors lead to disease.

Psychologists have developed a range of different perspectives on stress. Life events researchers claim that major life events are a key predictor of disease. Transactional researchers have focused on appraisals of stress and specifically the impacts of appraisals of minor day-to-day hassles and uplifts. Conservation of resource theorists focus on the impact of loss of resources as the main predictor of stressors. These approaches are sometimes seen as in conflict but can also be viewed as all contributing a useful perspective on a complex phenomenon. All have had some success in predicting negative health and psychological outcomes. However, links between stressors and major physical health outcomes such as breast cancer have not been established.

People do clearly differ in their individual responses to stress, so some will get ill in response to stressors while others will not. For example, it is likely that some people are physiologically more reactive to stressors and/or take longer to recover and worry, rumination and repetitive thought appear to play an important role in stress–disease relationships.

KEY CONCEPTS AND TERMS

- Allostatic load
- Conservation of resources (COR) model
- Diseases of adaptation
- General adaptation syndrome (GAS)

- Hassles and uplifts scale
- Hierarchical linear modelling
- Life events
- Perseverative cognition

- Social Readjustment Rating Scale
- Stress
- Stress diathesis
- Stress reactivity
- Stress recovery
- Transactional theory

SAMPLE ESSAY TITLES

- 'Having a stressful life increases the likelihood of contracting disease'. Evaluate this statement with reference to examples from the psychological literature.
- Compare and contrast the transactional approach and the conservation of resources approach to stress.
- Why do some people get ill in response to stress and others do not? Discuss.
- Critically evaluate two approaches to measuring the effects of stress on health.

FURTHER READING

Books

Folkman, S. (ed.) (2011). *Oxford Handbook of Stress, Health and Coping.* Oxford: Oxford University Press.

Journal articles

Chida, Y. and Steptoe, A. (2010). Greater cardiovascular responses to laboratory mental stress are associated with poor subsequent cardiovascular risk status: A meta-analysis of prospective evidence. *Hypertension*, 55, 1026–1032.

Hobfoll, S. (2001). The influence of culture, community and the nested-self in the stress process: Advancing conservation of resources theory. *Applied Psychology: An International Review*, 50, 337–421. (See also the subsequent articles in this journal by Lazarus, Schwarzer and others.)

Kamarck, T.W. and Lovallo, W.R. (2003). Cardiovascular reactivity to psychological challenge: Conceptual and measurement considerations. *Psychosomatic Medicine*, 65, 9–21.

Lazarus, R.S. (1990). Theory-based stress measurement. *Psychological Inquiry*, 1, 3–13.

McEwen, B.S. (1998). Protective and damaging effects of stress mediators. *New England Journal of Medicine*, 338, 171–179.

Segerstrom, S.C. and O'Connor, D.B. (2012). Stress, health and illness: Four challenges for the future. *Psychology and Health*, 27, 128–140.

Steptoe, A. and Kivimaki, M. (2013). Stress and cardiovascular disease: An update on current knowledge. *Annual Review of Public Health*, 34, 337–354.

Verkuil, B., Brosschot, J.F., Gebhardt, W. and Thayer, J.F. (2010). When worries make you sick: A review of perseverative cognition, the default stress response and somatic health. *Journal of Experimental Psychopathology*, 1, 87–118.

4 Stress and health in context

CHAPTER PLAN

Chapter 3 examined a range of different approaches to stress and considered the links between stress and health. In this chapter we look at the effect of environmental or contextual factors on stress and their relationship to health.

In the first section, we consider the effect of socio-economic status (SES) and social inequality on stress and health. It is well established worldwide that poverty and deprivation are associated with poor health and that even within affluent societies lower SES is linked to poorer health. We consider the role of stress in this relationship.

We then consider stress at work in a subsequent section. For most people, their job determines their income and therefore their SES. Indeed, researchers typically classify individuals into social classes based on their occupation using formal classification systems such as the UK National Statistics Socio-Economic Classification (NS-SEC; National Statistics, 2002). Most people spend a significant proportion of their lives at work and evidence suggests that many people feel that it is a major source of stress (Smith *et al.*, 2000). Work stress is also of great interest to employers who need to have healthy and productive workforces.

Work stress is also known to have implications beyond the work environment. If we feel stress at work this cannot always be easily switched off when we go home and similarly major problems in our personal lives may affect our work. Work stressors may impact even more on our home lives if we work long hours and take work home with us. Increasingly, the barriers between work and home are being eroded by new technology and changing working patterns (Major and Germano, 2006). Therefore, researchers have examined the relationships between work and home lives, looking at such concepts as work–family conflict, work–home spillover and work–life balance.

In the final section of the chapter we discuss ways to intervene to reduce stress, with a particular focus on work stress. This includes what governments, organizations and individuals themselves can do to reduce stress. Thus there are four sections to this chapter:

1 socio-economic status, stress and health;
2 work stress and occupational health psychology;
3 stressors in work and home life;
4 preventing and reducing stress at work.

LEARNING OUTCOMES

When you have completed this chapter you should be able to:

1 Discuss the impact and the causes of social inequality on health.
2 Describe and evaluate key theories of work stress.
3 Describe the impacts on well-being of a range of different types of stressor, e.g. family stressors, conflict between home and family, etc.
4 Discuss the ways stress can be reduced in the workplace.

SOCIO-ECONOMIC STATUS, STRESS AND HEALTH

Poverty is linked to poorer health within most countries. It is easy to think of reasons why this might be the case. Poorer housing conditions, inadequate diet and reduced access to health care services are just a few potential explanations. However, there is a difference between the relationship found within each country and what we observe when we compare one country with another (i.e. comparisons between countries).

We might expect that, even in the Western world, relatively more prosperous countries would have relatively lower mortality than poorer countries. However, comparing countries, we find that in poor countries increases in gross national product (and average income) over time are correlated with life expectancy but above a certain threshold this correlation disappears, that is, there is no further increase in longevity as people become richer. Wilkinson (1996: 29) calls this the 'epidemiological transition'. Yet within these countries there remains a strong link between income and mortality.

Wilkinson suggested that in affluent societies (beyond the epidemiological transition), health is affected less by changes in material standards and more by relative poverty (Wilkinson, 1992, 1996, 1997). Wilkinson argues that it is our position in this hierarchy, including our feelings of relative advantage/disadvantage within society, which causes stress and poorer health. He considered England and Japan to illustrate this phenomenon. In 1970 England and Japan had very similar life expectancies and similar income distribution. However, between 1970 and the 1990s Japan's income distribution shifted to become much narrower (that is, people had more similar incomes clustered around the mean), while in England the distribution became much wider (with increasing differences between the richest and poorest). At the same time, Japan's life expectancy increased dramatically while the UK moved down the international longevity league tables. Wilkinson argues that this phenomenon is not easily explained by factors such as health policies or nutrition.

Potential explanations of this effect include the role of psychological factors associated with the stress of relatively low social status in an affluent society. This explanation is bolstered by animal studies. For example, Wilkinson (1996) draws on Sapolsky's (1993) work, which reveals that baboons lower in dominance hierarchies show higher levels of glucocorticoids indicating more frequent stress responses that could be detrimental to immunological functioning. In addition these lower dominance animals have higher resting blood pressure and their blood pressure returns more slowly to resting levels following stressful encounters. High status animals also show changes in hormonal and cardiovascular functioning indicative of stress when their position in the hierarchy changes, for example, when a larger male is introduced into their group. Similar correspondence between such physiological indices of stress response and social position is observed in people, e.g. among civil servants working at different levels within government (Marmot et al., 1991; Wilkinson, 1996).

A further puzzling finding is that, while SES is strongly linked to mortality in men (when their SES is determined by their occupation) this is not the case for women. In fact, women's mortality is more strongly affected by socio-economic class when they are classified according to their husband's job and not their own (Bartley et al., 2004). One explanation is that, traditionally, a husband has been the main breadwinner and his participation in the workforce was often more enduring. Thus men's occupation has more influence on the overall living standards of the family and so determined family members' positions within the societal hierarchy.

Traditionally, it has been hypothesized that inequalities in health are due to material/structural and cultural/behavioural differences between socio-economic groups. However, researchers debated whether social inequality causes ill health or ill health causes social inequality (Carroll, Bennett and Davey Smith, 1993). This has given rise to two opposing explanations. The first is known as the social causation hypothesis, which states that low SES causes ill health. In other words, factors associated with occupying a low socio-economic position negatively impact on health. The alternative explanation is known as the social drift hypothesis, which states that ill health causes low SES, that is, when an individual becomes ill, they drift down the socio-economic hierarchy because they may be unable to hold down a job. In general, more evidence supports the former explanation. In longitudinal studies following large samples of individuals over time, baseline measures of SES have been found to be good predictors of subsequent health status, whereas health status has been found to be a weaker predictor of SES. Moreover, if ill health caused SES decline one might expect to see differences between fast-acting fatal illnesses (e.g. lung cancer) where there is usually little time to change SES and chronic illnesses (e.g. chronic bronchitis). Yet the SES gradient is seen equally strongly in both types of illness (Carroll et al., 1993).

Stress and social inequality

Cardiovascular disease has been found to be associated with SES and this relationship is not eliminated after conventional risk factors such as smoking are taken into account. This has led researchers to search for additional factors that explain these social inequalities. Two hypotheses have been suggested relating to the role of stress in contributing to social inequality (e.g. Adler et al., 1994). First, the differential exposure hypothesis maintains that the higher prevalence of health problems in low socio-economic groups may be associated with a greater exposure to psychological stressors in these groups. Second, the differential vulnerability hypothesis suggests that individuals in lower socio-economic groups are less well equipped to cope with stressors due to having fewer resources (e.g. having less money to buy healthy foods, choosing less effective coping strategies and having limited social support networks) and as such their impact is much greater in these groups. Evidence supporting both hypotheses has been found, although the most consistent findings relate to the differential vulner-ability hypothesis. However, Stronks *et al.* (1998) have suggested that the importance of the differential exposure hypothesis has been underestimated.

Cohen, Doyle and Baum (2006) investigated the link between SES and a number of stress hormones. After controlling for race, age, gender and body mass index, the results showed that lower SES was associated with higher levels of cortisol, adrenaline and noradrenaline, mirroring Sapolsky's work with baboons. More impressively, Cohen *et al.* (2006) also showed that the effects of SES on these stress hormones were mediated via smoking status, not eating breakfast and having a less diverse social network. These findings emphasize the importance of psychological, biological and behavioural factors in understanding the effects of SES on health. They suggest that health behaviours and social resources, typifying lower SES, explain why those in lower SES positions suffer greater stress-related illness.

WORK STRESS AND OCCUPATIONAL HEALTH PSYCHOLOGY

Investigating and reducing work stress has become a major focus of a newly established field of psychology known as occupational health psychology. The US National Institute of Occupational Safety and Health (NIOSH) states that 'Occupational Health Psychology concerns the application of psychology to improving the quality of working life and to protecting and promoting the safety, health and well-being of workers' (NIOSH, 2010). The emphasis here is on reducing occupational stress, injuries and illness and there are now a number of postgraduate courses, which are concerned with psychosocial and organizational issues relevant to occupational health and safety (see Chapter 11). The research literature on stress is vast but some key models of work stress can be identified.

Theories and models of work stress

A number of writers have produced useful frameworks and models summarizing key variables that might cause stress for individuals at work (Warr, 1987; Cooper, Sloan and Williams, 1988). For example, Warr (1987) listed nine key stressors, which are like vitamins, in that a certain amount is essential for good mental health. Thus, to minimize stress, a job needs to have (1) appropriate levels of personal control over activities and events; and (2) the right amount of opportunity to use existing skills and develop new skills. The job also needs to provide (3) opportunities to pursue goals or meet demands; and have the right amount of (4) variety; (5) clarity; and (6) opportunity for interpersonal contact. Like some vitamins (e.g. vitamins A and D), either too much or too little of these variables may be bad for well-being. However, the final three factors (like vitamins C and E) are only thought to be stressful if there is a shortage. These are (7) money; (8) physical security (e.g. job security or working conditions); and holding a (9) valued social position. This framework simply focuses on external environmental stressors. However, as we noted in Chapter 3, people vary in their perceptions of stressors and in their ability to cope, so what is a reasonable demand for one person will overload another.

FOCUS 4.1

What are theories and models? Why do we need them in health (and occupational health) psychology?

Theories are descriptions of how things, or people, are constructed and how they behave. Science is the process of generating theories and testing their capacity to account for observations of events. As scientists, psychologists use theory in their efforts to describe, explain, predict and change cognition, emotion and behaviour. In psychology, theory includes descriptions and categorizations that allow us to distinguish between types of people, for example in relation to cognition or personality and between types of social situation, for example in terms of work demands or role relations. Identifying correlations between characterizations of people (e.g. personality) or jobs (e.g. work demands) and health or health-related outcomes is the first step in theory development, which next proceeds to articulating processes that explain correlations. These causal explanations describe sequences of interconnected mechanisms underlying psychological responses and behavioural patterns. Once such processes are understood we can predict relationships between theorized variables and intervene to change such processes (Abraham, 2004). For example, see the development of psychological processes linking personality to coronary heart disease (as described in Chapter 6). Thus, developing and testing theory helps us explain why people behave differently and thereby facilitates prediction of the behaviour of particular types of people or people in particular roles and/or situations (Abraham, 2004).

The terms 'framework', 'model' and 'theory' are often used interchangeably in psychology and the distinctions are not clear-cut. However, generally speaking, a framework is a loose set of constructs that does not clearly specify linking mechanisms. Models may provide clearer links between constructs but theories should ideally specify interconnecting causal mechanisms, which can be experimentally tested (see our discussion of testing social cognition models in Chapter 7).

In research in the area of occupational health psychology, many theoretical constructions are more accurately described by the term 'model' than 'theory' and we still have few theories to help us understand the processes whereby work stressors may damage health. Better theories would help us to design more effective interventions. Arguably, theoretical development is more advanced in other areas of health psychology such as predicting and changing motivation and health behaviour (see, e.g. Chapters 7–9).

The limitations of such frameworks have prompted some researchers to develop more complex models incorporating all possible stressors and influences (Beehr and Newman, 1978; Cooper *et al.*, 1988). For example, the model developed by Beehr and Newman incorporated 150 variables. Unfortunately, such models are too complex to be easily testable or to provide practical guidance to those attempting to provide interventions to reduce stress. The breadth of the concept of stress and the large number of variables involved has undoubtedly rendered it challenging to develop concise and comprehensive theories of work stress.

ACTIVITY 4.1

Working in groups, make a list of all the things that you think are stressful about work (i.e. independent variables). Then note down individual characteristics that would allow some people to cope with these stressors better than others, for example, personality (see Chapter 6) or other resources they might have (i.e. moderators – see Focus 5.2). Then, finally, think of all the possible outcomes (i.e. physical, psychological and behavioural) that might result from high levels of stress (i.e. dependent variables).

Much has been written about the key elements of a good theory (e.g. Popper, 1963). Usually this includes that the theory should be falsifiable and concise (or parsimonious). Do you think it would be possible to produce a concise and falsifiable theory of the causes of work stress from your three lists of variables? Discuss why it might be difficult to produce a good theory of work stress.

Thus, most research has focused on more specific testable models focusing on a limited number of variables and potential interactions between them. Three such models have stimulated a great deal of research in recent years: the job demand–control (JDC) model (also known as the job strain model; Karasek, 1979; Karasek and Theorell, 1990), the job demand–resources (JD-R) model (Demerouti *et al.*, 2001) and the effort–reward imbalance (ERI) model (Siegrist, 1996).

Karasek's job demand–control model

In its original form this model focused on two key aspects of work – demands and control – as suggested by the name of the model (Karasek, 1979). A high demand job is a job with heavy workload, fast pace of work and conflicting demand (see Figure 4.1). A high control job means the employee has a say in decisions relating to their job. The model predicts that jobs that have a combination of high demand and low levels of control would result in high levels of psychological and physical strain for employees, i.e. they would be 'high strain' jobs (see Figure 4.2). Typical jobs of this type might include call centre work or being a junior doctor or nurse in a busy casualty department. The opposite combination, low levels of demand and high levels of control would result in low levels of strain. While there is a common view that it is senior

FIGURE 4.1 A high demand job is a job with heavy workload.

Source: Copyright otnaydur/Shutterstock.com.

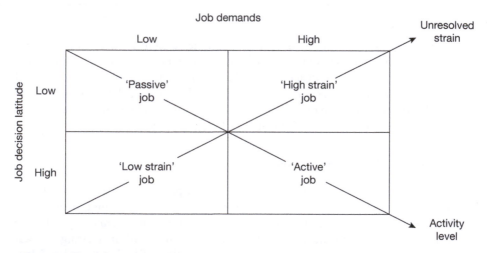

FIGURE 4.2 The job strain model.

Source: From Karasek, 1979.

executives in a company who are likely to experience stress, it is in fact the case that those lower down an organization suffer the most heart disease (e.g. Marmot *et al.*, 1991). The JDC model suggests that this is because they have low levels of control and may therefore be unable to moderate their job demands.

The JDC model also describes two further job types. Active jobs are those with high levels of demand and high control. These are hypothesized to be less stressful than high strain jobs because they offer the individual opportunities to develop protective behaviours, encourage active learning and motivate engagement in new behaviours (Karasek, 1979). Thus, for example, a high level manager or senior executive might have high job demands, but may also be in a position to delegate some of the work. By contrast, passive jobs, that is, those with low demands and low control (for example, an assistant in a seaside cafe out of season) are essentially boring and are suggested to result in learned helplessness and reduced activity. The original conceptualization of the model (Karasek, 1979) emphasized the importance of the interaction between the two variables in predicting strain. In a later publication, Karasek (1989) argued that this interaction is not of central importance. The model is, therefore, frequently considered supported if there is an additive effect of demands and control. However, van der Doef and Maes (1999) make a clear distinction between two alternative hypotheses, which are tested in different studies:

1   The *strain hypothesis* (the additive hypothesis), which states that greater psychological strain and physical illness will be suffered by those in the high strain quadrant of the model (see Figure 4.2).
2   The *buffer hypothesis*, which states that there is an interaction between demand and control (i.e. control moderates, or buffers, the impact of demand). This can be tested by entering a multiplicative interaction term into a multiple regression equation predicting strain outcomes after the main effects terms (of demand and control).

The model has subsequently been expanded by the addition of social support to form the job demand–control–support model (Johnson and Hall, 1988) and both forms of the model have stimulated considerable research looking at a wide range of physical and psychological outcomes (for reviews see van der Doef and Maes, 1998, 1999; de Lange *et al.*, 2003; Hausser *et al.*, 2010). This has been facilitated by the availability of measures of the core variables. The 'job content questionnaire' (Karasek, 1985) aims to measure demand and control as objectively as possible using a self-report questionnaire to tap the existence of particular stressors using items such as 'my job requires working very fast' or 'my job allows me to make a lot of decisions on my own'. People are asked to respond to these items by ticking one of four options ranging from 'strongly agree' to 'strongly disagree'.

The JDC model has been successful in predicting cardiovascular disease (Kivimaki *et al.*, 2012) and associated risk factors (e.g. ambulatory blood pressure levels) as well as psychological well-being (van der Doef and Maes, 1998, 1999; O'Connor *et al.*, 2000a) although there is less support for the buffer hypothesis. There is also evidence that it predicts health behaviours such as physical activity (e.g. Kouvonen *et al.*, 2007; Fransson *et al.*, 2012). However, evidence is often complex and inconsistent (Jones, Kinman and Payne, 2006). Indeed, a study of daily health behaviours suggested that, on a day-to-day basis, within-person fluctuations in mood and work hours were more important than the stable features of the work environment (Jones *et al.*, 2007).

The model has been influential and it has inspired a number of successful interventions to increase control and reduce demand e.g. see Bambra *et al.* (2007), discussed later in this chapter. However, job redesign attempts have not always been successful (van der Klink *et al.*, 2001). Critics have suggested that the key variables are too broad and/or confounded with other work characteristics, leaving the precise nature of required interventions unclear (e.g. Jones *et al.*, 1998; O'Connor *et al.*, 2000b). The model has also been criticized for not including individual differences (e.g. coping characteristics), which have been found to buffer the relationship between work features and employee well-being (Parkes, 1991; de Rijk *et al.*, 1998). In these respects the next two models have some advantages.

The job demand–resources model

The job demand–resources model (JD-R) is one of the most recent approaches to work stress (Demerouti *et al.*, 2001). It addresses some of the criticisms of the above model. It was originally proposed as a model of burnout. This is a syndrome consisting of exhaustion, depersonalization and lack of personal accomplishment (Maslach, 1982). Those working in human service occupations (social workers, teachers, etc.) were assumed to be particularly vulnerable to burnout but more recently the concept has been extended to other occupations as the core dimensions of exhaustion and disengagement may be found in many occupations (Bakker and Demerouti, 2007). The model has since been used to predict other outcomes, such as depression (Hakanen *et al.*, 2008) and job satisfaction (Nielsen *et al.*, 2011).

Like the JDC and the ERI, the JD-R model suggests that stress results from a lack of equilibrium between sets of broadly positive and broadly negative variables. This model focuses on the equilibrium between *job demands* and *resources*. *Job demands* are defined as the 'physical, social, or organizational aspects of the job that require sustained physical and/or psychological (cognitive and emotional) effort or skills and are therefore associated with certain physiological and/or psychological costs' (Bakker and Demerouti, 2007: 312). *Job resources*, on the other hand consist of a broad range of aspects of the job that serve to either help the individual to achieve their work goals, help reduce their job demands or facilitate personal growth and development (Bakker and Demerouti, 2007). This may include control and rewards as well as social resources. The model has also been expanded to include personal resources such as optimism and self-efficacy (Xanthopoulou *et al.*, 2007). It is consistent with the tenets of the conservation of resources theory (see Chapter 3).

The model suggests two processes, *the health impairment process* whereby excessive demands may lead to exhaustion and health problems and the *motivational process* whereby job resources may lead to increased work engagement and performance (Bakker and Demerouti, 2007). A number of studies have now supported these two core processes in relation to psychological burnout and job engagement (e.g. Schaufeli, Leiter and Maslach, 2009, Xanthopoulou *et al.*, 2007).

In addition to these main effects, the JD-R model, like the JDC model, proposes that interactions between the core variables are also important in predicting strain and motivation. Because of the large number of potential resources and demands, a range of interaction effects are possible whereby specific job resources (control, support, feedback, role clarity, etc.) may buffer the impact of different types of demands (Bakker and Demerouti, 2007). Not only may the effects of job resources reduce the negative impact of high demands, but the model also proposes that resources may aid motivation when demands are high. Studies by the model's originators have found many significant interaction effects, though a large cross-national study has been unable to replicate these (Brough *et al.*, 2013).

Unlike the JDC and the ERI model, the JD-R has so far primarily been tested on psychological outcomes such as burnout and work engagement (e.g. Hakanen *et al.*, 2008), for which it was designed, rather than health outcomes. It has, however, been useful in predicting work–home interference (Bakker *et al.*, 2011) and organizational outcomes such as turnover intention and low organizational commitment (Hu, Schaufeli and Toon, 2011).

Effort–reward imbalance model

The effort–reward imbalance (ERI) model (Siegrist, 1996) assumes that people involved in social exchanges (such as the employer–employee relationship) expect reciprocity, i.e. mutual give and take. If these expectations are not met they experience the situation as stressful. Thus, the model proposes that an imbalance between the efforts that employees believe that they put into their work and the rewards they receive results in negative outcomes for health and well-being (see Figure 4.3). Efforts follow from work demands including time pressure, responsibilities or physical

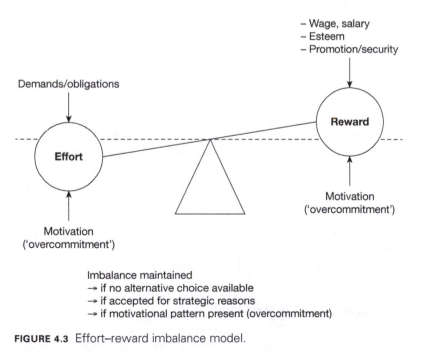

FIGURE 4.3 Effort–reward imbalance model.

Source: Reproduced with permission from Johannes Siegrist.

demands. Rewards stem from the nature of the social contract and include money (adequate salary), esteem (respect and support) and career opportunities (including security) (Siegrist, 2002, 2005). However, Siegrist (2005) suggests that the kind of person who is likely to suffer particularly from feeling that their work is associated with high costs and low gains is the individual who suffers from 'overcommitment', that is, they may overestimate the demands upon them or underestimate their ability to cope. Siegrist (2005) suggests that people remain in situations where efforts are high and rewards are low where there are no alternative job choices available or where they may have a strategic reason to do so (for example, because of long-term anticipated benefits) or where they are overcommitted to work.

Like the JDC model, the ERI has its own standardized questionnaire (Siegrist, 1996). While it has been less frequently tested than the JDC, the evidence is generally supportive. For example, the potential impact of lack of reciprocity (i.e. jobs that combine high effort and low rewards) has been highlighted in research conducted by van Vegchel *et al.* (2001). In this study, the risk of health symptoms was between six and nine times higher for employees who reported high efforts and low rewards than those with low efforts and high rewards. There is also evidence that an imbalance between efforts and rewards is associated with heart disease (Kivimaki *et al.*, 2002; Aboa-Éboulé *et al.*, 2011).

Siegrist (2005) suggests that the model may be useful for designing worksite interventions. For example, improving leadership skills of supervisors and increasing their awareness of the need for recognition and constructive feedback may help increase perceptions of rewards among employees. He also suggests that structural interventions designed to increase non-monetary incentives, e.g. flexible working time, job security and increasing contractual fairness, may also reduce imbalance.

While the ERI model focuses primarily on the workplace, van dem Knesebeck and Siegrist (2003) suggest that the model may be relevant in other social contexts. For example, they found that elderly men and women who reported non-reciprocal social exchange in social relationships (e.g. in marital, parental and other social roles) were twice as likely to experience depressive symptoms.

Some researchers have combined the JDC and ERI to predict psychological and physical health outcomes (e.g. Bosma et al., 1998; van Vegchel, De Jonge and Landsbergis, 2005). Studies have typically indicated that variables from the ERI, i.e. effort–reward imbalance (and in some cases overcommitment), together with low job control (from the JDC model), predict negative health outcomes.

Overall, research based on all these models has told us a great deal about the range of factors that are stressful at work and how they impact on our health. They also suggest ways in which work can be structured and organized to reduce stress. A limitation of all these models is that they focus on work stressors in isolation, failing to take into account how work and other roles are interlinked. Stressors in home and family life cannot be clearly separated from those in work life.

STRESSORS IN WORK AND HOME LIFE

How does work life or university life affect you during your leisure time? If you are stressed during the day do you worry in the evening and feel low, or do you switch off and make sure you do something pleasant to compensate for the hard day you have had? These kinds of questions have interested researchers investigating the relationships between stressors in different domains of life and they are becoming increasingly important as the boundaries between work and home life are reduced. More women (including those with young children) are now working so both men and women occupy potentially conflicting roles. Furthermore, new technologies such as laptop computers, emails and mobile phones mean that employees can work anywhere. This is linked to a trend for work to be more flexible with more people working outside the traditional 9-to-5 day to cater for demands for 24-hour services (e.g. supermarkets, call centres) as well as to facilitate working in global organizations operating across time zones. This has led to an increasing concern among employees about lack of work–life balance (Major and Germano, 2006).

Three types of relationships between work and home life have been considered (Staines, 1980). First, the impact of work was hypothesized to spillover to affect the individual at home. For example, those experiencing negative emotions at work would take these to the home environment. However, this hypothesis has been extended beyond stressors and is assumed to also apply to activities and behaviour. So those with active and stimulating jobs would seek similar types of experience out of work. In contrast the compensation hypothesis, suggested that, for example, those with active stimulating jobs might seek calm and undemanding leisure activities and vice versa. A third hypothesis, the segmentation hypothesis, suggested no relationship, implying that work and non-work domains are independent (Staines, 1980). Early studies have tended to support the spillover hypothesis. For example, Meissner (1971) found that individuals who were isolated at work were also isolated at home. However, most studies were cross-sectional leaving the direction of causation unclear. Did work stressors spillover to the home or were home stressors affecting people at work, or was a third variable (such as personality) responsible for the link? Longitudinal studies have helped clarify these relationships. For example, Williams and Alliger (1994) showed that spillover occurs in both directions, with moods experienced in one environment influencing those in the other. However, in common with most other studies, they found that work seems to interfere more with family life than vice versa.

More recently these findings have been extended by examining crossover of stress. This is the idea that stressors in one environment (usually work) not only affect the individual directly experiencing them when that person is at home but also affect others who share the home environment. Support for this phenomenon has now been found in numerous studies (Bakker, Westman and van Emmerik, 2009). For example, a study of more than 2,000 couples found striking evidence that workplace aggression experienced by one member of a couple was associated with an increase in psychological distress in their partner (Haines, Marchand and Harvey, 2006). Song *et al.* (2011) got couples to complete daily diaries and found crossover between unemployed and employed partners. Children have also been found to suffer from their parents' work stressors. Repetti and Wood (1997) studied working mothers and their pre-school children in a laboratory setting after work for five consecutive days. They found that on days when they reported heavier workloads, or where they had experienced interpersonal conflicts, the mothers were more withdrawn from their children. For men, the link between work stress and negative interaction with children seems to be moderated by neuroticism, that is, for men high in neuroticism job stress was linked to more negative emotional response to their children (Wang, Repetti and Campos, 2011).

Work–life conflict

Relationships between work and other aspects of life have been investigated in terms of role conflict, that is, when a person feels incompatible pressures from two separate roles. Most commonly this has focused on work–family conflict (Greenhaus and Beutell, 1985). For example, it may be that time spent at work prevents people from participating in family activities, or it may be that strain experienced at work affects people psychologically at home, or that particular behaviours found useful at work spill over and cause problems in the home environment. Thus, Greenhaus and Beutell (1985) introduced the concepts of time-based, strain-based and behaviour-based conflict. Like spillover, conflict can occur in two directions, work may affect family life (work-to-family interference) and family issues may impact on work (family-to-work interference: O'Driscoll, Brough and Kalliath, 2006). Recently, there has been some criticism of the emphasis on 'family' implied by the term 'work–family conflict', as increasing numbers of people live alone but nevertheless may experience conflicts with personal life and leisure activity. Many researchers now prefer to look at 'work–life' conflict (e.g. Siegel et al., 2005).

Research suggests that in the past, work-to-family conflict was typically higher among men than women, while family-to-work conflict was higher in women. However, research suggests that these effects are now levelling out (O'Driscoll et al., 2006). This is probably due to more equal roles in both work and home life. The negative effects of work–family conflict include increased work turnover and poorer work performance, reduced job satisfaction, increased distress and depression, poorer physical health and increased alcohol consumption.

Grandey and Cropanzano (1999) suggest that the effect of work and family stress can be explained by conservation of resources theory (Hobfoll, 1989; see Chapter 3). For example, conflict arising in the work role may result in fewer resources (such as time) being available to spend in the other role. However, those with additional resources such as marital partners may suffer less than those with fewer overall resources. Consistent with this, research has found that long work hours are linked to work–family conflict (e.g. Major, Klein and Ehrhart, 2002) and that having a partner is linked to reduced conflict both from work to family and family to work (Brough and Kelling, 2002).

Work–family and family–work facilitation

Positive experiences at work may also spill over and lead to greater happiness at home and vice versa. In the past, the bulk of research focused on stress and role conflict. With current trends towards a more positive psychology, however, researchers are looking at these beneficial impacts. A range of terms have been used to describe this process including positive spillover, work–family (and family–work) facilitation, enhancement or enrichment (O'Driscoll et al., 2006). These terms all broadly refer to the idea that engagement in work has beneficial impacts on engagement in the family and vice versa. For example, skills and knowledge gained in one domain may be beneficial in the other. Similarly, affective assets (positive moods or confidence) or capital assets (e.g. financial or social) acquired in one domain may help in the other (Carlson et al., 2006). Grzywacz and Bass (2003) have found that optimal adult mental health is found in conditions where both work–family and family–work facilitation is high and work–family conflict is low. We await further research to find out how we can achieve this optimal state.

RECOVERY FROM WORK STRESS

In recent years, interest in the work–family interface has led to a focus on recovery from work stress. Jobs that are high in demand and low in control (i.e. high strain jobs), for example, have been found to be linked to a high need for recovery (Sonnentag and Zijlstra, 2006). Sonnentag and Zijlstra define 'need for recovery' as 'a person's desire for being – temporarily – relieved from exposure to stressors in order to replenish his or her resources' (2006: 330). This in turn was linked to poorer well-being and fatigue (i.e. recovery mediates the relationship between demands and control and well-being outcomes). Psychological detachment, relaxation, mastery and control experiences in time off work have been show to help recovery (e.g. Sonnentag, Binnewies and Mojza, 2008). Engaging in pleasant activities is also related to greater recovery (Van Hooff et al., 2011), as is physical activity (Rook and Zijlstra, 2006). The presence of children in the family, not surprisingly, helps detachment (Hahn and Dormann, 2013). Researchers are starting to look at whether training can help recovery. A recovery training program with modules promoting psychological detachment, relaxation, mastery and control (Hahn et al., 2011) led to increased recovery experiences during time off-work time and improved sleep quality and reduced perceptions of work stress.

More commonly, interventions for work stress deal with reducing or managing the stress in the workplace. These are examined in the next section.

PREVENTING AND REDUCING STRESS IN THE WORKPLACE

A number of different types of intervention have been used in the work setting. Organizational change and job design interventions reduce stress by modifying the job to remove stressors. Other types of intervention aim at modifying the individual's ability to cope with stress, for example, by training, counselling or by changing the individual's physical fitness. These are described in further detail in the following sections.

Preventing or reducing stress by changing the work environment

Removing or reducing stressors at source wherever possible seems both sensible and ethically desirable. Furthermore, the focus of the work stress models discussed above is to determine sources of stressors with, by implication, a view to intervening to change the nature of jobs. This may be done by, for example, changing task characteristics such as job control as suggested by the JDC model.

This type of intervention has gained in importance with the increased public and governmental pressure to reduce work stressors throughout Europe, Australia and North America. For example, in the UK, the Health and Safety at Work Act

(1974: 2) states that employers have a duty 'to ensure as far as is reasonably practicable, the health, safety and welfare at work of all employees'. Since the 1990s this has been interpreted to include work demands, organization and work relationships (HSE, 1995). UK employers are now also required to assess the risk of stress-related ill health arising from work and to take steps to control such risks. This approach is now formalized within the Management Standards approach to work stress advocated by the UK Health and Safety Executive (see Table 4.1). For each of the standards listed there is the additional standard that 'systems are in place locally to respond to any individual concerns' (HSE, 2007). These standards are not legally enforced, rather they are recommendations to help employers meet legal obligations.

Interventions aimed at changing the workplace and thereby reducing or removing causes of stress are perhaps the most challenging type of stress management both to conduct and to evaluate rigorously and thus there is less research evidence in this area (Randall, Griffiths and Cox, 2005). For example, a meta-analysis (see Research methods 8.1) by van der Klink *et al.* (2001) considered 48 experimental evaluations of stress reduction interventions to be of sufficient rigour to be included (see also the discussion of intervention evaluation in Chapter 9). However, only five of these were organizational interventions aimed at reducing stressors (the rest being interventions targeting the individual). These researchers found no overall significant effect across the five studies. However, a more recent review (Bambra *et al.*, 2007) looked at 19 studies of interventions to restructure tasks and found that interventions which increased demand and reduced control (i.e. the opposite of the recommendations of the JDC), resulted in poorer health, as the JDC predicts. There were also health benefits where interventions increased control and reduced demands but these were less marked. A study by Bond and Bunce (2001) found that increases in job control were related not only to improved well-being but also to better self-rated performance and reduced sickness absenteeism. It is likely that the extent to which organisational interventions are of benefit to health will vary from person to person and researchers have started to consider the effects of individual differences. For example, those with greater psychological flexibility have been found to benefit more from an intervention to increase job control (Bond, Flaxman and Bunce, 2008)

Overall, organisational interventions face numerous challenges. For example, uncontrolled variables, such as changes in market conditions causing job insecurity, may undermine positive influences. Furthermore, organizational change may itself be stressful. Murphy (2003) suggests that simultaneous individual interventions may be needed to help people adjust to planned organizational change. Nevertheless, while evidence concerning such interventions is as yet limited, the pressure to reduce the causes of stress in the workplace remains high.

In recent years, the call for greater work–life balance has led to new organizational interventions aimed at helping people to manage the interface between home and work, for example the introduction of policies enabling employees to work more flexibly both in terms of working hours and work location. Such interventions might be expected to enhance employees' control and thereby reduce stress. While there is little evidence concerning the stress reducing effects of interventions to increase flexibility, studies indicate that perceptions of work flexibility are linked to improved well-being and health behaviours (Grzywacz, Casey and Jones, 2007) and improved perceptions of health (Butler *et al.*, 2009).

TABLE 4.1 UK Health and Safety Executive Management Standards (HSE, 2007)

Stressor area	Description	The standard
Demands	Includes workload, work patterns and work environment	Employees indicate that they are able to cope with the demands of their jobs
Control	How much say the person has in the way they do their work	Employees indicate that they have a say about the way they do their work
Support	Includes the encouragement, sponsorship and resources provided by the organization, line management and colleagues	Employees indicate that they receive adequate information and support from their colleagues and superiors
Relationship	Includes promoting positive working to avoid conflict and dealing with unacceptable behaviour	Employees indicate that they are not subjected to unacceptable behaviours, e.g. bullying at work
Role	Whether people understand their role within the organization and whether the organization ensures that the person does not have conflicting roles	Employees indicate that they understand their role and responsibilities
Change	How organizational change (large or small) is managed and communicated in the organization	Employees indicate that the organization engages them frequently when undergoing an organizational change

Reducing stress by stress management training

A common approach to reducing stress in the workplace is to offer employees stress management training courses, a form of intervention that is not unique to the workplace. There is no set format for these courses and they are likely to include information about the nature of stress and a series of emotion-focused and problem-focused coping strategies (see also Chapter 5).

Emotion-focused techniques typically involve some form of relaxation training. This frequently involves a technique known as progressive muscle relaxation, in which individuals are instructed to focus on specific groups of muscles in turn and progressively tense them and then release the tension (e.g. 'clench your fist as tight as you can, then let it go'). Finally, they aim to tense and release all muscles together. Relaxation may be accompanied by the use of music or visualization techniques (e.g. 'imagine you are lying on a beach, you can hear the waves in the distance and feel the gentle breeze'). Tapes are also available for people to use these techniques at home. Biofeedback is also sometimes used as an adjunct to relaxation. This gives individuals continuous feedback throughout a relaxation session about physiological processes such as muscle tension or blood pressure.

Problem-focused techniques can include techniques such as assertiveness or teaching time management skills (see Chapter 9). However, the most commonly used techniques are derived from cognitive behaviour therapy, which seek to alter people's appraisals of stressful situations, inhibit automatic thoughts and enhance coping skills. Some people exacerbate the stress they experience by negative cognitions. Thus, for example, when faced with a disagreement with a work colleague about how to do a piece of work, a typical thought might be 'he obviously does not like me, maybe no-one likes me'. This irrational response illustrates personalizing and catastrophizing. This would be explored with the individual and different responses considered, e.g. 'We obviously do not see eye to eye on this task. How can we resolve this difference?' This response is much less likely to generate stress and depression and more likely to lead to constructive problem solving. Stress management techniques that draw on cognitive behaviour therapy involve people examining their reactions and developing skills to stop what for many are automatic negative thoughts and to replace them with more constructive cognitions. This then leads to rehearsal of different appraisals and new coping skills. These kinds of techniques have been demonstrated to be effective in therapeutic interventions (e.g. DeRubeis and Crits-Christoph, 1998).

Stress management training courses vary greatly in the length of the course and the components used within the course. In the workplace they may consist of very brief one-off sessions for participants who are not particularly stressed at the outset. It is not surprising if evaluations of such interventions show little improvement. However, rigorous evaluations of longer training interventions for individuals with high levels of anxiety show significant improvements in well-being (e.g. Ganster *et al.*, 1982). Identifying which components are responsible for benefits has proved more difficult (see Chapter 9). Comparisons between different methods often show all techniques to be equally successful. However, meta-analytic reviews of workplace interventions have found those based on cognitive behavioural approaches to be most effective though other techniques such as relaxation also show benefits (e.g. van der Klink *et al.*, 2001; Richardson and Rothstein, 2008).

A number of new developments in stress management training have been introduced in recent years. The success of therapies based on the concept of mindfulness has meant this has inevitably had an influence on approaches to dealing with employees. 'Mindfulness' involves deliberate focus on an awareness of what is happening in the present moment (Kabat-Zinn, 2003). Mindfulness-based therapies (such as mindfulness-based stress reduction and mindfulness-based cognitive therapy) aim to help people to cope more effectively with experiences, by accepting emotions and discomforts and paying attention to experiences without analytic or dysfunctional thought processes. Mindfulness exercises utilize meditation extensively to encourage focus on the present moment. Clinical trials have shown these approaches to be effective in reducing anxiety and depression (Piet, Wurtzen and Zachariae, 2012). In the work environment, mindfulness approaches have successfully been used as stress management training for local government employees (e.g. Flaxman and Bond, 2010) and as part of an intervention to help people return to work after stress-related sickness absence (Netterstrom, Friebel and Ladegaard, 2013). Mindfulness interventions have also been shown to be helpful in improving balance between work and home life (Michel, Bosch and Rexroth, 2014) and to be effective when delivered online (Morledge et al., 2013).

Counselling

The provision of counselling services for distressed employees is now a popular form of intervention that primarily aims to treat rather than prevent stress. This is now typically provided via Employee Assistance Programmes available to employees and (frequently) their families. Such services are provided by a specialist provider and retained by companies. The level of service offered is variable and may range from telephone counselling and advice to the provision of a series of face-to-face counselling sessions. Typically employees are provided with a card offering a 24-hour telephone service. The best services offer a range of help, which may include specialist legal and financial advice, relationship support and trauma counselling. Some are also providing online support and support for health behaviour change. It has proved difficult to rigorously evaluate these schemes because random allocation to treatment and control groups is not possible when individuals refer themselves for services. Furthermore, withholding treatment from distressed employees would be unethical. However, studies do suggest that employees find such services useful and they report improved well-being (e.g. McLeod and McLeod, 2001) and that they are cost-effective for the organizations employing them (Csiernik, 2011).

Worksite lifestyle change interventions

Physical fitness is the main lifestyle intervention that has clear benefits in terms of stress reduction as well as its more obvious benefits for health (see Chapter 1). It can be seen as both an emotion-focused and a problem-focused strategy (Long and Flood, 1993). It can distract the individual from stressful emotions and invoke a relaxation response that is incompatible with stress. However, it can also increase people's confidence and self-esteem, which may affect appraisal of their ability to cope with problems, that is, it may increase task-specific self-efficacy (see Chapter 8). Many workplaces now encourage physical activity by provision of sports facilities on site or negotiated rate reductions with local facilities. It is in an employer's interest to have a healthy workforce who will

ACTIVITY 4.2

Chris is a qualified social worker with a good track record. He is one of the most experienced workers in his team. He therefore has one of the heaviest caseloads including a number of children who are at risk of child abuse. He frequently works long hours and faces aggressive clients alone. He is feeling increasingly overloaded and most days can do little more than respond to crises. He often has to cancel routine visits and is unable to make constructive plans to work towards improving his clients' situations. Because he does not have time to get round to all his clients, he is anxious that one of the children in his care may be harmed before he has the chance to intervene. He feels that he does not get adequate support from his manager and gets little feedback about how well he is doing. Recently the situation has become so bad that Chris feels perpetually anxious and unable to sleep. He is beginning to feel that he can no longer cope with the job and is considering looking for alternative employment.

What do you think Chris' managers should do to alleviate the problem? Consider the role of each of the types of interventions described in this chapter.

be less prone to sickness absence and it may also have other organizational benefits in terms of employee relations. Exercise can be promoted at an individual or organizational level. While large-scale, good quality evaluations of outcomes of worksite interventions are rare, indications are that such interventions can be effective for both improving physical health and reducing stress (Conn et al., 2009).

What type of intervention is most successful?

Removing stressors at source seems the most desirable and ethically acceptable approach but there have been relatively few successful interventions of this kind because job redesign operates in a complex context in which other factors can cancel out potential benefits. This weak evidence base is not a justification to abandon this type of intervention. Indeed, in the UK, any company that did so would be likely to fall foul of the Health and Safety at Work Act (1974). Instead Murphy (2003) advocates using a range of interventions. Many jobs are inherently stressful at times or include elements that will be stressful for some employees, while other employees will be suffering as a result of unavoidable stressors outside of work. The provision of a range of interventions that are based on the best possible evidence and that combine both organizational change and individual support would seem likely to offer the best chance of success.

SUMMARY

Social inequality is linked to poorer health within countries around the world, even within affluent countries. In richer countries ill health and mortality are associated with relative poverty. Evidence suggests that it is low SES causing ill health rather than vice versa. Stress is implicated in this relationship. Those in lower SES positions are exposed to more stressors and tend to be more vulnerable to their effects.

The workplace has been a dominant focus of stress research and a number of models of work stress have been proposed. The JDC, JD-R and the ERI models have been particularly influential. Together these models highlight the importance of having a manageable level of work demands (or efforts) and the need for these to be balanced by appropriate rewards, including recognition and status and the importance of adequate levels of control over your job as well as other resources such as adequate support from colleagues and management. There is evidence that a lack of these components is related to increased coronary heart disease.

Changes in the nature of work have led to an increase in concern about poor work–life balance. When work and family demands conflict or when work spills over into home life it can have negative impacts on individuals and on other family members. However work can also bring psychological benefits that may have positive effects on home life.

There are a range of interventions to reduce stress, which include removing stressors by organizational interventions such as job redesign, reducing the impacts of stressors by stress management training, treating stressed individuals by counselling and changing aspects of lifestyle to help people to be able to resist or cope with stress. All can play a useful part in reducing the effects of stress at work as well as in other environments.

KEY CONCEPTS AND TERMS

- Biofeedback
- Cognitive behaviour therapy
- Compensation
- Counselling
- Employee assistance programmes
- Job redesign
- Mindfulness
- Recovery
- Relative poverty
- Segmentation
- Social causation hypothesis
- Social drift hypothesis
- Social inequality
- Socio-economic status
- Spillover
- Stress management training
- Work–family conflict
- Work–family and family–work facilitation
- Workplace counselling

SAMPLE ESSAY TITLES

- Does being poor make people less healthy? Discuss with reference to psychological research.
- Evaluate current theoretical approaches to work stress. How useful have they been for guiding interventions to improve the work environment?
- 'Work stress is unpleasant for employees but it has no real implications beyond the workplace'. Discuss.
- Imagine you have been asked by a company management team to advise on how they should reduce stress among their employees. What evidence-based advice would you offer?

FURTHER READING

Books

Brough, P., O'Driscoll, M., Kalliath, T., Cooper, C.L. and Poelmans, S. (2009). *Workplace Psychological Health: Current Research and Practice*. Cheltenham, UK: Edward Elgar.

HSE (2014). *The Management Standards*. Retrieved 12 March 2014 from www.hse.gov.uk/stress/standards

Journal articles

Bakker, A.B., and Demerouti, E. (2007). The job demands–resources model: State of the art. *Journal of Managerial Psychology*, 22, 309–328.

Bosma, H., Peter, R., Siegrist, J. and Marmot, M. (1998). Two alternative job stress models and the risk of coronary heart disease. *American Journal of Public Health*, 88, 68–74.

Heikkila, K., Fransson, E.I., Nyberg, S.T., Zins, M., Westerlund, H., Westerholm, P., Virtanen, M., Vahtera, J., Suominen, S., Steptoe, A., Salo, P., Pentti, J., Oksanen, T.,

Nordin, M., Marmot, M.G., Lunau, T., Ladwig, K.-H., Koskenvuo, M., Knutson, A., Kittel, F., Jockel, K.-H., Goldberg, M., Erbel, R., Dragano, N., DeBacquer, D., Clays, E., Casini, A., Alfredsdon, L., Ferrie, J.E., Singh-Manoux, A., Batty, G.D. and Kivimaki, M. (2013). Job strain and health-related lifestyle: Findings from an individual-participant meta-analysis of 118,000 working adults. *American Journal of Public Health*, 103, 2090–2097.

van der Klink, J.L., Blonk, R.W.B., Schene, A.H. and van Dijk, F.J.H. (2001). The benefits of interventions for work-related stress. *American Journal of Public Health*, 91, 270–276.

Wilkinson, R.G. (1997). Health inequalities: Relative or absolute material standards? *British Medical Journal*, 314, 591–595.

3 | Coping resources: Social support and individual differences

5 Coping and social support

Chapters 3 and 4 examined a range of theories relating stress to health outcomes. However, not everyone reacts in the same way to the pressures of life. This chapter explores ways in which different approaches to coping and the availability of social support can affect health.

In the course of normal life we are all faced with a range of stressors and challenges. When faced with a threat such as failing an important exam or having an argument with a friend, how do you cope? Do you try to think calmly about how you can address the problem, do you feel angry and distressed and express your feelings, do you talk to a friend or do you go for a drink or cigarette? Perhaps you use several of these strategies? These are just a few of the many ways of coping that have been identified by researchers in a range of different typologies of coping strategies. Does the way you cope depend on the circumstances or do you behave consistently across different situations? For example, do you tend to adopt a problem-solving approach or, alternatively, deny the threat? Consistent (or dispositional) coping tendencies are known as coping styles that are related to personality. How we cope affects the outcomes we experience. In this chapter we will consider a range of coping approaches and their implications for health.

Friends, family and work colleagues are, for most people, particularly important in times of stress. We may seek out our friends to listen to us express our feelings, distract us from insoluble problems or help us to find solutions. Thus, for many people, using social support is an important coping strategy and most measures of coping ask people about the extent to which they use social supports. Of course, social support depends on having a friend or network of friends who we can call on. Thus friends and family are regarded as coping resources. The availability of these resources seems to be important for our well-being regardless of whether they are providing social support in times of stress or whether we deliberately draw on them as a coping strategy. The chapter is divided into two sections: (1) coping; and (2) social support.

LEARNING OUTCOMES

When you have completed this chapter you should be able to:

1 Describe and critically evaluate studies of coping and social support, including strategies and styles of coping.
2 Discuss the implications of coping and social support for health.
3 Discuss the mechanisms by which coping and social support affect health.
4 Suggest ways to intervene to help individuals to cope with stressful situations.

COPING

Coping is a key element of Lazarus and Folkman's (1984) transactional theory of stress, described in Chapter 2. In this theory, coping is viewed as part of the stress process, defined as 'constantly changing cognitive and behavioural efforts to manage specific external and/or internal demands that are appraised as taxing or exceeding the resources of the person' (Lazarus and Folkman, 1984: 141). You may recall the two types of appraisal. Primary appraisal involves the individual assessing the potential harm, loss, threat or challenge imposed by the stressor, that is, what's at stake. This leads to secondary appraisal in which the individual evaluates the coping options and resources available. In the case of potentially failing an exam, primary appraisals might range from 'this does not matter too much, it's just a setback' to 'this means I am hopeless and my future is bleak'. Secondary appraisals will depend partially on the primary appraisal but also on the resources the individual feels they have (including their confidence, their intellectual resources, financial resources, etc.). In relation to the exam threat, secondary appraisals could include investigating the possibility of re-sitting the exam and planning how to do more work in future or eliciting the support of others to go out and 'drown your sorrows'. Thus appraisal provides the basis for coping and so leads finally to the outcome that may involve emotional responses, behaviour and health. Arranging to re-sit the exam and/or planning to do more work would both be described as problem-focused strategies. These are strategies that involve trying to obtain information and formulate actions that will change the situation, e.g. to reduce or remove the impact of the stressor. However, 'drowning your sorrows' would be an example of an emotion-focused strategy that simply aims to regulate the emotions generated by the stressor, in this case, by avoiding thinking about it. An alternative emotion-focused approach would be to think about the problem in a different light (i.e. appraising it more positively, e.g. 'this has taught me a lesson I won't forget'). Thus coping is a mediator between the stress appraisal and the final outcome (see Focus 5.2 for a further discussion of mediation).

To assess how people cope, Folkman and Lazarus (1988) developed a measure called the Ways of Coping (WOC) Questionnaire. They used factor analysis of responses to a range of coping items to produce eight overall measures. These are (1) confrontative coping; (2) distancing; (3) self-controlling; (4) seeking social support; (5) accepting responsibility; (6) escape avoidance; (7) planful problem solving; and (8) positive reappraisal. Some subsequent researchers have criticized these measures on the grounds that other studies have failed to replicate these eight factors. For example, in a review of coping measures, Skinner *et al.* (2003) argue that eight studies that used the WOC produced eight different sets of categories based on factor analyses with the number of categories ranging from two to nine. Carver, Scheier and Weintraub (1989) also criticized the model for its lack of comprehensive coverage of coping methods.

To overcome this problem, Carver *et al.* (1989) produced an alternative, theory-based questionnaire called the COPE. This is based on both Lazarus' theory and their own model of behavioural self-regulation. The strategies measured by this questionnaire are shown in Research methods 5.1. The measure includes more distinct types of

RESEARCH METHODS 5.1

Measuring coping using the COPE (adapted from Carver *et al.*, 1989)

The COPE questionnaire consists of sub-scales to assess each of the following types of coping. The response scale can be adjusted to apply to a particular situation or to assess dispositional coping. The measure (or sometimes specific sub-scales) is still frequently used in a wide range of research e.g. Beatty *et al.*, 2011; Alarcon, Edwards and Clark, 2013).

Primarily problem-focused coping
- *Active coping*, e.g. 'I take direct action to get around the problem'.
- *Planning*, e.g. 'I make a plan of action'.
- *Suppression of competing activities*, e.g. 'I put aside other activities in order to concentrate on this'.
- *Restraint coping*, e.g. 'I hold off doing anything about it until the situation permits'.
- *Seeking instrumental social support*, e.g. 'I try to get advice from someone about what to do'.

Primarily emotion-focused coping
- *Seeking emotional social support*, e.g. 'I discuss my feelings with someone'.
- *Focus on and venting emotion*, e.g. 'I get upset and let my emotions out'.
- *Behavioural disengagement*, e.g. 'I give up the attempt to get what I want'.
- *Mental disengagement*, e.g. 'I go to the cinema or watch television, to think about it less'.
- *Positive reinterpretation and growth*, e.g. 'I learn something from the experience'.
- *Denial*, e.g. 'I act as though it hasn't even happened'.
- *Acceptance*, e.g. 'I learn to live with it'.
- *Turn to religion*, e.g. 'I try to find comfort in my religion'.
- *Alcohol/drug use*, e.g. 'I use alcohol and drugs to help me get through it'.
- *Humour*, e.g. 'I make jokes about it'.

strategies than the WOC questionnaire. However, there is considerable overlap between these two measures and both have proved popular and have been widely used in coping research over the last 20 years.

Lazarus (1999) argues that there is no universally effective (or ineffective) coping strategy. What works in one situation will not work in another. Furthermore, Lazarus suggests that the effectiveness of coping strategies will depend on the type of person and the outcome they are considering. Different coping strategies may also be useful at different stages of dealing with a stressor. Folkman and Lazarus (1985) found that just before an exam, problem–focused coping strategies are used most, whereas in the period waiting for results, emotion-focused strategies predominate. Emotion-focused approaches, such as denial, are often unhelpful because they leave the threat unchanged. However, in some situations, they may be useful in the short term. For example, when experiencing the symptoms of a heart attack, denial is likely to be dangerous and even life threatening because it may lead to delay in seeking treatment. However, once in hospital, denial may be helpful in reducing the anxiety that is likely to exacerbate the medical condition. Once the patient is discharged from hospital denial again may be dangerous as it may lead to resistance to modifying health behaviours.

Lazarus (1999) suggests that when there is nothing that can be done to alter the stressor or reduce the harm (i.e. when there is little control) then denial can be beneficial. Emotion-focused coping may also be important for people with high trait anxiety who are more likely to become anxious when faced with potential stressors. In a prospective study, Sultan *et al.* (2008) found that emotion-focused coping enhanced glycaemic control among diabetics high in trait anxiety (so that trait anxiety moderated the emotion-focused coping–health outcome relationship). However, problem-focused coping was also found to reduce trait anxiety, suggesting that for this highly anxious group of patients both coping strategies were important.

Critical evaluation of coping research

The literature on coping is extensive and complex and has been much criticized, not least because it has provided limited information on which to base interventions (e.g. Somerfield, 1997). The limitations of classification systems and the over-reliance on questionnaires are key problems.

In this chapter we have considered two well-established classification systems but many others have been proposed. In a review, Skinner *et al.* (2003) found over 100 different classification systems, which collectively generated more than 400 ways of coping. Typically, these are classified into a range of higher order categories. The three most common higher-level categories were (a) problem-focused versus emotion-focused; (b) approach versus avoidance; and (c) cognitive versus behavioural. Skinner *et al.* (2003) suggest that this range of diverse classifications has made it difficult to make progress. They argue that many systems such as the two discussed above are based on exploratory factor analyses and as a result have a number of flaws. First, there is often a lack of clarity or distinctiveness in the different categories. Second, it is difficult to ensure that the categories are comprehensive and finally, even where items do load onto a single category they may still represent more than one underlying category, which perhaps has a single underlying emotional tone. For example, both rumination and avoidance coping may load on to a single factor because worrying is common to both, even though the response is very different. Skinner *et al.* (2003: 248) suggest that there is a need for a comprehensive list of ways of coping that can then be classified into 'conceptually clear and mutually exclusive action types'. They identify 13 families of coping that fit this description. They are problem solving (e.g. direct action); support seeking; escape (e.g. avoidance, disengagement and denial); distraction; cognitive restructuring (e.g. positive thinking); rumination (e.g. worry and self-blame); helplessness (e.g. giving up); social withdrawal; emotional regulation (e.g. by emotional expression or self-calming); information seeking; negotiation (e.g. compromise or prioritizing); opposition (aggression or blaming others); and delegation (e.g. maladaptive help seeking).

Do we have consistent styles of coping across different situations?

When faced with a stressful situation, we do not all adopt the same coping strategy. Thus we need to consider individual differences or the ways personality affects choice of coping strategy. However, the extent to which coping is determined by stable factors, rather than varying across situations, has been a source of debate among researchers. Those such as Lazarus who are interested in the different strategies used in different circumstances take a situational view, while those who focus on consistency across different situations take a dispositional (or trait) approach to coping.

Carver and Scheier (1994) argue that there are dispositional tendencies to use emotion-focused or problem-focused coping. The COPE is designed to be used as either a dispositional or a situational measure, depending on whether the individual is asked to complete it in relation to specific situations or in relation to general tendencies.

Some researchers are sceptical about the accuracy of people's reports of their general coping tendencies (e.g. Coyne and Gottlieb, 1996). Lazarus (1993) suggested that dispositional tendencies to use particular coping strategies are better obtained by looking at the individual in a range of different situations. One study that compared people's ratings of how they generally coped with their average coping across a number of specific episodes found that asking people how they generally coped was a poor predictor of what they did in a specific situation, although the tendency to use escape-avoidance or religious coping showed more consistency across situations (Schwartz J.E. *et al.*, 1999). The tendency to use avoidance (versus approach) coping is a key feature of two coping trait classifications, namely, repressive coping and monitoring (versus blunting) coping.

Repressive coping

People who have a repressive coping style direct attention away from threatening information or stimuli or interpret such information in a non-threatening manner (Derakshan and Eysenck, 1997). This has clear links to the Freudian notion of repression and was originally contrasted with 'sensitizing', a form of approach coping. A person high on repressive coping will avert attention from negative feelings to the extent of being unaware that they feel anxious or depressed. However, this is different from intentional suppression of disturbing thoughts or feelings (Myers, Vetere and Derakshan, 2004). A characteristic of repressors is that, when faced with stressful tasks, there is a discrepancy between their self-reports of anxiety (that are low) and their scores on physiological indicators of anxiety (that tend to be high). This has been demonstrated in experimental studies where people have been asked to perform anxiety-provoking tasks such as public speaking (e.g. Newton and Contrada, 1992).

Measuring repression is problematic because repressive copers will, by definition, be unaware of their feelings of anxiety. In most cases they will not even know that they have tendencies to repress feelings. An early self-report measure of repression (the repression–sensitization scale; Byrne, 1961) was found to correlate so highly with measures of trait anxiety that repression was effectively equivalent to low anxiety (Eysenck and Matthews, 1987). However, for a measure of repression to be useful,

---

FOCUS 5.1

The alexithymic personality

A personality trait often considered alongside repressive coping is alexithymia. The term alexithymia, when literally translated, means 'lacking words for feelings' and relates explicitly to an individual's capacity to process and express emotion. Alexithymia can be assessed using the Toronto Alexithymia Scale that measures the extent to which respondents have difficulty in identifying, labelling and understanding emotions, thereby identifying individuals who show impaired capacity for emotional expression (Bagby, Taylor and Parker, 1994). However, unlike people with a repressive coping style who are unconsciously motivated not to recognize negative emotions such as anger, fear and stress, individuals with an alexithymic personality experience negative emotional states but are unable to identify, label and understand the emotion. Interestingly, the term alexithymia was introduced in the 1970s by psychodynamically oriented clinicians who noticed that many clients who presented with stress-related or psychosomatic illnesses exhibited little insight into the causes of their stressful experiences or negative moods (see Lumley, Tojek and MacKlem, 1999). Typically when an individual with an alexithymic personality is asked about a significant relationship or an emotionally charged situation, they will be unable to answer (e.g. 'I don't know'), or they will provide simple and non-specific responses (e.g. 'I felt bad').

It has been suggested that this emotional deficit may negatively impact on an individual's ability to cope with stressful and traumatic events. Evidence indicates that the alexithymic personality is associated with mortality and morbidity from all causes. In particular, research has shown a link between alexithymia and increased risk of developing cardiovascular disease (e.g. Waldstein et al., 2002; Tolmunen et al., 2010). The alexithymic personality has been found to be associated with cancer pain (Porcelli et al., 2007). These findings suggest that alexithymic individuals may be more likely to use maladaptive coping and engage in more health risk behaviours.

repressors need to be distinguishable from those who are simply not anxious. Weinberger, Schwartz and Davidson (1979) have developed a method of measuring repression using a measure of anxiety together with a measure of defensiveness. This is the most frequently used approach. To be defined as a repressor a person must have a low score on anxiety and a high score on defensiveness. The measure of defensiveness often used is the Marlowe–Crowne measure of social desirability (Crowne and Marlowe, 1960).

Repression has been linked to poorer immune functioning (e.g. Esterling *et al.*, 1993) and to increased coronary heart disease risk factors such as high cholesterol (Niaura *et al.*, 1992). A recent meta-analysis (Mund and Mitte, 2012) looked at 22 studies of repressive coping and somatic illness and found that repressive coping was associated with cancer and heart disease. However, the findings for cancer suggest that repressive coping does not precede cancer diagnosis, but is likely to develop subsequently in order to cope with the diagnosis. Furthermore, it was not possible to draw any conclusions about the relationship between repression and cancer progression. Mund and Mitte (2012) also found that repressors were at increased risk of hypertension and cardiovascular disease, however, this result was based on only a single study and remains to be confirmed. Thus exact implications of this coping style for health remain unclear.

Monitoring and blunting

Monitoring and blunting coping styles refer to the information-processing style of people facing threats. It has typically been studied in medical situations with a view to ascertaining the appropriate type of information to give to patients to help them cope with impending medical or surgical interventions. Those with a monitoring style will tend to seek out information about the threat and amplify or worry about it (e.g. Miller, Summerton and Brody, 1988) whereas those with a predominantly blunting style will actively avoid it. Typically, these two dimensions are treated as independent (rather than being opposite poles of a single dimension) so that individuals are divided into high and low monitors and high and low blunters.

Research suggests that monitors and blunters react differently to medical stressors. For example, high monitors go to the doctor with less severe medical problems and demand more tests and information than low monitors (Miller *et al.*, 1988). Miller *et al.* (1988) suggest that this is not accompanied by any greater wish for control, rather it is to reduce uncertainty and lower arousal.

Miller and Mangan (1983) suggested that a patient's level of arousal was lower if the level of information given was matched to their coping style (i.e. monitors require much more detailed information). This theory has been used to inform the design of appropriate health messages (see also Chapter 8). Williams-Piehota *et al.* (2005) matched messages about mammography to women's coping styles. They hypothesized that matched messages would be more effective in persuading women to attend for mammography. The leaflet designed for those classified as blunters was short and to the point. It gave basic facts such as 'the key to finding breast cancer is early detection and the key to early detection is getting regular screening mammograms'. In contrast, the leaflet for monitors gave details of symptoms and risk factors for cancer and explanations of mammography procedures, e.g. 'for some women early detection may prevent the need to remove the entire breast or to receive chemotherapy'. Both leaflets included information to reassure and address anxiety. Messages that were matched to monitoring style were more effective in promoting uptake of mammography during the following six months. However, the difference was only significant for blunters, for whom it may be particularly important to provide messages that are appropriate. A similar approach was also useful in promoting fruit and vegetable consumption, though here the monitor message was particularly successful (Williams-Piehota *et al.*, 2009). Furthermore, Kola *et al.* (2013) found that matching information to suit the monitoring/blunting coping style of patients minimized the distress of patients undergoing colposcopy (an investigative procedure commonly used following abnormal cervical smears). Overall, these studies suggest tailoring messages to be appropriate to the coping styles of recipients is important for health psychologists and medical practitioners.

Personality, coping dispositions and situational coping

We have discussed situational and dispositional approaches to coping, separately. However, coping styles and strategies are interrelated and function within the context of general personality. Many studies have examined links between personality and coping strategies, especially neuroticism and optimism. Hewitt and Flett (1996) suggest that the relationship between personality and coping can be conceptualized in terms of the three types of relationships between variables shown in Focus 5.2. Thus for the mediational model, personality would determine coping style or strategy, which then determines adjustment. In the additive model, personality and coping have independent effects and in the interactive (or moderation) model coping may buffer the impact of personality on adjustment.

Bolger (1990) found that coping strategies mediated the relationship between personality and anxiety in the face of medical school entrance exams such that the personality trait of neuroticism led to ineffective coping. Specifically, they found that two ineffective coping strategies (wishful thinking and self-blame) mediated over half of the effect of neuroticism on anxiety. Fortunately, they found no effect of neuroticism on exam mark! Coping styles may also moderate the effects of personality. For example, O'Connor and O'Connor (2003) found that the negative effects of trait perfectionism on psychological well-being were moderated by coping styles. Specifically, the maladaptive effect of self-oriented perfectionism (i.e. having unrealistically high expectations for one's self) was reduced by the adaptive effects of positive reappraisal, while the harmful effect of socially prescribed perfectionism (i.e. the belief that others hold unrealistically high standards for one's behaviour) was exacerbated by the presence of an avoidance coping style.

Optimists and pessimists have also been shown to adopt markedly different coping styles and strategies (for a review see Carver, Scheier and Segerstrom, 2010). For example, pessimists tend to be more avoidant copers, whereas optimists are more likely to use approach styles and strategies such as problem-focused coping, cognitive restructuring and acceptance (Solberg Nes and Segerstrom, 2006). Optimism is generally linked to more positive approaches to coping that are considered in the next sections.

FOCUS 5.2

Direct effects, mediation and moderation

Researchers examining coping and social support have investigated the mechanisms by which these factors influence relationships between stressors and outcomes such as health and well-being. There are three main types of mechanisms that are examined in this research and in other areas of health psychology (see Figure 5.1).

1   *Direct effects.* In this case coping or social support, for example, has a direct impact on the outcome. For example, having good social support or a positive approach to coping could lead to better health irrespective of the amount of stress the person is experiencing. Figure 5.1a illustrates a situation where a high level of stress and poor coping strategies would both independently act to decrease well-being (and vice versa). This is sometimes also described as an additive effect.

2   *Mediated effects.* This occurs when one variable has its effect on another via an intervening variable. In Figure 5.1b coping acts as an intervening variable through which the stressor exerts its effects on the level of strain. For example, the experience of stress could result in poor coping (e.g. use of alcohol or drugs), which leads to deteriorated well-being. Social support could be said to be a

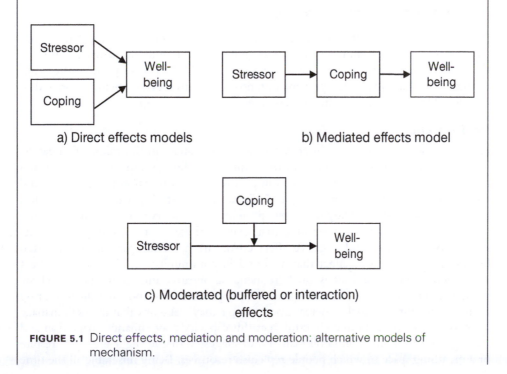

a) Direct effects models

b) Mediated effects model

c) Moderated (buffered or interaction) effects

FIGURE 5.1 Direct effects, mediation and moderation: alternative models of mechanism.

mediator in circumstances where, for example, a breast cancer diagnosis leads to someone joining a support group, which in turn reduces their anxiety or depression. Alternatively, a stressor such as marital breakdown may lead to a reduction in support (through loss of a previously supportive partner and perhaps the partner's family and friends) that may increase anxiety and depression.

3 *Moderated effects.* Moderators, unlike mediators, change the nature of the relationship between two variables, e.g. the stressor–strain relationship. Moderators may alter either the strength or direction of this relationship. Thus coping would be described as moderating the relationship between a stressor such as bereavement and an outcome such as well-being if, for example, bereavement led to poor health only for those who did not use social support or emotional expression as coping strategies. This kind of moderator is also referred to as a buffer because it reduces the impact of the stressor. This effect can be identified as an interaction effect (e.g. in a regression equation) because social support affects the association between stress and well-being. Other variables such as gender or personality may also act as moderators because, for example, some stressors may only result in strain for those scoring highly on a certain personality trait (e.g. neuroticism). Logically, however, fixed traits such as gender cannot act as mediators.

Positive approaches to coping

It has been argued that coping research has focused unduly on the causes and consequences of stress and negative affect (e.g. Folkman and Moskowitz, 2000). In recent years there has been a move towards considering the role of positive affect and cognitions, which may help prevent potentially negative events being appraised as stressful. Three such approaches are considered below.

Positive affect

Research has highlighted the importance of positive affect in the midst of threatening events. This work is in line with the positive psychology movement, which is a recent branch of psychology interested in positive human functioning (Seligman and Csikszentmihalyi, 2000). For example, Folkman (1997) studied care-giving partners of men dying of AIDS. They interviewed the carers at intervals before and, in many cases, after bereavement and reported that, even in these most distressing of circumstances, both positive and negative affect co-occurred. While participants reported higher levels of negative affect than is found in community samples, positive affect was experienced with at least as much frequency as negative affect among those whose partners did not die. Even after bereavement people still report positive affect. During difficult circumstances such as bereavement people may feel guilty that they still manage to enjoy a joke or feel quite cheerful. Yet this capacity may enhance adaptation and coping. Lazarus, Kanner and Folkman (1980) suggested that it might provide a respite or a breathing space in which people replenish resources. Being miserable all the time may simply become too tiring. Folkman and Moskowitz (2000) summarize other potential functions. These include (a) helping us to build social, intellectual and physical resources; (b) helping to provide a buffer against physiological consequences of stress; and (c) helping prevent clinical depression by interrupting negative rumination spirals. They further point out that when people report more negative events they tend to also report more positive events. It may be that in bad times we create more positive events, or we may interpret neutral events more positively, to offset our negative experiences and induce positive affect.

Positive affect has been related to three particular types of coping (Folkman, 1997; Folkman and Moskowitz, 2000). First, it has been linked to positive reappraisal, which is defined by Folkman and Moskowitz (2000: 650) as 'coping strategies for reframing a situation to see it in a positive light (seeing a glass half full as opposed to half empty)'. This coping strategy is incorporated in the COPE questionnaire (see above) as positive reinterpretation and growth. Second, positive affect is associated with problem-focused coping that involves direct efforts to solve or manage the stressor, i.e. by gathering information, planning, decision-making. Third, positive affect is associated with a tendency for 'the infusion of ordinary events with positive meaning' thereby generating good feeling about oneself or one's life (Folkman and Moskowitz, 2000: 650).

Research attention has also focussed on the possible health benefits of positive affect. At the daily level, positive affect has been shown to have a beneficial influence on physiological processes such as cortisol levels and ambulatory blood pressure (Steptoe and Wardle, 2005). Research reviews suggest that positive affect can have significant effects on health both at the daily level *and* in the longer term with an effect size comparable to negative affect (Chida and Steptoe, 2008; Howell, Kern and Lyubomirsky, 2007; Steptoe, Dockray and Wardle, 2009). For example, Ong *et al.* (2006) have suggested that the ability to maintain positive emotions in the face of stress is one pathway through which people can successfully adapt to stress and experience better health outcomes.

Researchers from the University of Kansas have recently taken the exploration of positive affect and positive psychology one step further (Kraft and Pressman, 2012). The authors in question investigated the effects of manipulating smiling and facial expressions on participants' responses to stressful tasks. In this innovative study, participants held chopsticks in their mouths to either produce a smile or a neutral expression. The results were startling and showed that participants who were smiling had lower heart rate during the recovery from stress compared to the participants in the neutral condition! More importantly, it did not matter if they were aware of whether they were smiling or not.

Benefit finding

Most people, faced with even the most serious of stressors, try to identify some benefit. For example, when faced with a stressor such as breast cancer a patient might identify benefits such as improvements in relationships or a greater appreciation of day-to-day experiences. Finding such benefits has been related to improved mental health (see Helgeson, Reynolds and Tomich, 2006, for a meta-analysis). In addition, longitudinal research has suggested benefits in terms of objective measures of physical health. For example, Affleck *et al.* (1987) found that men who found more benefits 7 weeks after a heart attack had lower incidence of further heart attacks during the next 8 years.

There is also evidence suggesting that benefit finding is related to improved immune functioning (see Bower and Segerstrom, 2004) and a range of objective indicators of health in HIV and cancer patients (for a review see Bower, Moskowitz and Epel, 2009).

Benefit finding is linked to optimism and positive affect, i.e. those with higher optimism scores and positive affect are more likely to find benefit in adversity (Hart, Vella and Mohr, 2008). It is also linked to positive reappraisal, though these are all distinct constructs (Sears, Stanton and Danoff-Burg, 2003). The mechanism whereby benefit finding affects health is not yet known. However, Bower *et al.* (2009), suggest a model whereby benefit finding is linked to changes in appraisal and coping processes, social relationships and/or priorities and goals. Changes in these factors in turn leads to more adaptive responses to future stressors thus minimising the stress experienced and the harmful physiological effects of stress hormones. They further suggest that effects on health may also be mediated by positive affect.

Benefit finding is sometimes examined within the context of emotional writing interventions (see Focus 5.3).

FOCUS 5.3

Written emotional disclosure interventions

In 1986, James Pennebaker developed the 'emotional writing paradigm' in which he explored the effects of writing for 15–20 minutes on three consecutive days about stressful or traumatic events on a range of health outcomes. Typically, individuals in the experimental group are asked to write about their deepest emotions and thoughts about the most upsetting experience(s) in their life. They are encouraged to really let go and to link their writing to other aspects of their life such as relationships, their childhood, their careers and who they would like to become, who they were in the past and who they are now. In the control group, individuals are asked to write about what they have done the previous day and to describe their plans for the following day.

Research has found that emotional disclosure through expressive writing can produce clinically significant changes on a number of physiological and psychological health outcomes such as enhanced responses to hepatitis B vaccination in healthy adults, improvement in lung function in asthmatic patients and increased lymphocyte counts in HIV patients (Petrie *et al.*, 1995; Smyth *et al.*, 1999; Petrie *et al.*, 2004). Emotional disclosure through writing has also been found to reduce physician visits at follow-up, increase exam performance, reduce psychological distress and increase re-employment following job loss (see Pennebaker, 1997).

Support for the benefits of emotional writing has also been found in meta-analyses (Smyth, 1998; Frisina, Borod and Lepore, 2004). However, two more recent reviews have shown that the effects of emotional disclosure are likely to be smaller than previously hoped and its impact is moderated by individual differences variables (e.g. personality and previous experience of trauma) and by the characteristics of the writing task (e.g. time spent writing, instructions received) (Frattaroli, 2006; Merz, Fox and Malcarne, 2014; Nazarian and Smyth, 2013). In addition, in some cases, the beneficial effects of writing may only be observed when using more sensitive and subtle outcome measures such as implicit measures that are not contaminated by self-report bias or expectations (O'Connor et al., 2011a).

How does emotional writing influence health? Several mechanisms have been suggested. For example, writing may reduce the cumulative physiological drain of not confronting upsetting experiences or facilitate cognitive processing of traumatic memories, which in turn leads to affective and physiological change. One of the current mechanisms proposed to account for the positive effects of emotional disclosure involves exposure and cognitive processing (Sloan and Marx, 2004). By accessing the emotions, feelings and cognitions linked to a stressful or traumatic event, memory begins to be restructured. Through such restructuring the individual assimilates the stressor into their own self-schema and beliefs system, becomes aware of the associated feelings and considers methods of coping with the traumatic or stressful encounter.

An important line of work has concentrated on understanding the psychological processes associated with the beneficial effects of emotional disclosure. For example, Creswell et al. (2007) content analysed the essays of early-stage cancer survivors and showed that essays that included self-affirmation writing (i.e. evidence that an important personal value was affirmed as a result of their cancer) were associated with fewer physical symptoms at 3 months' follow-up. In other work, O'Connor and Ashley (2008) have explored the importance of the emotional characteristics of disclosure essays together with the alexithymic personality trait. Using the computer programme, Linguistic Inquiry and Word Count (LIWC), they found that alexithymic participants who disclosed more negative emotion words compared to positive emotion words exhibited reduced blood pressure responses to stress two weeks after writing. Yet non-alexithymic participants who disclosed more positive and less negative emotion words displayed reduced blood pressure responses to stress.

RESILIENCE

The term 'Resilience' as a psychological construct was first used in the developmental literature to describe the ability to overcome negative childhood experiences. In recent years it has gained popularity in adult psychology in the context of loss and other traumatic events (Bonanno, 2012) and like the other approaches discussed above is linked to the growth in more positive approaches in psychology and the move away from an emphasis on negative well-being outcomes. It has spawned a complex literature on what factors contribute to resilience. Bonanno (2012: 754) defines resilience as a 'stable trajectory of healthy functioning in response to a clearly defined event'. Typically resilience is defined by this successful outcome. It is not a personality construct though personality traits (e.g. optimism) are predictors of the outcome (Carver *et al.*, 2005; Zautra and Reich, 2011). Other factors seen as contributing to resilience include resources such as social networks, income and education (Zautra and Reich, 2011; Bonanno *et al.*, 2007).

However, in addition to these variables, processes of coping with stressful events are central to achieving successful outcomes. Researchers have investigated the links between coping strategies and resilience. For example, Bonanno *et al.* (2012) investigated the coping strategies (using the COPE scale) that predicted resilience (i.e., a stable pattern over time of low symptoms of anxiety and depression) in the face of spinal cord injury. They found that resilient patients were more likely to appraise the spinal cord injury as a challenge rather than a threat and were more likely to cope using strategies of acceptance and fighting spirit and less likely to use behavioural disengagement. A study of child caregivers also showed that resilience is associated with higher levels of benefit finding (see above; Cassidy, Giles and McLaughlin, 2014).

FOCUS 5.4

Building resilience

The American Psychological Association (2014) has produced a list of 10 ways to build resilience:

1 *Make connections*: building relationships, accepting and giving help and support.
2 *Avoid seeing crises as insurmountable problems*: change how you interpret and respond to difficult events.
3 *Accept that change is part of living*: this includes accepting circumstances that cannot be changed.
4 *Move toward your goals*: develop realistic goals and take steps to move towards them.
5 *Take decisive actions*: act on difficult situations rather than detaching from them or wishing they will go away.
6 *Look for opportunities for self-discovery*: try to learn from difficult experiences.
7 *Nurture a positive view of yourself*: develop confidence in your abilities to solve problems and trust your instincts.
8 *Keep things in perspective*: avoid blowing problems out of proportion.
9 *Maintain a hopeful outlook*: be optimistic. Visualise what you want rather than worrying about what you fear.
10 *Take care of yourself*: for example, engage in activities you enjoy, exercise, etc.

Source: From American Psychological Association (2014). Copyright © 2014 by the American Psychological Association. Reprinted with permission.

ACTIVITY 5.1

Consider each of the 10 ways of building resilience listed in Focus 5.4. How do each of these relate to the coping strategies discussed earlier in this chapter?

Throughout this section on coping, we have seen that drawing on social support resources can make a positive contribution to coping. The role of strong social networks and other types of social supports are explored in further detail in the next section.

SOCIAL SUPPORT

What do we mean by social support? What should researchers be measuring when they look at social support? Is it important to be part of community networks with large numbers of social contacts, or is it more important to have one close relationship perhaps with a spouse, cohabiting partner or close friend? Maybe the crucial issue is not the nature of the relationship but whether people perform behaviours that help out in a stressful situation. These are key questions addressed by social support research.

Types of social support

Various classifications of social support exist. Researchers have distinguished between structural and functional approaches to support (e.g. Uchino, Cacioppo and Kiecolt-Glaser, 1996). Structural approaches examine the simple existence of networks and friendships, whereas functional approaches look at the actual function that such social contacts serve (e.g. providing practical help versus emotional support). Supports have further been categorized into perceived and received supports, with perceived support tending to show stronger relationships with health than received support (Uchino, 2009). In this section we examine research demonstrating the importance of being part of a social network followed by some studies examining the importance of having a small number of quality relationships. We then examine studies examining a range of different functions of social support.

Social networks

In 1979, Berkman and Syme published what is now regarded as a classic study demonstrating the value of social networks for health. The study, conducted in the USA, followed up a random sample of almost 5,000 adults (aged 30–69) for 9 years from 1965. At the start of the study the researchers recorded the presence and the extent of four types of social ties – marriage, contact with the extended family and friends, church membership and other formal and informal group affiliations. These were combined to form a social network index. They found that both the individual ties and the combined index predicted mortality over the next 9 years. Those with low scores on the index were about twice as likely to die as those with high scores, even after controlling for self-reports of social class, smoking, obesity and health at the outset. One limitation of this study was the use of self-reports of health in the initial measurements but findings were later replicated using physical examinations. In a review of a range of such studies, House, Landis and Umberson (1988) concluded that evidence consistently supports the view that there is an increased risk associated with having few social relationships even after adjusting for other risk factors. However, there are gender differences. In particular, marriage has more health benefits for men than for women and bereavement is more harmful for men. More recently poor social networks, or social isolation (as it is now more frequently called), have been linked to strokes (Rutledge et al., 2008), decline in cognitive functioning (Shankar et al., 2013) and depression (Golden et al., 2009).

Quality of relationships

Being part of a large social network does not guarantee that people will receive greater help when they need it. The correlation between the number of connections people have and the actual support they receive tends to be quite low, perhaps because one good relationship may provide better support than a large number of more superficial contacts (Cohen and Wills, 1985). The importance of quality rather than quantity of relationships is demonstrated by a well-known sociological study conducted by Brown and Harris (1978), who studied the origins of depression in women. They interviewed 400 women about the life events they had experienced in the past year. They also asked the participants to name the people they were able to confide in about their worries. Women were classified into one of the four following categories: (a) those who had a close relationship with someone in the same household; (b) those without such a relationship who had a friend or relative they saw at least weekly; (c) those with a close friend or relative they saw less than weekly; and (d) those with none of these relationships. The study found that having a confiding relationship protected the women from depression following major life events. Among the women who experienced a stressful life event, only 1 in 10 of those in category a developed depression, compared to 1 in 4 of those in category b and 1 in 2.5 of those in categories c or d. This suggests that having confiding social support buffered the impact of life stressors.

Functional social support

None of the above measures taps specific supportive behaviours. However, it is important to consider what types of behaviour may be most helpful if we wish to develop effective social support interventions (e.g. Dakof and Taylor, 1990). For example, what type of support would be most helpful when an individual received a diagnosis of cancer? Various types of specific social support have been assessed, including emotional support (helping the person to feel accepted or valued), instrumental support (i.e. practical support) and informational support (e.g. Cohen and Wills, 1985). The match between support provided and an individual's need may be crucial to effectiveness. For example, a study of support from family and friends provided for breast cancer sufferers (Reynolds and Perrin, 2004) compared a range of provided support with the support desired by the women. The study found that two behaviours that were intended to be supportive were unwelcomed by over 90 per cent of the women. These both related to trying to find causes or explanations for the cancer. However, reactions to other types of support varied greatly between women. Using cluster analysis, a statistical technique that classifies people into groupings according to specified characteristics, they found four different patterns. Group 1 wanted many types of support, which focused on reassurance that everything would be OK; group 2 wanted people to act normally and did not want to talk about cancer; group 3 wanted facts, information and general advice; and group 4 wanted to talk but did not want advice. The four groups did not differ on measures of adjustment to breast cancer. However a mismatch of support was associated with poorer adjustment, particularly where people received support they had not wanted.

Health impact of social support

There is strong evidence for positive effects of social support. For example, a thorough review of 81 studies (Uchino *et al.*, 1996) indicated that social support was related to beneficial effects on cardiovascular, endocrine and immune functioning. These researchers also found that interventions to improve social support had beneficial impacts on heart disease risk factors such as blood pressure.

The mechanisms whereby social support impacts on health have been discussed at length. Cohen and Wills (1985) suggested two alternative pathways. First, social support may have a direct effect on well-being and health, i.e. it is beneficial regardless of the

FIGURE 5.2 Greater social support is associated with better health.

presence of stressors. Second, social support may buffer or moderate the impact of stressors on health so that it only benefits those facing threats (see Focus 5.2). In a review of early literature, Cohen and Wills (1985) found evidence of direct effects for structural supports (e.g. when measures of social networks are used), but buffering was sometimes found when studies focused on close relationships. Uchino *et al.* (1996) confirmed this finding. Studies tend to find buffering effects when measures of en-acted supports are used. It is perhaps not surprising that, when close family or friends provide specific supports in response to a particular stressful situation, this buffers the stress, while simply having a large social network may not have the same effect. Social support may also have a positive impact on health through its effect on health behaviour (i.e. the social support–health relationship is mediated by health behaviours). Finally, it is also possible that the level of social support available to an individual is a stable individual difference that is linked to personality traits (e.g. agreeableness or lack of hostility, see Chapter 6). However, Uchino *et al.* (1996) concluded that relationships between social support and health occur even where personality variables are controlled.

Finally, it is also worth considering the impact of social support on the provider of the support. We saw in Chapter 2 that carers of Alzheimer's patients showed slower wound-healing than matched controls (Kiecolt-Glaser *et al.*, 1995), a clear instance of

---

FOCUS 5.5

Can social support ever be bad for you?

In some situations social support can be unhelpful. We have seen that this is the case where there is a mismatch between our needs and the support provided. It is also not unusual for researchers to find that social support provided in the work situation is not beneficial (e.g. Uchino *et al.*, 1996). Support at work, especially from a supervisor, may make the recipient feel incompetent and so is not experienced as helpful. This idea was tested in an experimental study by Deelstra *et al.* (2003), which imposed instrumental support and found that negative affect was higher and self-esteem was lower when support was given, except when the problem could not have been solved without it. These effects were confirmed by physiological indicators (e.g. pulse rate).

Similarly, social networks may not always be supportive For example, in a study of widowed women (aged 60–69), Rook (1984) found a stronger relationship between problematic relationships and reduced well-being than between positive relationships and improved well-being. Furthermore, most of those relationships identified as 'problematic' were friends or relatives. The researchers suggested that many of these unhelpful relationships were not seen to be egalitarian, i.e. others were making decisions for them. There is also evidence from a meta-analysis that negative aspects of social relationships may have a negative impact on the immune system (Herbert and Cohen, 1993).

negative impact of offering social support. This may be an extreme example where giving support is damaging because it is extremely stressful. Generally, social psychologists researching reciprocity in social support have suggested that the feeling of giving more support than you receive is beneficial for health (e.g. Liang, Krause and Bennett, 2001). However, there do seem to be gender differences. Vaananen *et al.* (2005) examined the long-term effects of perceived reciprocity in intimate relationships on sickness absence and found that women who gave more support than they received were healthier (compared to those who received more than they gave), whereas men who received more than they gave were healthier. They suggested that giving support was associated with enhanced self-esteem for women.

In summary, many of the findings in studies discussed in this section emphasize the importance of providing social support in a way that does not undermine individuals' self-esteem and feelings of competence.

RECENT DEVELOPMENTS IN SOCIAL SUPPORT RESEARCH

Loneliness and social isolation

In recent years research has focused on the effects of social isolation and loneliness. Social isolation refers to a lack of social networks. For example, those living alone with few friends and family and limited contact with others are regarded as isolated (Shankar *et al.*, 2011). As we have seen earlier in this chapter it is well established that such isolation is associated with a range of cognitive and health problems and with increased mortality.

Loneliness is the perception of social isolation and is not necessarily the same as objective isolation. Feelings of loneliness may occur in those who have considerable social contacts while some quite isolated people do not feel lonely. Social isolation is a particular risk for older people as they frequently live alone and may have lost partners or suffer deteriorating mobility. Loneliness in this group is also a matter of concern. A survey of older people (over age 65) in the UK found that 7 per cent reported being often or always lonely (Victor *et al.*, 2005). Loneliness is found to show a U-shaped relationship with age, being higher among those aged under 25 and those aged over 65 years (Victor and Yang, 2012).

Loneliness, like social isolation, has been linked to an increase in physical illness and mortality (for reviews see Hawkley and Cacioppo, 2010 and Cacioppo and Cacioppo, 2014). Hawkley and Cacioppo (2010) also report evidence of devastating effects of loneliness on mental well-being and cognitive functioning. It has been associated with increased risk of depression, cognitive decline and Alzheimer's disease. So serious are these effects that Hawkley and Cacioppo (2010: 209) conclude that 'A perceived sense of social connectedness serves as a scaffold for the self – damage the scaffold and the self starts to crumble'.

Recent research has investigated the mechanisms whereby both loneliness and social isolation are linked to illness and mortality. It is unclear whether they have independent effects or whether loneliness mediates the relationship between social isolation and health (see Focus 5.2) and few studies examine both variables in conjunction. Cornwell and Waite (2009) found that loneliness and isolation have independent effects on self-rated health, but loneliness appeared to mediate the association between isolation and mental health. Both have been linked to physical inactivity, smoking and other health behaviours (Shankar *et al.* 2011). However, Shankar *et al.* (2011) found that social isolation was linked to blood pressure and a number of inflammatory markers. This suggests that both loneliness and social isolation may affect health through their effects on health behaviour but that social isolation may have direct effects on biological processes implicated in heart disease development. Steptoe *et al.* (2013) also found that loneliness was not independently associated with mortality among older adults and also did not appear to mediate the link between social isolation and mortality suggesting social isolation is associated with ill health and mortality regardless of whether a person experiences loneliness. Steptoe *et al.* (2013) suggest that while reducing both social isolation and loneliness would benefit individuals' well-being, interventions to reduce isolation would be more important for reducing mortality.

Social isolation and social support in cyberspace

Over the last century the nature of social networks has gradually changed for many people. Greater social mobility means that many people work away from home and families are often dispersed around the world. At the same time new technologies have made it possible for people to maintain contact, at first by phone and more recently via the Internet (e.g. by email, social networking, instant messaging and use of webcams). Opportunities to build new networks, often based on specific interests, are also offered via Internet chat rooms or discussion forums. In recent years there has been a rapid growth in studies examining the impact of the Internet for social networks and social support.

Whether the Internet has a positive or negative impact on social networks and individuals' well-being has proved controversial. Kraut *et al.* (1998) studied 179 people in 73 households over the first year or two of their Internet use. They found that greater use of the Internet was linked to reductions in communication with others in their household, a decline in the size of their social circle and increases in feelings of depression and loneliness. This was true even though they used the Internet predominantly for communication purposes. They labelled this phenomenon the 'Internet paradox'. They followed up the same sample three years later (Kraut *et al.* 2002) and found that the negative effects had generally been replaced by positive effects in that more use of the Internet was associated with improved psychological well-being and more social involvement, although, on the negative side, there was also an increase in stress. However, there were important individual differences in the long-term effects of Internet use with better outcomes for extroverts and those who already had good social support but poorer outcomes for introverts and those lacking social support. Overall, they suggest that the Internet may have improved in the 3 years of the study, offering better information and communication services (e.g. instant messaging) that help maintain social contacts. There were also gender differences in Internet use such that women were more likely to use email to keep in touch with family and friends who live far away (Boneva, Kraut and Frohlich, 2001). It is clearly likely that the effects on social contacts are very dependent on type of use made of the Internet and whether it is a replacement for social contact or for other individual activities.

ACTIVITY 5.2

It has been suggested that excessive Internet use makes people isolated and withdrawn. Discuss whether you think this is the case. Do you think it is possible to improve your social support via the Internet?

For people who are perhaps isolated by illness or disability, the Internet can provide a unique and invaluable source of support. It can provide informational support and can also put people in touch with others experiencing similar circumstances, who may be able to provide emotional support. Researchers have examined Internet social support for a range of illnesses, including breast cancer or HIV/AIDS, as well as sites offering support for behaviour change such as quitting smoking or losing weight. For example, Fogel *et al.* (2002) found that women with breast cancer who used the Internet for information on breast health issues reported greater social support and less loneliness. This was true even when the use of the Internet was less than 1 hour a week. Similarly, Kalichman *et al.* (2003) reported greater perceptions of social support, as well as greater active coping, among HIV-positive people who used the Internet for health-related information. Mo and Coulson (2012) suggest that participating in online support groups help individuals living with HIV/AIDS by four empowering processes, i.e. receiving useful information, receiving social support, finding positive meaning and helping others.

Researchers using qualitative methods to content analyse communications in Internet social support groups have shed light on the types of social support available. For example, Coulson, Buchanan and Aubeeluck (2007) analysed communications online in a support group for people affected by Huntington's disease (an inherited degenerative neurological disorder). They found that informational and emotional supports were most commonly offered. Just less than 10 per cent offered tangible help and this included indirect help such as advising someone of sources of direct help. Other studies confirm the finding that informational and emotional supports are the dominant forms of support in online communications.

Further research by Coulson (2013), using qualitative methods, has shown the value of membership of a web-based community for those with inflammatory bowel disease. The majority accessed the site daily and to obtain information and emotional support. They reported that it helped them to accept their illness and learn to manage it. It also helped them view their disease more positively and improved their subjective well-being. However, some disadvantages were also reported. For example, a focus on the negative side of the disease could be demoralising.

In some cases there may be more worrying disadvantages to Internet use. For example, there has been considerable concern in the media and medical profession about pro-anorexia websites that provide support for life-threatening behaviour (e.g. Christodoulou, 2012). In an experimental study of exposure to such websites, Bardone-Cone and Cass (2007) found evidence of negative effects on viewers' affect, self-esteem and perceived weight. Similarly, Whitlock, Powers and Eckenrode (2006) analysed self-injury message boards for adolescents and suggested that while they may provide valuable support they may also normalize and so encourage damaging behaviour.

ACTIVITY 5.3

Search for support groups online (e.g. type 'support group' into Google). Pick three support groups for physical or psychological disorders and evaluate them. What kind of support do they offer? How likely is it to fit the needs of the target group?
  See Kiesler and Kraut (1999) for a discussion of the value of such groups.

SUMMARY

Coping can be viewed both as a situational and dispositional variable. Researchers have identified a wide range of coping strategies that are typically measured using standard coping questionnaires. These have been used to explore coping in response to particular situations and to examine dispositional tendencies to use particular coping strategies. These strategies are often further grouped into overarching categories, e.g. emotion-focused or problem-focused coping.

Repressive coping is a form of avoidant coping style that is linked to health outcomes. The distinction between monitoring and blunting coping styles addresses people's information processing preferences and is useful in helping to design strategies to communicate medical information to patients. General personality styles are also linked to coping strategies. Coping strategies can be seen as mediators of the relationship between personality and well-being outcomes.

A positive or optimistic approach to the experience of threat has coping benefits. People typically report feeling positive affect (as well as negative affect) even in the most stressful times. This is thought to provide respite and help build resources. Positive affect and looking for benefits in stressful situations also benefits health. Positive approaches to coping are also central to developing resilience.

Social support has been classified into functional and structural forms of support and a distinction has also been made between perceived and received support. Types of functional support have also been identified e.g. emotional, instrumental and informational supports. Most types of support have been linked to positive health outcomes. Having good social networks has been shown to be beneficial for health and mortality but having one or two close confiding relationships may be more important in a crisis. Both direct and stress-buffering effects have been found depending on the type of support considered. However, there are also some instances when social support may not be helpful. This may be particularly the case where social support is damaging to the self-esteem of the recipient. In some circumstances it may also be harmful to the support giver.

Recent developments in social support research discussed in this chapter include research on loneliness and isolation and on the role of new technologies for the provision of social support.

KEY CONCEPTS AND TERMS

- Benefit finding
- Blunter
- Coping resources
- Coping strategies
- Coping style
- Emotion-focused

- Emotional writing
- Loneliness
- Monitor
- Primary appraisal
- Proactive coping
- Problem-focused

- Repressive coping
- Resilience
- Secondary appraisal
- Social isolation
- Social networks
- Social support

SAMPLE ESSAY TITLES

- Moving house is generally considered to be a stressful experience. How does psychological theory and research help to explain why one person may cope with this experience better than another?
- 'Coping is personality in action under stress.' Evaluate this statement with reference to situational and dispositional approaches to coping.
- Are personal relationships helpful in reducing stress? Discuss with reference to the psychological evidence.
- Is the Internet a valuable resource in the provision of social support to isolated individuals? Discuss giving examples from the research literature.

FURTHER READING

Books

Folkman, S. (ed.). (2011). *The Oxford Handbook of Stress, Health and Coping*. Oxford: Oxford University Press.

Journal articles

Carver, C.S., Scheier, M.F. and Weintraub, J.K. (1989). Assessing coping strategies: A theoretically based approach. *Journal of Personality and Social Psychology*, 56, 267–283.

Folkman, S. and Moskowitz, J.T. (2004). Coping: Pitfalls and promise. *Annual Review of Psychology*, 55, 745–774.

Hawkley, L.C. and Cacioppo, J.T. (2010). Loneliness matters: A theoretical and empirical review of consequences and mechanisms. *Annals of Behavioral Medicine*, 40, 218–227.

Kiesler, S. and Kraut, R. (1999). Internet use and ties that bind. *American Psychologist*, 54, 783–784.

Steptoe, A., Shankar, A., Demakakos, P. and Wardle, J. (2013). Social isolation, loneliness and the all-cause mortality in older men and women. *Proceedings of the National Academy of Sciences*, 110, 5797–5801.

Uchino, B.N. (2009). Understanding the links between social support and physical health: A life-span perspective with emphasis on the separability of perceived and received support. *Perspectives on Psychological Science*, 4, 236–255.

6 Personality and health

CHAPTER PLAN

In this chapter we examine the ways in which personality dimensions or traits can determine health outcomes. These effects of personality on health include direct effects through physiological mechanisms and indirect effects through health behaviours.

Personality traits refer to stable individual differences in thinking, feeling and behaving across a range of different situations. Research in the health domain has found that particular dimensions of personality are associated with poor health and reduced longevity, while others are linked to good health and increased length of life. The magnitude of these effects can be similar to those of known biological risk factors such as cholesterol (Caspi, Roberts and Shiner, 2005). The personality dimensions associated with poor health outcomes include neuroticism (or negative affect), type A personality and hostility. The dimensions associated with good health outcomes include optimism, extraversion and conscientiousness. In this chapter we consider the evidence linking these personality variables to health outcomes and some of the mechanisms by which personality affects health. For example, personality traits might lead to greater exposure to stressful events, to a reduction in the effectiveness of coping strategies, or a change in coping resources such as social support. These explanations of the personality–health link build on the discussion of the impact of personality on coping in Chapter 5. Other personality traits such as hostility may affect health through changing the intensity and duration of physiological reactions to stress, linking personality to the biopsychosocial pathways considered in Chapter 2.

In this chapter we will consider (1) optimism and health; (2) type A behaviour and coronary heart disease; (3) hostility and coronary heart disease; (4) neuroticism and health; (5) extraversion and health; and (6) conscientiousness and health.

INTRODUCTION

This chapter reviews evidence suggesting that stable individual differences in the way people think, feel and behave (i.e. personality traits) are predictive of various health outcomes. We explore how these stable individual differences can predispose individuals to respond to life challenges in a manner, which, over time, damages or protects their health. Much research on personality in recent years has focused on five broad personality types: openness to experience (or intellect), conscientiousness, extraversion, agreeableness and neuroticism (or emotional stability) (McCrae and Costa, 1987; Digman, 1990). This is often referred to as the Big Five Taxonomy or the OCEAN model of personality. A growing body of research now relates traits from the Big Five Taxonomy to various health behaviours and health outcomes. For example, Booth-Kewley and Vickers (1994) suggest that the Big Five personality traits may determine the extent to which people engage in general clusters of health-related behaviours such as substance use risk behaviours (e.g. smoking). However, there has been less research on how openness and agreeableness link to health outcomes so we will focus on extraversion, neuroticism and conscientiousness. The Big Five model is based on the assumption that a range of more specific personality traits can be understood as blends of the different Big Five traits. Some of the best evidence for the impacts of personality on health outcomes arises from work looking at more specific personality traits. So, for example, work has examined the impact of optimism or positive affect on health. We will consider work on optimism, type A behaviour pattern and hostility as important areas of research relating personality traits to health outcomes. Some research has also suggested a cancer or type C personality type (see Focus 6.1) and a distressed or type D personality type (see Focus 6.3).

Since the magnitude of personality effects on health outcomes can be comparable to known biological factors, these effects must be taken seriously by health psychologists (Ferguson, 2013; Hampson *et al.*, 2006; Hampson, 2012). In the Western world the leading causes of morbidity and mortality in middle and later life are now various chronic diseases such as coronary heart disease, cancer and diabetes, while in children, adolescents and young adults unintentional injuries are the leading causes of death. Personality traits may have important roles to play in both these periods of life.

LEARNING OUTCOMES

When you have completed this chapter you should be able to:

1 Explain how optimism is related to positive health outcomes and the role of attributional styles in this relationship.
2 Discuss the effects of type A personality and hostility on coronary heart disease and potential mediation of these effects through physiological reactions.
3 Describe the role of neuroticism (or negative affect) on poor health and the explanations of this effect through perceptions of stress, ability to cope and social support.
4 Describe the impact of extraversion on positive and negative health outcomes through effects on mood and health risk behaviours.
5 Describe the relationship between conscientiousness and positive health outcomes and the mediating effects of health behaviours.
6 Evaluate the different mechanisms through which personality variables affect health outcomes.

FOCUS 6.1

Type C personality

This chapter reviews work on the 'type A' or coronary prone behaviour pattern. The type A individual appears to be hostile, easily angered, competitive and hard-driving. Research by oncologists interested in the behavioural causes of cancer has suggested a 'type C' or cancer risk pattern (Temoshok *et al.*, 1985). Type C individuals are characterized by high levels of denial and suppression of various emotions, in particular anger. Type C includes a number of other features including 'pathological niceness', conflict avoidance, high social desirability, harmonizing behaviour, over-compliance, over-patience, as well as high rationality and a rigid control of emotional expression. It is suggested that the excessive denial, avoidance, suppression and repression of emotions that characterize type C over time weaken the individual's natural resistance to carcinogenic influences. Support for the link between type C personality and cancer is found in studies relating different immune parameters (natural killer cell activity, lymphocytes, serotonin uptake, mean platelet volume) to mood states, coping styles and personality traits (Cunningham, 1985). Alexithymia is a related personality type (a literal translation is the lack of words for emotions), characterized by difficulty identifying, labelling and understanding emotions, which is also found to be associated with negative health outcomes. Evidence exists to suggest that alexithymia is linked to an increased risk of developing cardiovascular disease (Waldstein *et al.*, 2002). It has also been found to be associated with blood pressure reactivity following written emotional disclosure (O'Connor and Ashley, 2008; see also Focus 5.1).

In relation to the development of chronic diseases, personality traits may play an important role in the maintenance of behaviours that are health-promoting or health-damaging when engaged in over time (e.g. smoking and unhealthy eating). Similarly, accidents and unintentional injuries are usually a consequence of repeated exposure to risky situations rather than a single chance event. Personality traits may also influence health through a variety of other mechanisms such as increasing perceptions of stress. A key theme in this chapter is the different mechanisms by which personality traits affect health outcomes. In considering each personality trait and its impact on health we discuss potential explanations and then in a final section consider these explanations collectively. Table 6.1 (below) provides a summary of key explanations of the relationships between personality traits and health.

OPTIMISM

Optimism refers to the expectation that in the future good things will happen to you and bad things will not. While we all may be optimistic in some areas of our lives and pessimistic in others, optimism taps the extent to which an individual is optimistic in general across a range of domains and across time. A number of measures of optimism have been developed. Scheier and Carver (1992) developed a measure that focuses on optimistic expectations. This includes items such as 'In uncertain times, I usually expect the best' and 'I always look on the bright side of life'. Optimism has also been assessed using indices of an individual's sense of hope. A measure developed by Snyder et al. (1996) focuses on the extent to which individuals pursue their goals and their beliefs that their goals can be realized. Items include 'I energetically pursue my goals' and 'There are lots of ways around any problem'. Other researchers have focused on how people explain the causes of bad events (Peterson, 2000). Such explanations or 'attributions' can be classified along a number of dimensions such as whether they are internal or external to the individual (e.g. whether the cause is something about the individual versus their environment), whether they are likely to be stable or unstable over time (e.g. the extent to which the cause will affect most/all similar future outcomes or just this specific one) and whether they are general or specific causes (e.g. will the cause affect a range of life events for that individual or just this particular event). Optimists tend to attribute bad events to external, unstable and specific causes while pessimists see the same events as resulting from internal, stable and global causes (Peterson, Vaillant and Seligman, 1988). For example, an optimist might believe that they got a minor illness because they were 'run down' after an unusually busy time at work. In contrast, a pessimist might believe they contracted a minor illness because they are always susceptible to such things no matter what they do.

The outcomes of optimism include increased psychological well-being, better physical health and even greater longevity. For example, in relation to psychological well-being, Litt et al. (1992) found that optimistic individuals were less depressed after unsuccessful in vitro fertilization. Similarly, Carver et al. (1993) reported that optimism in women with breast cancer was associated with less distress following surgery and that this effect persisted one year later. Alloy, Abrahamson and Francis (1999) found that students with a pessimistic explanatory style were more likely to subsequently experience depression.

Research also demonstrates that high levels of optimism are associated with better physical health. Those with high levels of optimism have fewer infectious illnesses and report fewer physical symptoms even during periods of stress (Peterson and Seligman, 1987). They are also more likely to recover from surgery more quickly and less likely to be re-hospitalized (Scheier et al., 1999). Peterson et al. (1988) provide an impressive demonstration of the effects of optimism on physical health. In a sample of men, an attributional style measure of optimism assessed at age 25 was found to predict health status 35 years later as judged by doctors; the optimists were more likely to be in better health even when initial physical and mental health were statistically controlled.

Most impressively, those with high levels of optimism may even live longer. Danner, Snowdon and Friesen (2001) coded pieces of text that a sample of 180 Catholic nuns had written about themselves on entering the church as young women, for emotional content. The research then examined the survival rates of these same women when they were 75–95 years of age. Those who wrote sentences containing self-descriptions with the most positive emotions (e.g. happiness, pride, love) were more likely to live longer than those containing the fewest positive emotions. Comparison of the top and bottom 25 per cent (quartiles) indicated that 24 per cent of those in the top quartile had died compared to 54 per cent of those in the bottom quartile. Similar results have been reported for men. Everson *et al.* (1996b) examined the relationship between hopelessness and health outcomes in a large sample of men. Comparing the top and bottom 33 per cent (tertiles) showed that those in the top tertile compared to the bottom tertile for hopelessness were 3.5 times more likely to die from all causes of death, 4 times more likely to die from cardiovascular disease and 2.5 times more likely to die from cancer. Similarly, men with AIDS who are optimistic live twice as long as men who are pessimistic (Reed *et al.*, 1994). More generally, among older individuals, those with positive attitudes towards ageing live an average of 7.5 years longer than those with more negative attitudes (Levy *et al.*, 2002).

These studies on health outcomes highlight an important but subtle distinction between optimism and positive affect. Whereas optimism refers to positive beliefs and feelings about the future, positive affect reflects a level of pleasurable engagement with the environment such as happiness, joy, excitement, enthusiasm and contentment. These two tendencies may overlap substantially as is shown in the Danner *et al.* (2001) study. However, recent research has begun to examine the effects of positive affect independently of optimism (see Pressman and Cohen, 2005, for a review of positive affect and health; see also Chapter 5). One important issue here is the extent to which positive affect is the opposite of, or alternatively distinct from, negative affect, a personality trait we consider below. Currently there is evidence supporting each view as we discuss below.

The explanation for the relationship between optimism and various health outcomes is still unclear. One interesting suggestion is that those high in optimism may be more likely to avoid certain high-risk situations. Some supporting evidence for this view comes from Peterson *et al.* (1988) who showed that those with an optimistic attributional style were less likely to die from accidental or violent causes than those with a pessimistic style, while the two groups did not differ in respect of mortality from cancer or cardiovascular disease. A further explanation for the relationship between optimism and health is through the effects of optimism on coping strategies. Those high in optimism are more likely to use adaptive and functional strategies for coping with problems such as acceptance, rational thinking, social support and positive reframing. For example, Scheier, Weintraub and Carver (1986) conducted a study in which students had to write about coping with stressful situations. Optimists were found to be more likely to use strategies such as making a plan and sticking to it, focusing intently on the problem and seeking social support. Optimists were also less likely to distract themselves from thinking about the problem. Scheier *et al.* (1989) reported similar differences between optimists and pessimists in the way they coped with recovery from surgery that resulted in faster recovery among the optimists. The use of more constructive coping strategies may lead to better health outcomes, partly by helping individuals to avoid negative life events and also by helping them to confront and deal with problems earlier and more effectively. A further explanation focuses on the effect of pessimism on physiological reactions to stress in terms of immune functioning and cardiovascular response (Scheier and Carver, 1987). Some support of this explanation can be found in studies that have shown immune responses to be lower in pessimists (Segerstrom *et al.*, 1998).

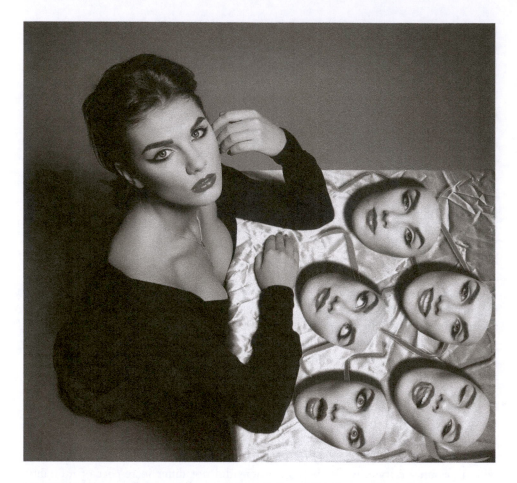

FIGURE 6.1 We can all show different 'faces' to the world. Personality traits tap consistencies in how we respond and behave. Such consistencies have been found to be important to the maintenance of health and the development of illness.

Source: Copyright Elaine Nadiv/Shutterstock.com.

TYPE A BEHAVIOUR

Type A behaviour pattern is typified by a competitive drive, aggression, chronic impatience and a sense of time urgency (Rosenman *et al.*, 1976). This type of behaviour is contrasted with the opposite cluster of characteristics, type B behaviour pattern, which leads to a more relaxed, laid-back approach to life. The concept of type A behaviour originated from the work of two cardiologists, Meyer Friedman and Ray Rosenman, who realized that their patients' disease was not fully explained by conventional risk factors such as dietary cholesterol and smoking. For years they failed to look beyond the physical symptoms and to consider the signs of stress in their patients, even though patients tended to sit on the edge of waiting room chairs to the extent that an upholsterer commented that the front edges of the waiting room chairs were unusually worn (Friedman and Rosenman, 1974). Eventually, however, they sent out a questionnaire asking 150 businessmen what they believed had precipitated a heart attack in a friend. Few thought it was due to diet or smoking and most felt it was due to 'excessive competitive drive and meeting deadlines' (Rosenman et al., 1964: 73). A subsequent study suggested that physicians agreed even though this was not a recognized cause in the medical literature of the time. This and subsequent research ultimately led to the identification of the constellation of characteristics described above and its long-term investigation in a large prospective study known as the Western Collaborative Group Study. This examined risk factors for coronary heart disease (CHD) in a sample of over 3,000 healthy middle-aged men. The study started in 1960 and followed participants for more than 27 years. Rosenman and colleagues assessed the participants in the study using a structured interview, in which the interviewer asked questions in a confrontational manner (including interrupting the participant) with the aim of provoking the participant in order to assess aggression and time urgency (Chesney, Eagleston and Rosenman, 1980). The men were then followed up at 8.5 and 22 years. The researchers found after 8.5 years that those men who were classified as type A had around twice the risk of developing CHD as those who were type B, even after controlling for other risk factors. At this stage it appeared that type A was a risk factor that was as important as smoking or high blood pressure for the development of CHD. However, on follow-up after 22 years, the researchers found that type A behaviour no longer showed a significant relationship with CHD (Ragland and Brand, 1985). Thus, after the initial enthusiasm about the importance of this risk factor, doubts were raised.

Many other research teams around the world were also conducting studies of type A behaviour during the 1960s and 1970s and in the early years (pre-1978) these tended to support the idea that type A was linked to CHD (Miller et al., 1991). However, after this time, the majority of subsequent studies, like that of the Western Collaborative Group itself, failed to support the original findings. As a result the role of type A in heart disease became a controversial issue. A number of meta-analyses have been conducted over the years (e.g. Booth-Kewley and Friedman, 1987; Miller et al., 1996; Myrtek, 2001). For example, Miller et al. (1996) suggested that the null findings were due to a range of methodological differences between the early studies and those conducted later. First, the more recent studies often looked at samples that were already at high risk of heart disease. Second, over time, questionnaire measures (e.g. the Jenkins Activity Survey; Jenkins, Zyzanski and Rosenman, 1971) have been used rather than the structured interview, which allows assessment of behaviour in interaction. Compared to the interview, questionnaire items have limitations in terms of assessing behaviour and tend to be less effective in predicting CHD. Overall, Miller et al. (1996) concluded that type A behaviour was a risk factor for heart disease as, across studies based on structured interviews, about 70 per cent of middle-aged males with CHD were type As, as opposed to 46 per cent of healthy males.

Myrtek (2001) reviewed all prospective studies (a total of 25) published up to 1998 investigating coronary heart disease and type A behaviour. They concluded that taking all studies together there was no significant association between type A behaviour and heart disease and hence that type A is not a risk factor for heart disease. Since that time there seems no further evidence to support a link. Perhaps most damning of all for the type A construct has been a paper by Petticrew, Lee and McKee (2012), which suggests that the initial positive results were due to the fact that much of the early research was funded by the tobacco industry and 'selected results used to counter concerns about tobacco and health' (2012: 2018). Evidence that type A caused disease could be used to suggest that smoking was merely a result of type A and not itself a risk factor.

However, interest in at least one aspect of type A continues as a number of meta-analytic reviews (e.g. Booth-Kewley and Friedman, 1987; and Matthews 1988) raised the possibility that one component of type A behaviour (hostility) is predictive of heart disease. While a certain amount of research continues into the type A behaviour pattern the emphasis has now shifted towards investigating hostility.

HOSTILITY

Hostility, like type A, is a complex and multidimensional construct. It has been defined as 'a negative attitude towards others, consisting of enmity, denigration and ill will' (Smith, 1994: 26). Components of this characteristic are cynicism about others' motives, mistrust and hostile attributional style, i.e. a tendency to interpret other people's actions as aggressive (Smith et al., 2004). While this definition is primarily cognitive, the associated emotional and behavioural constructs of anger and aggression are often incorporated within the construct (Miller et al., 1996). The construct is measured using items such as 'Some of my family have habits that bother and annoy me very much' and 'It is safer to trust no-one'; with a response of 'true' indicating higher levels of hostility. These items are taken from the Cook–Medley hostility scale, which is a commonly used measure (Cook and Medley, 1954). Hostility has been found to be correlated quite highly with the hard-driving component of type A behaviour ($r = .44$). It is also positively correlated with a range of measures of neuroticism ($r = .27$ to $.54$) and negatively with measures of extraversion ($r = -.48$) (Carmody, Crassen and Wiens, 1989). Some authors discuss hostility as one (negative) expression of the Big Five personality trait agreeableness (Ozer and Benet-Martinez, 2006), i.e. hostility is low agreeableness.

Following from the tradition of research in type A behaviour, most research in this area has focused on the role of hostility in CHD. As for the research on type A, meta-analyses have assessed the strength of effects (Miller et al., 1996). Miller et al. (1996) included 45 studies in their review and concluded that hostility was an independent risk factor for CHD. As was the case with the research into type A, they found that the strongest relationships were found using structured interviews to assess hostility, which emphasize the expressive component of hostility (i.e. verbally and physically aggressive behaviour). These studies suggested that the effects were at least similar in magnitude to those reported for traditional risk factors such as smoking, high blood pressure and cholesterol. Even among studies using self-report measures (the Cook–Medley scale: Cook and Medley, 1954), the review found small but consistent relationships with heart disease. It should be noted, however, that a more recent meta-analysis offers a less positive interpretation based on a smaller subset of papers (Myrtek, 2001), i.e. they suggest that while the effects are significant they are very small indeed. Furthermore, Petticrew *et al.* (2012) suggest that large amounts of tobacco industry funding also supported early research into hostility. In the main however, studies and reviews continue to suggest that hostility plays a role in causing CHD (e.g. Gallo and Matthews, 2003) and hypertension (Rutledge and Hogan, 2002). Most recently, Chida and Steptoe (2009) reviewed prospective studies of the role of anger and hostility in heart disease including a number of studies published since the previous reviews. They conclude that both anger and hostility are associated with an increase in CHD events in those who were initially healthy, but also poorer prognosis for CHD patients. They suggest that interventions to reduce anger and hostility may help prevent and treat CHD. Focus 6.2 considers one such intervention.

The possible mechanisms underlying the effects of hostility have also been discussed in some detail. Smith *et al.* (2004) discuss five possible models:

FOCUS 6.2

Interventions to reduce hostility

There is now evidence suggesting that a hostility-reduction intervention aimed at CHD patients with high levels of hostility may reduce risks for heart disease. Gidron, Davidson and Bata (1999) conducted a randomized controlled trial in which 22 hostile male patients were assigned to either a treatment or control group. Hostility was assessed by observation during a structured interview and by self-ratings. The hostility-reduction intervention involved eight 90-minute weekly group meetings using cognitive behaviour techniques. Participants were taught skills to reduce antagonism, cynicism and anger. They were also asked to rate their hostility in a daily log and to record their use of the skills they had learnt. The control group had a one-session group meeting giving information about the risks of hostility and about basic hostility-reduction skills. The participants were followed up immediately after the trial and again after 2 months. Those in the intervention group were observed to be, and rated themselves to be, less hostile at follow-up than the controls. They also had lower diastolic blood pressure. Furthermore, reductions in hostility were correlated with reductions in blood pressure.

In a subsequent paper, Davidson *et al.* (2007) conducted secondary analysis of the data from the above study. They found that patients who received the intervention tended to have fewer hospital admissions in the 6 months following the intervention, and, importantly, had significantly fewer days in hospital (a mean of 0.38 days compared with a mean of 2.15 days for the control group). Consequently, their hospitalization costs were less. While more studies are needed with larger and more diverse groups, these findings suggest there may be potential to design efficacious and cost-effective hostility-reduction treatments.

1   *Psychophysiological reactivity model*: suggests that hostile individuals show exaggerated cardiovascular and neuroendocrine responses to stressors.
2   *Psychosocial vulnerability model*: suggests that hostile individuals experience more interpersonal conflict. Hostility may lead to more stress and also be associated with less social support.
3   *Transactional model*: combines the above two models and suggests that hostile individuals experience more interpersonal conflict and also have greater physiological reactivity – a 'double whammy' effect.
4   *Health behaviour model:* suggests that hostility affects health because hostile individuals engage in health-risk behaviour patterns that mediate the effects of hostility on health. For example, hostile people may be cynical about health warnings or resistant to medical advice.
5   *Constitutional vulnerability model*: raises the possibility that individual differences (which might be genetic) are associated with both the personality tendency and the disease risk, i.e. the association between hostility and CHD is due to a third variable.

Overall, Smith *et al.* conclude that there is considerable support for a number of these models. Hostile people do display heightened physiological responses; they also experience increased levels of conflict and less social support. However, research has not yet established whether these tendencies mediate the relationship between hostility and health. There is some evidence that hostile people do display poorer health behaviour patterns but it is also clear that this does not wholly account for the relationship between hostility and health. Finally, the development of molecular genetics offers opportunities to explore the constitutional vulnerability model. Further research is awaited on these mechanisms. However, it is possible that several mechanisms play a part in explaining the association between hostility and health.

An interesting possibility in relation to the development of hostility is suggested by the work of Matthews *et al.* (1996). In this work, negative behaviours during parent–son discussions aimed at resolving disagreements were observed in 51 Caucasian adolescent (12–13 years of age) boys. Results showed that the frequency of negative behaviours in the family discussions predicted hostility and expressed anger assessed three years later even after controlling for baseline hostility. This would suggest that hostility may be nurtured within particular family backgrounds that are characterized by negative behaviours during interactions. In contrast, work by Caspi *et al.* (1997) shows that measures of temperament taken at 3 years old predict later health-related risk behaviour in early adulthood and that this effect is mediated by personality measures taken in late adolescence. This would appear to be good evidence that personality traits are something we are born with or at least develop very early in life and remain stable throughout our lives. Together, however, these studies suggest that, while certain aspects of personality may be stable from a very young age, other aspects change and develop over time as a result of our interaction with our environment. Thus both 'nature' and 'nurture' explanations may be needed to account for personality trait development.

FOCUS 6.3

Type D personality

Similar to type A, type D personality is a risk factor for coronary heart disease. The type D, or distressed, personality describes individuals who experience high levels of negative emotions (negative affectivity) and inhibit the expression of these negative emotions in social interactions (social inhibition). The concept was introduced by Johan Denollet, of Tilburg University in the Netherlands.

Type D personality can be assessed by a self-report questionnaire containing items that tap negative affectivity (e.g. 'I often make a fuss about unimportant things' or 'I often feel unhappy') and social inhibition (e.g. 'I often feel inhibited in social interactions' or 'I find it hard to start a conversation'). A type D individual would be someone who scores highly on both of these dimensions. This is important because previous research has shown negative affectivity or neuroticism to be related to various negative health outcomes.

Denollet and colleagues have shown the type D personality to be a risk factor for adverse health outcomes in cardiac patients. So, for example, Denollet et al. (1996) assessed type D in a sample of 286 cardiac patients who were receiving treatment. Approximately one-third of the sample were classified as type D. Approximately 8 years later, the patients were followed up. Among those classified as type D a total of 27 per cent had died compared with a total of 7 per cent of the rest of the sample. A majority of the deaths were due to heart disease or stroke. This translated into an odds ratio of almost four (i.e. being four times more likely to die if classified as type D compared to those not classified as type D). These effects were replicated in several studies. However, a meta-analysis including more recent studies suggested this was an overestimate and gave an odds ratio of 2.28 (Grande, Romppel and Barth, 2012). More recent studies have often found smaller effects, a pattern seen in research in other areas discussed above and have questioned the definition of the construct (see Ferguson et al., 2009).

The explanation for the relationship between type D and risk of death is not entirely clear. Those with type D personalities appear to have more highly activated immune systems and more inflammation (perhaps indicating more damage to blood vessels in the heart and throughout the body). They also show greater increases in blood pressure in reactions to stress. Recent research has suggested that type D individuals engage in fewer health behaviours and experience lower levels of social support and that these effects remain after controlling for neuroticism (Williams *et al.*, 2008).

NEUROTICISM

Neuroticism is one of the Big Five personality traits. It refers to the tendency to commonly experience negative emotions such as distress, anxiety, fear, anger and guilt (Watson and Clark, 1984). Because of the focus on negative emotions it is sometimes referred to as negative affect. Those high in neuroticism or negative affect worry about the future, dwell on failures and shortcomings, and have less favourable views of themselves and others. There are a number of well-established measures of neuroticism. For example, the International Personality Item Pool (www.ipip.ori.org/ipip), which contains a set of public domain measures of the Big Five personality traits, includes statements such as 'worry a lot' and 'get upset easily'; those high in neuroticism are more likely to consider these statements as good self-descriptions. A variety of studies show that those high in neuroticism report themselves as experiencing more physical symptoms and that these symptoms are more intense (Affleck *et al.*, 1992). For example, Costa and McCrae (1987) reported neuroticism to be related to frequency of illness, cardiovascular problems, digestive problems and fatigue across a sample of women with a wide variety of ages. These effects have been demonstrated in various cross-sectional and longitudinal studies.

Similar to the case for hostility, a number of mechanisms by which neuroticism might influence health outcomes have been suggested. One potential mechanism relating neuroticism to health outcomes might be through perceived or actual stress experienced. For example, those high in negative affect tend to perceive events as more stressful and difficult to cope with than those who are low in negative affect (Watson, 1988). In addition, those high in negative affect may experience more prolonged psychological distress after a negative event (Ormell and Wohlfarth, 1991). However, an important alternative suggestion in relation to neuroticism is that the reported impact on health symptoms may be attributable to the use of self-report measures of health. The hypothesis is that high levels of neuroticism lead to an individual noticing or complaining more about symptoms without this influencing the symptoms he or she experiences. Work that has objectively assessed physical health has indeed tended to report little association between such measures and neuroticism (Watson and Pennebaker, 1989). This importantly suggests the need to measure and control for the effects of neuroticism in any studies using symptom reports as outcome measures.

A further mechanism by which neuroticism may lead to negative health outcomes is through impact on coping mechanisms. Neuroticism might be related to maladaptive coping strategies in a similar way to pessimism. For example, Costa and McCrae (1990) showed that those high in neuroticism were more likely to engage in self-blame and less likely to engage in problem solving in response to a scenario describing a nuclear accident. Another mechanism by which neuroticism influences affect health outcomes is through social support. It has been suggested that those high in neuroticism may have greater difficulties in forming and maintaining close relationships and may experience higher levels of interpersonal conflict. In support of this view those high in negative affect have been shown to have lower marital satisfaction (Burke, Weir and DuWors, 1980). These effects of neuroticism may have the result that those high in neuroticism experience less social support and so are less likely to experience the health protective effects associated with social support (see Chapter 5).

Neuroticism may also influence an individual's health behaviour patterns and, thereby, their health outcomes. Neuroticism is associated with more smoking and alcohol abuse and less healthy eating and exercise (Booth-Kewley and Vickers, 1994). For example, in relation to smoking, longitudinal studies have found that those with higher neuroticism scores are more likely to take up smoking and maintain the habit (e.g. Canals, Bladé and Domènech, 1997). Thus negative health outcomes associated with higher levels of neuroticism might be due, in part, to those with higher levels of neuroticism being more likely to smoke. Thus smoking may mediate the neuroticism–health relationship. Shipley *et al.* (2007) recently reported the impact of neuroticism on mortality in a sample of over 5,000 UK adults over a period of 21 years. High neuroticism was associated with mortality from all causes and with mortality from cardiovascular diseases. However, these effects became non-significant after controlling for age, gender, social class, education, smoking, alcohol consumption and physical activity. This would suggest that the effects of neuroticism on mortality may be explained by socio-demographic factors and health behaviours. A final mechanism by which neuroticism may impact on health is through physiological changes. Research has highlighted the impact of high levels of neuroticism on reduced immune function (Kiecolt-Glaser *et al.*, 2002) suggesting another potential mechanism through which neuroticism impacts on various health outcomes.

EXTRAVERSION

Extraversion is a further Big Five personality trait where those with high levels of the trait are referred to as extraverts and those with low levels referred to as introverts. Extraverts tend to be outgoing, social, assertive and show high levels of energy; they also tend to seek stimulation and so enjoy new challenges but get easily bored. In contrast introverts tend to be more cautious, serious and avoid over-stimulating environments and activities (Eysenck, 1967; Costa and McCrae, 1992). There are a number of well-established measures of extraversion–introversion. For example, Eysenck and Eysenck's (1964) measure contains items such as 'Are you usually carefree?' and 'Do you enjoy wild parties?' with extroverts more likely to agree with these types of items (see Figure 6.2). Extraversion has been found to be associated with positive psychological well-being and better physical health. For example, extraverts report more positive moods and higher levels of pleasure and excitement. Costa and McCrae (1980) showed that extraversion measured at one time point significantly predicted happiness 10 years later. Extraverts tend to report lower rates of coronary heart disease, ulcers, asthma and arthritis (Friedman and Booth-Kewley, 1987). Some research has reported effects for extraversion on mortality. For example, Shipley *et al.* (2007), in addition to examining the impact of neuroticism on mortality, also examined the impact of extraversion. In their sample of over 5,000 UK adults examined over a 21-year period, extraversion was found to be significantly associated with a reduced risk of respiratory disease.

The explanation for the relationship between extraversion and health is not entirely clear. It is possible that this relationship is attributable to extraverts experiencing lower levels of stress, better coping strategies or more social support compared to introverts but there is as yet no strong evidence to support these explanations. Similarly, in

FIGURE 6.2 The Rorschach ink-blot test for personality. Most modern personality tests employ questionnaires to assess different personality traits. Earlier tests employed more projective tests such as the Rorschach ink-blot test shown here where respondents were required to interpret ink blots and their responses used to classify their personality. Such tests however have low reliability and scores tend to vary depending on the psychologist doing the interpretation.

ACTIVITY 6.1

The accident-prone personality?

Some research has addressed the idea that certain personality traits are precursors of accidents or unintentional injuries, i.e. the accident-prone personality. The best evidence supporting such a personality type comes from studies focusing on impulsivity. This research shows that childhood impulsivity predicts injuries both during childhood and later life (Caspi *et al.*, 1997; Cooper *et al.*, 2003).

What mechanisms might explain how impulsivity is related to injuries? Try reading these two articles and coming up with a list of potential mechanisms.

relation to health behaviour patterns, extraversion appears to be associated with both health-protective behaviours like exercise (Rhodes, Courneya and Hayduk, 2002) and health–risk behaviours like smoking (Booth-Kewley and Vickers, 1994)!

CONSCIENTIOUSNESS

Conscientiousness refers to the ability to control one's behaviour and to complete tasks. Highly conscientious individuals are more organized, careful, dependable, self-disciplined and achievement-oriented than those low in conscientiousness (McCrae and Costa, 1987). High conscientiousness has also been associated with a greater use of problem-focused, positive reappraisal and support-seeking coping strategies (Watson and Hubbard, 1996) and a less frequent use of escape-avoidance and self-blame coping strategies (O'Brien and Delongis, 1996; see Chapter 5). In addition, conscientiousness is associated with a propensity to follow socially prescribed norms for impulse control (John and Srivastava, 1999; Bogg and Roberts, 2004, 2013). Recently, measures of conscientiousness with good levels of reliability and validity have become available. For example, the International Personality Item Pool contains statements such as 'am always prepared' and 'am exacting in my work' in order to tap conscientiousness. Those high in conscientiousness are more likely to consider these statements as accurate self-descriptions. A growing body of research shows conscientiousness to be positively associated with health-promoting behaviour patterns, health outcomes and even longevity prompting much recent research into the relationships between conscientiousness and health.

The key evidence for an effect of conscientiousness on longevity comes from the Terman Life-Cycle personality cohort study. In this highly regarded study, a sample of over 1,000 children born around 1910 completed various measures every 5 to 10 years from the age of 11. The original sample of children selected had above average IQ and were drawn from the area around the Californian cities of San Francisco and Los Angeles. The personality assessments included measures of conscientiousness, optimism, self-esteem, sociability, stability of mood and energy level. Friedman *et al.* (1993) reported that of these variables only conscientiousness was significantly associated with lower mortality over time. The degree of association was such that those high in conscientiousness were more likely to live longer (by about 2 years) compared to those low in conscientiousness. Comparing the top and bottom 25 per cent (quartiles) on conscientiousness indicated that those in the bottom quartile were one and a half times more likely to die in any one year compared to those in the top quartile. Figure 6.3 shows the survival curves for participants in the Terman sample separately for males and females and for those with and without divorced parents among those with high and low levels of conscientiousness. Hampson *et al.* (2013) using a different cohort showed that childhood conscientiousness predicted objectively measured health when members of the cohort were in their fifties. Those with lower childhood conscientiousness were observed to have higher levels of obesity and worse blood lipids. Reviews have shown low conscientiousness to be a consistent risk factor for developing obesity across populations (Jokela *et al.*, 2013a). Most recently, in the largest study of its kind, conscientiousness has been shown to be the only higher-order personality trait to be related to mortality risk across populations (Jokela *et al.*, 2013b; see also Kern and Friedman, 2008).

An important mechanism by which conscientiousness may influence health is through health behaviour patterns. Friedman *et al.* (1995) showed that the impact of conscientiousness on longevity in the Terman sample was partly accounted for by its effect on smoking and alcohol use, that is, conscientious children were less likely to become heavy smokers and drinkers. Consistent with these findings, Booth-Kewley and Vickers (1994) found that conscientiousness was more strongly correlated with clusters of health-related behaviours than the other Big Five traits and was particularly strongly associated with health protection and accident control behaviours. Similarly, Courneya and Hellsten (1998) reported that, of the Big Five traits, conscientiousness was most strongly related to engaging in exercise behaviours, while Siegler, Feaganes and Rimer (1995) showed that regular mammography attendance was predicted by conscientiousness and extraversion. A comprehensive meta-analysis of work on the

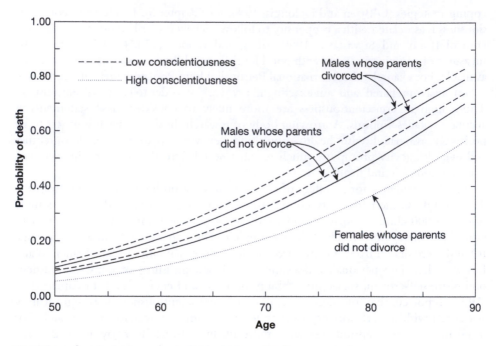

FIGURE 6.3 Survival curves for individuals from the Terman study.

Source: Copyright Howard S. Friedman and Joseph Schwartz.

relationship between conscientiousness and behaviours (Bogg and Roberts, 2004) showed conscientiousness to be positively related to a range of protective health behaviours (e.g. exercise) and negatively related to a range of health-risk behaviours (e.g. smoking). In a recent cohort study, school-related conscientiousness was found to be predictive of alcohol consumption and cigarette smoking in adolescents confirming its importance early in the lifecourse (Hagger-Johnson *et al.*, 2012). Table 6.2 shows the size of these effects for a range of different health behaviours (the impact of health behaviours on health is further considered in Chapter 7). A further way in which conscientiousness may impact on health outcomes is through modifying behaviour following illness. So, for example, some studies have demonstrated that individuals high in conscientiousness are more likely to follow health care advice and that this difference is particularly apparent when the advice is difficult or time consuming to follow (Christiansen and Smith, 1995; Schwartz J.E. *et al.*, 1999). A recent study (Booth *et al.*, 2014) has shown that lower conscientiousness was associated with increased brain ageing (e.g. objectively measured brain tissue loss) using the Lothian Birth Cohort Study 1936 when the participants were in their seventies. Importantly this effect of conscientiousness on brain ageing appeared to be partly explained (i.e. mediated) by differences in health behaviours such as smoking, alcohol use, physical activity and diet.

Recent research has begun to examine how personality traits may produce changes in health behaviours through shaping the way in which individuals think about these behaviours. This work suggests that our thoughts and feelings about performing a particular health behaviour (e.g. exercising) are a primary determinant of whether we perform that behaviour. That is, we tend to engage in behaviours that we have positive thoughts and feelings about (see Chapter 7). Consequently, conscientiousness may influence the amount of exercise we do by shaping our thoughts and feelings about exercising (i.e. thoughts and feelings mediate the impact of conscientiousness on exercise). Such mediation effects have been demonstrated by Siegler *et al.* (1995), who found that the effect of conscientiousness on mammography attendance was mediated by knowledge of breast cancer and the perceived costs of seeking mammography. Similarly, the impact of conscientiousness on the self-care activities of patients with type 1 diabetes has been found to be mediated by treatment beliefs (e.g. Christensen, Moran and Wiebe, 1999). However, other research has found both mediated and direct effects for conscientiousness when predicting health behaviour (Conner and Abraham, 2001; O'Connor *et al.*, 2009; Vollrath, Knoch and Cassano, 1999).

In addition to mediation effects, conscientiousness might also operate as a moderator changing the relationship between health beliefs and health behaviour patterns. A few studies have examined the moderating role of conscientiousness. For example, in a retrospective study, Schwartz M.D. *et al.* (1999) found that conscientiousness moderated the relationship between breast cancer-related distress and mammography uptake such that, among those with high levels of distress, those with high conscientiousness scores were more likely to have attended mammography screening than those with low conscientiousness scores. Conscientiousness scores had no effect on attendance among those with low levels of distress. Hampson *et al.* (2000) reported a similar significant interaction between conscientiousness and perceived risk in relation to changes in indoor smoking behaviour in response to the threat from radon gas, with greater response to risk among the more conscientious. In relation to exercise, Rhodes

TABLE 6.1 Relationship between conscientiousness and various health behaviours based on a meta-analysis of available studies

Behaviour	Effect size	Total sample size
Physical activity	.05	24,259
Excessive alcohol use	−.25	32,137
Drug use	−.28	36,573
Unhealthy eating	−.13	6,356
Risky driving	−.25	10,171
Risky sex	−.13	12,410
Suicide	−.12	6,087
Tobacco use	−.14	46,725
Violence	−.25	10,277

Note: Cohen (1992) suggests that $r = 0.1$ equates to a small effect size, 0.3 to a medium effect size and 0.5 to a large effect size; so these effect sizes for conscientiousness are mostly in the small to medium range.

Source: From Bogg and Roberts (2004). Copyright © 2004 by the American Psychological Association. Reprinted with permission.

et al. (2002) reported conscientiousness to significantly moderate the intention–behaviour relationship, with higher levels of conscientiousness associated with stronger intention–behaviour relationships (see also Conner, Rodgers and Murray, 2007). Conner *et al.* (2009) showed intentions to be stronger predictors of resisting initiating smoking for an adolescent sample with high rather than low levels of conscientiousness.

CONCLUSIONS

We have reviewed relationships between key personality traits and health outcomes and considered some of the explanations of this relationship. Out of the Big Five personality framework we noted that although there was as yet less evidence linking openness to health outcomes, there was more evidence in relation to conscientiousness, extraversion, neuroticism and agreeableness (when defined as high hostility), with better health outcomes associated with high conscientiousness, high extraversion, low neuroticism and high agreeableness (or low hostility). We also noted that a body of research supports a link between optimism and positive health outcomes. The negative impacts of type A behaviour pattern and hostility on health were also noted, particularly in relation to the risk of coronary heart disease.

While discussing the effects of individual personality traits on health outcomes we also noted a number of important explanations for the relationship between the two. Table 6.1 provides a summary of these explanations and is worth reviewing now.

Not all these explanations constitute true causal mechanisms. Indeed part of the problem in interpreting any relationship between personality and health is that the data obtained is usually correlational (see Research methods 6.1).

A further explanation of the relationship between personality traits and health outcomes is a measurement artefact explanation. Here the suggestion is that the personality trait may cause differences in the way certain health outcomes (e.g. symptoms) are reported. For example, we noted that, at least in relation to neuroticism, some of the relationship between the personality trait and health outcomes may be artefactual, caused by a reliance on self-report measures of symptoms (see Chapter 4). This would account for the stronger relationship between neuroticism and symptom reports compared to the relationship between neuroticism and non–self-report health outcomes (e.g. illness).

The remaining explanations of the relationship between personality traits and health outcomes are more easily interpreted as causal relationships. A key explanation may be that personality traits can lead to health outcomes through physiological mechanisms. So, for example, hostility might cause damage to arteries, which in turn leads to a greater likelihood of heart disease. Another explanation focuses on the idea that certain personality traits may be associated with approaching certain risky situations. Friedman (2000) has referred to this idea as tropisms. Drawing on the analogy of phototropic plants that move towards sources of light, the suggestion is that certain personality types are drawn to particular situations, which then pose a risk to the individual's health. For example, extraverts might be more likely to seek out situations where the risk of accidental injury is higher or where health risk behaviours such as smoking or drug use are common. Relatedly, personality traits may lead to negative health outcomes through changing engagement in health-related behaviours. We noted that conscientious individuals appear to be less likely to engage in health-risking behaviours such as smoking and more likely to engage in health-protective behaviours such as exercise. As we have already suggested, this might be through exposure to such behaviours in situations individuals are drawn to. Alternatively, personality traits like conscientiousness might make some health behaviours more likely by changing the way conscientious individuals think about behaviours such as exercise (Conner and Abraham, 2001). Thus conscientious individuals might value health-protective behaviours more or might just be better at planning how best to engage in such behaviours. These cognitions about health behaviours are the focus of Chapter 7.

A final set of explanations for the relationship between personality traits and health outcomes relates to stress and the variables that protect against the effects of stress. So, for example, individuals high in neuroticism may perceive themselves as experiencing more stress. Such individuals may also be less likely to employ appropriate coping mechanisms or have access to coping resources such as social support to deal with this stress. In this case it may be the stress that causes the negative health outcomes, but it is high levels of neuroticism that cause the stress and the inability to cope appropriately with the stress. Penley and Tomaka (2002) provide an interesting discussion of the relationship between all of the Big Five personality traits and both stress and coping. While Ferguson (2013) has proposed a theoretical model explaining the role of personality in the illness process and identified six routes through which personality can have an influence on health (see also Bogg and Roberts, 2013 for a discussion of conscientiousness and health).

RESEARCH METHODS 6.1

Correlation and inferences of causation

When an independent (or predictor) variable (e.g. social support or attitude) is measured at the same time as a dependent (or outcome) variable (e.g. immune functioning or condom use) this is known as a cross-sectional study. When the dependent variable is measured at a later time then this is known as a longitudinal or prospective study. For example, if we measure job stress and then follow up our participants a year later this is a prospective study. Prospective studies offer more reassurance regarding the direction of causation because we know that the independent variable measure preceded the dependent variable measure in time. Prospective studies also allow us to control for levels of a dependent variable at time 1 so that we can predict change in the dependent variable from an independent variable. For example, we might find that lower reported social support (at time 1) predicts increases in stress over the following year (i.e. changes from time 1 to time 2). Thus while we might use analysis of variance (ANOVA) to test whether an association between an independent and dependent variable is likely to be replicable, we can use analysis of covariance (ANCOVA) to assess the degree to which an independent variable can predict change in a dependent variable over time by including a baseline measure of the dependent variable as a covariate.

The direction of causation is ideally assessed in an experimental study in which we manipulate (rather than measure) the independent variable. In health psychology, interventions such as behaviour change interventions provide good examples of experimental methodology. For example, one group may receive an intervention to change attitudes or reduce work stress while another (control) group receives no intervention. If participants are randomly allocated to these two groups (to try to evenly distribute confounding factors across groups) or matched (to balance confounding factors) then any difference in the dependent variable following the manipulation (that is, the intervention) can be reasonably attributed to that manipulation. The classic use of experimental methodology in health psychology is the randomized controlled trial (RCT). It is of course worth noting that such experimental methods merely establish one causal determinant of the dependent variable, they do not necessarily demonstrate that this is the one and only causal determinant.

Unfortunately, we often cannot manipulate independent variables in health psychology and so must infer underlying causal mechanisms from correlational data. For example, in relation to smoking, the majority of the evidence supporting an impact of smoking on cancer and cardiovascular disease outcomes is correlational, at least for studies in humans. Similarly, the relationship between personality and health is based on correlational data.

There are well-known dangers in drawing causal inferences from correlational data. Two key issues are causal direction and the third variable problem. Causal direction refers to the issue of the direction of effect being unknown when two variables are correlated: did A cause B or B cause A? For example, in relation to personality and health this issue becomes one of whether a personality trait resulted in a health outcome or the health outcome produced the personality trait. So, for example, some patients with serious illnesses such as cancer may become anxious and neurotic. This might lead us to the erroneous conclusion that neuroticism played a role in causing the cancer when in fact the cancer had produced increased neuroticism.

Third variable problems refer to the possibility that a correlation between two variables might be due to both variables being caused by a third variable. So, for example, there is some evidence that a hyper-responsive nervous system is an underlying factor in both the development of an anxious personality (high neuroticism) and the development of heart disease. Here an anxious, reactive personality would be related to (that is, correlated with) heart disease without being a causal determinant of heart disease (McCabe et al., 2000). Similarly, Eysenck (1967) argued that extraversion relates to differences in the sensitivity of the nervous system that influences emotional reactions and reactions to socialization. Extraverts may also be more likely to seek stimulation through behaviours such as smoking. In both these cases it is not the personality trait itself that causes the health outcomes but an underlying biological mechanism that causes both the personality trait and the health outcome.

TABLE 6.2 Explanations of the relationship between personality traits and health outcomes

Non-causal explanations	
Causal direction problem	Health outcome causes personality change (e.g. illness affects perceptions and behaviour)
Third variable problem	Both the personality trait and health outcome are caused by another underlying variable (e.g. disease)
Measurement artefact	The measurement of the health outcome is contaminated by the personality trait
Causal explanations	
Physiological changes	The personality trait causes physiological changes that in turn influence health outcomes
Tropisms	The personality trait means the individual is more likely to be exposed to risky situations
Health behaviours	The personality trait makes the individual more likely to engage in health-risk behaviours and less likely to engage in health-promoting behaviours
Stress impacts	The personality trait makes the individual more likely to experience stress and/or less likely to be protected from the effects of stress through coping mechanisms or social support.

SUMMARY

A number of personality traits show significant relationships with various health outcomes such as morbidity and mortality. Indeed some of these relationships are of a similar size to those reported for more well-known risk factors like blood cholesterol levels. Of the Big Five personality traits that form much of the focus in modern-day personality research there is good evidence relating low levels of neuroticism and high levels of extraversion and conscientiousness to health outcomes (e.g. lower levels of illness and greater longevity). Evidence also suggests that optimism is positively related to health outcomes, while type A behaviour and hostility (low agreeableness) tend to be negatively related to health outcomes. In some cases (such as type A and type D) recent studies have shown declining effects and the importance of such variables remains a controversial issue.

The explanations of these relationships between personality and health are many and varied. They range from artefactual explanations, through mediating mechanisms, to direct biological or physiological effects. So, for example, much of the observed impact of neuroticism on self-reported illness is probably attributable to those higher in neuroticism being more likely to report symptoms. In relation to conscientiousness and health, for example, there is evidence of a mediating mechanism through greater engagement in health-protective behaviours and less engagement in health-risking behaviours, whereas in relation to hostility there is evidence of a direct effect through damage to arteries caused by over-reactivity to stress among those high in hostility. Detailing the range of effects that different personality dimensions can have on health and assessing the explanations of these effects is an exciting area of current research in health psychology.

KEY CONCEPTS AND TERMS

- Achievement-striving
- Agreeableness
- Big Five personality traits
- Conscientiousness
- Cynicism
- Direction of causation
- Extraversion
- Hope/Hopelessness
- Hostile attributional style
- Hostility
- Impatience–irritability
- International Personality Item Pool
- Measurement artefact
- Mistrust
- Negative affect
- Neuroticism
- Openness to experience
- Optimism
- Optimistic attributional style
- Positive affect
- Psychophysiological reactivity model
- Psychosocial vulnerability model
- Third variable problem
- Tropisms
- Type A behaviour pattern

SAMPLE ESSAY TITLES

- Describe the evidence relating key personality traits to different kinds of health outcomes.
- Critically evaluate the mechanisms by which personality traits might have impacts on health.
- Do personality differences predict health? Discuss relevant findings and mechanisms.

FURTHER READING

Journal articles

Bogg, T. and Roberts, B.W. (2013). The case for conscientiousness: Evidence and implications for a personality trait marker of health and longevity. *Annals of Behavioral Medicine*, 45, 278–288.

Ferguson, E. (2013). Personality is of central concern to understand health: Towards a theoretical model for health psychology. *Health Psychology Review*, 7, S32–S70.

Hampson, S.E. (2012). Personality processes: Mechanisms by which personality traits 'get outside the skin'. *Annual Review of Psychology*, 63, 315–339.

Pressman, S.D. and Cohen, S. (2005). Does positive affect influence health? *Psychological Bulletin*, 131, 925–971.

Smith, T.W., Glazer, K., Ruiz, J.M. and Gallo, L.C. (2004). Hostility, anger, aggressiveness and coronary heart disease: An interpersonal perspective on personality, emotion and health. *Journal of Personality*, 72, 1217–1270.

4 | Motivation and behaviour

7 Health cognitions and health behaviours

CHAPTER PLAN

In Chapter 6 we examined the part that personality plays in determining health outcomes. In this chapter we examine health cognitions, foundational to motivation, which have been found to differentiate between people who do and do not perform health behaviours. This is followed by an examination of how health-related motivation can be changed in Chapter 8 and how health-related behaviours can be changed in Chapter 9.

The prevalence of health-related behaviours varies across social groups. For example, smoking is more prevalent among those from more economically deprived backgrounds. This would suggest that these factors might be the focus of interventions to change health-related behaviours. However, socio-demographic factors may be impossible to change or may require political intervention at national or international levels (such as changes in income distribution or taxation). For that reason a considerable body of research has examined more modifiable factors that may mediate (and explain) the relationship between socio-demographic factors and health-related behaviours. A particularly promising set of factors are the thoughts and feelings the individual associates with the particular health-related behaviour. These are known as *health cognitions* and are the focus of this chapter. We will consider (1) predicting health behaviours; (2) social cognition models; (3) a critical appraisal of social cognition models; and (4) the intention–behaviour gap.

LEARNING OUTCOMES

When you have completed this chapter you should be able to:

1 Describe the key health cognitions associated with performing health behaviours.
2 Explain what the cognitive determinants of health behaviours are according to (a) the health belief model; (b) protection motivation theory; (c) theory of planned behaviour; and (d) social cognitive theory.

3　Evaluate the contribution of stage models to the understanding of change in health behaviours.
4　Critically evaluate the contribution of social cognition models to understanding the determinants of health behaviours.
5　Describe the intention–behaviour gap in relation to health behaviours.

PREDICTING HEALTH BEHAVIOURS

Can we predict who will perform health behaviours? Such knowledge might help us understand variations in the distribution of health across society and suggest targets for interventions designed to improve health through changing health behaviours. As you might expect, a range of differences exist between those who do and do not engage in health behaviours such as smoking or exercise. These include demographic factors, social factors, personality factors and cognitive factors (Conner and Norman, 2005, 2015).

FOCUS 7.1

What are health behaviours?

The range of behaviours influencing health is extremely varied, from health-enhancing behaviours such as exercise participation and healthy eating, to health-protective behaviours such as health screening clinic attendance, vaccination against disease and condom use in response to the threat of AIDS, through to avoidance of health-harming behaviours such as smoking and excessive alcohol consumption and sick role behaviours such as compliance with medical regimens. A unifying theme across these behaviours has been that they each have immediate or longer-term effects upon the individual's health and are at least partially within the individual's control.

A number of definitions of health behaviours have been suggested. For example, Kasl and Cobb (1966: 246) defined them as 'Any activity undertaken by a person believing himself to be healthy for the purpose of preventing disease or detecting it at an asymptomatic stage'. Can you see any problems with this definition? A more recent definition is offered by Conner and Norman (2005: 2), who define health behaviours as 'any activity undertaken for the purpose of preventing or detecting disease or for improving health and well-being'. Behaviours encompassed in such a definition include medical service usage (e.g. physician visits, vaccination, screening), compliance with medical regimens (e.g. dietary, diabetic, antihypertensive regimens) and self-directed health behaviours (e.g. diet, exercise, breast or testicular self-examination, brushing and flossing teeth, smoking, alcohol consumption and contraceptive use).

Demographic variables show reliable associations with the performance of various health behaviours. Age, for example, shows a curvilinear relationship with many health behaviours, with higher incidences of health-risk behaviours such as smoking in young adults and much lower incidences in children and older adults (Blaxter, 1990). Health behaviours also vary between genders, with women being generally less likely to smoke, consume large amounts of alcohol or engage in regular exercise and more likely to monitor their diet, take vitamins and engage in dental care, although such patterns can change over time (Waldron, 1988). Differences predicted by economic and ethnic status are also apparent for behaviours such as diet, exercise, alcohol consumption and smoking (e.g. Blaxter, 1990). Generally, younger, wealthier, better-educated individuals are more likely to practise health-enhancing behaviours and less likely to engage in health-risking behaviours. Socio-economic status (SES) differences are particularly apparent with 'social class gradients' (i.e. increased longevity, better health and improved health behaviours as we move from lower to higher SES groups) apparent in most Western countries (Mackenbach, 2006). Social factors, such as parental models, are important in instilling health behaviours early in life. Peer influences are also important, for example, in the initiation of smoking (e.g. McNeil *et al.*, 1988). Cultural values also appear to be influential, for instance in determining the exercise behaviour of women across cultural groups (e.g. Wardle and Steptoe, 1991). We noted in Chapter 6 that personality traits are fundamental determinants of behaviour and that there is now considerable evidence linking personality and health behaviours (see Vollrath, 2006). For example, Friedman *et al.* (1993, 1995) found that childhood conscientiousness predicted longevity and that this was partly accounted for by conscientious individuals being less likely to engage in smoking and alcohol use.

None of the correlates of health behaviours mentioned above can be easily modified and therefore they do not represent useful targets for interventions designed to change health behaviours. This is not the case for the cognitive antecedents of behaviour. A variety of cognitive factors distinguish between those who do and do not perform various health behaviours. For example, knowledge about behaviour–health links (or risk awareness) is an essential factor in an informed choice concerning a healthy lifestyle (see Chapter 8). The reduction of smoking over the past 20–30 years in the Western world can be largely attributed to a growing awareness of the serious health risks posed by tobacco use brought about by widespread publicity. However, the fact that tobacco continues to be widely used among lower socio-economic status groups and the growing uptake of smoking among adolescent girls in some countries, illustrate that knowledge of health risks is not a sufficient condition for avoidance of smoking by all individuals.

Knowledge is just one of a number of cognitive correlates of health behaviours. Others include perceptions of health risk, potential efficacy of behaviours in reducing this risk, perceived social pressures to perform a behaviour and control over performance of the behaviour. The relative importance of individual cognitive factors in predicting performance of health behaviours has been the focus of numerous studies. For example, Cummings, Becker and Maile (1980) had experts sort 109 variables associated with performing health behaviours and derived 6 distinguishable factors:

1   accessibility of health care services;
2   attitudes to health care (beliefs about quality and benefits of treatment);

3   perceptions of disease threat;
4   knowledge about disease;
5   social network characteristics; and
6   demographic factors.

These six groups of correlates may not be independent. For example, there may be considerable overlap between perceptions of disease threat and knowledge of the disease. In order to account for such overlaps and describe the relationships between different influences on health behaviours a number of models have been developed. Such models have been labelled 'social cognition models' because of their use of a number of cognitive variables to predict and understand individual behaviours, including health behaviours. It is important to note at the outset that these models focus on behaviour-specific cognitions as determinants of the relevant behaviour. For example, on this view healthy eating is best understood in terms of cognitions about healthy eating rather than more general thoughts and feelings about health. In the health psychology area these are usually referred to as health cognitions.

FOCUS 7.2

How do health behaviours impact on health outcomes?

A great many studies have now looked at the relationship between the performance of health behaviours and a variety of health outcomes (e.g. Doll *et al.*, 1994). Large-scale epidemiological studies have demonstrated the importance of a variety of health behaviours for both morbidity and mortality. For example, the Alameda County study, which followed nearly 7,000 people over 10 years, found that seven key behaviours were associated with lower morbidity and longer life: not smoking, moderate alcohol intake, sleeping 7 to 8 hours per night, exercising regularly, maintaining a desirable body weight, avoiding snacks and eating breakfast regularly (Belloc and Breslow, 1972; Breslow and Enstrom, 1980).

Health behaviours are assumed to influence health through three major pathways (Baum and Posluszny, 1999): first, by generating direct biological changes such as when excessive alcohol consumption damages the liver; second, by changing exposure to health risks, as when the use of a condom protects against the spread of HIV; and third, by ensuring early detection and treatment of disease, as when testicular or breast self-examination leads to early detection of a cancer that can more easily be treated.

Can you think of further examples of the pathways through which health behaviours might exert their effects on health?

SOCIAL COGNITION MODELS

Social cognition models describe the important cognitions that distinguish between those who do and do not perform health behaviours. This approach focuses on the cognitions or thought processes that intervene between observable stimuli and behaviour in real world situations (Fiske and Taylor, 1991). This 'social cognition' approach has been central to social psychology over the past quarter of a century. Unlike behaviourism, it is founded on the assumption that behaviour is best understood as a function of people's perceptions of reality, rather than objective characterizations of environmental stimuli.

Research into social cognition models can be seen as one part of what has been called 'self-regulation' research. Self-regulation processes are defined as those 'mental and behavioral processes by which people enact their self-conceptions, revise their behavior, or alter the environment so as to bring about outcomes in it in line with their self-perceptions and personal goals' (Fiske and Taylor, 1991: 181). Self-regulation research has emerged from a clinical tradition in psychology, which views the individual as striving to eliminate dysfunctional patterns of thinking or behaviour and engage in adaptive patterns of thinking or behaviour (Bandura, 1982; Turk and Salovey, 1986). Self-regulation involves cognitive re-evaluation of beliefs, goal setting and ongoing monitoring and evaluating of goal-directed behaviour. Two phases of self-regulation activities have been defined: motivational and volitional (Gollwitzer, 1990). In the motivational phase costs and benefits are considered in order to choose between goals and behaviours. This phase is assumed to conclude with a decision or intention concerning which goals and actions to pursue at a particular time. In the subsequent volitional phase, planning and action directed towards achieving the set goal predominate.

Much of the research with health behaviours has focused on the important cognitions in the motivational phase, although recent research has begun to focus on the volitional phase. The key social cognition models in this area are:

1   *The health belief model* (HBM; e.g. Janz and Becker, 1984; Abraham and Sheeran, 2005, 2015).
2   *Protection motivation theory* (PMT; e.g. Maddux and Rogers, 1983; Norman, Boer and Seydel, 2005; Norman *et al.*, 2015).
3   *The theory of reasoned action/theory of planned behaviour* (TRA/TPB; e.g. Ajzen, 1991; Conner and Sparks, 2005; Norman *et al.*, 2015).
4   *Social cognitive theory* (SCT; e.g. Bandura, 2000; Luszczynska and Schwarzer, 2005, 2015).

A distinct set of models focus on the idea that behaviour change occurs through a series of qualitatively different stages. These so-called 'stage' models (Sutton, 2005, 2015) importantly include the transtheoretical model of change (Prochaska and DiClemente, 1984; Prochaska, DiClemente and Norcross, 1992). In the following sections we consider these different models and what they say about how cognitions help direct health behaviours. These social cognition models (SCMs) provide a basis for understanding the determinants of behaviour and also provide important targets, which interventions designed to change behaviour should focus on if they are to change motivation (see Chapter 8) and, thereby, behaviour (see Chapter 9).

The health belief model

The health belief model (HBM) is the earliest and most widely used SCM in health psychology (see Abraham and Sheeran, 2005, 2015 for a review). For example, Hochbaum (1958) found that perceived susceptibility to tuberculosis and the belief that people with the disease could be asymptomatic (so that screening would be beneficial) distinguished between those who had and had not attended for chest X-rays. Haefner and Kirscht (1970) took this research further by demonstrating that health education interventions designed to increase participants' perceived susceptibility, perceived severity and anticipated benefits resulted in a greater number of check-up visits to the doctor compared to controls over the following eight months.

The HBM suggests that health behaviours are determined mainly by two aspects of individuals' representations of health behaviour: perceptions of illness threat and evaluation of behaviours to counteract this threat (see Figure 7.1). Threat perceptions are based on two beliefs: the perceived susceptibility of the individual to the illness ('Am I likely to get it?'); and the perceived severity of the consequences of the illness for the individual ('How bad would it be?'). Similarly, evaluation of possible responses involves consideration of both the potential benefits of and barriers to action. Together these four beliefs are believed to determine the likelihood of the individual undertaking to perform a health behaviour. The particular action taken is determined by the evaluation of the available alternatives, focusing on the benefits or efficacy of the health behaviour and the perceived costs or barriers of performing the behaviour. Hence individuals are more likely to follow a particular health action if they believe themselves to be susceptible to a particular condition, which they also consider to be serious, and believe that the benefits of the action taken to counteract the health threat outweigh the costs. For example, an individual is likely to quit smoking if he or she: believes him or herself to be susceptible to smoking-related illnesses; considers the illnesses to be serious; and that, of the alternative behaviours open to him/her, considers quitting smoking to be the most effective way to tackle his/her susceptibility to smoking-related illnesses (i.e. greatest benefits and fewest barriers).

Two other variables often included in the model are cues to action and health motivation. Cues to action are assumed to include a diverse range of triggers to the individual taking action, which may be internal (e.g. physical symptom) or external (e.g. mass media campaign, advice from others) to the individual (Janz and Becker, 1984). An individual's perception of the presence of cues to action would be expected to prompt adoption of the health behaviour if the other key beliefs are already established in their mind. Health motivation refers to more stable differences between individuals in the value they attach to their health and their propensity to be motivated to look after their health. Individuals with a high motivation to look after their health should be more likely to adopt relevant health behaviours (i.e. more health-protecting and less health-risking behaviours).

The HBM has provided a useful framework for investigating health behaviours and has been widely used. It has been found to successfully predict a range of behaviours. For example, Janz and Becker (1984) found that across 18 prospective studies (that is, those in which behaviour was measured later, following an earlier measurement of beliefs) the four core beliefs were nearly always found to be significant predictors of health behaviour (82 per cent, 65 per cent, 81 per cent and 100 per cent of studies

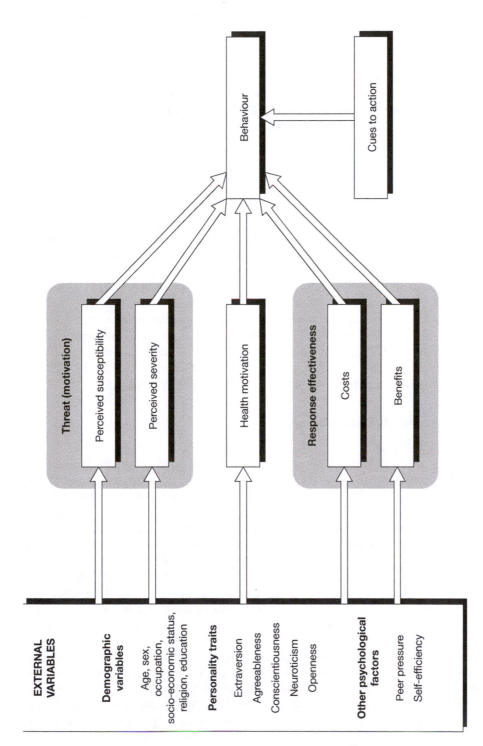

FIGURE 7.1 The health belief model (HBM).

report significant effects for susceptibility, severity, benefits and barriers, respectively). Some studies have found that these health beliefs mediate (or explain) the effects of demographic correlates of health behaviour. For example, Orbell, Crombie and Johnston (1995) found that perceived susceptibility and barriers entirely mediated the effects of social class upon uptake of cervical screening. However, the overall evidence for such mediation is somewhat mixed. In addition, the HBM has inspired a range of successful behaviour change interventions. For example, Jones *et al.* (1988) tested an intervention designed to encourage patients visiting an accident and emergency service to make a follow-up appointment with their own doctor. Patients were randomly assigned to a control (i.e. routine care) group or to the intervention group. The intervention involved meeting a nurse who assessed and challenged patients' health beliefs. For example, a patient who did not feel susceptible to reoccurrence of the emergency event (e.g. an asthmatic attack) might be told of the likelihood of reoccurrence without further treatment in order to increase perceived susceptibility. Results of this randomized controlled trial showed that while only 24 per cent of the control group subsequently attended a follow-up, a significantly greater 59 per cent of the intervention group did so.

The main strength of the HBM is the common-sense operationalization it uses, including key beliefs related to decisions about health behaviours. However, further research has identified other cognitions that are stronger predictors of health behaviour than those identified by the HBM, suggesting that the model is incomplete. This prompted a proposal to add 'self-efficacy' (see Chapter 8 and below) to the model to produce an 'extended health belief model' (Rosenstock, Strecher and Becker, 1988), which has generally improved the predictive power of the model (e.g. Hay *et al.*, 2003).

Protection motivation theory

Protection motivation theory (PMT; Norman *et al.*, 2005, 2015) is a revision and extension of the HBM, which incorporates various appraisal processes identified by research into coping with stress (see Chapter 3). In PMT, the primary determinant of performing a health behaviour is protection motivation or intention to perform a health behaviour (see Figure 7.2). Protection motivation is determined by two appraisal processes: threat appraisal and coping appraisal. Threat appraisal is based upon a consideration of perceptions of susceptibility to the illness and severity of the health threat in a very similar way to the HBM. Coping appraisal involves the process of assessing the behavioural alternatives, which might diminish the threat. This coping process is itself assumed to be based upon two main components: the individual's expectancy that carrying out a behaviour can remove the threat (response efficacy); and a belief in one's capability to successfully execute the recommended courses of action (self-efficacy).

Together these two appraisal processes result in either adaptive or maladaptive responses. Adaptive responses are those in which the individual engages in behaviours likely to reduce the risk (e.g. adopting a health behaviour), whereas maladaptive responses are those that do not directly tackle the threat (e.g. denial of the health threat). Adaptive responses are held to be more likely if the individual perceives him or herself to be facing a health threat to which he or she is susceptible and which is perceived to be severe and where the individual perceives such responses to be effective in

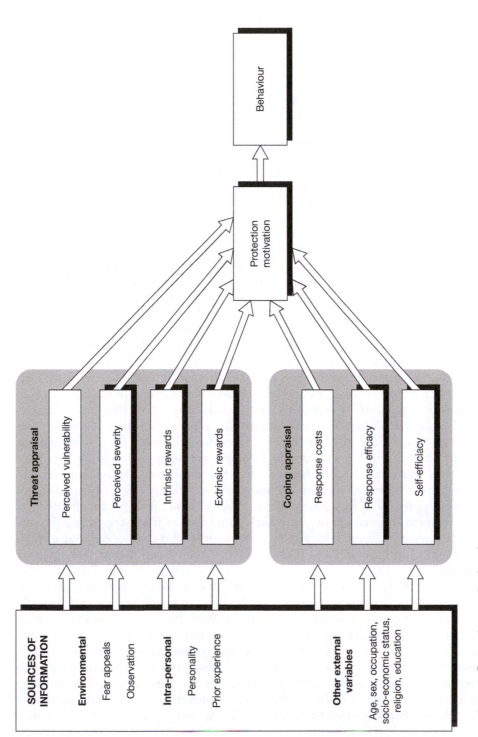

FIGURE 7.2 Protection motivation theory.

reducing the threat and believes that he or she can successfully perform the adaptive response. So, for example, smokers will try to quit smoking when they believe themselves to be susceptible to smoking-related illnesses that they think to be serious and where quitting smoking is perceived to be effective in reducing the threat and perceived to be something they have confidence they can achieve. The PMT has been successfully applied to the prediction of a number of health behaviours (for recent reviews see Norman *et al.*, 2005, 2015).

Theory of planned behaviour

The theory of planned behaviour (TPB) was developed by social psychologists and has been widely applied to understanding health behaviours (Conner and Sparks, 2005, 2015). It specifies the factors that determine an individual's decision to perform a particular behaviour (see Figure 7.3). Importantly this theory added 'perceived behavioural control' to the earlier theory of reasoned action (Ajzen and Fishbein, 1980), which continues to be applied (Ajzen, 2001; Fishbein and Ajzen, 2010). The TPB proposes that the key determinants of behaviour are intention to engage in that behaviour and perceived behavioural control over that behaviour. As in the PMT, intentions in the TPB represent a person's motivation or conscious plan or decision to exert effort to perform the behaviour. Perceived behavioural control (PBC) is a person's expectancy that performance of the behaviour is within their control and confidence that they can perform the behaviour. PBC is similar to Bandura's (1982) concept of self-efficacy used in the PMT and the extended HBM.

In the TPB, intention is itself assumed to be determined by three factors: attitudes, subjective norms and PBC. Attitudes are the overall evaluations of the behaviour by the individual as positive or negative (and so include beliefs about benefits and barriers included in the HBM). Subjective norms are a person's beliefs about whether significant others think they should engage in the behaviour. PBC is assumed to influence both intentions and behaviour because we rarely intend to do things we know we cannot and because believing that we can succeed enhances effort and persistence and so makes successful performance more likely (see Chapter 8). Thus, according to the TPB, smokers are likely to quit smoking if they form an intention to do so. Such an intention to quit is likely to be formed if smokers have a positive attitude towards quitting, if they believe that people whose views they value think they should quit smoking and if they feel that they have control over quitting smoking.

Attitudes are based on behavioural beliefs, that is, beliefs about the perceived consequences of behaviours. In particular, they are a function of the likelihood of a consequence occurring as a result of performing the behaviour and the evaluation of that outcome (i.e. 'Will it happen?' and 'How good or bad will it be?'). It is assumed that an individual will have a limited number of consequences in mind when considering a behaviour. Thus a positive attitude towards quitting smoking will result when more positive than negative consequences are thought to follow quitting. Subjective norm is based on beliefs about salient referents' approval or disapproval of whether one should engage in a behaviour (e.g. 'Would my sexual partner approve?' and 'Would my best friend approve?'). These beliefs are weighted by the 'motivation to comply' with each salient other on this issue (e.g. 'Do I care what my sexual

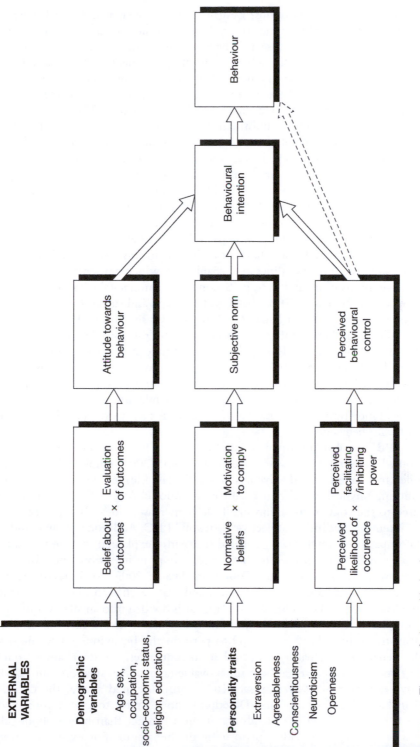

FIGURE 7.3 Theory of planned behaviour.

partner/best friend thinks about this?'). Again, it is assumed that an individual will only have a limited number of referents in mind when considering a behaviour. Thus the more people (whose approval is seen to be important) who are thought to approve of the action, the more positive the subjective norm. Judgements of PBC are influenced by control beliefs concerning whether one has access to the necessary resources and opportunities to perform the behaviour successfully, weighted by the perceived power, or importance, of each factor to facilitate or inhibit the action. These factors include both internal control factors (information, personal deficiencies, skills, abilities, emotions) and external control factors (opportunities, dependence on others, barriers). As for the other types of beliefs, it is assumed that an individual will only consider a limited number of control factors when considering a behaviour. So, for example, in relation to quitting smoking, a strong PBC to quit smoking would be expected when a smoker believes there are more factors that facilitate than inhibit quitting smoking, especially if the inhibiting factors do not have strong effects on the feasibility of quitting.

The TPB has at least two advantages over the extended HBM. First (as in PMT), health beliefs are seen to affect behaviour indirectly, in this case through attitude and intention. Thus the model outlines a mechanism by which particular beliefs combine to influence motivation and action. Second, the model takes account of social influence on action. The TPB has been widely tested and successfully applied to the understanding of a variety of behaviours (for reviews see Ajzen, 1991; Conner and Sparks, 2005, 2015). For example, in a meta-analysis of the TPB Armitage and Conner (2001) reported that across 154 applications, attitude, subjective norms and PBC accounted for 39 per cent of the variance in intention, while intentions and PBC accounted for 27 per cent of the variance in behaviour across 63 applications. Intentions were the strongest predictors of behaviour, while attitudes were the strongest predictors of intentions (see McEachan *et al.*, 2011 for a review of applications of the TPB to health behaviours).

The TPB has also informed a number of interventions designed to change behaviour. For example, Hill, Abraham and Wright (2007) employed a randomized controlled trial to test the effectiveness of a TPB–based leaflet compared to a control in promoting physical exercise in a sample of school children. The leaflet condition compared to the control condition significantly increased not only reported exercise but also intentions, attitudes, subjective norms and PBC. Additional analyses indicated that the impact on exercise was mediated (i.e. partly explained) by the increases the leaflet had produced (compared to the control group) in intentions and PBC.

Recent work with the TPB (see Conner and Sparks, 2005, 2015) has suggested the value of dividing attitude, subjective norm and PBC each into two components to form the 'two-factor TPB' (Figure 7.4). Attitude is divided into an affective or experiential component and a cognitive or instrumental component. The first concerns beliefs and evaluations about how it will feel to perform the behaviour while the second includes beliefs and evaluation about other consequences. So, for example, quitting smoking might be perceived as both unenjoyable (affective evaluation) but beneficial (cognitive evaluation). As well as subjective norms (defined above) the two-factor model includes descriptive norms. Descriptive norms refer to perceptions of what others are doing ('e.g. all my friends are doing it') rather than beliefs about others' approval of the target individual performing the behaviour. For example, a smoker might believe that important others approved of him or her quitting but those other

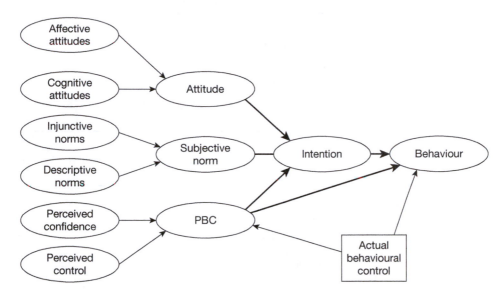

FIGURE 7.4 The two-factor theory of planned behaviour.

individuals to have not quit smoking themselves. PBC is divided into perceived control and perceived confidence. So, for example, one might perceive that quitting smoking is within one's control but not feel confident that one can easily quit smoking. The latter factor is most like self-efficacy and has been found to be the stronger predictor of intentions and behaviour (Rodgers, Conner and Murray, 2008).

Social cognitive theory

In social cognitive theory (SCT; Bandura, 1982) behaviour is held to be determined by three factors: goals, outcome expectancies and self-efficacy (see Figure 7.5). Goals are plans to act and can be conceived of as intentions to perform the behaviour (see Austin and Vancouver, 1996; Luszczynska and Schwarzer, 2005, 2015). Outcome expectancies are similar to behavioural beliefs in the TPB but here are split into physical, social or self-evaluative depending on the nature of the consequences considered. Thus, in this model, beliefs about others' approval (subjective norms in the TPB) are grouped with beliefs about other consequences. Self-efficacy is the belief that a behaviour is or is not within an individual's control and is usually assessed as the degree of confidence the individual has that they could still perform the behaviour in the face of various obstacles. This is very similar to PBC in the TPB and particularly the perceived confidence component in the two-factor TPB. Bandura has recently added socio–structural factors to his theory. These are factors assumed to facilitate or inhibit the performance of a behaviour and affect behaviour via changing goals. Socio–structural factors refer to the impediments or opportunities associated with particular living conditions, health systems, political, economic or environmental systems. They are assumed to inform goal setting and be influenced by self-efficacy.

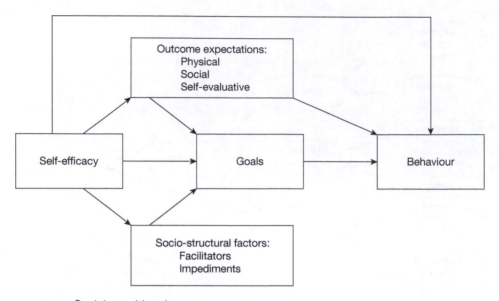

FIGURE 7.5 Social cognitive theory.

Source: From Luszczynska and Schwarzer (2005), reproduced with permission from McGraw-Hill.

The latter relationship arises because self-efficacy influences the degree to which an individual pays attention to opportunities or impediments in their life circumstances. For example, self-efficacious individuals intending to exercise might be expected to focus on exercise cues in the environment such as running or cycling routes. This component of the model incorporates perceptions of the environment as an important influence on health behaviours. In overview, the SCT predicts that quitting smoking, for example, is more likely for individuals who have a goal of quitting smoking, who perceive that various positive physical (e.g. health), social (e.g. positive regard from others) and self-evaluative (e.g. feeling good about yourself) outcomes will follow from their quitting smoking and who perceive they have the confidence to quit smoking in the face of various obstacles.

SCT has been successfully applied to predicting and changing health behaviours. (e.g. Luszczynska and Schwarzer, 2005, 2015). However, unlike a number of the other models we have considered, many of the applications of SCT only assess one or two components of the model rather than all components. Self-efficacy and action-outcome expectancies along with intentions have been found to be important predictors of a range of health behaviours in a diverse range of studies (for reviews see Bandura, 2000; Luszczynska and Schwarzer, 2005, 2015; see Chapter 8 on changing self-efficacy).

Stage models of health behaviour

The models considered above assume that the cognitive determinants of health behaviours act in a similar way during initiation (e.g. quitting smoking for the first time) and maintenance of action (e.g. trying to stay quit). In contrast, in stage models psychological determinants may change across such stages of behaviour change (see Sutton, 2005, 2015 for a review). An important implication of the 'stages' view is that different cognitions may be important determinants at different stages in promoting health behaviour. The most widely used stage model is Prochaska and DiClemente's (1984) transtheoretical model of change (TTM). Their model has been widely applied to analyse the process of change in alcoholism treatment and smoking cessation. DiClemente *et al.* (1991) identify five stages of change: pre-contemplation (not thinking about change), contemplation (aware of the need to change), preparation (intending to change in the near future and taking action in preparation for change), action (acting to change) and maintenance (of the new behaviour) (see Figure 7.6). Individuals are seen to progress through one stage to the next to eventually achieve successful maintenance. In the case of smoking cessation, it is argued that in the pre-contemplation stage the smoker is unaware that their behaviour constitutes a problem and has no intention to quit. In the contemplation stage, the smoker starts to think about changing their behaviour, but is not committed to try to quit. In the preparation stage, the smoker has an intention to quit and starts to make plans to quit. The action stage is characterized by active attempts to quit and after 6 months of successful abstinence the individual moves into the maintenance stage. This stage is characterized by attempts to prevent relapse and to consolidate the newly acquired non-smoking status.

While the model is widely applied, the evidence in support of stage models and different stages is relatively weak (see Sutton, 2000, 2005, 2015). Sutton (2000) concludes that the distinctions between TTM stages are 'logically flawed' and based on 'arbitrary time periods'. Moreover, even Prochaska and DiClemente's (1984) own data do not suggest that smokers typically progress through the TTM stages sequentially. For example, in one study, Prochaska *et al.* (1991) found that only 16 per cent of participants progressed from one stage to the next without reversals over a two-year period and that 12 per cent moved backwards during the same period! In addition, it has proved especially difficult to support the key prediction that there are different determinants of behaviour change in different stages. The best evidence for stage models would be where we showed that interventions matched to individuals' stage of change were more effective in producing behaviour change than interventions mismatched to an individual's stage (although see also Abraham, 2008). So, for example, in a matched intervention, outcome expectancies might be targeted in individuals in

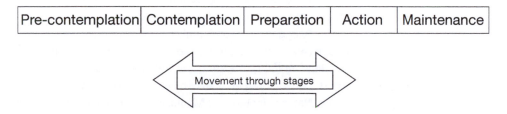

FIGURE 7.6 The transtheoretical model of change stage theory.

the contemplation stage, while self-efficacy was targeted in individuals in the action stage and this would be reversed in a mismatched intervention. Unfortunately, few such matched–mismatched studies have produced evidence supportive of stage models (see Littell and Girvin, 2002 for a systematic review of the effectiveness of interventions applying the TTM to health-related behaviours). Thus, at present, research findings do not support the added complexity and increased cost of stage-tailored interventions. West (2005) in reviewing stage models has recently suggested that work on the TTM should be abandoned.

It is difficult to usefully categorize people as 'pre-contemplators' or those 'in preparation' because people frequently cycle between such states as their motivation to change shifts. Nonetheless, an individual at a particular time may be more focused on deciding whether or not to act or on ensuring that they act on a prior decision to act (i.e. an intention). This is captured by the terms 'motivational phase' and 'volitional phase', respectively. This two-phase conception of action readiness suggests that health promoters need to think about how they can consolidate people's motivation to act and how they can help people to enact their intentions (see Chapters 8 and 9). In general, the social cognition models considered in this chapter have focused on the former. For example, the TPB does not help us distinguish between intenders who do and do not take action. Thus there is a need to better theorize the processes that determine which intentions are translated into action. As Bagozzi (1993) argues, the variables outlined in the main social cognition models are necessary, but not sufficient, determinants of behaviour. In other words, they can provide good predictions of people's intentions (or motivation) to perform a health behaviour, but not always their actual behaviour. This area of research has been referred to as the 'intention–behaviour gap'.

FOCUS 7.3

Deciding between social cognition models

Although a great deal of research has been devoted to testing individual social cognition models, little research has compared the relative predictive power of different SCMs. For example, Reid and Christensen (1988) found that while the HBM explained 10 per cent of the variance in adherence among women taking tablets for urinary tract infections to a tablet regimen, the variance explained increased to 29 per cent when cognitions specified by the theory of reasoned action were added.

Another approach to the variety of SCMs is to integrate them. This may be valuable, especially since many include similar cognitions. For example, commentators agree that the key cognitions prominently include intention, self-efficacy and outcome expectancies (or attitudes). An important attempt to integrate these models was made by Bandura (SCT), Becker (HBM), Fishbein (TRA), Kaufen (self-regulation) and Triandis (theory of interpersonal behaviour) as part of a workshop organized by the US National Institute of Mental Health in response to the need to promote HIV-preventive behaviours. The workshop sought to 'identify a finite set of variables to be considered in any behavioral analysis' (Fishbein *et al.*, 2001: 3). They identified eight variables, which, they argued, should account for most of the variance in any (deliberative) behaviour. These were organized into two groups. First were those variables that were viewed as necessary and sufficient determinants of behaviour. Thus, for behaviour to occur an individual must (1) have a strong intention; (2) have the necessary skills to perform the behaviour; and (3) experience an absence of environmental constraints that could prevent behaviour. The second group of variables were seen to primarily influence intention, although it was noted that some of the variables may also have a direct effect on behaviour. Thus, a strong intention is likely to occur when an individual (4) perceives the advantages (or benefits) of performing the behaviour to outweigh the perceived disadvantages (or costs); (5) perceives the social (normative) pressure to perform the behaviour to be greater than that not to perform the behaviour; (6) believes that the behaviour is consistent with his or her self-image; (7) anticipates the emotional reaction to performing the behaviour to be more positive than negative; and (8) has high levels of self-efficacy. Figure 7.7 illustrates this integrated model.

If you were trying to identify the determinants of condom use, which cognitions would you focus on? Would this be any different if you were trying to predict smoking cessation?

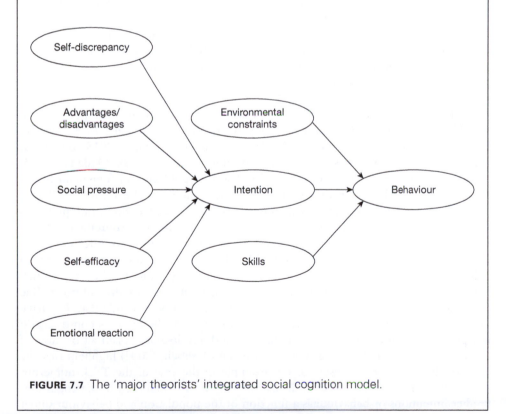

FIGURE 7.7 The 'major theorists' integrated social cognition model.

A CRITICAL APPRAISAL OF SCMs

The use of SCMs to predict health behaviour has a number of advantages and disadvantages. Below we outline the main advantages of a social cognition approach before considering a range of specific and more general criticisms that have been made of this approach.

There are four clear advantages of using SCMs to predict and understand health behaviours. First, they provide a clear theoretical background to any research, guiding the selection of cognitions and providing a description of the ways in which these constructs combine in order to determine health behaviours. Second, because the models have been repeatedly tested they provide reliable and valid measures of selected cognitions (for example, see Ajzen's website for guidance on developing TPB measures at www.people.umass.edu/aizen/tpb.html). Third, SCMs provide us with a description of the motivational and volitional processes underlying health behaviours. As a result, they add to our understanding of the proximal determinants of health behaviour and, because of this, they, fourth, identify key targets for interventions designed to change motivation (see Chapter 8).

The use of SCMs could also limit our understanding of health behaviour. For example, because SCMs provide clearly defined theoretical frameworks, their use may lead to the neglect of other cognitions. For example, moral norms (i.e. doing what you think is the right thing to do) are not included in the main SCMs but have been shown to be important in behaviours such as blood donation (Godin, Conner and Sheeran, 2005). Another limitation of SCMs is that while they usefully identify cognition change targets, they commonly do not specify the best means to change such cognitions. Moreover, an over-exclusive focus on SCMs may lead to the neglect of other potentially effective behaviour change interventions, such as increased taxation or legislation, which may not or may not have their effects through the cognitions specified by the SCMs (see Chapter 9).

In the health psychology area there has been one widely cited critique of SCMs written by Ogden (2003) with a response by Ajzen and Fishbein (2004) (see also Fishbein and Ajzen, 2010; Greve, 2001; Norman and Conner, 2015; Sniehotta, Presseau and Araujo-Soares, 2014 and associated commentaries). Ogden's (2003) critique is based on a review of 47 empirical studies published in four main health psychology journals over a four-year period and focuses on the HBM, PMT and TRA/TPB. Ogden raised four issues: use in developing interventions, interpretation of empirical testing, analytical versus synthetic truths and mere measurement. Ogden first concluded that SCMs were useful to researchers and 'to inform service development and the development of health-related interventions to promote health behaviors' (2003: 425). However, she also made three key criticisms. First she argued that SCMs cannot be empirically tested, that is, confirmed or disconfirmed. She supported this point by pointing out that researchers do not conclude that they have disconfirmed SCMs when they find that one or more of the theory's constructs do not predict the outcome measure or that the findings do not explain all or most of the variance in intentions or behaviour. Ajzen and Fishbein (2004) highlight that the logic of this argument is unsound. For example in the case of the TPB, numerous descriptions of the theory make clear that the extent to which each of the cognitions predicts intentions or behaviour is a function of the population and behaviour under study. For a specific behaviour and population one or more antecedents may indeed not be predictive, without disproving the theory. For example, social approval may be crucial to some health behaviours but not to others. Thus finding that a particular cognition is not relevant to a particular behaviour does not disconfirm the theory. However, finding that none of the cognitions specified by the theory predicted useful proportions of the variance in intention or behaviour across behaviours would indeed disconfirm the theory. In fact, available evidence suggests that the theory is very useful, explaining on average 40–50 per cent of the variance in intention and 21–36 per cent of the variance in behaviour across studies (Conner and Sparks, 2005; McEachan et al., 2011).

Ogden also claimed that the theories contain only analytic truths (as opposed to synthetic or empirical truths that are based on evidence) because the correlations observed between measured cognitions are likely to be attributable to overlap in the way the constructs are measured. She claimed that this argument extends to measures of behaviour because these are often based on self-report. This interpretation of the literature has been disputed for two main reasons. First, it is not at all apparent that this explanation would account for the observed patterns of correlations among cognitions that are commonly reported in the literature. Second, high levels of prediction of behaviour are also found with objective measures of behaviour that do not rely on self-report and thus cannot be biased in the way Ogden describes. For example, Armitage and Conner (2001) in their meta-analysis of the TPB showed that intention and perceived behavioural control still accounted for an impressive 21 per cent of variance in behaviour when behaviour was objectively measured across a number of studies (see also McEachan et al., 2011 who reviewed prospective tests of the TPB to a range of health behaviours using either self-reported or objectively measured behaviour).

This examination of the percentage of variance explained by SCMs has discouraged some health psychologists. For example, Mielewczyk and Willig (2007: 818–819) in reviewing this evidence conclude that:

> the TPB is therefore unable to account for around 60 per cent of the variance in intentions and for up to almost 80 per cent of that in behaviour. Since the SCM approach is directed purely at providing explanations of variance in outcomes, the extent of that unexplained across such a large body of literature is highly damning.

This pessimism is unfounded for a number of reasons (see Abraham, Sheeran and Orbell, 1998, for a useful discussion). First, as Sutton (1997) notes, the percentage of variance explained by any model, including physiological models of symptom appearance, is directly related to the reliability of the measures employed. The maximum variance that can be accounted for will always be the square root of the product of the two reliabilities. Thus there are inherent measurement limitations on the percentage of variance that any model can explain. Second, when cognition and behaviour measures are not 'compatible' (i.e. do not refer to the identical action, target, time and context), the R^2 will be reduced (Ajzen and Fishbein, 1980). Similarly, if the number of response options used to measure cognitions and behaviour is not equal (e.g. if attitude is measured on a 7-point scale and behaviour on a 3-point scale), this will also reduce R^2. Finally, when sampling biases lead to a restricted range in either the independent (cognition) or the dependent (behaviour) variable compared to the actual range in the population (e.g. if the sample drink more alcohol than the sampled population) then the observed R^2 will underestimate the real cognition–behaviour relationship. Thus it is methodologically unrealistic to expect predictive models to explain 100 per cent of the variance in measures of behaviour.

We would claim that explaining 21 per cent of the variance in objectively measured behaviours is 'impressive' (rather than 'damning') because of the potential for behaviour change intervention that this figure represents. Rosenthal and Rubin (1982) translate percentages of explained variance into expected increases in outcome or success rates using their 'binomial effect size display'. This approach indicates that even when 19 per cent of the variance in behaviour is explained we would expect an increase in that behaviour from 28 per cent in a control group to 72 per cent in an intervention group (who had adopted the cognitions that explained the 19 per cent). This would indeed be an impressive finding for any evaluation of a behaviour change intervention (see Godin and Conner, 2008, for an examination of different indices of the intention–behaviour relationship for physical activity). Of course, changing the cognitions specified by the SCMs is a challenging endeavour (see Chapter 9) but the predictive success of SCMs strongly indicates that models such as the TPB can specify change targets that (if successfully changed) could make important differences to the prevalence of health behaviours in the population and, thereby, public health. Consequently, after reviewing available evidence and providing guidance for behaviour change interventions in the UK National Health Service, the National Institute of Health and Clinical Excellence (2007: 10–11) noted that 'a number of concepts drawn from the psychological literature are helpful when planning . . . behaviour change with individuals'. This list included 'positive attitude', 'subjective norms', 'descriptive norms', 'personal and moral norms', 'self-efficacy', 'intention formation' and 'concrete plans'.

Finally, returning to Ogden's critique, she suggested that measuring such cognitions as the TPB suggests, prompts their creation rather than simply recording pre-existing thoughts and perceptions. As Ajzen and Fishbein (2004) point out this is a common concern in questionnaire and interview studies. Recent research has in fact supported this concern. The effect has been referred to as the 'question-behaviour effect' meaning that measurement by itself prompts behaviour change. The strongest effects appear to be associated with the measurement of intentions. In Sherman's (1980) original demonstration of the effect, one group of participants was asked to predict how likely they would be to perform a socially desirable or socially undesirable behaviour (volunteering for the American Cancer Society or singing the Star Spangled Banner down the phone, respectively), while a second group made no prediction about their behaviour. The results indicated that participants asked to predict their behaviour were more likely to perform the socially desirable behaviour (31 per cent versus 4 per cent) and were less likely to perform the undesirable behaviour (40 per cent versus 68 per cent) compared to control participants making no prediction. Recent research has shown that completing a TPB questionnaire about blood donation led to a 6–9 per cent increase in attendance of blood donation 6–12 months later compared to groups who did not complete such a questionnaire (Godin et al., 2008). Other research has shown the question-behaviour effect can be used to change behaviours such as health screening attendance and influenza vaccination (Conner et al., 2011). Reviews of the question-behaviour effect indicate a significant but small effect on subsequent behaviour (Rodrigues et al., 2015; Wood et al., in press). However, rather than invalidating the use of SCMs, these findings point to the need for the use of more sophisticated designs to distinguish measurement and predictive effects, e.g. including conditions without baseline (time 1) questionnaires for comparative purposes. Moreover, the question–behaviour effect suggests that SCMs are indeed tapping psychological processes crucial to behaviour change.

THE INTENTION–BEHAVIOUR GAP

The intention–behaviour gap refers to the fact that intentions are far from perfect predictors of behaviour. In this section we review two areas of research exploring this gap. The first focuses on the stability of intentions across time while the second examines the volitional processes that might be important in determining whether intentions get translated into action.

Intention stability

In the vast majority of applications of SCMs the predictors of behaviour are measured by questionnaire (at time 1) and then behaviour is measured at a second time point, thereby employing a prospective survey method. One important requirement of such a design is that the measured constructs (e.g. attitudes) will remain unchanged between the measurement and the opportunity to act. So, for example, in using the TPB the assumption is that intentions to exercise will remain the same from when the (time 1) questionnaire is completed to the time points at which the respondent has the opportunity to engage in exercise. This is one of the limiting conditions of the TPB. However, cognitions including intentions may indeed change in this time period and such change provides one important explanation of the intention–behaviour gap. Several studies have now demonstrated that the intention–behaviour gap is indeed reduced for individuals with intentions that are more stable over time. For example, Conner, Norman and Bell (2002) found that intentions were stronger predictors of healthy eating over a period of 6 years when these intentions were stable over a 6-month time period. These findings show that intention stability moderates the relationship between intention and behaviour.

A number of other factors have been found to influence the size of the intention–behaviour gap. For example, anticipating feeling regret if one does not perform a behaviour or perceiving a strong moral norm (that is, believing that one is morally obliged to act) have both been found to significantly reduce the intention–behaviour gap (see Cooke and Sheeran, 2004, for a review). Like Conner et al. (2002), Sheeran and Abraham (2003) found that intention stability moderated the intention–behaviour relationship for exercising but, more importantly, found that intention stability mediated the effect of other moderators of the intention–behaviour relationship, including anticipated regret. This suggests that the mechanism by which a number of these other moderators may have their effect on intention–behaviour relationships is through changing the temporal stability of intentions. Hence, factors that might be expected to make individual intentions more stable over time would be expected to increase the impact that these intentions have on behaviour and so reduce the intention–behaviour gap.

FOCUS 7.4

Impact of socio-economic status on the intention–behaviour gap

A variety of studies have reported that as socio-economic status increases engagement with health-enhancing behaviours like exercise also increases while engagement with health-risking behaviours like smoking decreases. This could be because of weaker intentions to engage in health enhancing and stronger intentions to engage in health-risk behaviours in lower socio-economic status groups, although there is little evidence to support this view. A more interesting possibility is that lack of available resources in lower socio-economic status groups interferes with their ability to translate healthy intentions into health behaviours (e.g. intending to exercise more or smoke less). This would be a moderating effect of socio-economic status on the intention–behaviour relationship and would help explain the large intention–health behaviour gap in lower socio-economic status groups. Conner *et al.* (2013a) showed such a moderation effect for physical activity, breastfeeding and smoking initiation, in each case the intention–behaviour relationship was significantly weaker in the lower socio-economic status group compared to the high socio-economic status group. This finding would suggest that interventions targeting intentions in lower socio-economic status groups need to be supplemented by interventions designed to tackle the problems have in enacting such intentions (e.g. by providing better access to exercise facilities).

If you were trying to increase physical activity in lower socio-economic status groups what strategies would you use to try to increase intentions to exercise and reduce the intention–behaviour gap?

Implementation intention formation

A variety of factors that affect the enactment of intentions have been investigated including personality traits, self-efficacy and planning. For example, we noted in Chapter 6 that conscientious individuals may possess skills that help them to enact their intentions (see Chapter 8 for more on self-efficacy and Chapter 9 for more on planning). However, another factor may relate to the nature of the intention formed.

Gollwitzer (1993, 1999) makes the distinction between goal intentions and implementation intentions. While the former is concerned with intentions to perform a behaviour or achieve a goal (i.e. 'I intend to do X'), the latter is concerned with if-then plans, which specify an environmental prompt or context that will determine when the action should be taken (i.e. 'I intend to initiate the goal-directed behaviour X when situation Y is encountered'). The important point about implementation intentions is that they commit the individual to a specific course of action when certain environmental conditions are met. Sheeran *et al.* (2005: 280) note that:

to form an implementation intention, the person must first identify a response that will lead to goal attainment and, second, anticipate a suitable occasion to initiate that response. For example, the person might specify the behaviour 'go jogging for 20 minutes' and specify a suitable opportunity 'tomorrow morning before work'.

Gollwitzer (1993) argues that, by making implementation intentions, individuals pass control of intention enactment to the environment. The specified environmental cue prompts the action so that the person does not have to remember or decide when to act.

Sheeran *et al.* (2005) provide an in-depth review of both basic and applied research with implementation intentions (see also Prestwich *et al.*, 2015). For example, Milne, Orbell and Sheeran (2002) found that an intervention using persuasive text based on protection motivation theory prompted positive pro-exercise cognition change but did not increase exercise. However, when this intervention was combined with encouragement to form implementation intentions, behaviour change was observed (see Gollwitzer and Sheeran, 2006, for a meta-analysis of such studies; Prestwich *et al.*, 2015 for a review of the use of implementation intentions to change health behaviours). Thus implementation intention formation moderates the intention–behaviour relationship demonstrating that two people with equally strong goal intentions may differ in their volitional readiness depending on whether they have taken the additional step of forming an implementation intention. Implementation intention formation has been shown to increase the performance of a range of behaviours with, on average, a medium effect size. Implementation intentions appear to be particularly effective in overcoming a common problem in enacting intentions, that is, forgetting. Provided effective cues are identified in the implementation intention (i.e. ones that will be commonly encountered and are sufficiently distinctive), forgetting appears to be much less likely. Implementation intentions also appear to help individuals resist negative health behaviours (e.g. smoking initiation in adolescents; Conner and Higgins, 2010) and recent research has suggested that pairs of individuals can form joint implementation intentions that can be particularly effective (referred to as collaborative implementation intentions; Prestwich *et al.*, 2012).

SUMMARY

There is considerable variation in who performs health behaviours. Demographic differences explain part of this variation, although such factors are not easily modifiable. Various modifiable cognitions have been identified, which explain differences in who performs health behaviours. Key cognitions include intentions, self-efficacy and outcome expectancies (or attitudes). Cognitions have been incorporated in a number of social cognition models (SCMs) that describe the key cognitions and how they are interrelated in the determination of behaviour. The most important SCMs include the health belief model, protection motivation theory, theory of reasoned action/theory of planned behaviour and social cognitive theory. These models focus on the cognitive antecedents of motivation. Stage models attempt to describe the process of behaviour change from first consideration to maintenance of change but there is limited evidence to suggest that people remain in stable stages of action readiness over time. While SCMs have a number of advantages, criticisms of SCMs suggest the need for further sophistication in the testing of such models. SCMs are limited in their capacity to explain why some intentions are translated into behaviour while others are not. Various factors explaining this intention–behaviour gap have been explored and the important role of the temporal stability of intentions has been identified. Research has also investigated volitional processes, which facilitate the enactment of intentions. Implementation intentions, that is, if-then plans situating an intended action in a specific context, have been shown to reduce the intention–behaviour gap.

KEY CONCEPTS AND TERMS

- Critique of SCMs
- Health behaviours
- Health belief models
- Implementation intentions
- Intention–behaviour gap

- Mere measurement
- Protection motivation theory
- Self-regulation
- Social cognition models (SCMs)
- Social cognitive theory

- Stage models
- Theory of planned behaviour
- Transtheoretical model of change

SAMPLE ESSAY TITLES

- Critically evaluate the use of social cognition models in understanding health behaviours.
- Compare and contrast the health belief model and the theory of planned behaviour as explanations of why people do and do not perform a range of health behaviours.
- What do we know about the antecedents of intention? Discuss with reference to available empirical evidence.

FURTHER READING

Books

Abraham, C. and Sheeran, P. (2015). Health belief model. In M. Conner and P. Norman (eds) *Predicting and Changing Health Behaviour: Research and Practice with Social Cognition Models* (3rd edn). Buckingham: Open University Press, 30–69.

Abraham, C., Norman, P. and Conner, M. (2000). Towards a psychology of health-related behaviour change. In P. Norman, C. Abraham and M. Conner (eds) *Understanding and Changing Health Behaviour: From Health Beliefs to Self-Regulation*. Switzerland: Harwood Academic, 343–369.

Conner, M. and Sparks, P. (2015). The theory of planned behaviour and the reasoned action approach. In M. Conner and P. Norman (eds) *Predicting and Changing Health Behaviour: Research and Practice with Social Cognition Models* (3rd edn). Maidenhead: Open University Press, 142–188.

Norman, P. and Conner, M. (2015). Predicting and changing health behaviour: Future directions. In M. Conner and P. Norman (eds) *Predicting and Changing Health Behaviour: Research and Practice with Social Cognition Models* (3rd edn). Maidenhead: Open University Press, 391–430.

Journal articles

Ajzen, I. and Fishbein, M. (2004). Questions raised by a reasoned action approach: Reply on Ogden (2003). *Health Psychology*, 23, 431–434.

Ogden, J. (2003). Some problems with social cognition models: A pragmatic and conceptual analysis. *Health Psychology*, 22, 424–428.

8 Changing motivation

CHAPTER PLAN

In Chapter 7 we studied cognitions that have been found to differentiate between people who do and do not perform health behaviours. In this chapter we focus on interventions designed to change cognitions in order to promote health-related behaviours.

Learning about a health risk can change people's attitudes, intentions and behaviour. Therefore, provision of accessible and easily understood information is an important part of health promotion. Information is evaluated by the receiver and if it is judged to be mistaken, not personally relevant or implying difficult or costly actions it may be ignored. Consequently, health promoters also need to persuade individuals and groups to take health-promoting action. Successful persuasion depends on anticipating how recipients will perceive and respond to the persuasive attempt. Successful persuasion is likely to result in attitude change and (as we saw in Chapter 7) attitudes provide an important foundation for the motivation to change one's behaviour. However, when people feel they cannot make a change they are unlikely to pursue it. Consequently, ensuring high perceived control and self-efficacy is crucial to maintenance of motivation and the translation of intentions into action. In this chapter we will consider how motivation can be bolstered and changed in five sections: (1) providing information; (2) persuading others; (3) changing attitudes; (4) enhancing self-efficacy; and (5) from motivation to behaviour change.

LEARNING OUTCOMES

When you have completed this chapter you should be able to:

1 Describe how information and advice should be presented to maximize its impact on health-related motivation and action.
2 Explain how social influence techniques can be applied to maximize the impact of health-promotion advice on recipients' motivation, in mass media, one-to-one and group communication.

3   Explain how the manner in which messages are processed (i.e. the degree of cognitive elaboration) determines which message features have most impact on attitude change. Use this explanation to provide evidence-based advice on how health promoters can maximize attitude change.

4   Illustrate the importance of self-efficacy to motivation, health behaviour and health and explain how self-efficacy can be enhanced.

PROVIDING INFORMATION

If people become aware of a health risk from a source they perceive to be trustworthy and they also believe they can easily protect themselves, information alone can prompt behaviour change. For example, media coverage about food scares such as bovine spongiform encephalopathy (BSE) can lead to widespread change in behaviours such as beef purchase (e.g. Swientek, 2001; Tyler, 2001). Inaccurate information can also promote behaviour changes that increase health risk. For example, when a highly regarded medical journal (*The Lancet*) published an article linking the measles, mumps and rubella vaccine (MMR) with autism and inflammatory bowel disease in 1998, MMR vaccination uptake fell and cases of measles increased. Although the validity of the research was subsequently questioned by the journal's editor as well as being denounced by 10 of the 13 original authors and the UK prime minister (see *The Guardian*, Tuesday 24 February 2004), it proved difficult to re-build public confidence in the safety of MMR and raise vaccination uptake to previous levels. Further research found no immunological response differences to MMR in children with and without autism (Baird *et al.*, 2008) but in 2008 national vaccination uptake levels still remained lower than the optimal 95 per cent levels. This example emphasizes the power of a credible source. When scientists and government ministers offer contradictory information or when advice is perceived to serve the interests of the source (e.g. industry), information and reassurance may not be believed. People may interpret, 'there is no cause for concern', as, 'there must be a problem' or, similarly, 'this is dangerous' as 'just more state interference'. Consequently, as well as the ethical imperative for health professionals, scientists and government to ensure that information available to the public is not misleading, there is a need to ensure information is accurate and evidence-based to maintain future credibility.

Source credibility may also be enhanced by presentation of two-sided arguments. Presenting the disadvantages as well as the advantages of a product or recommended action has been found to be more persuasive because two-sided presentations result in greater perceived credibility of the source (e.g. Crowley and Hoyer, 1994; Eisend, 2006). This may be especially true for sceptical audiences. Two-sided arguments may also increase the perceived novelty of the message, which, in turn, enhances attention and interest and so may promote positive attitude change (Eisend, 2007). Thus, being open about the costs or side effects of a recommended action may be more effective in changing attitudes and intentions because the audience is more likely to believe that the highlighted benefits are real.

Making information accessible and easy to understand

Information can only change motivation and behaviour if people can access it and understand it. Thus providing accurate information in the right place for the target audience is crucial if information is to affect action. Information providers need to know where and when the target audience will seek information before designing an information campaign. Will the target audience seek information on the web or just before they take their medication or, for example, when they are about to use a sunbed? Preliminary research with the target audience can answer such questions and so help guide effective information provision.

Once the most appropriate context for information presentation is established, information providers must ensure that what they say is easily understood. For example, if patient information leaflets provided with medications are written in tiny writing and include technical terms patients do not understand then they are not likely to enhance adherence. Ease of comprehension is partly determined by what the recipient already knows. If you want to give someone good directions (e.g. in a city) you ideally want to be aware of what landmarks they already know. Yet evidence suggests that health professionals often overestimate patients' knowledge and, therefore, their ability to understand health-related information. For example, Boyle (1970) found that only 20 per cent and 42 per cent of patients, respectively, were able to accurately identify the position of the stomach and heart. Similarly, Hadlow and Pitts (1991) found that while the vast majority of doctors were able to select correct clinical definitions of conditions such as stroke, eating disorder and depression, only 18 per cent, 30 per cent and 32 per cent of patients were able to do so, respectively. Thus prior explanation of medical and unfamiliar terms is required if they are to be used in information designed for the general population.

Text can also be more or less difficult to read depending on how it is written and the words that are used. The level of reading difficulty can be assessed using a variety of measures. For example, the Flesch Reading Ease measure (FRE) (Flesch, 1948) assesses the average number of syllables in words used and the average sentence length. A score between zero and 100 is generated with higher scores denoting easier texts (e.g. scores of 65 and above are acceptable for literate adults). Media professionals regularly edit text to achieve good readability. For example, the most popular newspaper in the UK is said to have a reading age of 9! Considerable additional effort is required to ensure that health information is readable by the vast majority of the population. For example, in a survey of more than 1,000 leaflets provided by palliative care units in the UK and Ireland, Payne et al. (2000) found that 47 per cent were printed in less than font 12. Two-thirds had poor readability scores as assessed by the FRE, which implied that they would only be understood by 40 per cent of the UK population.

Providing wanted information

Health professionals tend to underestimate patients' desire for information. Even when they are facing bad news and potential terminal diagnoses, evidence indicates that patients want to know as much as possible (e.g. Jenkins, Fallowfield and Saul, 2001) – but what do they want to know? Coulter, Entwistle and Gilbert (1999) reviewed

54 sources of information, including information leaflets and listened to patients in focus groups to discover what kind of information they wanted. These researchers found that the sources of information they reviewed did not correspond to patients' desires for information. They generated a list of 22 questions that patients commonly want answered (reproduced in Activity 8.1) and recommended that the patient information resources be written and revised to ensure that they answer these questions.

ACTIVITY 8.1

What do patients want to know?

Coulter *et al.* (1999) suggest that patients typically want answers to the following questions:

- What is causing the problem?
- How does my experience compare with that of other patients?
- Is there anything I can do myself to ameliorate the problem?
- What is the purpose of the tests and investigations?
- What are the different treatment options?
- What are the benefits of the treatment(s)?
- What are the risks of the treatment(s)?
- Is it essential to have treatment for this problem?
- Will the treatment(s) relieve the symptoms?
- How long will it take to recover?
- What are the possible side effects?
- What effect will the treatment(s) have on my feelings and emotions?
- What effect will the treatment(s) have on my sex life?
- How will it affect my risk of disease in the future?
- How can I prepare myself for the treatment?
- What procedures will be followed if I go to hospital?
- When can I go home?
- What do my carers need to know?
- What can I do to speed recovery?
- What are the options for rehabilitation?
- How can I prevent recurrence or future illness?
- Where can I get more information about the problem or treatments?

Examine the NHS 'Choices' website (www.nhs.uk/Pages/homepage.aspx). Do you think this website provides the answers to patient questions identified by Coulter *et al.* (1999)? For example, have a look at the body map and the areas it highlights (e.g. head and neck) and/or look at explanations of specific conditions, e.g. 'chlamydia'? How readable is the website? Do you have ideas for improving this website? Note you can send your feedback to the NHS.

Organization of information

In addition to providing easy to understand information that is wanted by the target audience and presented in the right context, information providers can make information easier to understand and remember by organizing it in a manner that is easy to process. Providing information in a logical order facilitates processing. For example, clarifying the cause of an illness before explaining how a treatment works can help a patient understand why the treatment is necessary or why it should be administered as recommended. Telling the audience what you are about to tell them can also enhance recall. This is often referred to as 'explicit categorization'. For example, a nurse might say 'First, I am going to tell you what I think is wrong, . . . now I'm going to tell you about the treatment . . ., etc.' Highlighting and repeating important points also helps people pay particular attention to them ('This is important so I'm going to say it again'). Finally, when giving advice, it is important to be specific, e.g. 'You need to lose one stone in weight' is much easier to remember and act on than 'You need to lose weight'. Ley *et al.* (1976) wrote a manual for GPs explaining these simple techniques and assessed patient recall for information provided in consultations with four GPs before and after they read the manual. Results showed that recall increased from 52–59 per cent across the four doctors at baseline to 61–80 per cent after the GPs had read the manual. Thus, these five simple presentation techniques (logical order, explicit categorization, specific advice, emphasizing and repeating important points) make information easier to process and recall.

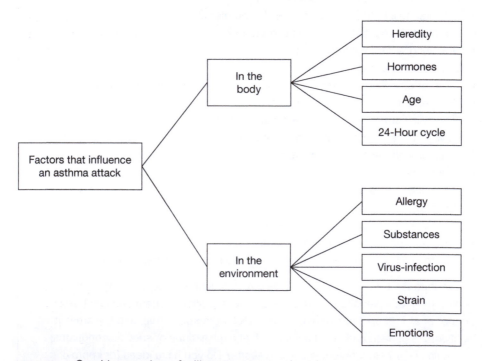

FIGURE 8.1 Graphic organizers facilitate text comprehension.

Source: Kools *et al.* (2006). Reprinted with permission of SAGE Publications.

Visual aids can make written materials easier to understand. For example, an experiment conducted by Kools *et al.* (2006) showed that participants who read text describing asthma care extracted from a health promotion leaflet had poorer comprehension of the text than participants who read the same text modified by the addition of graphic organizers (including the one in Figure 8.1). Pre-testing of such materials is important to ensure that they are appropriate for the target audience.

The way in which risk information is presented can also determine its impact on motivation and action. As we shall see in Chapter 11, risk information can be more or less persuasive depending on whether it is framed in terms of gains or losses (even when the same information is included).

Information knowledge and motivation

Unfortunately, information is often not enough to change behaviour because even those who understand and have a good knowledge of the consequences of their actions fail to follow advice. Why? Can you think of a health-related behaviour that you know you should change?

Using meta-analysis (see Research methods 8.1), Sheeran, Abraham and Orbell (1999) examined psychosocial factors associated with heterosexual condom use in 121 empirical studies. Effect sizes for 44 separate factors correlated with condom use could be calculated. These analyses revealed an average weighted correlation of 0.06 (a small effect size) for the relationship between knowledge and reported condom use. Thus increasing knowledge by itself is unlikely to be enough to promote condom use. By contrast, the average weighted correlations for attitude towards condom use (0.32), others' approval of use (0.37) and intention to use (0.43) were equivalent to medium effect sizes. These findings indicate that changing perceived approval and attitudes towards condoms is much more likely to impact on heterosexual condom use than is changing knowledge. Sheeran *et al.* (1999: 126) concluded that these results 'provide empirical support for conceptualizing condom use in terms of . . . an extended theory of reasoned action' and argued that these correlates specify important targets for safer sex promotion. A similar meta-analysis of studies applying the theories of reasoned action (Fishbein and Ajzen, 1975) and planned behaviour (TPB, Ajzen, 1991) to condom use confirmed the utility of these theories as models of cognitive antecedents of condom use (Albarracín *et al.*, 2001). Thus for many behaviours changing cognitive elements of motivation is critical to behaviour change. This may not be achieved by simply providing good information.

PERSUADING OTHERS

We have seen that providing information can sometimes be persuasive in itself but that, more often, even when people understand information and have good knowledge of health risks, this may not be enough to motivate change. So how can we overcome resistance to change? How can health professionals move beyond providing information to persuading target audiences to change? Persuasion is social influence (one person or group influencing another) and there is a considerable body of research on how social influence works. For example, Pratkanis (2007) lists 107 potentially effective

RESEARCH METHODS 8.1

Meta-analysis

Meta-analysis allows researchers to examine the average size of associations (or differences) between two measures or conditions across a series of studies. When combining effect sizes (e.g. the size of an association between two measures) across studies it is important to weight studies for the number of participants because a finding based on 100 participants is likely to be more reliable than one based on 10. For example, if a correlation study found that knowledge and behaviour were correlated at $r = .05$ among a sample of 100 people and another study found the correlation to be $r = .07$ among a similar sample of 100 people then the average weighted correlation (r^+) would be 0.06, across these two studies. However, if the second study had only recruited a sample of 50 then r^+ would be 0.0425. In this way, meta-analyses allow researchers to combine results across studies to calculate average 'effect sizes'. Cohen (1992) has provided guidelines for interpreting the size of sample-weighted average correlations (r) suggesting that $r^+ = .10$ is 'small', $r^+ = .30$ is 'medium', while $r^+ = .50$ is 'large'.

Meta-analyses can also be used to estimate the average impact that behaviour change interventions (see Chapter 9) have on a particular outcome (such as physical activity levels). In this case, the most usual measure is d (rather than r). d is calculated by subtracting the behavioural outcome score of one condition from another (for each study) and dividing this by the standard pooled deviation, that is, the standard deviation for both conditions combined (Hedges and Olkin, 1985). For example, if, at follow-up, those who had received an intervention were found to exercise 3 times a week on average while those in a no-intervention control group exercised only 1.5 times a week on average and there was an overall standard pooled deviation of 1.5 this would generate a d value of 1.0. Cohen (1992) suggests that ds of 0.2 are 'small' while ds of 0.5 are of 'medium' size and ds of 0.8 are 'large' effect sizes. Thus this would be a large and impressive effect size. This is not surprising because in this example the intervention doubled the rate of the target behaviour compared to the control group, indicating an unusually successful intervention.

social influence tactics, including being a credible source, being empathetic, using flattery, agenda setting, using metaphor, using story telling, fear appeals and making people feel guilty. Here we will consider some key principles that need to be followed if you want to motivate someone else to change their behaviour.

Message framing

Prospect theory (Tversky and Kahneman, 1981) predicts that people process information differently depending on whether it relates to losses (or costs) or gains (or benefits). Specifically, people tend to be 'risk averse', that is they want to avoid risk, when thinking about gains but, when thinking about potential losses, people tend to be open to taking risks, or risk seeking. Consequently, a behaviour that is not associated with risk may seem more attractive when thinking about gains (because we tend to want to avoid risk when thinking about gains), while a behaviour that is perceived to be risky may be more attractive when people are thinking about losses or costs (when people favour risk). Preventive behaviours including condom or sunscreen use are undertaken to reduce the risk of ill health and so tend to be perceived as low risk. By contrast, detection behaviours such as breast or testicular self-examination are thought to be high risk because, despite the potential long-term benefits, there is an immediate risk of discovering a worrying problem. It has been predicted, therefore, that health promotion information about preventive behaviours will be most effective when it focuses upon potential gains, while health promotion information about detection behaviours will be most effective when it focuses upon potential losses or costs (see Rothman and Salovey, 1997). There is some evidence to support this. For example, Detweiler *et al.* (1999) gave people going to the beach messages that either emphasized gains associated with sunscreen use (e.g. 'If you use sunscreen with SPF 15 or higher, you increase your chances of keeping your skin healthy and your life long') or losses associated with not using sunscreen (e.g. 'If you don't use sunscreen with SPF 15 or higher, you decrease your chances of keeping your skin healthy and your life long'). They found that those who read the gain-focused messages were more likely to redeem a coupon to collect sunscreen. Moreover, this (gain-focused) group were more likely to intend to use sunscreen with a sun protection factor of 15 and to intend to apply sunscreen repeatedly.

However, framing effects do not always produce the desired effects on motivation and behaviour. One of the main reasons is that not all preventive behaviours are perceived as low risk and not all detection behaviours are perceived as high risk. For example, consider parents' decisions to have their children vaccinated against measles, mumps and rubella using the combined MMR injection. It is likely that after the publication of the now refuted report linking MMR vaccination with autism and inflammatory bowel disease (see above) parents perceived this preventive behaviour as high risk and therefore, might be more likely to respond to loss-focused messages rather than gain-focused messages. Abhyankar, O'Connor and Lawton (2008) tested this hypothesis and found that, as predicted, a loss-framed message (e.g. 'by not vaccinating your child against mumps, measles and rubella, you will fail to protect your child against contracting these diseases') was more effective in increasing women's MMR vaccination intentions than a gain-focused message (e.g. 'by vaccinating your child against mumps, measles and rubella, you will be able to protect your child against contracting these diseases'). Similarly, when a detection behaviour is perceived to result in a safe or certain outcome, then a gain-focused message is likely to be most effective. A study by Apanovitch, McCarthy and Salovey (2003) found that women who felt safe about the outcome of a HIV test because they considered themselves to be at no risk were more likely to report having the test six months after watching a gain-focused video message compared to those who saw the loss-focused message.

Other factors influence the extent to which messages are processed. For example, the degree to which an individual is involved with an issue has been found to influence the effectiveness of gain- and loss-focused messages. Rothman *et al.* (1993) found that framed messages only worked as predicted for people who were concerned with the target health behaviour (e.g. skin cancer detection). The extent to which a person holds a positive or negative attitude towards the target health behaviour is also important. In a study of intentions to use hormonal male contraception, O'Connor, Ferguson and O'Connor (2005) found that the hypothesized framing effects were only observed in men with a positive attitude towards the behaviour. Thus personal involvement and positive attitude towards the behaviour facilitate framing effects and thereby moderate the relationship between framing and motivation.

Thus framing information and advice in terms of benefits or gains so that this corresponds to how a recommended action is perceived (i.e. low risk behaviours are prompted using gains) can enhance the impact of risk information on motivation and behaviour. However, framing effects should be pre-tested on the target audience and individual characteristics considered before materials are produced.

Since Rothman and Salovey introduced their framing postulate in 1997, a number of important reviews of the scientific literature testing the effectiveness of message framing in relation to promoting health behaviours have been published (e.g. Covey, 2014; Gallagher and Updegraff, 2012; O'Keefe and Jensen, 2009; O'Keefe and Nan, 2012). Specifically, researchers have been interested in examining whether gain frames always facilitate prevention behaviours and loss frames always encourage detection behaviours. The accumulated evidence suggests that the findings are mixed and that they are influenced by important dispositional variables and individual differences. For example, in a meta-analysis of 53 studies aimed at encouraging disease detection behaviours, the results showed that loss-framed messages (highlighting the disadvantages of noncompliance with the communicator's recommendation) were only slightly more effective than gain-framed messages, though, the difference was statistically significant (O'Keefe and Jensen, 2009). More recently, another meta-analysis of the persuasive impact of message framing on attitudes, intentions and behaviours also concluded that the loss-frame appeals were not very effective for promoting detection behaviours (Gallagher and Updegraff, 2012). However, these authors did find that gain-framed messages were significantly more effective for promoting prevention behaviours.

Dispositional factors might account for these mixed findings. It is possible that the relative persuasiveness of gain- and loss-framed health messages will be influenced by fairly stable dispositional factors and/or individual differences (e.g. need for cognition, self efficacy). This was the focus of an influential recent review conducted by Covey (2014) that identified a number of important moderators of message framing effects. Specifically, she reported that factors such as ambivalence, approach–avoidance motivation, need for cognition and self-efficacy beliefs influenced the effectiveness of the different health messages. The major conclusion of this work suggests that health messages will be most influential and persuasive if the frame is tailored to the individual.

Social influence motives and principles

Social influence can be understood in terms of the key underlying motives that facilitate cognitive change (Cialdini and Trost, 1998). First, people want to access valid sources of information about their reality. When we see other people looking behind us we sensibly want to turn around to see what is there. This type of influence has been referred to as informational influence (Deutsch and Gerard, 1955) and is the basis of expert power (French and Raven, 1960). If we believe that someone else is better informed and better able to predict what will happen to us then they have the potential to exert informational influence over us. Doctors are a good example of experts with informational power in relation to health issues. Second, we are motivated to feel positively about ourselves, that is, to maintain positive self-esteem. Third, we want to have good relationships with other people (sometimes referred to as the 'affiliation motive'). Acceptance by other people is critical to our sense of self-worth so these motivations combine to facilitate normative influence. For example, we are reluctant to lose friends' approval so we are willing to do what they want rather than following our own preferences. In doing so we are subject to normative influence.

Research supports a series of principles concerning social influence processes (Cialdini, 1995), which relate directly to these two types of influence (i.e. informational and normative). First, as we have seen, ensuring that the message source is perceived to be credible and expert enhances persuasive impact. Our perception of a message source also depends on how we categorize ourselves in relation to the source (whether this is an individual or group). People seen as similar to ourselves or belonging to the same group are more likely to be liked, viewed positively and able to validate our experiences (Turner, 1991). Therefore, such people have a greater potential to exert normative influence. Consequently, it has been proposed that peers (people belonging to the target audience) are the most persuasive communicators. However, evidence indicates that this is only true if these communicators are also seen to be experts. Those perceived to be expert and whose gender and ethnicity match the target group are most persuasive and helpful (Durantini *et al.*, 2006).

Cognitive dissonance theory (Festinger, 1957) proposes that we are motivated to maintain a consistent view of the world because cognitive inconsistency creates dissonance, which is inherently unpleasant. Consequently, when the opinions of others or persuasive messages appear consistent with what we already know and believe, they are more likely to be persuasive. Thus consistency, that is, ensuring that a health message does not contradict existing beliefs, commitments or obligations (and thereby generate cognitive dissonance) is an important second feature of communications likely to persuade. See Focus 8.1 on how self-affirmation can be used to help increase the effectiveness of persuasive messages that potentially challenge self-worth.

A third, and related, principle is the perception of consensus. If a proposed change is supported by everyone (and this emphasizes the importance of not providing contradictory advice) and is adopted by others we are more likely to want to join in. Thus believing that others are performing an action that we are considering (that is holding a positive descriptive norm – Rivis and Sheeran, 2003 – see Chapter 7) is likely to facilitate persuasion and bolster motivation. This may be even more persuasive if we categorize ourselves as belonging to the same group as those adopting the change (e.g. 'other people like you have already adopted this behaviour') because such identification is likely to enhance the self-worth/validation impact of the message. Thus informational influence (and to some extent normative influence) can be strengthened by three key features of persuasive messages: (1) source credibility and expertise; (2) perceived consistency with current world view; and (3) perceived consensus/identification.

People we like and identify with can exert greater normative influence over us. Thus persuasion is more likely when the source is seen as enjoying a good relationship or good image with the target audience. This emphasizes the importance of good social and communication skills among professionals involved in face-to-face health promotion activities and of enhancing the brand value of organizations offering health advice such as the National Health Service (NHS) in the UK. We tend to like those who offer us things of value, so people are more open to social influence from those who have provided something for them. Therefore, reciprocation, through offering services or products that are seen as valuable, may be a useful way of encouraging a target group to listen to health-related advice. In addition, we value approval so believing that those who are important to us approve of a particular course of action (i.e. holding a positive subjective norm; Fishbein and Ajzen, 1975, see Chapter 7) is likely to facilitate persuasion and affect motivation. Thus normative influence can be strengthened by three key features of persuasive messages: positive relationships, reciprocation and the approval of valued others.

Persuasion in groups

Both informational and normative influence act on people in groups but persuasion in groups differs depending on whether it is persuasion by the majority (that is, more than half the group), called conformity (Asch, 1952), or conversion to a minority view or action. Majority influence or conformity is strengthened by consensus. A large and consistent majority exerts considerable informational and normative influence. By contrast, a minority challenges our usual assumptions and leads us to evaluate the contrast between majority and minority views (Moscovici, 1976; Moscovici and Lage, 1976). Conversion to a minority view does not work through consensus influence and is determined instead by how the minority act. If members of a minority group are seen to be consistent, committed, confident and fair they prompt others to think carefully about their alternative position. This systematic consideration and evaluation of the minority view means that, when minorities are persuasive, the attitude change that results from such conversion is likely to be longer-lasting and less subject to counter-persuasion than attitude change due to conformity (Martin, Hewstone and Martin, 2007).

Persuasion and influence in groups have important applied implications because group discussions are regularly used by researchers and health services including the UK NHS. Discussions in focus groups and so-called 'citizen's juries' are regularly used to discover what people want and the results are used to draw conclusions about public opinion and popular policy development. One problem associated with this methodology is that the way in which groups are managed and facilitated may affect what people say. For example, the questions posed and choices offered shape responses. Moreover, powerful majorities or confident and committed minorities may limit the number of viewpoints considered through conformity and conversion. Are group discussions the best way of sampling public opinion (see e.g. *The Observer*, Sunday 30 September 2007 for comment)?

FOCUS 8.1

Using self-affirmation to help increase the effectiveness of persuasive messages

Self-affirmation involves reflecting on one's cherished values, actions or attributes. As a result of such self-reflection individuals recall the sense of who they are and what they stand for in the face of perceived threats to their identity (Steele, 1988). Self-affirmation theory suggests that people are strongly motivated to maintain self-integrity and that because health messages are often perceived as threatening to self-integrity (e.g. suggesting the individual is not engaging in healthy behaviours) individuals may be motivated to find fault with such messages. So, for example, a smoker exposed to a health message about the risks of smoking may protect his/her self-integrity in one of two ways, either play down the potential risks of smoking set out in the message or make renewed efforts to quit smoking. Unfortunately from the point of view of the originator of the message it is often the former response that is adopted. Self-affirmation theory offers a useful way round this problem. It is suggested that self-integrity can be restored or reinforced by affirming sources of self-worth that are important to the person's identity but unrelated to the threat. For example, a smoker may remind herself of her strengths as a mother leading to the self-concept of being a smoker becoming less threatening to her self-integrity. Importantly, self-affirming thoughts can reduce the likelihood of self-threatening information in persuasive messages being dismissed. The idea is that self-affirming can promote more objective appraisal of threatening material in persuasive messages and so lead to more behaviour change consistent with the content of the message.

Epton *et al.* (2015) reviewed 144 studies testing the effects of self-affirmation on health-related cognition, affect and behaviour. Overall there appeared to be good evidence that self-affirming promotes greater general and personal acceptance of health-risk information and less playing down of message content. For example, Armitage *et al.* (2008) reported self-affirmation to promote acceptance of information about the health risks of smoking among a sample of smokers. Several studies also show that self-affirmation led to stronger intentions to change health risk behaviours (Armitage *et al.*, 2008) and even health-relevant behaviours (Armitage *et al.*, 2008; Sherman, Nelson and Steele, 2000). For example, Sherman *et al.* (2000, study 2) showed that compared to the non-self-affirmed the self-affirmed took more leaflets about HIV and purchased more condoms. Ferrer *et al.* (2012) recently reported that among female student drinkers compared to non-self-affirmed those who self-affirmed were more likely to form implementation intentions about reducing alcohol consumption following reading an article linking excessive alcohol consumption to breast cancer (see Sweeney and Moyer, 2015 for another recent review of the effects of self-affirmation on responses to health messages).

Obedience and informed decision-making

We have seen how important the source of a message is to persuasion. Holding legitimate authority is an especially powerful attribute in relation to social influence. When people occupy a role in which they accept that another person has the right to direct other people's actions, they are more easily persuaded. This was powerfully demonstrated in Milgram's (1974) experiments in which he showed that people would deliver (what they thought were) electric shocks to others to a much greater extent than was predicted, so long as they accepted the experimenter (ordering the shocks) as a legitimate authority figure. Following this work, Rank and Jacobson (1977) investigated nurses' obedience to an apparent order from a doctor to administer a drug in too large a quantity, that is to give a patient a drug overdose. They concluded that nurses were less likely to obey the mistaken order if they were familiar with the drug and had time to confer with other nurses. This emphasizes a more general point relevant to all those involved in health care decisions, namely, that being well informed and having time to confer before decisions are made and action is undertaken is likely to minimize mistakes, whether the decision-makers are managers, doctors, nurses or patients.

Overcoming resistance to change

Persuasion is necessary because often people do not want to change. We do not like others trying to influence us, we often find persuasive communications threatening or unbelievable and we feel it is too difficult to change everyday routines in the face of many competing demands. Reactance (Brehm, 1966) is an emotional response to attempts at coercion, prohibition and regulation. Reactance leads people to take the opposite view to that imposed and motivates people to do the opposite of what is recommended. Thus it is important to prepare for and manage social influence attempts. If a persuasion attempt is insensitive to the needs of the target audience it may have no impact or even be counterproductive.

We have noted the importance of perceptions of the message source and this extends to the way in which the persuasive attempt is delivered. Explicit persuasive attempts may be resisted. For example, it means that tone of voice and non-verbal indicators of power within a relationship can undermine social influence in one-to-one settings. For example, Ambady et al. (2002) taped surgeons' consultations with patients and, on the basis of 10-second clips, rated dominance and concern/anxiety in their voices (regardless of content). Higher dominance and lower concern were significantly associated with greater number of previous malpractice claims initiated by their patients! This has important implications for doctor–patient communication, which we will consider in Chapter 10.

Governments need to persuade populations that public health legislation is in the public interest before enacting such legislation (e.g. necessitating seat-belt wearing in cars or banning smoking in public places). Otherwise enforcement may be costly and there is a risk that unpopular legislation may be overturned. Thus reassuring a target audience that what is offered is caring advice, which is primarily in their own interest, is a crucial foundation for persuasion.

Reactance and resistance can be minimized by presenting persuasion attempts as choices, by highlighting the ease with which change can be managed and by focusing on what people can do rather than telling them what they should not do (e.g. 'you can choose to be smoke free', 'you can choose to eat a healthy diet and feel and look better') (Knowles and Rinner, 2007). Presenting health advice as choice has been widely adopted by the UK NHS. For example, it has established a 'choices website' described as 'the new service that helps you to make the most of your health and get the best out of the NHS' (www.nhs.uk/pages/homepage.aspx). While the intention here is to promote health behaviour change, the persuasive attempt is presented as offering new opportunities and increasing the recipient's freedom.

ACTIVITY 8.2

Design a brief set of arguments that could be used to persuade young people to donate blood, drawing on evidence-based principles of persuasion.

ATTITUDE CHANGE

Did you think about a health-related behaviour you feel you should change? Have you not changed because you expect this change to result in negative outcomes? Evaluating action positively, that is, holding a positive attitude towards it is critical to change. Consequently, attitude change is a key target for those wishing to persuade others to adopt healthier lifestyles.

Message processing and attitude change

Attitude change is dependent on how a recipient responds to a persuasive message. For example, some evaluative responses are based on superficial impressions while others are the result of systematic consideration. This has important implications for persuasive techniques. Petty and Cacioppo (1986) argue that although we are all motivated to hold valid attitudes, which help us make reliable predictions about our reality (hence the power of informational influence), we can have more or less motivation and capacity to devote to the systematic processing of messages we receive. They refer to the amount of systematic processing devoted to a message as 'cognitive elaboration' and, consequently, their model is known as the 'elaboration likelihood model' (ELM).

   The ELM refers to systematic processing of messages as central route processing and processing of messages in a superficial manner as peripheral route processing. Central route processing involves greater cognitive elaboration and the meaning of the message is critical to persuasion. By contrast, peripheral route processing involves little systematic processing (low cognitive elaboration) and other characteristics of the message are more likely to determine whether or not it is persuasive.

   When people are under time pressure, do not understand a message, think that the issue is not relevant to them or are distracted by something else they may evaluate a message on the basis of simple cues rather than considering its meaning in detail. For example, people use simple rules or decision-making heuristics to evaluate messages. These include 'expertise = accuracy', that is, she is an expert so what she says must be right, or 'consensus = correctness', that is, if so many people agree they must be right and 'length = strength', that is there are lots of arguments so it must be true. Sometimes situational constraints force people into peripheral route processing. For example, the message may be presented quickly amid distractions as is the case in many television advertisements. In addition, individual differences mean that some people are more or less likely than others to engage in systematic processing. For example, Chaiken (1980) identified people who agreed or disagreed with the length = strength heuristic (using agreement with questionnaire items such as 'the more reasons a person has for some point of view the more likely he/she is correct'). These people were then presented with a message containing 6 arguments in favour of cross-course, end-of-year examinations for students. However, the message was described to participants as either containing 10 or 2 arguments (although it always contained the same 6 arguments). The results showed that those who endorsed the length = strength heuristic were more likely to be persuaded when the message was described as having 10 arguments than were those who did not endorse the heuristic.

Central route (systematic) processing is unlikely among message recipients who do not understand a message. Figure 8.2 shows results from a study by Wood, Kallgren and Mueller Preisler (1985). Among message recipients with poor knowledge, attitude change was almost as likely whether a message contained weak or strong arguments because the ability to engage in systematic, central route processing was compromised by lack of knowledge. These recipients relied on peripheral processing and so failed to differentiate between strong and weak arguments. By contrast, those with good knowledge clearly differentiated between strong and weak arguments and were only

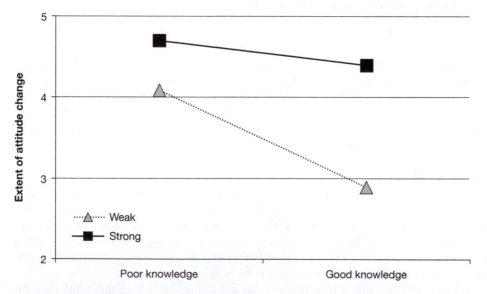

FIGURE 8.2 Prior knowledge and the effect of argument strength (Wood *et al.*, 1985).

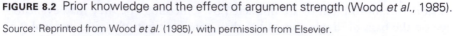

Source: Reprinted from Wood *et al.* (1985), with permission from Elsevier.

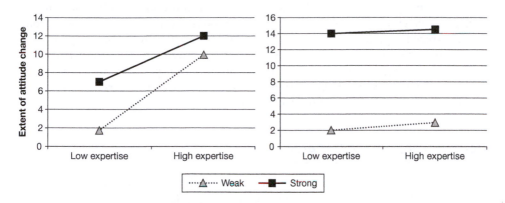

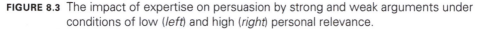

FIGURE 8.3 The impact of expertise on persuasion by strong and weak arguments under conditions of low (*left*) and high (*right*) personal relevance.

Source: Reprinted from Petty and Cacioppo (1986), with permission from Elsevier.

persuaded by the former. These results emphasize the importance of knowledge (and, therefore, high quality information) in allowing people to evaluate messages about their health.

When people have time to process messages or make time because they see the message as personally relevant, they are more likely to engage in systematic processing so that the content of the message is more important than other characteristics. Figure 8.3 shows how perceiving the message source to be an expert has different effects depending on whether recipients regard a message as high or low in personal relevance. The low relevance participants are strongly affected by perceived expertise and are more persuaded by an expert (rather than inexpert) source whether strong or weak arguments are used. However, for those who see the message as personally relevant (and so engage in systematic processing) only the quality of argument determines persuasion. Strong arguments are persuasive for this group, regardless of source expertise, and even an expert cannot persuade this group with weak arguments. This does not mean that source expertise is unimportant but rather that for those with the ability and motivation to engage in systematic processing poor quality arguments cannot be compensated for by the impression of expertise. In terms of the ELM this means that persuasion does occur through *both* the central and peripheral routes simultaneously but that one or other route will be dominant depending on factors such as message relevance. Individual characteristics also affect whether people are likely to engage mainly in systematic processing (Briñol and Petty, 2005). For example, some people have a high 'need for cognition' (i.e. like thinking about the content of persuasive messages) and so, in general, are motivated to make time for central route processing (Cacioppo, Petty and Morris, 1983).

Overall then, research suggests that if you do not have strong arguments then you are better discouraging systematic processing and relying instead on numerous arguments, consensus and perceived expertise. Perhaps fortunately, attitude changes resulting from peripheral route processing are less likely to be stable (that is, long-lived) and more likely to further change due to counter-persuasion, whereas attitude change resulting from systematic (central route) processing is more likely to be stable and to influence behaviour. Consequently, health promoters should ensure they use strong evidence-based arguments, encourage systematic processing by ensuring appropriate prior knowledge, emphasizing personal relevance, providing distraction-free presentations, using repetition and encouraging confidence in people's own judgement. Having facilitated systematic processing we must ensure that our persuasive messages are easily understood if we are to change attitudes.

ENHANCING SELF-EFFICACY

Perhaps you have not changed the health-related behaviour you thought of earlier because you think it would be too difficult to change. Self-efficacy (SE) is the belief that one has the ability and resources to succeed in achieving a goal despite environmental barriers. Perceived behavioural control and SE are important prerequisites of intention (see Chapter 7). SE promotes intention and performance so consideration of SE enhancement bridges our discussion of changing motivation (this chapter) and behaviour (Chapter 9). SE is important to many areas of health psychology. For example, in Chapter 3 we discussed how secondary appraisals determine our experience of stress. When we believe we can competently manage an environmental demand it becomes a challenge, otherwise it is a stressor. SE can sometimes depend on perceived social support (see Chapter 5), that is, we believe we can competently manage an environmental demand because we know others will help us.

Self-efficacy and performance

SE is correlated with performance across a range of behaviours from academic performance to health-related behaviours (Bandura, 1997). For example, in a meta-analysis (see Research methods 8.1) of 114 studies of SE and work-related performance, Stajkovic and Luthans (1998) found an equivalent effect size of $d = .82$, which corresponds to an increase of 28 per cent in performance due to higher SE. This is an impressive effect size. Such findings recommend SE-enhancing interventions to improve work performance. However, SE varies across behaviours. For example, DiClemente (1986) noted that the correlation between SE for stopping overeating and quitting smoking was small ($r = .21$) (Bandura, 1997), emphasizing that interventions designed to enhance SE need to be behaviour-specific.

While there is little evidence for distinct stages of behaviour change (see Chapter 7), people face different challenges as they progress from action (e.g. jogging for the first time) through to maintenance (e.g. habitually jogging regularly three times a week). Thus SE-enhancing interventions should target challenges relevant to particular target audiences (Abraham, 2008). To facilitate this, different types of SE measures have been defined. For example, Schwarzer (2008) distinguishes between action SE (believing one can succeed in completing a planned behaviour), maintenance SE (believing one can maintain the action over time) and recovery SE (believing one can adopt the behaviour again after a relapse).

Those who believe they can succeed set themselves more challenging goals. They exert more effort, use more flexible problem-solving strategies and are more persistent because they believe they will eventually succeed. By contrast, low SE undermines striving. High SE also minimizes stress (because of favourable secondary appraisals, see Chapter 3), which enhances skilled performance (Bandura, 1997). Moreover, high SE facilitates concentration on the task rather than concerns about personal deficiencies or exaggeration of task demands (Wood and Bandura, 1989) thereby minimizing anxiety during performance. Thus SE affects how people conceptualize a task, how confident they feel during performance, how persistent they are in the face of setbacks, how much effort they invest and how they feel about themselves during performance.

Self-efficacy and health

As well as affecting performance, SE levels affect health directly by moderating the impact of potential stressors on physiological systems. Low SE generates stress, which elicits a variety of physiological responses (see Chapter 2). These include the release of catecholamines into the bloodstream, such as adrenaline and cortisol, from the adrenal gland. This, in turn, increases heart rate, blood pressure, sugar levels and blood flow to large muscle groups. SE changes have been found to be associated with catecholamine activation (Bandura, 1997) providing a plausible mechanism by which SE levels alter the physiological impact of environmental demands on the body. It is unsurprising, therefore, that high SE is associated with less down-regulation of the immune system in response to stressors (Wiedenfeld et al., 1990). It has also been argued that intermittent (as opposed to chronic) stress responses may 'toughen' physiological systems by dampening down stress responses over time (Dienstbier, 1989), i.e. periodic increases in sympathetic nervous system arousal train the body to respond less extremely to subsequent stressors. However, this effect depends on these intermittent stressors being perceived as challenges (rather than threats), which, in turn, depends on high SE in relation to actions required by such stressors.

ACTIVITY 8.3

Identify three television advertisements that illustrate application of evidence-based principles of persuasion.

Enhancing self-efficacy

Bandura (1997, 1999) argues that there are four main approaches to enhancing self-efficacy:

1   mastery experiences;
2   vicarious experience;
3   verbal persuasion; and
4   perception of physiological and affective states.

First, and most powerful, mastery experiences (i.e. experience of successfully performing the behaviour) give people confidence that they can tackle new tasks because they know they have previously succeeded with similar challenges. This recommends that teachers and trainers guide learners towards success by identifying manageable tasks and only increasing difficulty as confidence and skill grow, that is by use of graded tasks (see Figure 8.4). Moreover, helping someone practise a manageable task and providing feedback can consolidate skills and enhance SE. Failure undermines SE and focusing on past failure can be self-handicapping.

FIGURE 8.4 Direct experience of success enhances self-efficacy.

Source: Copyright oliveromg/Shutterstock.com.

Second, SE can also be enhanced through observation of others' success, especially if we categorize the models as being like ourselves. For example, Bandura (1997) notes that observing failure in a model judged to have less skill than ourselves has little or no impact on SE but observing the same failure in a model judged to have similar skills is likely to undermine SE. Health promoters should conduct preliminary research into when positive and negative models are helpful to people establishing new goals, building SE and acquiring new skills. Positive models (that is, observation of successful others) are likely to be SE-enhancing (e.g. in the case of physical fitness), although in some cases, for example when undesirable body image is salient, negative models (that is, use of models failing to establish physical fitness) may be motivating (Lockwood *et al.*, 2005). Moreover, contrasts between current self and desired or ideal self can be motivating, that is, negative self models (i.e. an undesirable self) may have positive effects on changing motivation when combined with realistic goal-setting opportunities (Oettingen, 1996).

Third, when direct experience and modelling are not available, SE can be enhanced through verbal persuasion. People can be persuaded by arguments demonstrating that others (like them) are successful in meeting challenges similar to their own (thereby changing descriptive norms) as well as persuasion highlighting the individual's own skills and past success. Tailoring communication to enhance persuasiveness (as discussed in this chapter), including, for example, maximizing source trustworthiness and expertise is likely to enhance the effectiveness of such interventions.

Finally, our own physiological reactions and our interpretations of these reactions affect SE. Mood, stress and anxiety during performance can bolster or undermine self-efficacy. For example, although arousal is normal during demanding performances, it can be interpreted as a sign of panic or incompetence. Such interpretations are likely to disrupt and undermine performance. By contrast, acknowledging arousal as a natural response to performance demands may add to excitement and commitment. Thus interventions designed to reduce negative moods and anxiety and to reinterpret destructive interpretations of arousal are likely to enhance SE and facilitate skilled performance.

FROM MOTIVATION TO BEHAVIOUR CHANGE

In this chapter we have considered the use of evidence-based techniques to enhance motivation to perform health-related behaviours. In Chapter 7 we noted that motivation alone may not be enough to prompt action. Research on the intention–behaviour gap and implementation intention formation indicates that interventions focusing on post-intentional or volitional processes may be critical to prompting already motivated people to adopt health-promoting behaviours. Thus the challenge for health promoters is to generate the motivation to perform target health behaviours and also to help motivated people develop volitional capacities (e.g. bolstering self-efficacy and prompting implementation intention formation).

In the face of growing health care demands from ageing populations and increasing prevalence of long-term illnesses (see Chapter 10) health services have begun to supplement one-to-one professional–patient models of health care delivery with group and volunteer delivery modes (Whelan, 2002). Such programmes aim to develop health care self-management skills including illness-specific competencies and generic decision-making skills. Evaluations of these interventions have found that they can be both effective in changing behaviour and also cost-effective. For example, Lorig, Mazonson and Holman (1993) found that a self-management course for patients with chronic arthritis resulted in increased self-efficacy, reduced pain and produced a 43 per cent reduction in consultations with doctors. The course was delivered to groups by trained volunteers who were themselves arthritis sufferers. For patients suffering from rheumatoid arthritis, the reduction in health service usage constituted a saving of $162 per patient. Since there are about 386,600 people with rheumatoid arthritis in the UK (Symmons *et al.*, 2002), then, even using 1993 figures with current currency conversion rates, this intervention has the potential to save the UK National Health Service £32 million if it were provided for all sufferers. Other evaluations have identified a variety of health care gains from participation in such group-based self-management training. Barlow *et al.* (2002) reviewed 145 evaluations and concluded that self-management training led to increases in patients' knowledge and SE, better symptom management, adoption of appropriate coping techniques and enhancements in health status. Other studies have found reduced hospitalization (e.g. Lorig *et al.*, 1999a) and enhanced physical and psychological well-being following attendance at such courses (Wright *et al.*, 2003).

Evaluation of health interventions of this kind illustrates one area in which quantitative and qualitative research complement each other (see also Chapter 10). Quantitative research is required to assess effectiveness in terms of predefined criteria from health care usage figures, through to attitudes and quality of life using previously validated measures. However, qualitative research, usually using interviews or focus groups (where a group discusses a series of questions), can examine the perspective of the individual user in detail (Payne, 2004). Here the focus is not on the significance of mean differences but on detailed similarities and differences between users' accounts of the intervention. Such research might, for example, reveal which intervention techniques were especially valued or disliked by users and also highlight the range of individual responses in terms of cognition, emotions and behaviour. This could help intervention designers understand why some users respond positively and others negatively and imply modifications to the delivery or content of an intervention. Qualitative analysis of interview data could also reveal positive or negative experiences not previously considered by researchers and, thereby, imply new theoretical advances and/or new outcomes. For example, an intervention targeting motivation change might be found to work for many people through new social relationships and changes in identity. Researchers regularly judge the methodological adequacy of quantitative studies but this is more challenging in the case of qualitative studies. An interesting guide to judging the quality of qualitative studies relevant to health care has been proposed by Daly *et al.* (2007). For a useful introduction see Payne (2004) and for further details on qualitative theory and methods see Murray and Chamberlain (1999) and Smith (2003).

Influenced by the results of quantitative and qualitative evaluation research, the UK Department of Health began to develop the Expert Patient Programme (EPP) in 2001. This is a generic self-management training intervention designed to empower patients to effectively manage chronic health conditions and associated symptoms (see Chapter 10). The longer-term aim of the EPP was to facilitate patients becoming key decision-makers in the treatment process and gaining greater control over their lives through improved resourcefulness and self-efficacy, as well as reducing health service demand (Department of Health, 2001). EPP was based closely on the previously evaluated Chronic Disease Self-Management Course (Lorig, Gonzalez and Laurent, 1999b; see also Bandura, 1999), which developed from the successful interventions with arthritis patients. EPP was implemented throughout the NHS in 2007.

An EPP course comprises six weekly structured self-management training sessions delivered to groups of 6–15 patients with heterogeneous health conditions, led by trained, lay tutors with chronic health conditions. Patients also receive a self-help manual containing further information. The programme includes information provision and cognitive and behavioural modification techniques as well as prompting action planning and problem solving, providing support for taking exercise and eating a healthy diet as well as coping with depression. Course sessions are held in community settings and tutors are volunteers, thus keeping administration costs low. Early evaluations have been encouraging. Barlow *et al.* (2005) observed a number of benefits including increased SE in managing symptoms, reduced fatigue and depressed moods and better communication with doctors. Moreover, benefits were sustained 12 months after attending an EPP course. A randomized controlled trial found improvements in SE and psychological well-being, together with reduced anxiety and greater levels of physical activity, at six-month follow-up (Kennedy *et al.*, 2007).

SUMMARY

Health-related information needs to be accessible, originate from a credible source, minimize use of jargon, be easily readable and answer the questions the target audience are interested in. Simple techniques including logical order, explicit categorization and repetition enhance recall.

Persuasion is a form of social influence that can be understood in terms of underlying motives. We are motivated to access valid sources of information and this facilitates informational influence. We are also motivated to feel positively about ourselves and to have good relationships with others. This facilitates normative influence. Informational influence is strengthened by source credibility and expertise, consistency and consensus. Normative influence is strengthened by positive relationships, reciprocation and approval. Persuasion in groups can be understood in terms of conformity and conversion (in the case of minority influence). Avoiding prohibition and presenting advice as easy-to-implement choices can minimize reactance.

Attitude change based on systematic (or central route) processing is more stable and less susceptible to counter-persuasion than attitude change following from peripheral route processing. Central route processing is more likely when people are informed, motivated (e.g. they think the message is relevant to them) and have the capacity (e.g. distraction-free time to consider arguments) to process messages. During central route processing the meaning or quality of arguments is critical to persuasion.

Self-efficacy is correlated with performance across a range of behaviours but tends to be behaviour-specific. SE leads to greater effort, persistence and flexible responding. SE needs to correspond directly to the challenges faced by particular individuals or target audiences. SE can be enhanced by mastery experiences, vicarious experience (i.e. modelling), verbal persuasion and perception of physiological and affective states.

KEY CONCEPTS AND TERMS

- Central and peripheral route processing
- Cognitive dissonance
- Cognitive elaboration
- Conformity
- Conversion
- Decision-making heuristic

- Effect size
- Explicit categorization
- Flesch Reading Ease measure
- Graded tasks
- Graphic organizer
- Informational influence

- Mastery experience
- Need for cognition
- Normative influence
- Reactance
- Self-affirmation
- Self-efficacy

SAMPLE ESSAY TITLES

- Information isn't enough: health psychology research provides a new basis for health promotion. Discuss.
- Attempts to persuade people to avoid unhealthy behaviours often fail. How can health promoters persuade people to look after their health more effectively?
- What lessons can health promoters learn from the psychology of attitude change?
- Why is self-efficacy important to health and health-related behaviour?

FURTHER READING

Books

Cialdini, R.B. (1995). Principles and techniques of social influence. In A. Tesser (ed.) *Advanced Social Psychology*. New York: McGraw-Hill, 257–281.

Knowles, E.S. and Rinner, D.D. (2007). Omega approaches to persuasion: Overcoming resistance. In A.R. Pratkanis (ed.) *The Science of Social Influence: Advances and Future Progress*. New York: Psychology Press, 83–114.

Maio, G.R. and Haddock, G. (2015). *The Psychology of Attitudes and Attitude Change* (2nd edn). London: Sage.

Petty, R.E. and Cacioppo, J.T. (1986). The elaboration likelihood model of persuasion. In L. Berkowitz (ed.) *Advances in Experimental Social Psychology*. New York: Academic Press, 19, 123–205.

Journal articles

Bandura, A. (1999). Health promotion from the perspective of social cognitive theory. *Psychology and Health*, 13, 623–650.

Coulter, A., Entwistle, V. and Gilbert, D. (1999). Sharing decisions with patients: Is the information good enough? *British Medical Journal*, 318, 318–322.

9 Changing behaviour

CHAPTER PLAN

Human beings are, above all, adaptable. Climatic and ecological shifts in the Rift Valley in East Africa some 2 million years created natural selection pressures resulting in the evolution of our reprogrammable brains (Maslin and Christensen, 2007; Shultz and Maslin, 2013). Consisting of approximately 86 billion neurons, the human brain has the capacity, over time, to rewrite the regulatory processes that direct our cognitions, emotions and behaviour patterns (Herculano-Houzel, 2009; Doidge, 2007). As we practise new skills, form new relationships and develop new routines we re-programme ourselves so altering what we are able and likely to do in the future. The challenge for psychologists is to model the dynamism of cognitive, emotional and behavioural change (Reynolds and Branscombe, 2015).

In this chapter we consider how an understanding of regulatory processes can help us design and evaluate behaviour change interventions that may promote public health. We will see how experimental testing of precisely defined change techniques combined with systematic intervention design can be combined to create interventions that have the potential to improve everyday health promotion and health care. The chapter is presented in ten sections: (1) behaviour change and public health; (2) a framework for designing behaviour change interventions; (3) regulatory processes operating at different levels; (4) dual process models of intra-personal regulatory processes; (5) information, motivation and behavioural skills; (6) information and threat messages; (7) changing impulsive processes; (8) from specification of change processes to complex interventions; (9) evaluation of behaviour change interventions; and (10) taxonomies of intervention content characteristics and evidence of effectiveness from data syntheses.

LEARNING OUTCOMES

When you have completed this chapter you should be able to:

1 Explain, with examples, how individual behaviour patterns relate to health and public health provision.
2 Outline a scientific approach to designing a behaviour change intervention drawing upon the 'intervention mapping' framework and detailing key intervention features.
3 Describe a series of process or mechanisms that may regulate individual behaviour patterns including intra-personal, interpersonal, organizational and community level processes drawing on the 'social ecological' model.
4 Discuss the role of organizational and community development in health psychology practice.
5 Describe the two regulatory systems characterized by the 'reflective impulsive model'.
6 Articulate key questions that can be answered by elicitation research prior to intervention design, with reference to the 'information, motivation and behavioural skills' model.
7 Describe different types of skills that may be targeted in behaviour change interventions.
8 Discuss when fear appeals may or may not be effective with reference to protection motivation theory and illustrate the importance of carefully designed theory-based materials.
9 Describe a variety of techniques that may be employed to alter impulsive regulatory processes.
10 Illustrate how theoretical specification of regulatory processes facilitates identification of change techniques and how techniques are tailored to target populations and behaviour patterns using the intervention mapping procedures.
11 Discuss the importance of message source, delivery methods, facilitator characteristics and facilitator competences in intervention mapping.
12 Explain what is meant by choice architecture and discuss the implications of effective choice architecture engineering for government policy.
13 Explain the purpose of outcome, process and economic evaluations of interventions.
14 Explain why detailed descriptions of interventions and active control groups are needed and discuss available reporting guidelines, including the RE-AIM model.
15 Apply and critically evaluate taxonomies of characteristics describing behaviour change intervention content.
16 Explain and critically evaluate the use of meta-analyses to identify potentially effective behaviour change intervention content.

BEHAVIOUR CHANGE AND PUBLIC HEALTH

Individual behaviour patterns affect health. Across populations, these patterns shape public health and determine health care costs. For example, rising obesity rates have resulted in increases in type 2 diabetes, coronary heart disease, hypertension, osteoarthritis and some cancers (Allender *et al.,* 2006; Guh *et al.*, 2009; Whitlock *et al.*, 2009). Excess weight increases one's risk of premature death and accounts for at least 2.8 million premature annual deaths worldwide (World Health Organization, 2013). In the UK in 2013, for example, 61 per cent of adults were overweight or obese costing the health services an additional £5 billion annually (Department of Health, 2013). By 2050, rising UK obesity levels may result in increased national health costs of up to £45.5 billion per year (Kushner and Foster, 2000; Butland *et al.*, 2007). Yet the risk of obesity-related health problems can be substantially reduced with weight loss of as little as 5 per cent of body weight (Jensen *et al.*, 2014) and reviews suggest that interventions aiming to generate daily energy deficits can result in clinically meaningful weight loss (of at least 2–3kg) in the short term (Greaves *et al.*, 2011). So how can we intervene to change dietary and physical activity patterns to reduce obesity levels?

In many countries, the age of sexual debut has decreased over time and the range of sexual activities engaged in by young people has increased leaving young people at greater risk of sexually transmitted infections (STIs) and young women at risk of unwanted pregnancies (Mercer *et al.*, 2007). In the US, nearly half of the 19 million new sexually transmitted infections (STIs) are among young people aged 15–24 years (Hamilton, Martin, and Ventura, 2014). While, in the UK in 2012, there were more than 27,800 under-18 conceptions with more than half of these being terminated (The Office for National Statistics, 2014). Many STIs, such as Chlamydia, may not be diagnosed in young people but still affect future health and fertility. So how can we intervene to protect young people from the risk of STIs and unwanted pregnancy?

The examples above are just two global public health challenges calling for behaviour change interventions that could change population-level behaviour patterns.

A FRAMEWORK FOR DESIGNING BEHAVIOUR CHANGE INTERVENTIONS

We know that interventions to support people changing health-related behaviour patterns can be effective. Increases in physical activity and consumption of healthy diets, reductions in risky sexual behaviour and in smoking, improved self-care for chronic conditions and uptake of health screening have all been observed following targeted interventions (Denford *et al.*, 2015; Greaves *et al.*, 2011). For example, the UK's National Institute of Health and Care Excellence (NICE) commissioned a review that included data from 103 systematic reviews of interventions targeting 1 of 6 behaviours (cigarette smoking, alcohol consumption, physical activity, healthy eating, drug use and sexual risk taking). This review found that, although the degree of effectiveness varied between populations and intervention characteristics, overall, interventions were found to be successful in changing behaviour patterns (Jepson *et al.*, 2010 and see also Johnson *et al.*, 2003).

Producing effective interventions depends on careful, systematic design. A number of useful frameworks have been developed to support intervention design (e.g. Craig *et al.*, 2008; Centres for Disease Control and Prevention, 2012). In this chapter we focus on the intervention mapping approach (IM) (Bartholomew *et al.*, 2011; www. interventionmapping.com) because it provides a comprehensive and practical guide to optimal design and evaluation procedures.

Table 9.1 lists 12 broadly defined characteristics of any behaviour change intervention. This list is adapted from a similar table presented by Davidson *et al.* (2003) and provides a useful checklist for intervention designers. The characteristics are listed in the order they are usually considered in the IM process. Consideration of these characteristics clarifies at a glance why planning stages in intervention design must be inter-linked and iterative. For example, if those who need to deliver the intervention do not have the skills to do so or if the proposed delivery methods are unacceptable in the intended setting, then a rethink of the planning process is needed. Similarly, an evidence-based intervention that cannot be sustained in context over time due to a lack of resources will not have ongoing real-world impact and so is unlikely to contribute to public health improvement (Glasgow *et al.*, 2002). Without anticipation of implementation in early planning, interventions may not be adopted or may be partially delivered and so be ineffective.

Figure 9.1 summarizes the six design stages constituting IM and is derived from a more detailed model presented by Bartholomew and colleagues. First a needs assessment determines what (if anything) needs to be changed for whom. Second, primary and secondary intervention objectives are defined. This involves specifying precisely the behaviour changes participants will be expected to make (1 in Table 9.1). Third, identification of underlying regulatory processes or mechanisms that maintain current

TABLE 9.1 12 broad characteristics of behaviour change interventions

1	Specific behaviour change/s targeted
2	Modifiable processes (or mechanisms) operating at different levels that regulate relevant behaviour patterns
3	Change techniques known to alter identified regulatory process/mechanisms
4	The delivery methods or formats used (e.g. face-to-face meetings, telephone calls, interactive online programmes, leaflet distribution, etc.)
5	Intervention components, that is, the collection of materials and methods employed
6	The setting in which the intervention will be delivered (e.g. worksite, school, etc.)
7	The fit between intervention components and the cultural and practical context in which it will be used
8	Characteristics, qualifications and training of those delivering the intervention (e.g. relationship to recipients, skill bases, etc.)
9	Intensity (e.g. contact time in each session)
10	Duration (e.g. number of sessions and overall period of intervention)
11	Fidelity of delivery (e.g. were lessons/meetings delivered as designed)
12	Evaluation, including outcome, process and economic evaluations

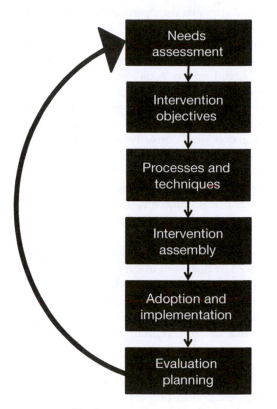

FIGURE 9.1 The intervention mapping approach to behaviour change intervention design.

Source: Bartholomew *et al.*, 2011.

(unwanted) behaviour patterns and/or are capable of generating new (wanted) behaviour patterns are identified. This allows identification of change techniques that have been found to alter those identified regulatory processes (2–4 in Table 9.1). Fourth, having identified evidence-based techniques relevant to the intervention's behaviour change objectives, practical ways of delivering these techniques are developed and assembly of the intervention can begin (4–7 in Table 9.1). Fifth, implementation planning involves anticipating how the intervention will be used or delivered in everyday contexts (7–11 in Table 9.1). For example, is the intervention attractive, acceptable, practical and sustainable? The final stage is evaluation (11 and 12 in Table 9.1). Does the intervention change the specified behaviours in context? Tortolero *et al.* (2005) and Lloyd, Wyatt and Creanor (2012) describe how the intervention mapping approach can facilitate systematic intervention design and planning.

A needs assessment involves identifying the health problem and behaviour patterns exacerbating that problem. This usually involves consulting or undertaking literature reviews and holding discussions with stakeholders. In some cases a needs assessment may reveal that intervention is not necessary or feasible, that dissemination of best practice/usual care is the optimal response. A thorough needs assessment can avoid wasting time and resources on unnecessary or ineffectual intervention development.

Defining intervention objectives in stage 2 depends on a precise definition of the behaviour changes required. These vary across interventions but, for example, in a sexual health intervention, the design group might consider a series of behaviours that facilitate successful condom use. For example, discussing condom use with a potential partner, acquiring condoms (which may depend on price and accessibility), storing and carrying condoms, negotiating condom use in intimate interactions and correct use of condoms. This could generate a series of interventions targeting, for example, accessibility and price, knowledge of correct use, attitudes towards carrying condoms, normative beliefs about carrying and using condoms correctly and skills in sexual negotiation and condom handling.

We will illustrate stage 3 of the IM process in more detail later below when we discuss regulatory processes and the selection of corresponding change techniques. This stage must be informed by anticipation of practical constraints that are the focus of stage 4 when selected change techniques are embedded in practical components and materials that constitute the intervention.

In the fifth stage of IM, implementation planning takes place. This involves anticipating how the intervention will be used or delivered in everyday contexts. For example, what are the motivations, skills and resources of those who will deliver the intervention? Will the recipients like the intervention and be able to engage with it? Will those meant to deliver the intervention be able to do so? Once developed, interventions should be piloted to ensure that the intervention is acceptable to the target population. Co-creation with recipients and those who will deliver the intervention not only facilitates ownership of the intervention, but can highlight practical challenges that need to be overcome during the design phases. For example, in creating the Healthy Lifestyles Programme (HeLP), designed to prevent weight gain among school children (Wyatt *et al.*, 2013), the designers held regular discussions with key stakeholders, including children, teachers and parents. This ensured that the choice of change techniques and delivery modes were engaging and sustainable. The final intervention involved a combination of different approaches including drama workshops in which children interact with and advise characters such as 'Snacky Sam' and 'Active Amy'. This important design feature might not have been included had the designers not been closely involved with schools during stage 5.

The final stage is evaluation, which we will also consider in further detail below. Although listed last, it is critical to anticipate evaluation from the outset. For example, when the desired behaviour changes are defined in stage 2, designers can address the challenge of measuring those changes to determine whether or not the intervention has been effective. For example, how should we measure normative beliefs about condom carrying and use (see Chapter 7). Similarly, in stage 3, when modifiable regulatory processes and change techniques capable of altering them are identified, measures of process/mechanism change need to be considered.

REGULATORY PROCESSES OPERATING AT DIFFERENT LEVELS

Specifying the target behaviour(s) in stage 2 of intervention mapping is important. For example, if we wish to increase physical activity to prevent obesity, we would need to consider which activities, how many times a week, for what duration and at what intensity by whom will make a difference to health. An intervention will only contribute to public health if the behaviour changes are sufficient to improve individuals' health prospects and are maintained over time. It is equally important to be clear about *who* an intervention will target. For example, an intervention designed to reduce unwanted teenage pregnancies is unlikely to be optimally effective if it targets all teenagers because most are not at risk of unwanted pregnancy. Subgroups of people differ in their cultural backgrounds, their knowledge, motivation and skills. So imprecise targeting may result in mismatched and ineffective interventions.

The scientific design of any intervention begins with an understanding of the processes or mechanisms that regulate the system (or systems) we hope to change. To create a new antibiotic biochemists must first understand and map interactions between organic molecules and bacteria. Similarly, psychologists need to understand the processes that regulate behaviour. In previous chapters we have reviewed individual, intra-personal processes that distinguish between people's behaviour patterns, including processes that result in greater or lesser intention or motivation (see Chapters 7 and 8). In addition to these processes, behaviour patterns and behaviour change may be regulated by inter-personal (between-people) and inter-group processes. For example, Haslam *et al.* (2014) studied residents of care homes and compared three conditions, in which (1) residents formed groups to redesign the home environment; (2) care staff redesigned the home environment for the residents; and (3) there was no change. These researchers found that people in the residents-redesign condition had significantly greater, clinically important increases in cognitive functioning and also increased use of resident lounges (compared to the other two conditions), indicating that involvement in the redesign group changed residents' thinking and behaviour. In this example, group and organizational processes, rather than intra-personal processes, such as attitudes towards socializing with other residents seem to be critical to intervention effectiveness (see too Tarrant, Hagger and Farrow, 2011).

Organizational rules, norms and resources may create stress (see Chapter 4) and impede health behaviour change. They are, therefore, often targeted both in community interventions and in single-organization worksite interventions. Worksite interventions may aim to integrate physical activity into employees' days including exercise breaks and promotion of walking and stair use or change the availability of healthy food and/or how food is labelled (Engbers *et al.*, 2005). Worksite interventions have been found to be effective in increasing physical activity and fitness as well as promoting weight loss (Proper *et al.*, 2003). Those focusing exclusively on physical activity (as opposed to general lifestyle changes) and especially those promoting walking appear to be most effective in promoting employee fitness (Abraham and Graham-Rowe, 2009; see also Taylor, Conner and Lawton, 2012).

Lack of resources, lack of skills and social norms at community level can also sustain health-risk behaviours. Consequently, interventions to promote health behaviours may need to be based in, and engage, communities. This often necessitates meetings and discussion with local people and organizations. It may also entail persuading local government to change policies, enforce existing legislation or provide new resources. In addition, such interventions may utilize local media campaigns and educational programmes. This work merges health psychology practice with community development work. Community development seeks to involve local people in identifying local assets and needs and facilitating action to create or acquire new resources and/or skills.

It is based on choice and participation and aims to extend opportunities and social justice for participants (Durie and Wyatt, 2007).

Community interventions to promote health-related behaviour patterns may target particular health-promoting or illness-management behaviours. By contrast, comprehensive interventions may target a range of health-related behaviour patterns. For example, the North Karelia Project, which began in Finland in 1972 included education on smoking, diet and hypertension using widely distributed leaflets, radio and television slots and education in local organizations. Voluntary sector organizations, schools and health and social services were involved and training was provided for personnel in various contexts. The intervention included education of school students about the health risks of smoking and the social influences that lead young people to begin smoking, as well as training for students in how to resist such social influences. This comprehensive intervention was found to be effective in changing a series of outcome measures including smoking reduction and serum cholesterol levels. For example, 15 years later, smoking prevalence was 11 per cent lower among intervention participants compared to controls (Vartiainen *et al.*, 1998).

In a review of evaluations of comprehensive community interventions (including the North Karelia Project), Hingson and Howland (2002) found that greater effectiveness was observed when interventions (1) targeted behaviours with immediate health consequences such as alcohol misuse or sexual risk taking; (2) targeted young people to prevent uptake of health-risk behaviours; (3) combined environmental and institutional policy change with theory-based behaviour change interventions; and (4) involved communities themselves in intervention design.

We considered the important role that social support plays in moderating stress (in Chapter 5). Social support can be crucial to behaviour change. Motivation to change can be undermined if changes are disapproved of, or resisted, by valued others, including family members or opinion leaders. Consequently, additional social support can enhance the effectiveness of interventions both in initiating and maintaining behaviour change. For example, planning how barriers to change may be overcome or the signing of behavioural contracts are change techniques facilitated by interpersonal interaction. Moreover, community and worksite interventions (such as the Expert Patient intervention we considered in Chapter 8) can provide social support by establishing buddy systems or support groups in which two or more people work together to support initiation and/or maintenance of behaviour change. Establishing how interpersonal processes influence a target behaviour and assessing skills in managing relevant social interactions and available social support is important when designing such interventions.

Societal structures and processes also regulate our behaviour patterns. We saw in Chapter 4 how relative poverty arising from the distribution of wealth within a country can affect health (Whitehead and Dahlgren, 1991). The management of taxation and benefit systems have large effects on health and longevity within countries (Wilkinson, 1996) but such change requires action by legislators. So, in certain cases, effective health promotion necessitates lobbying politicians and legislators and presenting the results of research to decision-makers in government (e.g. Schaalma *et al.*, 2004). Legislative change can have far-reaching and immediate effects on health. For example, in the UK in 2007, smoking in public places was banned and it became illegal to sell tobacco to people below the age of 18 years. Evaluating a similar legislative change, Sargent,

Shepard and Glantz (2004) found that myocardial infarction admissions to a hospital in Montana, USA fell significantly over 6 months during a smoking ban in public places, while at the same time, surrounding areas (without a smoking ban) experienced non-significant increases. In some cases, international legislation may be necessary. For example, while taxation can be effective in reducing smoking, raising the price of cigarettes in one country might have limited impact if it encouraged cigarette smuggling from neighbouring countries in which cigarettes were cheaper.

The 'social ecological' model (Bartholomew *et al.*, 2011) presented in Figure 9.2 illustrates different levels at which processes that regulate behaviour patterns can operate. The model reminds us that individual behaviour patterns can only be adequately understood by also taking account of the interpersonal, organizational, cultural, economic and legislative contexts in which that behaviour develops and is maintained. Acknowledging this point, in this chapter we will focus primarily on interventions targeting intra-personal processes to bring about individual change. This simplified approach will allow us to illustrate principles of intervention design and evaluation that are generalizable across other levels highlighted by the 'social ecological' model.

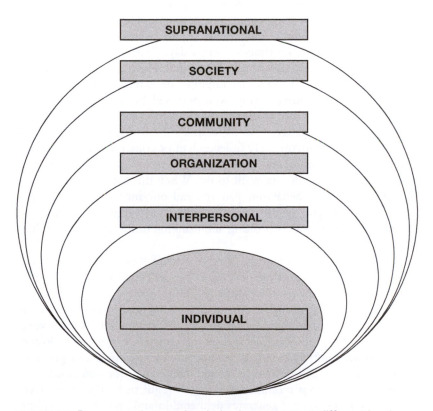

FIGURE 9.2 Processes that regulate behaviour operate at different levels.

Source: Adapted from Bartholomew *et al.* (2011).

DUAL PROCESS MODELS OF INTRA-PERSONAL REGULATORY PROCESSES

Our understanding of intra-personal behavioural regulation is best conceptualized in terms of two separate but interacting systems of regulatory processes. A series of 'dual-process' models have characterized these two systems (Borland, 2014; Kahneman, 2011; Strack and Deutsch, 2004). One system regulates conscious, deliberative control of action while the other operates automatic action involving low levels of conscious awareness and monitoring. The same behavioural sequence may involve one or both systems in different contexts. Consider, for example, leaving your home and locking the outer door. If you have lived in the same place for a while you may do this while thinking of other things. The behavioural sequence can be initiated and completed automatically with little conscious monitoring and consequently may be difficult or impossible to remember later. Of course, you are conscious while locking the door and so can engage in conscious control. For example, if, while you are leaving, a friend says, 'Don't forget to lock the door and take your key', then you may more carefully monitor your actions and make changes to your usual routine such as checking the door a second time. Such activation of conscious control facilitates change in routine or automatic behaviour patterns and enhances action recall.

Many of the behaviour patterns that affect our health can be enacted in an automatic manner. These include 'addictions', such as smoking, as well as many 'habitual' behaviour patterns, including eating, physical activity and computer use. For example, we may eat and drink many times during a day. Each one of these action sequences is unlikely to be carefully consciously monitored. Having another spoonful or another drink can be initiated by internal impulses or external cues with little conscious deliberation or monitoring. Many well-practised behavioural sequences are controlled automatically with low levels of conscious monitoring. The problem with such 'mindless' behaviour patterns (see Wansink's 2006 discussion of 'mindless eating') is they can become increasingly independent of conscious control, being prompted by well-learnt environmental cues. This can result in us doing things repeatedly that, on reflection, we do not want to do. When this happens we experience a lack of control over our behaviour patterns and our motivation no longer predicts our actions. For example, a person may be highly motivated to consume less calories but, nonetheless, find themselves eating and drinking more calories than they inteded to.

An important advance in conceptualizing these two regulatory systems was made by Strack and Deutsch (2004) when they developed the reflective impulsive model (RIM). This model has been elaborated by Borland (2014) as the context, executive and operational systems (CEOS) model. Both models highlight the operation of an automatic system referred to as the 'impulsive' (RIM) or 'operational' (CEOS) system. Both models describe how progressive activation of associative neuronal clusters linking perceptions, reward anticipation and learned motor responses can generate automatic behaviour. Both models describe a second deliberative (or conscious control) system that enables conscious monitoring of action regulation. This 'reflective' (RIM) or 'executive' (CEOS) system generates deliberation and reasoning including conscious attitudes and normative beliefs, feasibility assessments (resulting in greater or lesser self-efficacy), goals and intentions to undertake and prioritise actions (see

Chapters 7 and 8). We considered a similar dual system distinction in Chapter 8 when we discussed the ELM. In the ELM, systematic or central route processing involves reflective cognitive elaboration while peripheral route processing involves automatic processing which may occur with little conscious monitoring.

Borland's CEOS model provides new insights into the way in which the two systems interact to generate emotions. Here, however, we will use the original RIM terms and focus on what the RIM and CEOS have in common. The two systems operate in parallel on a moment-to-moment basis with the reflective system responding to aspects of impulsive functioning. For example, when people talk about 'urges' and 'cravings' they are referring to the reflective system's conscious awareness of the impulsive system regulating perceptions and action initiation processes. This is important because awareness of such 'urges' is critical to regaining control of impulsive behaviour patterns by deploying the reflective system to realign intentions and action sequences.

Understanding interactions between these two systems is foundational to the development of effective behaviour change interventions. Just as a friend's reminder can prompt monitoring of locking a door, so a food diary that is completed each time a person eats or drinks can change the regulation of eating and drinking. Deliberately monitoring and recording a particular set of actions reduces mindless or impulsive initiation and regulation. Using self-monitoring in this way illustrates how a change technique can be selected through our understanding of underpinning regulatory processes (Abraham and Michie, 2008; Michie et al., 2009). The use of conscious control to self-monitor is, however, taxing. By exerting conscious control over one set of actions we may reduce the reflective system's capacity to consciously regulate other action sequences (Baumeister, 2002). So while activation of the reflective system is critical to behaviour change, reliance on its capacity to override the impulsive system may be unsustainable. Sustainable behaviour change involves practice in context so that new behavioural routines become automatic and can be initiated and completed with little reflective control. Thus behaviour change involves both breaking unwanted habits and making new ones (Dean, 2013).

INFORMATION, MOTIVATION AND BEHAVIOURAL SKILLS

The information, motivation, behavioural skills (IMB) model (Fisher and Fisher, 1992 see Figure 9.3) provides a useful and well-tested model for designing individual-level behaviour change interventions targeting reflective regulatory processes. The model proposes that changes in the operation of the reflective system occur when individuals are well informed, highly motivated and have the skills necessary to perform a desired behaviour. Consequently, intervention designers should assess which informational, motivational or skill antecedents are lacking in a target population and target these in interventions designed to behaviour patterns within that population. This framework can be applied as designers work through the intervention mapping process.

Provision of information may be critical when motivated, skilled people lack an understanding of their behaviour or its consequences. For example, to lose weight, individuals may benefit from information about the number of calories in everyday foods and drinks and the amount and type of exercise needed to burn off the calories consumed

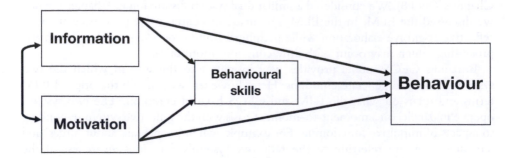

FIGURE 9.3 The information-motivation-behavioural skills (IMB) model.

Source: From Fisher and Fisher (1992). Copyright © 1992 by the American Psychological Association. Reprinted with permission.

so that they can develop everyday skills to create energy deficits (see Chapter 8 for a discussion about how to provide information effectively). Similarly, if people are not aware that their behaviour patterns may lead to long-term illness then providing such information allows people to choose to change their behaviour. For example, if a group of parents are not aware that children playing in the sun without sun protection may cause long-term skin cancer, providing this information is the first step in enabling change.

Some target audiences are well informed but, nonetheless, not motivated to change. In such cases, techniques known to change determinants of motivation can be employed. Determinants of motivation are described by a variety of models (as discussed in Chapter 7 e.g. the theory of planned behaviour). Combining key features of a number of social cognition models Fishbein and colleagues (2001) proposed that motivation is influenced by:

(a) an individual's beliefs about the advantages of changing their behaviour outweighing the disadvantages;
(b) the anticipation that changing behaviour will lead to a positive emotional reaction;
(c) the belief that others will approve of the proposed change;
(d) the belief that the behaviour change is consistent with the person's self-image or identity; and finally
(e) that the person feels capable of changing their behaviour, that is they have high self-efficacy.

Having established that the target audience is well informed or having decided how to provide appropriate information, assessing each of these five determinants of motivation can help identify any deficits in motivation. Once such deficits are identified then change techniques known to boost particular determinants of motivation can be selected. Early identification of population or subgroup deficits in this way has been referred to as elicitation research because it identifies the psychological targets, which, if changed, are most likely to result in behaviour change. Elicitation research forms part of stage 2 of the intervention mapping process.

Self-efficacy (see Chapter 8) is a key element of motivation but also a foundation for the development of behavioural skills. We do not usually continue to exert effort on unattainable goals. People who believe they can succeed (i.e. have high self-efficacy) set themselves more challenging goals, exert more effort, use more flexible problem-solving strategies and are more persistent (Bandura, 1997). The four techniques Bandura (1997) proposed as methods of enhancing self-efficacy (see Chapter 8) can be employed when elicitation research reveals that self-efficacy is low.

Well-informed, motivated individuals with high self-efficacy can fail to change their behaviour patterns because they lack the skills to undertake action sequences or to re-establish reflective control over impulsively regulated behaviour patterns. In such cases, information provision and motivation-building techniques are unlikely to lead to behaviour change. Sustained weight management, for example, may necessitate learning new cooking or exercising skills and skills to manage social situations that involve food (e.g. refusing a slice of cake a friend has baked or avoiding Saturday night takeaways with friends). The development of behavioural skills involves instruction and sometimes modelling, practice, receiving feedback on performance and where necessary further instruction and practice. This skill-development process ensures proficiency of execution and enhances self-efficacy.

Three broad classes of skills can be defined. First, self-regulatory skills. Control theory provides a useful way of thinking about self-regulation (Carver and Scheier, 1982). At its simplest the theory proposes that individuals' behaviour is goal directed: we set goals, assess how close (or far away) we are from attaining the goal, take action to get closer to the goal, monitor progress and again take action to bring reality closer to our goal. Control theory is based on a more general model of intelligent system operation, the test-operate-test-exit model (Miller, Galanter and Pribam, 1960), which proposes that systems test whether current stimuli (e.g. our perceptions) match a set standard (e.g. our goal) and, if the two are not matched, operate to bring stimuli in line with the set standard, before retesting. This feedback loop continues until the test shows that the stimuli matches the set standard (that is, we perceive ourselves to have attained the goal), at which point the system exits from the activity loop. So returning to self-efficacy, if the test indicates that the goal is unattainable then we may 'exit' from goal striving at an early stage. The test-operate-test-exit model and control theory provide a useful way of thinking about goal striving and the process by which we attain new skills, including self-regulatory skills.

A series of cognitive skills can be assessed and, where needed, taught to enhance self-regulation. For example, we can help people to (a) consider longer-term consequences of current action patterns; (b) set attainable goals; (c) self-monitor their behaviour; (d) evaluate their current behaviour against their goals; (e) set new goals in light of the feedback from self-monitoring; (f) prioritize goals in the face of other demands; (g) plan action before and during goal-relevant experiences; and (h) prompt exertion of appropriate effort when opportunities present themselves.

We can teach people to set SMART goals (Doran, 1981). The acronym stands for *Specific* (that is, specifying particular actions in particular contexts); *Measurable* (that is, we can test whether the goal has been attained); *Assignable* (that is, we know who will take action – although the 'A' is also sometimes used to stand for 'attainable' when it is already clear who needs to take action); *Realistic* (that is, the goal is attainable within the person's developing skill set and their environment); and *Time-specified* (that is, we know when or by what date action will be taken). A key part of realistic goal setting is beginning with easier tasks and only moving to more challenging goals as these are attained.

New motor skills constitute a second class of skills, which may be involved in adopting health-related behaviours. For example, before using a gym, people need to be taught to use exercise machines. Similarly, certain medication regimes necessitating using devices such as inhalers or needles that patients may need to be taught how to use (see Kools, 2012 for a discussion of how to provide such instruction in text). Even apparently simple skills such as hand washing, to avoid infection, may need special instruction to ensure competence (Pittet, 2002; Pittet *et al.*, 2000). Thus analysis of any health behaviour targeted in an intervention should involve an assessment of the motor skills required and the extent to which the targeted recipients are proficient or lacking in these skills. Of course, technological advances can make the skills involved in health behaviours easier to learn. Extra-fine needles make it easier for diabetics to inject themselves, alcohol wipes make hand washing easier and the development of a once-a-day single pill for HIV control makes adherence much easier than if patients have to take 36 pills a day! Sometimes skill deficits reveal an important role for organisational or technological change in supporting behaviour change.

Finally, we also require social skills to negotiate change in behaviour patterns with others and seek their support. For example, the skills to negotiate condom use with a reluctant partner or the skills to explain why we will not take part in alcohol drinking games or buying rounds of drinks, or eat traditional (but unhealthy) foods. These social skills required are likely to be determined largely by the target behaviour and the social resources available to individuals planning change. However, assertiveness training (that is, being able to express one's own wants and needs in an honest and non-aggressive manner) and negotiation skills are often prerequisite to managing interactions, which arise when individuals begin to change their behaviour patterns. Other useful techniques include role play, especially with modelling and video feedback, and live filming followed by video feedback and praise for interactions that demonstrate desired skills. This approach to skills development is exemplified in the practice of Video Interaction Guidance (Kennedy, Landor and Todd, 2011).

A number of successful behaviour change interventions have been based on the IMB, particularly in relation to HIV-preventive behaviour (e.g. Fisher *et al.*, 1994) and some of these have been evaluated using longer-term follow up (e.g. at 12 months in the case of Fisher *et al.*, 2002). Focus 9.1 provides an illustration of an IMB-based intervention. The IMB model is useful because it highlights the need to assess behaviour-relevant deficits among the target group prior to intervention design (stage 1 of intervention mapping) and provides a framework for defining the intervention objectives (stage 2), identifying key regulatory processes and, thereby, candidate change techniques that may be crucial to intervention effectiveness (stage 3). The model proposes that behaviour change intervention designers need to discover whether the (precisely defined) target group lack any behaviour-relevant information, whether the key determinants of motivation are in place among this target group and whether the target group lack any skills required to translate motivation into behaviour.

FOCUS 9.1

An information, motivation and behavioural skills intervention

In an intervention designed to reduce the risk of HIV infection, Fisher *et al.* (1994) included intervention components to address deficits in information, motivation and behavioural skills identified in previous elicitation research among US college students. Some of the targets they identified and the methods they used to achieve them are considered below.

Information component

A slide show followed by a large group discussion presented and consolidated information on HIV transmission and prevention, including the risk from different sexual behaviours, the effectiveness of condoms, where to buy condoms near campus, safer sex decision-making rules, HIV testing and facts and myths about HIV/AIDS.

Motivation component

Small group discussions led by a peer educator were followed by large group discussions led by a professional health educator. These incorporated a video narrated by people who were HIV positive. This was designed to provide persuasive arguments targeting key cognitions including perceptions of personal susceptibility to HIV and attitudes and subjective norms relating to condom use. Which of the five components in Fishbein's model of motivational determinants were targeted here?

Behavioural skills component

Negotiation self-efficacy was enhanced using peer-led role plays demonstrating safer sex communication. Students were encouraged by educators to practise safer sexual behaviours (e.g. condom handling skills and negotiation role playing) at home. Perceived effectiveness of condom use and self-efficacy in relation to condom use were bolstered by using a video in which peers modelled correct handling and use. In addition, group discussions were used to identify potential problems and reinforce newly learned negotiation skills.

When you finish reading this chapter return to this focus box and think about other change techniques that could have been included in an intervention of this kind.

PROVIDING INFORMATION AND USING FEAR APPEALS

Not all health promotion interventions, whether they are simple leaflets or more complex programmes, are developed using the intervention mapping approach. This can lead to mismatches between population needs and the content of interventions.

Abraham *et al.* (2002) surveyed widely available leaflets promoting condom use in the UK and Germany (gathering leaflets from general practitioners' surgeries, clinics for the treatment of sexually transmitted infections and from the largest publishers of such materials). The authors conducted a content analysis of the leaflets. This involved reading and re-reading the leaflets in order to identify distinct messages appearing across leaflet texts. Clearly defined, non-overlapping categories of message were defined and checked to see whether they comprehensively reflect the content of the leaflets. These category definitions were tested to see whether independent readers could assign the same message to the same category across leaflets (that is whether they could be used reliably). Such a set of text-derived categories can be reliably used to comprehensively describe the content of texts (in this case leaflets) and distinguish between the content of different texts can allow identification of intervention content that is or is not evidence based. Evidence-based messages (or more generally intervention components) can then be recommended for inclusion in subsequent interventions. This 'content analysis approach to theory-specified persuasive educational communication' has been used subsequently to improve the content of leaflets used in public health campaigns (e.g. Lake *et al.*, 2015; see Holsti, 1969 and Weber, 1990 for further guidance on content analyses of text).

These analyses found few differences in content between UK and German leaflets. In general, leaflets devoted most content to providing information on the transmission of sexually transmitted infections (STIs), people's risks of acquiring STIs, the effectiveness of condom use and on encouraging professional contact. This was disappointing because the apparent change targets of these leaflets, for example, knowledge and perceived susceptibility are not the strongest determinants of condom use. Sheeran *et al.* (1999) report average weighted correlations with condom use of 0.06 for both measures of knowledge and perceived susceptibility. Even perceived condom effectiveness was found to have an average correlation of only 0.10 with condom use. Thus the cognitions targeted most frequently by the majority of these leaflets were not those found to be those most strongly associated with condom use. By contrast, cognitions found to be stronger correlates of condom use such as those specified by the theory of planned behaviour were targeted less frequently by the leaflets (see Figure 9.4). The researchers identified 20 core messages that corresponded to the cognitive determinants significantly associated with condom use in previous studies. Seventy-five per cent of leaflets included less than half of these determinant-matched messages. However, a small number of illustrative leaflets were identified that included between 15 and 18 of the 20 core messages, demonstrating that safer sex promotion leaflets can include a range of messages matched to the cognitive determinants of condom use.

This study (and see too Abraham *et al.*, 2007) emphasizes two points. First, careful content analyses of intervention content can help identify change techniques (in this case messages included in text) that are more or less well matched to the findings of previous elicitation research. This is important in stages 2 and 3 of the intervention

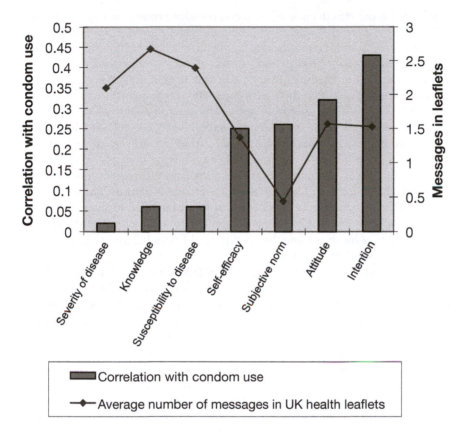

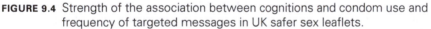

FIGURE 9.4 Strength of the association between cognitions and condom use and frequency of targeted messages in UK safer sex leaflets.

Source: From Abraham *et al.*, 2002. © British Psychological Society. Reproduced with permission from Wiley.

mapping process. Second, that interventions (in this case leaflets) designed on the basis of assumptions about what kind of intervention is required without adequate elicitation research may not identify change targets likely to optimize behaviour change. Many designers of condom-promotion leaflets appear to have assumed that the key deficit in the target population was information. Their 'logic models' explaining the theories of change implicit in these interventions were that being informed of one's susceptibility to a threat (STIs) would motivate condom use and that the skills necessary to use condoms were already in existence. Previous research had suggested that this was not the case. So many of these leaflets were not evidence-based and were not developed in a manner that optimized their behaviour change impact.

Public health campaigns frequently use messages that highlight health risk or threat and recommend protective action. Unfortunately, perceived threat does not always prompt behaviour change so fear appeals may be ineffective (e.g. Albarracín *et al.*, 2005). Protection motivation theory (PMT) (see Chapter 7) implies that fear appeals should incorporate threat and efficacy messages emphasizing perceived susceptibility and severity as well as the effectiveness of the recommended protection and self-efficacy enhancement (see Chapter 8). Collectively, these messages should prompt protective intentions. Such threat–inducing messages can enhance systematic processing of subsequent messages (as might be expected because of enhanced personal relevance – see ELM in Chapter 8). For example, Das, de Wit and Stroebe (2003) found that fear appeals generated favourable cognitive responses and consequent attitude change *if* participants felt susceptible to the threat (see too Witte and Allen, 2000). The way such warnings are presented, that is, the delivery method (see Table 9.1) also determines their effectiveness. A meta-analysis by Noar *et al.* (2015) (see Research methods 8.1 in Chapter 8) found that 12 of 17 experimental tests showed that fear appeals using pictures on cigarette packets generated greater change than warnings without pictures. Pictorial warnings held attention for longer, led to stronger cognitive and emotional responses and elicited more negative attitudes towards smoking and stronger intentions to avoid or quit smoking. Focus 9.2 presents different approaches to pictorial warnings for smokers. When you finish reading this section read Focus 9.2 and reflect on how we can best persuade smokers to quit.

Fear appeals may also fail to persuade. Two types of failure have been identified. First, if people are not persuaded that the threat is relevant to them this may undermine subsequent intervention and even threaten attitudes towards the recommended preventive action ('if the threat is not personally relevant why bother to take precautions?'). Second, if people do not believe they can protect themselves (i.e. they have low self-efficacy) they tend to protect themselves psychologically through defensive cognitive responses (see Chapter 8 on reactance and Chapter 5 on coping). When defensive processing (sometimes called fear control) occurs, then recipients may dismiss the message as untrustworthy – rejecting it altogether – or rejecting its relevance to them (Ruiter, Abraham and Kok, 2001). Whether threat-based messages prompt intention formation (as protection motivation theory would suggest) or result in undesirable defensive processing depends on the relationship between the perceived threat and efficacy information. When self-efficacy and the perceived effectiveness of the behaviour change to prevent negative consequences are more salient than perceived threat (e.g. 'I know I can do what I need to do to protect myself against the threat') then positive (danger control) motivational and behavioural change are likely. However, when self-efficacy is weak ('it's a threat I cannot manage') then coping is likely to be defensive (see Chapter 3). Thus fear appeals need to incorporate strong and persuasive threat information (to affect message processing) as well as strong self-efficacy and response efficacy messages (suggesting that behaviour change is feasible and effective against the threat) to be effective (Witte, 1992; Witte and Allen, 2000). Note too that the framing of risk awareness messages may also be crucial (see Chapter 8).

One approach to reducing the likelihood that threat messages will encourage defensive processing is to affirm valued images of the self before a threat message is presented. Self-affirmation (discussed in Chapter 8) reduces the need to defend the self against threat. One might prompt message recipients to think about positive aspects of themselves before receiving threat information. Affirmed participants have been found to be more convinced by threat information and more willing to accept risk or severity of threat (Steele, 1988). For example, in a study conducted by Harris and Napper (2005) male participants in a self-affirmation condition wrote about their most important value, why it was important and how it affected their everyday lives.

FOCUS 9.2

Promoting smoking cessation

The illustrations below are typical of those used in many anti-smoking campaigns (including those used on cigarette packets). How do these materials correspond to protection motivation theory specifications?

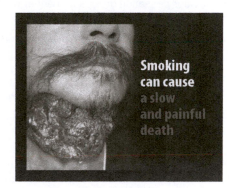

Most smokers want to give up and have tried to quit so motivation is not usually the main barrier to behaviour change. Instead, most smokers feel low self-efficacy in relation to quitting. The materials shown above do not bolster smokers' self-efficacy so smokers may dismiss them. Compare these to the 'Get unhooked' campaign below. This appeal offered smokers help by first acknowledging how painful and unpleasant quitting might be because of their addiction. Given what you know about fear appeals and smoking, which approach would you invest in pre-testing?

Smoking cessation also illustrates the biopsychosocial nature of health-related behaviour. Evidence suggests that participation in smoking cessation groups, which employ verbal persuasion as well as teaching self-regulatory skills, increases the chances of successful quitting and abstinence over six months. Moreover, because of the nicotine-based dependency helping maintain smoking, use of nicotine replacement therapy Zyban (Bupropion hydrochloride, which dampens appetite) is also effective. However, the most effective treatment is the combination of behaviour cessation groups and either nicotine replacement therapy or Zyban. This combination increases successful 6-month abstinence rates fourfold over that observed without help (West, McNeill and Raw, 2000). Thus by taking account of a variety of key cognitive determinants, important self-regulatory and social skills and critical biochemical processes a package of intervention components can be combined to tackle even complex and difficult-to-change behaviours.

Participants engaging in health–risk alcohol consumption who had been affirmed in this way reported greater ease of imagining developing breast cancer and higher perceptions of personal risk, suggesting that self-affirmation facilitated acceptance of personal risk (by reducing defensive processing). These high–risk, self-affirmed participants were found to have greater intentions to reduce their alcohol consumption at the 4–week follow up, compared to controls. Thus self-affirmation can change the way in which people process threat messages (Good and Abraham, 2011). In a very similar way, it appears that by enhancing self-efficacy before presenting threat information can also facilitate acceptance of threatening messages (Floyd *et al.*, 2000).

Two points emerge from our consideration of fear appeals. First, one cannot assume that raising people's awareness of a health threat will promote protective motivation. There may be more important determinants of the targeted behavioural change. Second, and more generally, messages based on particular mechanisms of change (such as those specified by PMT) need to be carefully designed to correspond to what is known about these change processes. Poorly designed fear appeals or other messages are likely to be ineffective or even counterproductive. Use of the intervention mapping framework and IMB can help optimize intervention design.

CHANGING IMPULSIVE PROCESSES

Fear appeals may elicit impulsive regulation through automatic activation of emotional responses, such as fear and disgust but the intervention techniques we have considered so far are hypothesized to work mainly by developing new reflective processing such as reasoning that, '*If I do X it will be bad for me*'. Can we instead work directly on the impulsive system to change unwanted behaviour patterns? Yes, psychologists have been doing so for decades.

Building on Pavlov's (1927) work, Skinner's (1938) *Behavior of Organisms* system-atically explained how the environment shapes behaviour. For example, we perceive aspects of the environment that, in the past, have been associated with rewarding experiences and we respond to repeat those experiences. Over time this process of conditioning establishes automatic responses to particular environmental stimuli, or cues, which, through sequencing, can be built up into complex impulsively regulated behaviour patterns. We can, for example, repeatedly pair a new cue with one that has been previously conditioned to elicit a particular response. Over time, perception of the new cue will elicit the conditioned response because of its association with the previously conditioned cue. This is Pavlov's (1927) classical conditioning often exemplified by the pairing of a sound with the presentation of food. Alternatively, we can alter the environmental consequences of a response. For example, by repeatedly pairing a rewarding consequence with a behaviour we can increase the frequency of that behaviour, especially in the environment in which the reward is presented. This is Skinner's (1938) operant conditioning as exemplified by a rat learning to press a lever to receive food. Pavlov and Skinner developed and researched the effectiveness of a sophisticated series of change techniques that can be used to recondition the impulsive system. For example, in classical conditioning the new cue may be presented simultaneously with, or just after, the conditioned stimulus, referred to as delay (where the conditioning stimulus and new cue are overlapping) and trace conditioning. Use of these different classical conditioning techniques can have different effects on emotional and behavioural responding (e.g. Burman and Gewirtz, 2004). The new consequence introduced in operant conditioning may be a reward or a punishment and both may have positive or negative effects on behaviour. For example, negative reinforcement can include the removal of an unpleasant experience in order to increase the frequency of the targeted escape behaviour. Repeated escapes reinforce avoidant responding including avoidance of classically conditioned emotional response, as when we avoid a cue that is associated with stress or fear (e.g. Delgado *et al.*, 2009). Substantial research effort has been devoted to identifying and cataloguing such reconditioning techniques but further research is needed to better understand how they can be applied (singly and collectively) to help people alter unwanted everyday behaviour patterns, especially habitual or mindless behaviour patterns initiated with little reflective control.

Research has been conducted into pairing a desired object that is usually approached with a stop signal so that rather than approaching the object the recipient ignores or rejects the object. If this is done repeatedly then the established (conditioned) impulse to approach may be inhibited because the object becomes associated with non–response or rejection. For example, in the 'go–no–go' paradigm pictures of food may be paired with cues that the recipient is asked to respond to, for example, by touching a screen, or refrain from responding to, for example, by not touching a screen. Two different tones can be used to signal whether the recipient should touch, or not touch, the image. If recipients are conditioned not to touch desirable food images over many pairings this may strengthen inhibitory control and, thereby, help people inhibit automatic approach responses in the real world (Lawrence *et al.*, 2015; Veling, Aarts and Stroebe, 2013). For example, if one is trained not to respond to pictures of doughnuts or chocolate this may make it easier to ignore or refuse these foods subsequently. A meta–analysis of 19 experimental studies, conducted mainly with undergraduates, suggested that inhibition training of this kind may be effective in changing health behaviour patterns (Allom, Mullen and Hagger, 2015). The analyses generated a small d value of 0.38 (see Focus 8.1) and found that effectiveness varied depending on the nature of the training, how long the training lasted and how the subsequent behaviour was measured.

Inhibition training is one of many change techniques that can be used to alter impulsive processes. A review of 92 studies focusing on changing unhealthy eating highlighted 17 separate techniques that have been tested, including inhibition training, implementation intention formation, avoidance training, cognitive restructuring, thought suppression and mindfulness training (van Beurden *et al.*, 2016, in press). This review highlighted the need for more research on these change techniques, especially experimental research with those at greatest health risk such as overweight and obese people.

Implementation intention formation, or if-then planning, has proved promising as a technique that can help the motivated change their eating patterns (see Chapter 7 and van Beurden *et al.*, 2016, in press in relation to unhealthy eating). Luszczynska *et al.* (2007) added a single training session focusing on if-then action planning to an existing group–based weight loss intervention. Recipients who were randomly assigned to receive this additional training session lost twice as much weight over a 2 month follow-up and 54 per cent lost 5 per cent of body weight compared to only 8 per cent in the unenhanced intervention. Moreover, increased self-reported planning was found to statistically mediate the effect of the enhanced intervention on weight loss, that is, the change in self-reported planning accounted for the difference in weight loss between the intervention and control group. This is consistent with the hypothesized mechanism of action, namely increased if-then planning led to improved behavioural control.

Consideration of if-then planning as a technique to change impulsively regulated behaviour patterns emphasizes two important points. First, when applying the IMB model to intervention mapping, we need to match change objectives and, therefore, our choice of change techniques to the needs of the target population. The intervention objective identified by Luszczynska *et al.* (2007) was not to increase knowledge (by providing information) or to increase motivation (by using fear appeals or other attitude-change techniques) because the target group was well informed and highly motivated. Instead, the training focused on acquisition of a particular cognitive skill (if-then planning), which has been found to help motivated people act on their intentions. Second, unlike the conditioning techniques we considered above, if-then planning involves *both* the reflective and impulsive systems. The plan is formulated by activating the reflective system but the pairing of a cue (the 'if') with an imagined response (the 'then') has the capacity to change impulsively regulated processes when the cue is encountered following training, which is to prompt a new response to the cue.

Breaking unwanted habits by changing the operation of the impulsive system may require use of multiple change techniques targeting various regulatory mechanisms delivered using various methods tailored to the target population (stages 3 and 4 of intervention mapping). Dean (2013) discusses the stages involved in 'habit reversal therapy' for people with Tourette's syndrome. The objective of this intervention is to reduce the incidence of unwanted, unconsciously elicited behavioural tics. The therapy focuses on becoming aware of the tics and the situations in which they occur and then practising a competing behaviour. The therapy is effective but is also intensive, involving more than 10 hours of therapeutic contact (McGuire *et al.*, 2014; Piacentini *et al.*, 2010). Reconditioning the impulsive system is rarely easy.

Habit reversal therapy employs behavioural replacement rather than any attempt to suppress unwanted behavioural responses. This is important because evidence suggests that thought suppression can have rebound effects, increasing the thoughts we wish to suppress (Wegner, 1994; Wenzlaff and Wegner, 2000). Consequently, techniques that involve acknowledgement or acceptance of unwanted thoughts or urges and planned responses may be more effective (Najmi, Riemann and Wegner, 2009; Sheeran, Aubrey and Kellett, 2007). For example, Erskine, Georgiou and Kvavilashvili (2010) evaluated the effects of smokers trying not to think about smoking and found that, compared to controls, smokers trying to suppress thoughts about smoking increased cigarette smoking.

There are interesting parallels between 'habit reversal therapy' and what Kessler (2009) calls 'food rehabilitation'. The latter also begins with building awareness, both of cues in our everyday environment that prompt overeating and of our own 'premonitionary urges' or feelings that we are about to revert to a habitual response. By training the reflective system to identify urges generated by the impulsive system just before we respond to cues, we can create space for reflective initiation of competing behaviours, just as a friend's reminder can change how we lock our front door. The next stage of food rehabilitation is the specification and learning of relevant competing behaviours, such as deliberately walking by the cake shop or taking another route to work. Kessler (2009) emphasizes cognitive and emotional reconstruction, that is, learning to reflectively nurture new thoughts and emotions in relation to conditioned cues. Over time this results in attitude change that further bolsters motivation to change. For example, one person having undergone food rehabilitation noted that, 'Once I thought a big plate of food was what I wanted and needed to feel better . . . now I see it for what it is . . . fat on fat on sugar on fat that will never provide lasting satisfaction and only keeps me coming back for more.' This is a radical cognitive and emotional reconstruction of food cues that might previously have prompted excitement and positive thoughts. Such reconstruction serves to sustain motivation to avoid unhealthy foods and reduce impulsive prompting of unhealthy eating. Reconditioning the impulsive system requires multiple learning opportunities because the associations that regulate the system have themselves developed through repeated pairings. Thus 'food rehabilitation' and other habit-breaking interventions require practice and more practice. Moreover, since such interventions can be very challenging to complete requiring considerable time and effort, people are likely to do better if they have good social support (see Chapter 5) to maintain training until the impulsive system has been successfully reconditioned.

FROM SPECIFICATION OF CHANGE PROCESSES TO COMPLEX INTERVENTIONS

We have seen how progress towards behaviour change intervention design proceeds from initial testing of predictive models (such as operant conditioning or protection motivation theory – see Chapter 7), through to experimental tests of techniques designed to change specified regularity mechanisms (e.g. the use of inhabitation training to reduce automatic responses to specified cues) through to more complex interventions such as Kessler's 'food rehabilitation'. Campbell et al. (2000) provide a useful five-step framework that allows researchers to situate their research along this developmental continuum. Initially, key theories need to be developed and tested to establish an understanding of determinants and change mechanisms. In this theory-building stage, small-scale experiments and surveys focus on mechanism rather than the testing of intervention techniques. Once a clearer idea of mechanism and regulatory processes emerges modelling phase work begins, which involves testing elements of the theory and particular change techniques. Once effective techniques are identified then exploratory trials and feasibility studies can be undertaken (e.g. Hill *et al.*, 2007; Luszczynska *et al.*, 2007). If these prove effective, particularly if data syntheses studies, such as systematic reviews and meta-analyses, demonstrate effectiveness across studies, then investment in larger-scale and definitive trials at national level with detailed, adequately powered outcome economic and process evaluations is warranted (e.g. Wight *et al.*, 2002; Wyatt *et al.*, 2013). Finally, if these demonstrate effectiveness then replicating this effect with sustainable interventions in routine practice is required to ensure adoption and faithful long-term implementation.

We considered cognitive dissonance theory in Chapter 8. Focus 9.3 presents an experimental test of a change technique derived from that theory. Specification of the process of dissonance induction allowed Stone *et al.* (1994) to develop a technique combining inducement of commitment to a behavioural standard (such as commitment to use condoms consistently) and enhanced awareness of personal failures to live up to that standard (such as a focus on past instances of unprotected intercourse) in order to generate cognitive dissonance. This cognitive change technique, known as the 'hypocrisy paradigm', has been tested in a series of studies with some evidence of effectiveness. It is not, however, the only technique that has been developed to induce cognitive dissonance. In a systematic review of such techniques, Freijy and Kothe (2013) assessed evidence for four additional techniques but concluded that overall, evidence favoured the hypocrisy paradigm. Thus theoretical specification of simple regulatory processes (such as dissonance induction) can generate quite distinct change techniques that may be more or less effective in changing targeted regulatory processes and, as a result, prompting behaviour change.

Selection of change techniques depends on identification of change objectives during stage 2 of the intervention mapping process. Consider the use of if-then planning. This simple technique may be applied differently to distinct real-world problems. Sheeran and Orbell (2000) found that inclusion of a planning prompt in a questionnaire increased attendance for cervical cancer screening. The prompt advised questionnaire recipients that they would be more likely to go for a cervical smear if they decided when and where to go. They were then given space to write 'when, where and how you will make an appointment'. In this case, motivated respondents who had not yet made an appointment were prompted to make specific action plans (e.g. specifying a time) to prompt a response that they had the skills to enact (making an appointment). The technique was effective in changing behaviour; 92 per cent of those offered this planning opportunity attended for screening compared to 67 per cent in the control group, despite equivalent levels of reported motivation across the two groups.

This when-where-and-how action-planning technique is distinct in form and targeted regulatory processes to that employed by Sheeran *et al.* (2007) to increase attendance at psychotherapy appointments among those who had already made appointments. These researchers undertook elicitation research to identify what could

FOCUS 9.3

Using cognitive dissonance to promote condom use

Cognitive dissonance theory (see Chapter 8) proposes that we are strongly motivated to avoid and eradicate contradictions in our world views. Consequently, it should be possible to motivate change by generating salient contradictions between beliefs and actions. In an experiment conducted by Stone *et al.* (1994) participants were randomly allocated to one of four conditions: (1) receiving information about condom use (information only); (2) receiving information and giving a talk promoting condom use that might be used in school health education (commitment); (3) being made aware of past failures to use condoms by recalling these failures (failure awareness); and (4) a combination of the commitment and failure awareness conditions. All participants were then given an opportunity to buy condoms cheaply. As the graph below shows, significantly more people in the combined commitment and failure awareness condition bought condoms (82 per cent) than in the failure awareness condition (50 per cent) or the commitment condition (34 per cent). The study also demonstrates that information alone is not enough. Significantly fewer people in the information-only condition bought condoms (44 per cent). This study illustrates how, applying cognitive dissonance

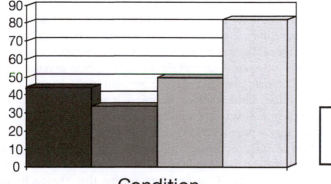

Condition

■ Information only ■ Commitment ▨ Failure awareness ☐ C + FA

theory, a cognitive contrast was created between people's representation of appropriate behaviour (which they were committed to by becoming an advocate of that position for school students) and their own health behaviour. This technique does not rely on a direct appeal, as in the case of persuasive argument designed to change people's perceptions of the outcomes of their action. It depends instead on the power of the salient contradiction between committed beliefs and the person's own past actions. Allowing people to take action that endorses their beliefs adds new cognitions relevant to the salient contradiction and helps resolve it through personal commitment to condom use in the future. Thus the strength of motivation to resolve the contradiction prompts a desirable change in motivation and in key preparatory behaviours (acquiring and carrying condoms).

A systematic review of experimental studies applying cognitive dissonance theory in this way found that, across studies, significant positive effects were observed across different cognitive and behavioural outcomes and suggested that the effectiveness of such interventions may be moderated by gender such that women tend to respond more positive to this technique than men (Freijy and Kothe, 2013).

potentially reduce missed appointments. This work highlighted a need to reduce concerns about their forthcoming appointment. Consequently, recipients were advised to use a self-talk technique in response to appointment anxiety, that is, 'as soon as I feel concerned about attending my appointment (the if) I will ignore that feeling and tell myself this is perfectly understandable (the then)'. Unlike the if-then planning technique employed by Sheeran and Orbell (2000), this is not an action planning technique – no behavioural response is targeted. It is a thought-regulation technique designed to reduce cognitive elaboration of specified anxieties. Note too that it is not an example of thought suppression (Wenzlaff and Wegner, 2000). Recipients were not advised not to think about their appointment but rather to avoid elaborating appointment-related concerns when they arose. By reducing the amount of time recipients spend worrying about their appointment the technique could make it easier for them to attend. Analyses showed that those who received a questionnaire containing this if-then thought regulation tip were more likely to attend their psychotherapy appointment with 75 per cent attending compared to 63 per cent in the control group.

These two experimental studies illustrate how simple self-regulatory techniques using an if-then structure can help motivated people act on their intentions. They also show how the needs of different groups (assessed in stage 1 of the intervention mapping process) leads to identification of different change objectives (stage 2). In one case the objective was to prompt appointment making, while in the other it was to increase keeping previously made appointments. This, in turn, meant that the techniques employed were designed to target distinct regulatory processes (stage 3) namely, detailed action planning versus distraction from specified anxieties. Consequently, the two techniques employed different practical delivery methods even though both were included in questionnaires. This comparison illustrates the detailed decision-making processes involved in intervention design even when short, simple techniques are employed. Not unlike rocket science, behaviour change design requires careful theoretical specification of mechanisms and processes combined with precise engineering of change techniques adapted to address specific real-world behavioural challenges facing particular target groups. Finally, these two studies illustrate how simple techniques have the potential to change our responses to health services in ways that could be cost-saving. We will consider outcome and economic evaluations when we discuss stage 6 of the intervention mapping process below.

Behaviour change interventions may employ multiple techniques targeting a range of different regulatory processes tailored to particular audiences. For example, Schinke and Gordon (1992) describe a culturally specific intervention including a self-completion book using comic strip characters and rap music verse to encourage effective safer sex regulation among black teenagers. The aim was to develop self-monitoring, self-regulatory and planning skills as well as rehearsal of verbal resources, which can be used to control and disrupt scripted interaction that could lead to unprotected sex. The acronym SODAS, standing for Stop, Options, Decide, Act and Self-praise, was used in this training. The first step, 'stop' explicitly elicits anticipated regret ('stop and think what these choices could really mean for you today, tomorrow . . . and for years to follow' – see Chapter 7) while the fourth step, 'act' involves the reader in generating if-then plans in relation to five types of verbal responses, which can be used when they are subjected to social pressure. This intervention highlights selection of delivery methods in the intervention mapping process. Cartoons, rather than questionnaires were used to deliver these techniques. Choice of delivery methods is critical because these methods determine recipients' engagement with the intervention and how the intervention affects processing of messages – see Noar et al.'s (2015) finding that use of pictures enhanced cognitive and emotional responses to fear appeals on cigarette packets. For example, drama-based techniques may be more engaging than reading written materials and so enhance intervention effectiveness (e.g. Wyatt et al., 2013). Consequently, the same technique delivered differently may have very different effects for the same target audience.

We have seen how many of the characteristics of an intervention listed in Table 9.1 become important during the intervention mapping process. The particular behaviour targeted leads to selection of specific techniques designed to alter particular change processes, which are delivered using methods appropriate to target group and setting. We noted in Chapter 8 that credibility of a message source (that is, who delivers the message – e.g. The Lancet article on MMRI) is critical to persuasion. Many communication models (see e.g. Berlo's Source, Message, Channel and Receiver model) have emphasized that the way in which recipients view the source influences how they respond (Hovland, Janis and Kelley, 1953). The title of a questionnaire or the name of the organization that produced a leaflet (e.g. a political party or a commercial organization) can critically affect how we process its content. This is even more important in interventions delivered face-to-face. How facilitators are viewed in terms of, for example, professional competence and whether they belong to the same group as the recipient (e.g. matched gender or culture) can strongly affect the way in which people respond to interventions (Durantini et al., 2006). The same technique or complex intervention delivered by two different sources (or facilitators) when viewed differently by intervention recipients may have very different effects on engagement, cognitive and emotional processing and, therefore, behaviour change.

The characteristics of facilitators are important, not only because of how they are viewed and responded to by recipients, but also because face-to-face intervention delivery depends on their abilities. An intervention that is not delivered as designed is said to have poor fidelity. The competence of those delivering interventions is critical to fidelity and, for complex interventions, this may be challenging to ensure through training. For example, a review of competence in motivational interviewing found that of 11 studies that had assessed clinician competence only 2 studies reported that

75 per cent of trained clinicians were proficient (Hall *et al.*, 2015). Thus, when developing complex interventions it is critical to develop and evaluate quality training programmes to ensure that intervention facilitators are competent to deliver the intervention, as designed, in practice contexts (such as schools or clinics). Only in this way can intervention design be translated into improved health promotion and health care delivery.

Governments are interested in effective behaviour change interventions, including those that could improve public health and reduce expenditure on health services. Both the UK and US governments were influenced by a book by Thaler and Sunstein (2008) describing how 'NUDGE's could be used to change behaviour. Both governments set up teams to develop and evaluate NUDGE interventions. What are NUDGE interventions? 'NUDGE' is an unusual acronym because, for example, the 'N' stands for incentives, that is, use of reinforcement to shape behavioural responses. Decades of work have shown that reinforcement, including use of financial incentives can change behaviour patterns. For example, if people can be persuaded to deposit savings, which they know they will subsequently lose if they fail to meet weight loss targets they lose more weight (Volpp *et al.*, 2008). Similarly, if pregnant women are paid to abstain from smoking they are more successful. In one study smoking cessation follow-up at 12 weeks post-partum found that 24 per cent of those receiving financial incentives had been successful compared to only 3 per cent in the control group (Heil *et al.*, 2008). Governments cannot pay everyone to improve their health-related behaviour patterns so the key research question here is, can reinforcement-based interventions initiate psychological changes that bolster intrinsic motivation and, through practice, develop skills and habits that allow behaviour change to be sustained (through impulsive regulation) – after incentives are removed. If so, such interventions have considerable potential but, if not, they are unlikely to have sustainable effects on public health. Further research is needed on the sustainability of incentive-based intervention but it seems unlikely that use of incentives is an effective way of motivating change and development in children (Kunz and Pfaff, 2002; Deci, Koestner and Ryan, 1999).

The 'D' in NUDGE stands for 'default'. This refers to the construction of systems that encourage the least effort option. For example, when subscription to a service is automatically renewed or tax is automatically deducted. Such systems make it easier for people to act as required by removing the costs of decision-making and action. There is evidence that such default opt-in, or assumed consent systems could benefit public health. Johnson and Goldstein (2003) argue that, in relation to organ donation, opt-in systems impose physical, cognitive and emotional costs on those wishing to donate organs and that these barriers reduce organ donation levels. They show that, in the UK, which uses an opt-in system, approximately 17 per cent of people donate their organs after death while in a range of European countries with assumed consent systems the figure is more than 99 per cent. It is likely, therefore, that legislation in the UK could increase organ donation dramatically. Note that this would be an intervention operating at the national level in the social ecological model (see Figure 9.2).

Use of reinforcement, including financial incentives and the construction of default opt-in systems are quite distinct approaches to encouraging population-level behaviour change. So NUDGEs include a variety of intervention types drawing on a range of change techniques and regulatory processes. Thaler and Sunstein (2008) characterize the interventions that they are interested in as altering 'choice architecture . . . without forbidding options or significantly changing economic incentives'. They say that NUDGEs are 'easy and cheap to avoid' and note that, 'putting fruit at eye level counts as a nudge . . . banning junk food does not'. It is possible to design interventions that use low value financial incentives but will they be effective? It is also possible to design easy default opt-in systems but, as with organ donation, some of these systems would require regulatory and legislative change (Marteau *et al.*, 2011). Given the diverse range of interventions that could be characterized as NUDGEs, it does not make sense to ask whether NUDGEs per se work but, instead, to evaluate each of these interventions. Some may work well in particular contexts, while others do not.

In this section we have seen how identification of regulatory processes can facilitate specification of a range of change techniques that may operate on aspects of the reflective or impulsive system or both. We have also seen how these techniques can be embedded in a range of delivery methods and delivered by a variety of sources and/or facilitators with particular competencies and relationships to recipients. Each of these separate intervention characteristics (see Table 9.1) needs to be carefully considered during the intervention mapping process so that relevant change techniques can be tailored to particular behaviour change problems within particular target groups.

EVALUATION OF BEHAVIOUR CHANGE INTERVENTIONS

The final stage of the intervention mapping process is evaluation. We can distinguish between three broad types: (1) outcome evaluations (that answer the question, did the intervention change the behaviour it targeted?); (2) process evaluations (that answer the question, how did the intervention work and did it change the regulatory mechanisms targeted?); and (3) economic evaluations (that answer the question, how much does the intervention cost for a given degree of effectiveness). We have noted that once the intervention objectives are defined in stage 2 of intervention mapping, it is important to identify measures to be used in the evaluation. Outcome measures may assess health or behaviour patterns or both, depending on the intervention objectives. Assessing health outcomes (such as weight loss or STI rates) allows tests of hypothesized links between behaviour change and health enhancement or disease incidence. For example, does increasing self-reported condom use among a target group decrease STI incidence?

When an intervention is found to be effective an economic evaluation can clarify how much it will cost to implement the intervention. This is important because health care funds are limited and implementing expensive interventions may require cuts in other services. It is worth noting, however, that when preventive health behaviour interventions are effective they are likely to be cost-effective because of high treatment costs. For example, the lifetime cost of treating a HIV positive person in the UK has been estimated at more than £240,000, so even expensive HIV-preventive interventions are likely to be cost-saving if they are effective in reducing HIV incidence. Similarly, an intervention that prevents obesity, heart attacks or falls among the elderly is very likely to be cost-saving and, therefore, cost-effective.

In this section we will not provide guidance on how to undertake evaluations. This is readily available elsewhere. A project funded by the UK School for Public Health

Research identified more than 400 evaluation training, support and guidance documents. For example, a guide to outcome evaluations has been developed by the US Centres for Disease Control and Prevention (2012). A useful guide to process evaluation has been produced by the UK Medical Research Council (Moore *et al.*, 2014) and the United States Department of Health and Human Services has provided guidance on economic evaluations (Honeycutt *et al.*, 2006). Instead, we will briefly highlight key aspects of outcome and process evaluations, focusing especially on the latter.

A rigorous outcome evaluation is likely to involve a randomized controlled trial. This may compare the intervention to a no-intervention control group or another intervention group (as is the case when an intervention is compared to routine or usual care), or both. Typically, post-intervention levels of outcome measures are compared, controlling for any pre-intervention differences. Ideally, we would observe no differences between intervention and control groups before the intervention but in practice these may occur. Randomization to intervention and control groups minimizes such differences and may be undertaken at an individual, or organizational level, as is the case in a cluster randomized trial when groups of individuals (such as schools or clinics) are randomized together. When, for policy or ethical reasons, all participants need to receive an intervention (so that there can be no no-intervention control group) then clusters can be randomly allocated to receive the intervention or not over a period of time so that all clusters are observed receiving and not receiving the intervention. In this design, called a step wedge design, each cluster acts as its own control. When randomization is impossible, matched groups need to be carefully scrutinized to ensure that differences other than exposure to the intervention are not responsible for observed differences in outcome.

Outcome evaluations usually calculate an effect size (e.g. standardized mean differences or Cohen's *d*) to indicate how effective the intervention was (Cohen, 1992). Anticipating the likely effect size in advance is important to ensure that enough participants are included to detect change. Attrition rates, that is the number of people who drop out of the study, are also important. For example, if an intervention requires persistence and 50 per cent of those in the intervention group drop out then, even if the intervention is very effective among the remaining 50 per cent (compared to no-intervention controls) the overall impact of the intervention may be limited. An intention-to-treat analysis is recommended in such instances. This involves retaining all randomized participants in the analyses and counting those who do not complete the intervention as showing no change. Note what a difference this makes when attrition in the intervention group is high.

The issue of active control groups in which the control participants are already receiving a service or intervention raises an important issue for trials that compare interventions to usual care. Comparison with high quality usual care can make an intervention appear less effective than comparison with a poor usual care group (de Bruin *et al.*, 2010). This can create problems for commissioners who may wish to implement effective interventions because it means that, unless we know what standard of usual care was used as a comparator, we cannot easily compare effect sizes across trials. An apparently very effective intervention (when compared to poor usual care) may add nothing to established best practice in another context. Yet the content of usual care, and control groups more generally, is rarely well described. Thus evaluation and implementation require accurate, detailed descriptions of the intervention – and control groups to which it has been compared.

Better reporting of behaviour change interventions and their evaluations would greatly enhance our capacity to translate evaluations of interventions into improved health care practice (Abraham *et al.*, 2014; Davidson *et al.*, 2003). Acknowledgement of inadequate scientific reporting has resulted in the development of many reporting guidelines (Simera *et al.*, 2013) including CONSORT (Consolidated Standards of Reporting Trials) for randomized controlled trials (Schulz *et al.*, 2010; Montgomery *et al.*, 2013), STROBE (Strengthening the Reporting of Observational studies in Epidemiology) for observational studies (Von Elm *et al.*, 2007) and guidance on the development and evaluation of complex interventions (Craig *et al.*, 2008). The TIDieR checklist (Template for Intervention Description and Replication; Hoffman *et al.*, 2014), the work of the WIDER group (Workgroup for Intervention Development and Evaluation Research; Abraham, 2012; Albrecht *et al.*, 2013) and more specific guidance such as that for the description of group-based behaviour change interventions (Borek *et al.*, 2015) extend this guidance. Currently there are more than 200 published reporting guidelines listed on the EQUATOR (Enhancing the QUAlity and Transparency Of health Research) website (www.equator-network.org), which was established to improve the reporting of health research.

Process evaluations are particularly important when evaluating complex interventions, which have a number of interacting components operating at different levels and that may address complex problems or seek to produce multiple outcomes (Campbell *et al.*, 2000; Craig *et al.*, 2008). Moore *et al.* (2014) provide a useful framework, which describes key elements that a process evaluation might investigate: *mechanisms of change*, *intervention delivery* and *contextual factors*. This guidance, like that of the Kellogg Foundation (2004) and intervention mapping recommends beginning with mechanisms, or processes, of change and suggests that intervention designers develop a 'logic model' that maps out the regulatory process(es) that the intervention is expected to change (see stage 3 of intervention mapping). This allows identification of meaures of processes or mechanisms that need to be included. Process measures may include cognition measures such as measures of attitude, self-efficacy or planning that can be assessed in both the control and intervention groups before and after intervention delivery. Such measurement allows mediation analyses to be conducted, testing whether the assumed change mechanisms account for the success of the intervention.

Process evaluations also investigate intervention delivery, trial management (such as the management of participant recruitment to a trail) and implementation processes (such as adaptations that were made when delivering the intervention in different contexts). A key part of process evaluation is the assessment of fidelity of delivery, that is, was the intervention designed as planned. This includes 'dose', that is, did recipients receive enough of the intervention? Glasgow *et al.* (2002) and Green and Glasgow (2006) provide a useful framework model for evaluating intervention delivery and implementation: the RE-AIM (Reach, Effectiveness, Adoption, Implementation and Maintenance) framework. *Reach* refers to how many of the target population were involved in an evaluation and how representative they were. For example, if an intervention was evaluated using economically advantaged participants then questions would arise as to whether it would also be effective for economically less advantaged people – or, for example, with those with more severe health problems than the intervention participants. *Effectiveness* relates to the range of effects an intervention might have. For example, even if it changed behaviour – did it enhance overall quality of life or have any unintended consequences (e.g. did participants find it onerous or upsetting)? *Adoption* refers to whether the users (e.g. nurses, teachers, managers, members of the public) are persuaded of the utility of the intervention and use it. Adoption depends on how easy the intervention is to implement, whether those who will deliver it and/or their clients like and value it and whether it is compatible with their other main goals (Paulussen, Kok and Schaalma, 1994). Since cost is important to most people, interventions are unlikely to be used if adopters cannot afford them. Understanding this adoption and diffusion process is critical to the overall impact of any intervention (Rogers, 2003). Even effective interventions have no impact on public health if they are not adopted and translated into everyday practice. *Implementation* refers to the ease and feasibility of faithful delivery. If an intervention is complex, expensive or requires specialist training or teams of people to deliver it then it is less likely to be sustainable in real-world settings so it may not be adopted or, if adopted, may be delivered with poor fidelity. *Maintenance* refers to the longer-term sustainability of the intervention in real-world settings. For example, if an organization or community does not have the resources to deliver an intervention then, no matter how effective, it will be dropped over time. Similarly, if implementation problems are encountered then even if the intervention is retained it may be changed and adapted to the setting, which may mean altering or dropping change techniques critical to its initial effectiveness, so rendering it ineffective. These practical, real-world considerations are critical to translating potentially efficacious interventions into sustainable enhancement of routine health preventive and health care services. They need to be carefully considered in stages 1 and 5 of the intervention mapping process.

Contextual factors may include an individual's characteristics, family, social network or organization (such as a school or community). Interventions may be differentially effective for different groups (e.g. men versus women, older or younger people or those high in conscientiousness versus those low in this trait). Such between-group analyses of effectiveness are called moderation analyses and can clarify for whom an intervention is most effective. Such analyses require large samples to provide the statistical power to identify group differences.

Process evaluations typically use mixed methods to answer multiple research questions about how an intervention operates. For example, quantitative data may be used in mediation and moderation analyses. Qualitative methods can be used to explore processes in detail, such as participant perceptions of interventions and how the intervention and its context interact with each other. If problems arise such as poor implementation or low recruitment levels, interviews with intervention staff or participants could be conducted to investigate the underlying reasons.

A useful distinction can be drawn between the function of process evaluations in relation to (1) pilot and feasibility studies and (2) definitive trials. In the former, findings from a process evaluation can be used to improve intervention development and redesign research methods, including outcome measures. In the latter the process evaluation should be conducted in a manner that does not alter the intervention or contaminate the outcome evaluation. Of course, the results of a process evaluation may necessitate intervention redevelopment, for example when an intervention is found not to alter targeted change processes. Close collaboration between process and outcome evaluators is needed to optimize intervention development in pilot and feasibility studies, while blinding and firewall procedures may be needed in definitive tests of a finalized intervention.

TAXONOMIES OF INTERVENTION CONTENT CHARACTERISTICS AND EVIDENCE OF EFFECTIVENESS FROM DATA SYNTHESES

We have noted that our behaviour is regulated by processes operating at different levels, from the intra-personal to international (see Figure 9.2) and that many distinct regulatory processes operate within these levels, including, at the intra-personal level, both reflective and impulsive processes. In stage 3 of the intervention mapping process, designers identify techniques that will effectively alter these regulatory processes. Researchers have developed useful lists, or taxonomies, of change techniques. Abraham and Michie (2008) named and defined 22 frequently employed change techniques linked to various theoretical accounts of regulatory processes as well as four packages of change techniques used together in more complex interventions. The utility of the taxonomy in categorizing intervention content was tested using 195 descriptions of interventions provided in scientific papers identified by three separate reviews, as well as a sample of 13 pairs of descriptions taken from published papers and detailed manuals. Both the taxonomy developers and trained coders were able to use technique definitions reliably to identify techniques in intervention descriptions. This taxonomy has been widely applied (see for example, Michie *et al.*, 2013) and further work has confirmed that it defines techniques that occur frequently in behaviour change interventions (Abraham *et al.*, 2015). The taxonomy includes four techniques derived from control theory and goal theory (Carver and Scheier, 1982; Locke and Latham, 2002), that is, goal setting or intention formation, self-monitoring, providing feedback on performance (that is, comparing it to a set standard or goal) and review and revision of previously set goals, to facilitate further goal setting. It also includes techniques designed to change the cognitive determinants of motivation including providing information about the consequences of action and about others' approval of the action (derived from the theory of planned behaviour and other similar models – see Chapter 7), as well as techniques useful for learning new skills such as providing instructions and modelling (derived from social cognitive theory). Four techniques based on operant conditioning processes were also included, that is, providing rewards directly following performance of the target behaviour (i.e. contingent rewards or reinforcement), teaching people to use environmental cues to prompt change (e.g. placing medication by one's toothbrush), setting up a behavioural contract that the individual signs to commit themselves to undertaking specified behaviours over a period of time and prompting practice, that is repeating a newly learned behaviour so that it becomes well learnt and habitual (and can be automatically triggered with little reflective processing). The taxonomy also includes four commonly employed technique packages, namely, relapse prevention (Marlatt and Donovan, 2005), stress management, motivational interviewing (Rollnick and Miller, 1995) and time management. Longer lists of change techniques have been provided by a series of subsequent taxonomies, some tailored to specific behaviour-change problems such as promoting sexual health (Abraham *et al.*, 2012) or promoting physical activity and healthy eating (Michie *et al.*, 2011) and general technique lists (Michie *et al.*, 2014).

Kok *et al.* (2015) present a taxonomy of change techniques linked to the intervention mapping approach used to structure this chapter. This taxonomy helpfully groups techniques (called 'methods' in this chapter) according to the change objectives, such as increasing knowledge, changing determinants of motivation (such as attitudinal and normative beliefs), enhancing self-efficacy and skills and changing impulsive regulatory processes (e.g. to break and make habits). The authors also include techniques operating at higher-order levels such as those that may be used to change organizations, communities and policy (see Figure 9.2). This taxonomy defines technique categories and helpfully specifies the conditions under which each technique is likely to be most effective.

Kok *et al.* (2015) noted that an effective technique must be able to change a specified regulatory process that shapes behaviour and must also be embodied in a delivery method that both preserves the technique and is acceptable and engaging for the target audience. As we have seen, Focus 9.3 includes only one of five techniques that have been tested as ways to induce cognitive dissonance (Freijy and Kothe, 2013). In this case different techniques have been used to target the same change process, hypothesized to change attitudes. We have seen too that if-then plans can be employed to prompt specific action planning or to rehearse focused cognitive distraction from potentially anxiety-provoking thoughts (Sheeran *et al.*, 1999; Sheeran *et al.*, 2007). In this case the same form of change technique is used to target distinct change processes and, consequently, delivered in different ways. In some cases the hypothesized change processes have implications for the delivery method. For example, we discussed framing effects in Chapter 8. In this case the delivery form of a message (e.g. an emphasis on gains versus losses) is determined by the theorized change process. It is important, therefore, not to mistakenly count distinct techniques as being the same when categorizing intervention content using taxonomies of change techniques.

Embodiment of a change technique in a delivery method may change its effectiveness. Consider, for example, making recipients aware of cues that may prompt impulsively regulated behavioural responses (as in habit reversal therapy and food rehabilitation). This could be done by inviting recipients to list relevant cues on a piece of paper or, in an application with children, recipients might be encouraged to make temptation T-shirts with pictures of snacks they want to reduce. In each case the technique targets cue awareness but the distinct methods of delivery are likely to affect technique effectiveness. Similarly, as we have noted, there are many forms of persuasive communication that may increase motivation or prompt action planning. For all of these techniques, the recipients' perceptions of the source of the communication (as sharing social identity, being expert or being trustworthy) is likely to influence effectiveness. Thus technique effectiveness depends on the particular delivery mode, including, in many cases, the source of communication. Schulz *et al.* (2010) highlight how interventions may differ according to method of delivery (e.g. face-to-face versus provision of written materials), type of materials (e.g. written versus video), location delivery (e.g. home versus school) and schedule of delivery (e.g. number and duration of exposures). Considering only interventions delivered in group settings, Borek *et al.* (2015) list 26 intervention characteristics that should be considered by designers and reported to enable replication with fidelity. Only one of these refers to the specific change techniques employed. We can see, therefore, that the list of characteristics provided in Table 9.1 is a useful starting point but detailed intervention planning can involve many different intervention characteristics.

One application of taxonomies of intervention content is a type of 'retrospective or archaeological process evaluation'. This is distinct from process evaluation proper conducted experimentally as part of a trial, as described above. The idea is to compare many published outcome evaluations and investigate whether the content of the reported interventions is associated with reported effectiveness using meta–analysis. Albarracín et al. (2005) provide a good example. Using 354 intervention descriptions and 99 control groups, spanning 17 years, these researchers asked which of 10 change techniques were most effective in promoting condom use among different target groups. The researchers identified five types of persuasive communication, which they referred to as 'passive' because these techniques could be employed without active involvement of the recipients (e.g. through a health promotion leaflet). These were provision of (1) information; (2) arguments designed to change attitudes; (3) arguments designed to change normative beliefs; (4) arguments designed to persuade recipients that they could perform successfully prerequisite tasks, that is, to enhance self-efficacy; and (5) threat or fear-inducing messages. In addition, the researchers considered five techniques that could be used in interventions involving 'active' or face-to-face interaction with recipients. These included three types of skill training, namely (6) condom-specific skill training; (7) self-management or self-regulatory skills training; and (8) interpersonal or social skills training. In addition, the researchers considered (9) provision of condoms; and (10) HIV counselling and testing. Results showed, perhaps unsurprisingly, that active interventions involving interaction with recipients were more effective in promoting condom use. The most effective interventions provided information, attitudinal arguments, behavioural skills arguments and provided self-management (or self-regulatory) skills training. In addition, provision of condoms and HIV counselling and testing enhanced intervention effectiveness.

Overall, these results offer support for targeting the change processes specified by the theory of planned behaviour, the information, motivation and behavioural skills model and social cognitive theory. By contrast, they suggest that the change processes specified by protection motivation theory may be less useful to intervention designers trying to promote condom use (see Chapter 7). It is worth noting too that given an average d of 0.38 for active interventions and assuming that, on average, 36 per cent of people in a target group use condoms at least sometimes (figures reported by Albarracín et al. (2005) – see Research methods 8.1 on d values) then an additional 17 per cent will use condoms at least sometimes following such active interventions. This is a sizable increase in the number of users following intervention and could impact on the prevalence of STIs and unwanted pregnancy rates. Interestingly, Webb and Sheeran (2006) conducted a similar review investigating how effective interventions that promoted intention formation (or goal setting) were in changing behaviour across behavioural targets. They found that medium to large changes in intention ($d = 0.66$) resulted in small to medium change in behaviour ($d = 0.36$); an effect size very similar to that observed for active interventions by Albarracín et al.

Albarracín et al. (2005) also found that some techniques were associated with effectiveness for some recipients but not others. Normative arguments targeting subjective and descriptive norms were found to promote behaviour change in audiences under 21 years of age but to reduce effectiveness among older recipients (perhaps due to reactance). Thus age moderates the relationship between inclusion of normative arguments and intervention effectiveness. Similarly, condom-use skills were effective for men but not women. Thus gender moderated the relationship between condom use skills training and intervention effectiveness. This emphasizes the importance of the technique–recipient fit in intervention design.

Albarracín *et al.* (2005) highlight the potential utility of meta-analyses when undertaking such 'retrospective process analyses'. The results help intervention designers identify candidate change processes and techniques in stage 3 of the planning process when targeting increased condom use. However, such reviews also need to be considered cautiously. Here we will highlight five questions that can be asked to assess the utility of such studies. First, is the sample of studies large enough? Albarracín *et al.* (2005) used a very large and representative sample of intervention descriptions. Small samples may generate results that could be reversed as more tests became available.

Second, are the intervention descriptions accurate? Content analyses of interventions may be based on categorization of the intervention material themselves (e.g. Abraham *et al.*, 2007) or detailed manuals. Descriptions from scientific papers may be less accurate and less comprehensive. For example, Abraham and Michie (2008) found that while approximately 9 change techniques per intervention were identified in descriptions included in manuals, only 6, on average, were identified when categorizing content of the same interventions from descriptions included in scientific papers.

Third, are the categorizations used derived from theorized change process and specific enough to provide guidance to designers? Albarracín *et al.* (2005) used a simple set of techniques derived from theorized change processes that were relevant to the behaviour change target of interest, namely, condom use. This is helpful to designers. However, when broad technique categories are employed this creates interpretation problems because researchers may have categorized distinct techniques into one category. This is sometimes referred to as the 'apples and pears' problem, that is, the specificity of the categorization operates at the level of 'fruit' rather than particular types of fruit. For example, Albarracín *et al.*'s (2005) results do not tell us whether normative arguments targeting descriptive and subjective norms (see Chapter 7) operate differently. Do both types of normative techniques promote condom use equally well and are both moderated in their effectiveness by age? Thus ideally technique categories used for intervention content analyses should be linked to particular change processes and be very specific. Even when this is achieved we need to be aware (as Albarracín *et al.*, 2005) note) that one change technique may operate through multiple change processes. For example, changing descriptive norms (that is promoting the belief that most people like me are doing X) may also change attitudes (doing X is rewarding).

Fourth, were the defined categories reliably applied by independent coders? Clearly if two people reading the same descriptions cannot easily agree on what it refers to then no further conclusions can be drawn about the categorizations undertaken (Abraham *et al.*, 2015).

Fifth, were all relevant characteristics of the intervention categorized? The answer to this question is unlikely to be 'yes' but the question highlights the importance of third variable effects, that is, where another feature of a set of interventions, other than those categorized, is responsible for an observed association between change technique inclusion and effectiveness. Albarracín *et al.* (2005) categorized aspects of the delivery method used (e.g. active versus passive methods) and the relationship between the source of the intervention and the recipients. They also categorized recipient type and showed moderation effects for age and gender. However, other aspects of interventions can affect intervention effectiveness such as the nature of comparison groups and how the intervention was designed. So conclusions are limited by the range of characteristics categorized. Nonetheless, when answers to all five of these questions are positive, such studies can identify 'best bet' intervention content for designers.

A different use of meta-analysis that may inform intervention design is the synthesis of experimental data to estimate the effect sizes that may be achieved by using particular change techniques. For example, in a large review of experimental tests, Sheeran *et al.* (2015) identified interventions capable of generating changes in attitudes, norms and self-efficacy (compared to control comparisons) and observed that changes in these processes (or determinants of motivation) generated medium-sized changes in intention (ds = 0.48, 0.49 and 0.51, respectively) and small to medium sized changes in behaviour (ds = 0.36, 0.38 and 0.47, respectively). In this type of meta-analysis the content of intervention is given by the primary studies and the review estimates the average effect sizes following observed change in a given change process. Again, the size of the study sample is important to robustness and, again, variation in type of recipient and mode of delivery (including source and context of delivery) may moderate observed effect sizes.

KEY CONCEPTS AND TERMS

- Adoption of interventions
- Behavioural contract
- Change objectives
- Change techniques
- Choice architecture
- CONSORT guidelines
- Control theory
- Default opt-in systems
- Delivery methods
- Elicitation research
- Evaluation – economic
- Evaluation – outcome
- Evaluation – process
- Fear appeals
- Feedback
- Food rehabilitation
- Goal setting
- Goal theory

- Habit reversal therapy
- If-then planning
- Information, moti-vation and behavioural skills model
- Inhibition training
- Instruction
- Intention-to-treat analysis
- Intervention mapping
- Modelling
- Motivational interviewing
- Motor skills
- Multi-level modelling
- Needs assessment
- NUDGE
- Organizational and community interventions

- Public health
- Reach and sustainability of interventions
- RE-AIM framework
- Reflective impulsive model
- Regulatory processes
- Reinforcement
- Relapse prevention
- Reporting guidelines
- Self-monitoring
- Self-regulation skills
- Social ecological model
- Social skills
- Source of persuasive communication
- Stress management

continued . . .

- Targeted change mechanisms or processes
- Taxonomies of intervention content characteristics
- Thought suppression
- Time management

SUMMARY

Planning behaviour change interventions requires precise identification of change objectives and theorizing of regulatory mechanisms. This allows selection of well-specified change techniques targeting relevant change processes. Elicitation research and co-development with intervention recipients and those who will deliver the intervention is critical to the design process. Behaviour change interventions may target both reflective and impulsive processes or both. Interventions may be simple (e.g. teaching specific action planning using if-then formats) or complex including many techniques and delivery methods. Evaluation is critical to knowing whether an intervention is or is not effective. Outcome, process and economic evaluations are important to identification of interventions capable to improving public health. Meta-analytic reviews can help intervention designers select change techniques and delivery methods but the results of such studies must be interpreted with caution. Those delivering the intervention are important to effectiveness both in their relation to recipients and their competence to deliver with fidelity.

SAMPLE GROUP EXERCISES (E.G. OVER TWO CLASS SESSIONS)

- Choose a health behaviour pattern (e.g. increasing physical activity) and design an evidence-based intervention to promote this behaviour among a specific target group.
- Draft a plan on how to intervene to enhance fitness among employees in a desk-based organization. Identify the defining features of your intervention (see Table 9.1) and draw upon intervention mapping procedures.
- Select a set of (e.g. 10) published intervention evaluations and try to identify the change techniques and delivery methods they employ.
- Select a set of (e.g. 10) published intervention evaluations and assess them in terms of the quality of evaluation and RE-AIM criteria (reach, effectiveness, adoption, implementation, maintenance). On the basis of your analysis, how useful do you think each is in terms of improving health or health care practice?

SAMPLE ESSAY TITLES

- How can health psychology inform the design of health promotion campaigns?
- What works in health behaviour change interventions? Discuss with reference to empirical research.

- How can behaviour change intervention evaluations help psychology develop better theories of change?
- How can research-based behaviour change interventions have more impact on routine practice in health care settings?

FURTHER READING

Books

Dean, J. (2013). *Making Habits, Breaking Habits*. Boston, MA: De Capo Press.

Kessler, D.A. (2009). *The End of Overeating: Taking Control of the Insatiable American Appetite.* Emmaus, PA: Rodale.

Journal articles

Borek, A., Abraham, C., Smith, J., Greaves, C. and Tarrant, M. (2015). A checklist to improve reporting of group-based behaviour-change interventions. *BMC Public Health*, 15, 963.

Kok, G., Gottlieb, N.H., Peters, G.J.Y., Mullen, P.D., Parcel, G.S., Ruiter, R.A.C., Fernández, M.E., Markham, C. and Bartholomew, L.K. (2015). A taxonomy of behaviour change methods: An intervention mapping approach. *Health Psychology Review*. doi: 10.1080/ 17437199.2015.1077155.

Luszczynska, A., Sobczyk, A. and Abraham, C. (2007) Planning to lose weight: RCT of an implementation intention prompt to enhance weight reduction among overweight and obese women. *Health Psychology*, 26, 507–512.

Marteau, T.M., Ogilvie, D., Martin, R., Suhrcke, M. and Kelly, M.P. (2011). Judging nudging: Can nudging improve population health? *British Medical Journal*, 342: d228.

5 | Relating to patients

10 Relating to patients

CHAPTER PLAN

We expect people to consult health services when they experience symptoms and to follow health care professionals' advice to avoid negative health consequences. In reality, however, professional help seeking is not easily predicted from clinical symptoms and people often do not follow health professionals' advice. In this chapter we explore how people's perceptions and beliefs affect help seeking and adherence. We also discuss how health care professionals can manage consultations effectively so that they maximize patient satisfaction, empowerment and illness management/recovery.

Half the UK population, especially those with long-term illnesses, report having used complementary therapies. We discuss what such therapies offer and consider the challenges involved in integrating them with traditional medical health care. We also examine the nature of placebo effects, their importance in assessing therapeutic effectiveness and what they teach us about the relationship between health and psychological care. Finally, we focus on the needs of people with long-term illnesses and how psychological interventions can help them.

The chapter is presented in six sections:

1 deciding to consult;
2 promoting adherence;
3 managing consultations;
4 patient-centredness and concordance;
5 complementary therapies and placebo effects; and
6 managing long-term illnesses.

LEARNING OUTCOMES

When you have completed this chapter you should be able to:

- Discuss who is most likely to consult health care services (such as a family doctor or general practitioner) and explain why.
- Identify key correlates of patient adherence and discuss how adherence can be maximized.
- Describe key tasks that need to be completed during consultations with patients.
- Identify key components of patient-centred consultations and discuss the findings of research into their effects on patients' well-being and health.
- Discuss the role of complementary therapies in health care.
- Define 'placebo effects' and explain how they occur.
- Discuss the needs of patients with long-term illnesses and illustrate the contribution that psychological interventions can make to caring for these patients.

DECIDING TO CONSULT

People frequently experience symptoms but do not consult health services. Estimates vary, but 50–75 per cent of the population experience one or more symptoms of ill health over any 2-week period (Demers *et al.*, 1980; Porter, 2004). Yet, as Porter (2004) notes, about one-third of these people do nothing about their symptoms, about one-third self-medicate using over-the-counter medications or use alternative therapies and only about one-third consult their doctor. Thus, even when health care is free at the point of delivery (as it is in the UK), there is far from a one-to-one correspondence between symptoms and consultation. This is problematic because people who need health care may not seek help and so worsen their prognosis and also because a substantial proportion of those who do consult have only minor symptoms that do not require medical intervention.

Why do people consult?

A number of consultation prompts have been identified (Porter, 2004; Zola, 1973). Unsurprisingly, symptoms that persist, that are perceived to be serious and thought to be amenable to treatment are more likely to lead to help seeking. Symptoms that interfere with other goals, for example, by inhibiting activities or reducing attractiveness, are also more likely to lead to consultation. Advice from others is an important additional trigger. Finally, ease of access to services and having time (e.g. away from work or child care) also make consultation more likely. In a study of 1,210 people, Berkanovic, Telesky and Reeder (1981) found that 64 per cent reported symptoms over 1 year. The researchers employed multiple regression analyses to discover which of a range of prompts were most strongly associated with consultation following symptom identification. Results showed that respondents who had greater numbers of long-term health problems, were older, had a regular doctor or had greater social support were more likely to consult (rs =.02–.19). However, consulting was most strongly predicted by advice to consult from a member of their social network (r =.35), the degree to which the symptom generated disability (r =.31), the perceived seriousness of the symptom (r =.56) and, especially, the perceived efficacy of care (that is, believing that medical intervention could alleviate or eradicate the symptoms) (r =.69). This study was based on the health belief model (see Chapter 7) but the results also support the theory of planned behaviour emphasizing the role of social norms and the perceived benefits of acting (that is, positive attitudes towards consulting). The results also emphasize the role of social support in consulting behaviour and the importance of perceptions of medical effectiveness.

Anticipated effectiveness of consultation was also found to be an important trigger in a population study of people with serious breathing difficulties, which compared people who had and had not consulted. Controlling for smoking status and perceived relative severity of symptoms, attribution of wheezing to smoking and lower self-efficacy in relation to explaining breathing difficulties to a doctor differentiated between those who did and did not consult (Abraham et al., 1999). The importance of perceived causation was also highlighted by King (1982) who found that perceived causes of elevated blood pressure predicted whether or not people attended for screening. Thus causal understanding of symptoms and anticipation of positive and effective interaction with health care professionals are also key determinants of health service use.

Symptoms are not always clear so people may struggle to understand what they mean. For example, Kendrick et al. (1993) found that, for 60 per cent of asthmatic patients, there was no significant correlation between ratings of severity and simultaneous peak flow measurements. This 60 per cent were not characterized by less severe symptoms (as measured objectively by peak flow) or by age or gender. The researchers concluded that a large proportion of asthmatic patients cannot reliably detect changes in their lung function. Similarly, Cantillon et al. (1997) found that, for 86 per cent of patients who believed they could predict changes in their blood pressure, there was no significant association between patients' assessments and clinical assessments. Patients' confidence in their ability to predict their blood pressure was, however, associated with higher anxiety. Thus, when symptoms are unclear, emotional responses to their detection are likely to be crucial to the effect that symptom perception has on health behaviour and health service usage.

Interpretation of symptoms

Leventhal and colleagues (e.g. Leventhal et al., 1997; Leventhal, Nerenz and Steele, 1984) have identified five broad dimensions within which beliefs about symptoms and illnesses can be categorized. First, *identity*, the way a symptom label is related to our perception of cause and has profound implications for how we respond. For example 'fatigue' or 'stress' have very different connotations to 'cancer'. Second, *cause*, refers to our understanding of the processes generating symptoms. For example, 'indigestion' has very different implications to 'heart attack' and believing that symptoms are due to one's own behaviour may lead to reduced motivation to seek professional help. Third, beliefs about *consequences*, including the perceived severity of symptoms. Fourth, *timeline*, refers to people's expectations regarding the duration of symptoms and their perceptions of whether symptoms (e.g. of diabetes or asthma) are chronic or acute can have important implications for health seeking and adherence. Finally, beliefs about *control and treatment effectiveness*, including, for example, perceptions of whether the illness can be cured strongly affect help seeking. For example, Leventhal *et al.* (1997) found that help seeking is more likely if ambiguous symptoms are detected when someone is also stressed but only if the stress has lasted for three weeks or more. Initially stress may be seen as the cause of a symptom and so it may be expected to be short-lived or to have only minor consequences but if the stress is perceived to be stable symptoms may be regarded as more serious and long term. Perception of bodily sensations and symptoms is also affected by individual goals and coping strategies (Cioffi, 1991).

Note how the findings of Berkanovic *et al.* (1981, see above) highlight two of the categories of beliefs proposed by Leventhal and colleagues, namely, perceived symptom seriousness (consequences) and perceived efficacy of care (control and treatment effectiveness). Note too that these five categories of illness beliefs overlap with beliefs specified by the social cognition models we studied in Chapter 7. For example, the health belief model and the theory of planned behaviour identify beliefs about consequences as important to intention and action and the theory of planned behaviour and social cognitive theory emphasize the importance of perceived control to action. Finally, look back at Activity 8.1 and compare patients' questions about medication to the beliefs associated with consultation.

Personality and emotional responses affect symptom interpretation

Emotional responses affect symptom reporting and health service usage. For example, Rietveld and Prins (1998) found that negative emotions did not affect objective measures of children's asthma but made it more likely that children would interpret normal exercise-related sensations (e.g. heart pounding and fatigue) as indicating asthma. Those experiencing more negative emotions reported greater breathlessness, regardless of objective symptoms. Patterns of emotional responding are predicted by personality assessments (see Chapter 6) so that, for example, those high in neuroticism report more symptoms (Watson and Pennebaker, 1989). For example, in a study of cold infections, Feldman *et al.* (1999) found that while neuroticism was not related to objective measures of infection, this trait was associated with symptom reporting among healthy people. Those scoring in the top third of the neuroticism distribution reported more than twice as many symptoms as those in the bottom third. These researchers suggest that this is because higher neuroticism leads to greater attention to somatic experiences and potential symptoms; a conclusion supported by other research (Kolk *et al.*, 2003).

Other personality factors shape symptom detection and perception. For example, while pessimism may be bad for one's health (see Chapter 6), pessimists seem to be more accurate in assessing their health. Leventhal *et al.* (1997) report that self-reported ratings of health were better predictors of mortality 5 years later among pessimists than optimists. Controlling for age and medical history and comparing those who reported their health to be fair or poor with those who reported their health to be excellent or very good, mortality was 8 times higher among pessimists but only 1.5 times higher among optimists. Here optimism moderates the relationship between self-reported health status and mortality (see Focus 5.2). More conscientious people tend to detect symptoms earlier because they have a lower threshold for symptom detection and are more concerned with self-protection (Feldman *et al.*, 1999).

Personality traits can affect decisions about service usage and adherence through specific symptom-related beliefs, that is, beliefs mediate the effect of personality on help seeking and adherence behaviour. For example, Skinner, Hampson and Fife-Schaw (2002) found that greater perceived consequences of diabetes symptoms and greater perceived effectiveness of available treatment were both associated with greater self-reported self-care among young people with diabetes. Thus, these beliefs are important both to consulting and adherence (see Berkanovic *et al.*, 1981 and above). Skinner *et al.* (2002) found that neuroticism was associated with beliefs about the consequences of diabetes but not with beliefs about the effectiveness of treatment. By contrast, conscientiousness was associated with stronger beliefs in the effectiveness of treatment. The researchers suggested that because conscientious people are more likely to engage in active problem-focused coping (see Chapter 5) they may access more information about their diabetes and its management, which in turn may result in more positive beliefs about treatment effectiveness.

Collectively then, research suggests that seeking help from health professionals and following their advice is strongly related to people's beliefs about their symptoms or illnesses. Consequently, understanding and intervening to change such beliefs could lead to more cost-effective use of health services. In particular, promoting accurate beliefs concerning the consequences of symptoms and the effectiveness of treatment has the potential to encourage those who need help to seek it and use it optimally and, at the same time, enable those with minor symptoms to self-manage their health.

PROMOTING ADHERENCE

'Adherence' means following advice given by health care professionals. This can involve a variety of behaviour changes including taking preventive action (e.g. reducing alcohol consumption or changing one's diet), keeping medical appointments (e.g. screening, physiotherapy or check-up appointments), following self-care advice (e.g. caring for a wound after surgery) and taking medication as directed (in relation to dose and timing). Non-adherence is usually defined as a failure to follow advice to an extent that causes a harmful effect on health or a decrease in the effectiveness of treatment. Most medical interventions rely on patient adherence. Yet about 50 per cent of patients do not take prescribed medications as recommended (Myers and Midence, 1998). This is not a new phenomenon. More than 35 years ago Sackett and Snow (1979) reported that only half of patients on long-term medical regimens were adherent. Across behaviours between 15 per cent and 93 per cent of patients do not follow the advice of health care professionals (Ley, 1988) and non-adherence is observed even when its consequences are fatal. In a prospective study of heart, liver and kidney transplant patients, Rovelli *et al.* (1989) found that 15 per cent were non-adherent, with non-adherence leading to organ rejection or death in 30 per cent of non-adherent cases, compared to only 1 per cent among adherent patients. Non-adherence is problematic because it means that when health care professionals make accurate diagnoses of a health problem and prescribe effective treatment their intervention may, nonetheless, be ineffective. Indeed, 10–25 per cent of hospital admissions have been attributed to non-adherence. Thus the potential cost-effectiveness of health care services is severely limited by non-adherence.

How can we measure adherence?

Simple self-report measures can provide good estimates of adherence (Morisky, Green and Levine, 1986) but when self-report measures are compared to objective measures, results indicate that patients overestimate their adherence (Myers and Midence, 1998). This can mean that treatment ineffectiveness is wrongly attributed to the treatment, rather than patients' failure to adhere (Blaschke *et al.*, 2012). Direct indicators such as analyses of urine or blood content and weight change as well as indirect objective measures such as pill counts, refill records and service usage records are also used to track adherence. In addition, indirect measures such as health improvement (e.g. blood pressure or hospitalization) may be employed as measures of adherence (Roter *et al.*, 1998).

Antecedents of adherence

Why do patients not follow advice? Patients are non-adherent for different reasons (Donovan and Blake, 1992). Some patients intend to take recommended actions but forget or find it difficult to do so, resulting in partial adherence. Others suspend medication or test their health or to avoid side effects that might impinge on important social events (Conrad, 1985). Some patients fear medication dependency while others disagree with the doctor's diagnosis or the prescribed treatment and deliberately take more or less than was advised. Knowing why patients do not adhere is important to designing interventions that may promote better adherence. Some key questions that influence patients' decisions to adhere are: Do I really need this treatment? Am I at risk of symptoms without doing what was advised? How effective/beneficial is the recommended action? What side effects will it have? To what extent will adherence conflict with other things I want to do? When consultations do not adequately answer these questions patients may reach their own conclusions and decide against adherence (see Activity 8.1).

In the past, adherence was referred to as 'compliance' but this term is rarely used now because it suggests that the patient's role is to follow orders given by health care professionals. In reality, patients decide whether the advice they receive is helpful and whether or not they will follow it. Consequently, health care professionals need to collaborate with and persuade patients if they are to shape their health-related behaviours.

If a patient feels her doctor is not interested in her problem or has not under-stood it, this will undermine confidence in the doctor's advice. Consequently, patient satisfaction is significantly correlated with adherence ($r = 0.26$, Ley, 1988). For exam-ple, in a well-known study of paediatric consultations, Korsch, Gozzi and Francis

(1968) found that mothers who were very satisfied with their doctor's warmth, concern and communication were three times more likely to adhere than dissatisfied mothers. Satisfaction depends upon the patient's perception of the doctor's sensitivity, concern, respect and competence. Reducing waiting time, taking time to greet the patient in a courteous manner and engaging in friendly introductory exchanges are all likely to increase satisfaction. Asking open-ended questions that cannot be answered 'yes' or 'no' and allowing the patient time to express his or her worries is also likely to make the patient feel satisfied with the consultation.

Given the importance of patient satisfaction it is interesting to note that doctors' own satisfaction with work is a predictor of patients' adherence. In a 2-year prospective study, DiMatteo et al. (1993) found that, controlling for adherence at baseline, doctors' satisfaction with their work was a significant predictor of patient's future adherence ($r = .25$). This study also showed that doctors' self-reported willingness to answer all their patients' questions, regardless of the time involved was positively associated with adherence. Doctors who are happier in their work may be more willing to answer questions and may engender greater satisfaction in their patients. Thus patient satisfaction may mediate the relationship between doctors' job satisfaction and their patients' adherence.

The social context in which people live including the social support they receive affects adherence. Indeed adherence may partially mediate the effect of social support on health. In a meta-analysis summarizing 122 studies reporting associations between social support and adherence, DiMatteo (2004) found that adherence (compared to non-adherence) was 3.6 times more likely among those receiving practical support than among those who did not have such support. Similarly, the risk of non-adherence was 1.35 times higher if patients were not receiving emotional support than if they were. Practical support increases self-efficacy and actual control over adherence (see the theory of planned behaviour and social cognitive theory – Chapter 8) thereby rendering recommended changes feasible. A lack of social support may also increase stress levels, which may, in turn, allow less priority for adherent goals (DiMatteo, 2004). This is consistent with a recent study that explored factors associated with non-adherence to medication among individuals with cardiovascular disease (Crowley et al., 2015). These authors found that higher life chaos (or stress), worry about having a stroke or heart attack and being younger predicted self-reported non-adherence to medication.

Can we improve adherence?

Available evidence suggests that we can improve adherence but that this may require interventions including multiple change techniques. For example, in a meta-analysis of 153 studies evaluating the effectiveness of interventions designed to improve patient adherence, Roter et al. (1998) found that interventions significantly improved adherence compared to control conditions with small to moderate effect sizes. The researchers reached four conclusions. First, while effect sizes were small, interventions were generally effective. For example, even the smallest effect size on measures of health outcomes translated into a 10 per cent increase compared to no-intervention controls. As Roter et al. (1998: 1150) note, a 10 per cent difference between an intervention and control group could 'save considerable cost and suffering'. Second, no particular intervention approach worked better than any one other but combinations were more effective than single techniques, especially if they simultaneously targeted education, behaviour change and emotional responses. Techniques targeting adherence behaviour included changing drug packaging, simplifying dose instructions, mailed reminders and skills development approaches. Third, adherence interventions were more effective for some conditions, especially diabetes, asthma, cancer and hypertension, suggesting that it may be easier to increase adherence for some patients than others. Finally, the researchers noted that a broader approach to identifying outcome measures could be beneficial. For example, as well as boosting adherence, interventions may affect patient satisfaction, patient understanding and quality of life. These may be important targets in themselves. This suggestion links to a more general question about the evaluation of health care interventions, that is, who decides what are the appropriate outcome measures? While physical health is very important, is it always the most important outcome? Consider the definition of health we began with in Chapter 1.

In a second meta-analysis, Haynes *et al.* (2005) examined the outcomes of randomized controlled trials, which measured adherence to medication and included a clinical or health outcome (that is, whether people in the intervention condition also showed greater health benefit). For short-term prescriptions they found that 4 of 9 interventions (44 per cent) had an effect on both adherence and at least one clinical outcome while, for longer-term treatment, 26 of 58 (45 per cent) led to improvements in adherence but only 18 interventions (31 per cent) led to improvement in at least one clinical outcome. The researchers concluded that for short-term drug treatments counselling, written inform-ation and a personal phone call could boost adherence, but for long-term treatments, no particular technique and only some complex interventions led to improvements in health outcomes. Those that were successful in improving health included combina-tions of more convenient care, providing information, counselling, reminders, self-monitoring, reinforcement, family therapy, psychological therapy, crisis intervention, telephone follow-up and additional supervision. Thus it is challenging to improve adherence to long-term medication to the extent that such improvements impact on clinical outcomes. However, while health improvement is a critical outcome it may not be the only one and it is a challenging target for interventions designed to change *behaviour* because even successful interventions (e.g. those generating increases of drug adherence using objective measures) may not make a difference to health.

Although it is sometimes challenging to promote improved adherence, health care professionals can maximize adherence by improving patients' understanding, recall and satisfaction. Patients must understand advice before they can follow it and they must remember it beyond the consultation if it is to shape behaviour. Both understanding and recall are associated with patient satisfaction. Consequently, combining these factors, Ley proposed the model of adherence shown in Figure 10.1. Understanding is correlated with adherence ($r = 0.36$) (Ley, 1988) and in Chapter 8 we discussed how health care professionals can enhance patient understanding. Even when information is understood it may be forgotten. For example, in an early study, patients were found to have forgotten around half of the verbal instructions given to them, after only 5 minutes (Ley, 1973). Again, we noted in Chapter 8 how recall could be improved (e.g. see our consideration of logical order, explicit categorization, specific advice and emphasizing and repeating important points).

In a review of reviews, van Dulmen *et al.* (2007) concluded that adherence can also be promoted by simplifying treatments, for example, reducing the numbers of pills or

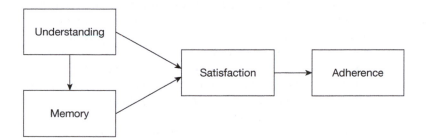

FIGURE 10.1 Antecedents of adherence.

Source: Adapted from Ley, 1988.

actions to be taken or simplifying schedules (e.g. once a day is much easier to achieve than three times a day). Providing patients with monitoring devices such as calendars or blister packs with named medication times also improves adherence. Thus technological advances play a part in improving adherence. Helpful instructions can also bolster adherence. For example, Kools (2012) found that adding illustrations to instructions led to better recall, fewer expressed doubts, that is, enhanced self-efficacy and a greater likelihood of correct use at first use.

Strategies that bolster memory for intentions and their subsequent enactment may also be used to increase adherence. For example, event-based recall is better than time-based recall (Ellis, 1998). So trying to remember 'take antibiotics twice a day' is likely to be less successful than trying to remember 'take antibiotics before breakfast and before dinner'. If one or more intentions have to be recalled, events can be more tightly specified, e.g. 'take blue pill before cereal and red pill with toast at breakfast'. This is very similar to the use of implementation intentions or if-then plans (as discussed in Chapter 7). Memory may also be enhanced by individualized feedback. For patients on long-term treatment medication, adherence can be monitored (e.g. by using electronic pill containers) and combined with individualized recommendations for remembering in relation to specific events that occur when the patient tends to forget their medication. Such interventions have shown some success with blood glucose control in diabetes, nebulizer use in people with obstructive lung disease, psychiatric medication, antiretroviral medication for HIV and oral anti-diabetic tablets (Rosen et al., 2004). Health care professionals can also assess motivation and self-efficacy. For example, patients could be asked if they intend to follow advice and if they see any barriers to doing so (e.g. 'Do you think you will take these tablets four times a day over the next two weeks?; Can you think of anything that might prevent you taking the medication?'). Such questions provide a check on the degree to which an agreed plan has been established and its feasibility in the context of the patient's life.

MANAGING CONSULTATIONS

Interactions between health care professionals (e.g. doctors and nurses) and their patients have the capacity to affect patient understanding, patient satisfaction, patient adherence and health outcomes. Consequently, the success and cost-effectiveness of health care services depends critically on consultation management. Use of good communication skills in consultations has been found to affect a range of health outcomes from emotional well-being to blood pressure and blood sugar concentration (Stewart, 1995). Yet it is all too easy for consultations to go wrong. The Toronto Consensus Statement on Doctor–Patient Communication (Simpson *et al.*, 1991) noted that 54 per cent of patient complaints and 45 per cent of patient concerns were not elicited by doctors and that in up to 50 per cent of consultations the patient and the doctor did not agree on the nature of the main presenting problem. This may be because patients are sometimes interrupted too quickly by health care professionals who want to identify and resolve patients' problems as efficiently as possible. Consultations serve different purposes and involve different groups of patients but key principles underlying effectiveness have been identified.

Many models of successful doctor–patient consultations have been developed. For example, after analysing 2,500 taped consultations, Byrne and Long (1976) identified six phases, which form the structure of successful consultations. They suggested that the doctor (1) establishes a relationship with the patient; (2) attempts to discover the reason for the patient's visit; (3) conducts a verbal and/or physical examination; (4) considers the diagnosis with the patient; (5) describes further treatment or investigation; and, finally (6) ends the consultation. Byrne and Long (1976) noted that consultations can go wrong in phase two

FIGURE 10.2 Doctor–patient interaction is crucial to patient satisfaction, patient adherence and health outcomes.

Source: © Joho/cultura/Corbis.

if the doctor fails to identify the true reason for consulting. Similarly, if the patient fails to understand the diagnosis in phase 4 this may undermine adherence.

The now more widely used Calgary-Cambridge consultation model provides a similar guide to structuring consultations (Silverman, Kurtz and Draper, 2005). Six stages are identified: (1) *initiating the consultation*, including establishing rapport (e.g. greetings and introductions) and identifying the reason(s) for the consultation (e.g. asking the patient what they would like to discuss); (2) *gathering information*, including understanding the patient's perspective (e.g. listening attentively without interrupting and using open questions to clarify what has been said); (3) *building the relationship*, including showing interest using non-verbal cues and communicating appreciation of the patient's concerns; (4) *providing structure* including summarizing what has been said; (5) *explanation and planning*, including providing the correct amount and type of information in a manner that aids recall and understanding and achieves a shared understanding and shared plan; and (6) *ending the consultation*.

Rather than focusing on sequence, Pendleton *et al.* (1984) identified seven tasks that need to be successfully completed in a health-focused consultation. These tasks, listed in Focus 10.1, overlap substantially with the Byrne and Long and Calgary-Cambridge models and, while developed as a learning aid for doctors, could be applied to many consultations between health care professionals and patients (including those conducted by health psychologists).

FOCUS 10.1

Seven key tasks to be accomplished in consultations

Pendleton *et al.* (1984) identified seven tasks that need to be completed successfully in a health-focused consultation:

1 Define the reason for the consultation including the nature and history of the problem, its effects and the patient's concerns and expectations.
2 Consider other problems including risk factors, which exacerbate the problem.
3 Choose an appropriate action for each problem in negotiation with the patient.
4 Develop a shared understanding of the problem(s).
5 Involve the patient in the management of problems and encourage acceptance of responsibility by the patient.
6 Use time and resources appropriately.
7 Establish and maintain a relationship with the patient.

Think about how these tasks relate to how a health psychologist would conduct a consultation with a manager referred because she was suffering serious stress at work (see Chapter 4).

PATIENT-CENTREDNESS AND CONCORDANCE

Byrne and Long (1976) contrasted doctor-centred and patient-centred consultations. Doctor-centred (or illness-centred) consultations focus on eliciting information necessary for precise diagnosis and prescription of appropriate treatment. The doctor tends to dominate such consultations asking direct, closed questions that demand short factual answers, which can clarify details (e.g. 'Where do you feel the pain?'). In such consultations, little time is spent eliciting or understanding the patient's ideas or providing information other than instructions on medical management of the problem. By contrast, in patient-centred consultations, doctors ask more open questions, which allow the patient to explain their perspective (e.g. 'So what do you think is wrong?'). The doctor also allows time to reflect back what the patient has said to demonstrate understanding and/or show empathy (e.g. 'you're worried about side effects') and to check that any treatment plans are acceptable to the patient. The Byrne and Long consultation phases, Calgary-Cambridge model of consultation management and Pendleton *et al.*'s seven-tasks model all highlight the importance of patient-centredness in consultations because evidence suggests that patients are less likely to be satisfied and less adherent following doctor-centred consultations.

Extending the work undertaken by Byrne and Long, Little *et al.* (2001) observed 865 consultations with general practitioners (or family doctors). These researchers identified five aspects of patient-centredness: (1) building a partnership, that is, being sympathetic, taking an interest in patients' worries and sharing planning; (2) taking an interest in the patient's life; (3) establishing a personal relationship, that is knowing the patient and their emotional needs; (4) providing health promotion, for example, addressing risk factors in the patient's lifestyle; and (5) taking a positive and definite approach including providing concrete guidance on what was wrong and when it would be resolved. Each of these five components could be reliably identified across consultations. They found that patient satisfaction was related to building a partnership and taking a positive approach. They also found that patients felt more empowered to deal with their problem when doctors had taken an interest in their lives, provided health promotion and adopted a positive approach. Patients also reported fewer symptoms one month after the consultation when doctors adopted a positive approach. Note how such results relate to the finding that doctor's concern/anxiety was associated with malpractice claims (see Chapter 8). It seems that patients expect partnership building and do not appreciate or benefit from doctors airing their uncertainties or concerns.

In most cases, including medication prescription, health care professionals can only contribute to improved health through shaping their patients' behaviour patterns. Consequently, consultation management involves a lot more than ticking off the phases or tasks highlighted by the models discussed above. If health care professionals are to change patients' behaviour patterns then it is important that those professionals are respectful and responsive to individual patients and ensure that patient values guide clinical decision-making (as was evident from Korsch *et al.*'s early work).

It has been proposed that health care professionals should strive to establish 'concordance' with their patients, that is, a mutual understanding and agreement about treatment and its implementation (Mullen, 1997; Bissell, May and Noyce, 2004). For example, using qualitative analyses of interviews with type 2 diabetic patients of

Pakistani origin, Bissell *et al.* (2004) found that some patients felt they could not discuss emotional, familial and financial factors that undermined their attempts to follow a diet appropriate to their condition. Being unable to discuss key barriers to adherence meant that doctors did not have the opportunity to offer advice on how to most closely approximate the recommended diets within everyday social constraints. Thus health care professionals need to consider real-world challenges the patient may face in following an agreed plan and allow time for such discussion and negotiation in consultations.

Patient-centredness and concordance are important because studies show that the relationship between health care professionals and their patients predicts patient satisfaction and adherence. This relationship is often been referred to as the 'working alliance' or 'therapeutic alliance' and Fuertus *et al.* (2007) found that patients' ratings of the working alliance and their self-efficacy predicted adherence and also satisfaction. Similarly, in a meta-analysis of 48 studies Arbuthnott and Sharpe (2009) found that better physician–patient collaboration is associated with better patient adherence and that this association was evident for paediatric and adult patient populations, for those with chronic and acute conditions and for family doctors (or general practitioners) and medical specialists. Similar findings have been reported for psychiatric consultations (McCabe and Priebe, 2004). Thus, across the board, sharing of views and establishing concordance within a therapeutic alliance appears to promote adherence.

In a related meta-analysis of studies of doctor–patient communication, Haskard Zolnierek and DiMatteo (2009) found a 19 per cent higher risk of non-adherence among patients whose doctor communicated poorly compared to patients whose doctor communicated well. They also found that training doctors in communication skills resulted in improvements in patient adherence. The odds of patient adherence were 1.62 times higher for patients whose doctor had received communication training compared to those whose doctor had not received such training. More generally a systematic review of 43 trials of interventions designed to promote 'patient-centred care', including shared control of the consultation and consideration of the person as a whole, found that such training is effective in transferring patient-centred skills to health care professionals. However, the effects of such training on patient satisfaction, patients' health behaviour and health varied across trials. Complex interventions directed at professionals and patients including condition-specific educational materials seemed to have greater effects on health behaviour and health status but the authors concluded that further trials were needed to confirm this latter conclusion (Dwamena *et al.*, 2012). Nonetheless, these findings strongly suggest that training health care professionals to communicate well and to build therapeutic alliances (or collaborations) with their patients could improve the effectiveness and cost-effectiveness of health services. Training is important because concordance may involve patients in sharing uncertainties about treatment outcomes (Elwyn *et al.*, 1999) and (as we have seen above) this needs to be managed in a positive manner by doctors and health care professionals to order to optimise adherence.

These findings suggest that the presenting problem (or illness) does not moderate the effectiveness of consultation styles. Yet a study by Savage and Armstrong (1990) suggests that it does. In this experimental study 200 patients were randomly allocated to two different consulting styles and followed up one week later. The styles were referred to as 'sharing' ('Why do you think this has happened?'; 'What do you think is wrong?'; 'Would you like a prescription?'; 'What do these symptoms or problems mean to you?') and 'directing' (e.g. 'This is a serious problem'; 'You are suffering from *X*'; 'It is essential that you take this medicine'; and 'You should be better in *X* days'). In all cases patients were allowed to complete their explanation of the problem and more than 80 per cent of those receiving each style reported that they had been able to discuss their problem well. Thus phase 2 in the Byrne and Long model was completed. The researchers found that a 'directing' style was associated with greater patient confidence that their doctor had understood their problem, perception of higher quality explanation by the doctor and greater reported health improvement one week later – but only among patients consulting about a physical problem or receiving a prescription. Among patients with a long–term or psychological illness and among those not receiving a prescription there was no difference between the two consulting styles. These findings mirror those of Little and colleagues emphasizing that, while patients need to be listened to, they expect positive, unambiguous expert advice from doctors reflecting their medical understanding of illness and treatments. However, where the problem has no clear physical diagnosis or cannot be treated using biomedical prescriptions a sharing style is likely to be especially beneficial to patient satisfaction and adherence. This does not mean that patient-centredness is unimportant for acute patients for whom there is a known remedy. As we have seen, the evidence suggests that patient-centred collaboration promotes adherence for all patients. However the degree of sharing and the extent of the therapeutic alliance required may differ across patients and may depend on the complexity of the problems that the patient and health care professional are facing. Training in patient-centredness could help health professionals with these assessments.

Patient empowerment

We have seen that communication and patient-centredness training can help health professionals manage consultations more effectively. Can we also empower patients in their interactions with health care professionals? On balance, the evidence suggests that we can. Robinson and Whitfield (1985) gave patients written information before their consultation reminding them that people may regret not asking questions after the consultation, advising them to check their understanding of instructions and the feasibility of those instructions and advising patients to ask about any discrepancies between recommendations made by the doctor and what they had expected. Compared to controls, these patients asked more questions in the consultation and gave more complete and accurate accounts of the recommended treatments after the consultation. Similarly, Cegala *et al.* (2000) found that patients receiving a training booklet designed to enhance patients' communication skills engaged in more effective information seeking, provided more detailed information about their condition to their doctor and used more summarizing utterances to check information provided by the doctor. Less encouraging results were reported by Kidd *et al.* (2004), who found that an intervention in which patients talked to a researcher about three or more questions they wanted to ask and were encouraged to rehearse these questions, did not increase question asking in the consultation. However, these researchers noted that question asking was higher than usual among their control group patients. The intervention did enhance self-efficacy to ask questions but had no impact on health outcomes. In a systematic review of 20 evaluations of interventions designed to increase patients' participation in medical consultations Harrington, Noble and Newman (2004) found that half of the interventions resulted in increased patient participation with greater effects being observed for clarification-seeking rather than question asking. They also noted a variety of other positive outcomes including perceptions of control over health, preferences for an active role in health care, greater recall of information, better adherence and improved clinical outcomes. Harrington and colleagues suggest that question asking may not be the best measure of whether consultation empowerment interventions are effective. They note, for example, that patients' perceptions of control over their health and preferences for an active role in their health care were found in all four studies that considered these outcomes. Given the importance of encouraging the general population to take a more active role in preventive health care (Wanless, 2002) further work on such interventions is warranted.

One objection to interventions designed to empower patients during consultations and to patient-centred consultations is that they are likely to be longer and doctors are already hard pressed to see patients who want consultations. Howie *et al.* (1999) examined nearly 26,000 randomly selected adult consultations across 53 medical practices and observed consultation times ranging from less than 5 minutes to more than 15 minutes with a mean of 8 minutes. These researchers administered a patient enablement measure, which resembles a measure of consultation-generated, health-related self-efficacy (see Chapter 7). It measured whether patients felt the consultation had made them better or worse at understanding their illness, coping with their illness, keeping themselves healthy and feeling able to help themselves. They found that patient enablement was associated with longer consultations and knowing the doctor better. They concluded that, 'It may be time to reward doctors who have longer consultations, provide greater continuity of care, and enable more patients' (Howie *et al.*, 1999: 738). Longer consultations may not only be associated with greater patient enablement. Reporting on a review of 14 studies Freeman *et al.* (2002) noted that longer consultations were associated with less prescribing, better recognition and management of psychosocial problems and better clinical care of long-term illnesses. Longer appointments may also be more likely to resolve problems and so reduce follow-up visits for the same problem (Hughes, 1983). Thus a shift to somewhat longer appointments and greater continuity of care (that is seeing the same doctor over time) could have beneficial effects on the effectiveness of health services.

COMPLEMENTARY THERAPIES AND PLACEBO EFFECTS

Poor patient satisfaction and uncertainty about the effectiveness of traditional medicine fosters demand for complementary or alternative medicine (CAM). Complementary therapies include a wide range of interventions based on different models of mind and body. The defining feature of such therapies is that they are not understood in terms of the evidence-based models of physiological systems (see Chapter 1). Many also differ from traditional medical care by focusing on the client's overall well-being rather than specific physical problems.

CAM use is widespread in developed countries. It has been estimated that 42 per cent of the US population have used CAM spending more than $21 billion annually

(White, 2000) and two-thirds of those receiving treatment for anxiety or depression report using CAM in the US (Bassman and Uellendahl, 2003). In Europe, 75 per cent of the French population and 50 per cent of the UK population report having used CAM (Murcott, 2006). Half of UK general practitioners (family doctors) provide CAM and more than 80 per cent of Australian general practitioners have referred patients for CAM (Murcott, 2006). Consequently, CAM has an important role in health care and many patients seen by psychologists will be using CAM.

The UK House of Lords Select Committee on Science and Technology (House of Lords, 2000) published a report on CAM, which distinguished between therapies that do and do not provide diagnoses. The report found that those that do include osteopathy, chiropractic (which are regulated by UK Acts of Parliament), acupuncture, herbal medicine and homeopathy; and those that do not include aromatherapy, hypnotherapy, reflexology and shiatsu. The Select Committee made a series of recommendations including (1) therapies that claim to treat specific conditions should have evidence of being able to do above and beyond the placebo effect (see below); (2) if a therapy does gain a critical mass of evidence to support its efficacy the UK National Health Service should provide access to it; (3) training in anatomy, physiology, biochemistry and pharmacology should be included within the education of CAM practitioners likely to offer diagnostic information; (4) CAM therapists should be trained in research methodology and have a clear understanding of the principles of evidence-based medicine; and (5) CAM therapists should encourage patients to see traditional health care professionals. These recommendations highlight the challenges of, on the one hand, providing access to effective treatments based on alternative models of health and, on the other, ensuring that such treatments are indeed effective.

Placebo effects

Placebo effects refer to health or well-being gains observed following administration of pharmacologically inert interventions such as saline injections or sugar pills (see Kaptchuk, 2009 for a brief and interesting historical perspective). In 1955, Beecher found that, across 15 clinical trials, 35 per cent of patients showed health gains in placebo conditions. In contrast, across 114 trails, Hróbjartsson and Gøtzsche (2001) found that when improvement was measured using a binary outcome (e.g. cured not cured) placebo treatments had no significant effect on outcome. Placebo conditions also showed no benefit when assessed using objective clinical outcomes. Placebo effects were observed on subjective, continuous outcome measures and in 27 trials assessing pain. Average placebo pain reduction was found to be equivalent to a 6.5 millimetre reduction on a self-report visual-analogue scale, measured on a 100 millimetre line. One weakness of such a review is that, if placebo effects are limited to particular types of health gain (such as reduced pain), these effects may not be evident when trials are pooled across conditions (Stewart-Williams, 2004).

Main effects of adherence have also been found in placebo conditions (Epstein 1984). For example, in a trial of beta blockers for women who had had a heart attack, Gallagher, Viscoli and Horwitz (1993) found that 5.6 per cent of those who took 75 per cent of the medication died within 26 months but 13.6 per cent of those who took less than 75 per cent died in the same period. Remarkably, this difference was not noticeably diminished in the placebo condition. In this case taking beta blockers was not found to be effective above and beyond the placebo effect. However, from a psychological perspective, the interesting question is, 'Why is adherence to placebo treatments associated with improved health outcomes?'

Placebo effects have raised doubts about a range of treatments. For example, although the UK National Institute for Health and Clinical Excellence (2004) recommended selective serotonin reuptake inhibitors (SSRIs such as Prozac) as the preferred treatment for mild to severe depression, their effectiveness has been questioned because depressed patients in placebo conditions show good levels of recovery (Kirsch and Sapirstein, 1998; Quitkin, 2000). Placebo responses raise the possibility that observed treatment effectiveness may not be due, or at least wholly due, to the pharmacological processes meant to explain the operation of a medication but to psychological changes initiated by beliefs that one is taking an effective treatment which, in turn, lead to health improvement (Moncrieff and Kirsch, 2005).

In trials that only compare a treatment with a placebo condition, numerous factors contribute to an observed 'placebo effect'. Natural fluctuations in physiological functioning mean that, for many conditions, some people spontaneously improve (so called spontaneous remission). This is especially true of long-term conditions when people are likely to seek medical help when their symptoms are most severe. People involved in intervention trials may also change how they assess their symptoms (cf. Norman and Parker, 1996). In addition, they may engage in new behaviours relevant to their treatment. Controlling for such effects necessitates a three-condition design in which treatment is compared to both placebo and a no-treatment control group (e.g. people randomly assigned to a waiting list for trial inclusion). The true placebo effect can then be defined as the additional gain seen in the placebo group over and above the no-treatment condition (Ernst and Resch, 1995). Note too that placebo conditions need to mimic the context in which treatment is administered. These so-called 'non-specific effects' include setting and communication. This is why health care professionals involved in trials should, ideally, be blind to which condition a patient has been allocated to.

Explaining placebo effects: patient expectations and anxiety reduction

Many explanations of placebo effects have been tested and it is likely that multiple processes are involved (see Stewart-Williams, 2004, for a clear summary). For example, placebo analgesic effects have been shown to be mediated by the release of endogenous opioids (Levine, Gordon and Fields, 1978) demonstrating that some placebo effects have measurable effects on the brain and endocrine system. However, such observations do not explain *how* placebo administration affects physiological systems. This may operate through patient expectations and anxiety reduction. When a health care professional (perceived to be competent) communicates to a patient that her problem is understood and that she is being prescribed (or advised to undertake) an effective, manageable treatment the patient will expect her condition to improve. Such expectations may have cognitive, physiological and behavioural effects. For example, believing that the worst is over could liberate the patient to devote time and energy to other life-enhancing pursuits. It could alter coping strategies, perhaps leading to more social support seeking. It is also likely to reduce stress and anxiety. Secondary appraisals (see Chapter 3) will be altered because patients believe they have an important new resource, namely, a treatment that will cure or alleviate adverse symptoms. Anxiety reduction is known to have physiological effects. For example, it is likely to affect endocrine functioning, reducing levels of cortisol and adrenalin in the bloodstream. This, in turn, may have positive effects on blood pressure and immune functioning (see Chapter 2) as well as on cognitive functioning (e.g. memory). Anxiety reduction is also associated with reduced pain because downward neural pathways from the brain can cut off or 'gate' incoming pain signals from peripheral nerves (Melzack and Wall, 1965). Thus a stress reduction explanation based on expectations of treatment efficacy provides a powerful explanation of some placebo effects. This explanation corresponds to Little *et al.*'s observation that patients reported fewer symptoms after consultations in which doctors adopted a positive and definite approach including providing guidance on when the problem would be resolved. Moreover, an expectation-based explanation could account for the direct effects of adherence because the more consciously one adheres to the apparently effective treatment the stronger one's expectation of relief or recovery should be. Nonetheless, this explanation does not account for all placebo effects. For example, objectively assessed bronchodilation placebo effect findings observed by Butler and Steptoe (1986) could not be explained by changes in expectations or anxiety.

Explaining placebo effects: classical conditioning

Classical conditioning theory may account for some placebo effects. In this model the 'real' drug is the unconditioned stimulus and beneficial physiological changes are the unconditioned response. Similarity of administration of the placebo treatment (e.g. context, nature of treatment, etc.) leads to an association between the placebo treatment (the conditioned stimulus) and the unconditional stimulus. Such effects have been observed in people and animals. For example, Benedetti, Pollo and Colloca (2007) examined the effect of repeated administrations of injected morphine during athletes' training sessions on placebo response. They found that athletes who had had morphine injections during training and who then received a saline injection (which they thought was morphine) showed greater pain endurance and physical performance during competition. This has interesting implications for drug testing in sport because it suggests that after appropriate drug conditioning it may be enough for an athlete to believe she is taking a performance-enhancing drug in order to enhance performance.

The placebo effect literature strongly emphasizes how important it is to provide patients with expectations of recovery (where it is reasonable and ethical to do so) and to encourage commitment to adherence. The psychological consequences of these processes may greatly enhance the pharmacological processes generated by available drugs. Practitioners able to harness and deliver the psychological and physiological effects evident in placebo responding will maximize the health impact of interventions. This was confirmed by a review of 19 trials. In this review Di Blasi *et al.* (2000) concluded that various contextual factors affected treatment effectiveness and that, in particular, there was evidence suggesting that cognitive care (that is managing expectations positively) and emotional care (communicating concern for the patient's problems) maximizes treatment effectiveness. Thus to optimize their effectiveness health care professionals need to be able to deliver such cognitive and emotional care. This is a critical element of patient-centredness.

Explaining placebo effects: neurobiological processes

In an interesting review, Finniss et al. (2010) point out that the physiological mechanisms underpinning placebo effects vary across conditions. So, for example, in pain relief these involve activation of endogenous opioids and dopamine systems while in depression they involve changes in electrical activity in parts of the brain. Thus placebo effects are observed because particular psychological processes initiated by interactions between health care professionals and patients activate particular physiological systems that have healing effects. If health care professionals understood better how their interactions with patients could initiate such activation they could, potentially, enhance traditional medical care. Moreover, CAM effects may be best explained by specific physiological activation effects. However, it is not clear how such effects can be reliably activated and it seems likely that the degree of activation may vary across patients. In addition, as Finniss et al. (2010) highlight, there are ethical issues about how such effects may be activated without deception. Finniss et al. conclude that further research on deliberate initiation of placebo effects in clinical practice is needed to fully understand how psychological changes may initiate these physiological healing responses. Such research could allow health care professionals to harness placebo effects to enhance patient care.

Understanding and testing complementary therapies

The assumptions underpinning many complementary therapies are incompatible with scientific findings. For example, some homeopathic treatments are diluted so many times that not a single molecule of the original substance remains. While homeopaths claim that water somehow 'remembers' the original active ingredient this makes no sense in terms of our understanding of the chemistry of water (Murcott, 2006). Similarly, as the UK NHS website explains, acupuncture is based on the assumption (first made 2,000 years ago in China) that health depends on a life force called Qi, which flows along 12 bodily meridians. Needles are inserted into the meridians to restore health by unblocking Qi flow. Yet anatomical research has found no evidence of these meridians.

Considerable effort has been devoted to evaluating the effectiveness of complementary therapies and acupuncture is especially well researched (see also Vickers and Zollman, 1999, for a useful introduction to osteopathy and chiropractic). Vas et al. (2004) found that combining acupuncture with pharmacological treatment for osteoarthritis of the knee led to greater pain reduction and increased physical functioning one week after treatment, controlling for placebo effects. However, Foster et al. (2007) found that adding acupuncture to advice and exercise for osteoarthritis of the knee did not enhance effectiveness. Interestingly, the acupuncture placebo condition in this study involved use of blunt needles, which collapsed into their handles to give the appearance of penetration, thereby controlling for some contextual effects. The UK NHS website notes that the UK National Institute for Health and Care Excellence (NICE) only recommends acupuncture as a treatment for chronic lower back pain, chronic tension headaches and migraines because evidence of effectiveness is only available for these conditions. Yet other claims have been made. For example, White (2000) and Bassman and Uellendahl (2003) present fairly positive reviews citing evidence for the effectiveness of acupuncture in treating depression and substance abuse. Murcott (2006) is more pessimistic even regarding the evidence on pain relief, noting that there are few studies of longer-term effectiveness. He compares the evidence available for the analgesic effects of aspirin and acupuncture and concludes that evidence for the latter is clearly weaker. Overall, he concludes that evidence for the effectiveness of complementary therapies generally is equivocal. However, here too there is debate about appropriate outcome measures. What if an alternative therapy was found to have no effects on clinical outcomes over and above placebo but was found to have a noticeable effect on patients' reported happiness or sense of empowerment? Would this constitute effective health care?

MANAGING LONG-TERM ILLNESS

In England, 15.4 million people have a long-term physical illness (LTI) and this is likely to rise to 18 million by 2025. About 60 per cent of those older than 65 have a LTI compared to 17 per cent of people under the age of 40. People with LTIs are intensive health care users accounting, in the UK, for more than half of general practice appointments and nearly three-quarters of inpatient days in hospital. LTIs include hypertension, asthma, diabetes, coronary heart disease, stroke, chronic obstructive pulmonary disease (COPD), cancer, heart failure, chronic pain and epilepsy (Department of Health, 2008).

LTIs affect people's lives in many ways. Sufferers are less likely to be in employment, more likely to be poor and more likely to need additional care and support from family members and others. With no medical cure in sight it is unsurprising that people with LTIs are also more likely to be CAM users. We have noted that people with LTIs may benefit from self-management interventions (see Chapter 8) and that longer consultations focusing on the patients' beliefs and feelings and prompting patients to take control of illness management may be especially important for these patients (see above). Empowering patients with LTIs to actively shape the consultations with health care professionals may optimize the health benefits of consultations (Michie, Mills and Weinman, 2003). Moreover, patient-centredness may need to be extended to become an 'empowering partnering approach' that acknowledges patients' independence in self-management of their illness (McWilliam, 2009).

The challenge for people with LTIs is to adapt to their illness, adopt the most effective coping strategies including social support seeking (see Chapter 4) and to maintain high self-efficacy (see Chapter 7) and the best possible quality of life (QoL). The extent to which they are able to do this and to enjoy life may predict longevity. For example, Moskowitz, Epel and Acree (2008) found that positive affect, including measures of enjoying life was associated with mortality among people with diabetes and people over 65 and especially among those reporting higher levels of stress. The findings suggested that positive affect may buffer stress (see Chapter 3). Consequently, psychological support is crucial to helping this group and some CAM practitioners may be able to offer such support more effectively than health care professionals because they employ longer consultations focusing on overall well-being. A UK Department of Health (2008) report notes that adherence among people with LTIs is poor and that people with LTIs want more health care services delivered in the community and in their homes. The report also notes that providing people with greater control over the services they use is likely to increase adherence, self-efficacy and quality of life.

Cognition and coping is critical to adaptation to LTI. For example, Scharloo *et al.* (2000) found that the five categories of beliefs about symptoms identified by Leventhal and colleagues (as discussed above) predicted coping and adaptation in COPD patients, emphasizing the importance of cognitive care and intervention for these patients. Qualitative methods can reveal the details of patients' of illness-related thoughts, including the burden that LTIs place on people's self-image. For example, Dovey-Pearce, Doherty and May (2007) show how diabetes can affect young people's self-concept, highlighting the desire to be 'normal', the additional adult responsibilities that diabetes places on young people and the importance of peer support. Similarly, Smith and Osborne (2007) illustrated the crushing effect that chronic pain can have on self-concept. Interviewees described how their pain led to social behaviour that they were ashamed of and wanted to distance themselves from their public persona. They expressed nostalgia for a past, pain-free self and were anxious about the self that others attributed to them as a result of their pain-directed behaviour. Patients with LTIs may also find engagement with traditional health services, which focus on diagnosis and treatment, challenging and alienating. For example, in a qualitative study of stories written by women with chronic pelvic pain, McGowan *et al.* (2007) found that women found consultations unsatisfactory especially when medical tests failed to validate their experience of pain. The failure to find a physiological explanation left women feeling powerless and devalued and concerned that they were not believed and perceived to be neurotic or depressed by health care professionals. In some cases this led to complete disengagement from health care services, despite ongoing pain.

Behaviour change interventions in long-term illnesses

Behaviour change interventions have much to offer people with LTIs. For example, in a systematic review, Glazier *et al.* (2006) found that 11 of 17 interventions improved diabetes care with intervention being associated with delivery by community educators or lay people, one-to-one interaction with individualized assessment, a focus on behaviour change, provision of feedback, use of 10 or more sessions and a duration of 6 months or more. While such interventions are expensive they are likely to be cost-effective because they could reduce visits to general practitioners by a quarter and hospitalization by a half among those with LTIs, while also enhancing participants' QoL (Department of Health, 2008). Note too that behaviour change interventions can prevent some LTIs. For example, Knowler *et al.* (2002) found that a lifestyle change programme including weekly exercise targets was more effective than medication in preventing diabetes onset over a 3-year period.

We noted above that clinical evidence of recovery may not always be the most important outcome measure, for example, in relation to interventions designed to increase adherence or patient involvement in consultations. In a classic paper, Kaplan (1990) argued that mortality and quality of life are always the most important outcome measures in health care and, certainly, quality of life improvement is a key measure of success in helping people with LTIs. There are a variety of quality of life and health-related quality of life measures available including one developed by the World Health Organization (WHOQOL Group, 1995) and the Short-Form Health Survey (Ware, Kosinski and Keller, 1996), which assess the degree to which illness imposes on everyday life and how patients' feel about their everyday life.

Managing chronic pain

Chronic pain provides a useful illustration of the importance of psychological theory and intervention to LTI. In a comprehensive review, Gatchel *et al.* (2007) indicate how a biopsychosocial approach to understanding pain emphasizes the role of psychological care in treatment. They note, for example, that anxiety reduction interventions can result in reduced distress and interference with daily living. They also note that enhanced self-efficacy in relation to controlling the impact pain has on everyday living affects the body's opioid and immune systems, reduces pain, improves recovery after surgical procedures and improves overall psychological adjustment. Higher levels of pain-related self-efficacy increase motivation to follow through with goals that become challenging and so reduce activity avoidance and may increase social engagement and support. Consequently these researchers note that, 'pain cannot be treated successfully without attending to the patient's emotional state' (Gatchel *et al.*, 2007: 602). Current treatment of pain focuses on multidisciplinary programmes, which incorporate a combination of approaches including psychological interventions. Turk and Burwinkle (2005) highlighted the effectiveness and cost-effectiveness of such programmes compared to traditional approaches. They list commonly used measures of pain assessment and show that multidisciplinary programmes are effective, not only in reducing pain but in improving employment status and reducing medication and medical services usage. They also emphasize the role of psychologists both in designing and evaluating interventions within such multidisciplinary contexts.

There are a range of change techniques that may be used by psychologists working with patients experiencing pain (see Chapter 2). The gate-control theory of pain perception (Melzack and Wall, 1965) clarified how the brain is able to control pain sensation providing a clear pathway for psychological moderation of pain experience. Cognitive intervention techniques involve teaching patients to identify and change cognitions and emotions that increase pain. So, for example, challenging catastrophic or hopeless thoughts may reduce anxiety and enhance self-efficacy. Such interventions have been shown to be effective, especially with chronic pain patients and can be more effective than pharmacological interventions (Morley, Eccleston and Williams, 1999; see also Andrasik and Schwartz, 2006). Patients may also be taught new coping strategies including distraction (i.e. patient focuses on a non-painful stimulus in their nearby environment in order to distract attention away from pain); non-painful imagery (i.e. patient focuses on a positive, imagined event/scene unrelated to pain); pain redefinition (i.e. patient learns to redefine negative thoughts about the pain experience using positive self-statements); and hypnosis (i.e. patient experiences less pain while in a relaxed, hypnotic state). Each of these cognitive techniques has been found to be effective in reducing pain experience but the evidence is stronger for acute pain than for chronic pain (Fernandez and Turk, 1989). Such cognitive techniques can, of course, be combined with behaviour change techniques (see below) and, for headache pain, this combination has been found to be as effective as conventional analgesics (Holroyd *et al.*, 1991). Moreover, an influential recent review or reviews found that, for chronic pain, the strongest evidence for effectiveness across all psychological interventions was for cognitive behavioural therapy with a focus on cognitive coping strategies and behavioural rehearsal (Eccleston, Morley and Williams, 2013).

Change techniques can also focus directly on pain-related behaviour with a view to enhancing activity and quality of life rather than pain reduction. Application of change techniques based on the principles of operant conditioning such as extinction and reinforcement were pioneered by Fordyce (1976). Central to this approach is the assumption that pain behaviours (e.g. withdrawal, lying down, crying, limping, reliance on medication) are learned responses that become conditioned through reinforcement (e.g. receiving attention, sympathy and care in response to pain behaviour and avoiding anticipated pain by taking analgesic medication). Therefore, this approach seeks to:

1   reinforce adaptive 'well' behaviours such as walking without limping after a minor operation;
2   encourage family and friends not to attend to or reward pain behaviours; and
3   provide analgesic medication on a fixed schedule (e.g. every 4 hours) and not when the patient requests it or is in pain.

Each of these change techniques has been found to successfully reinforce new adaptive behaviour patterns and to extinguish previous maladaptive behaviour (Horn and Munafo, 1998). For example, patients' reliance on medication can be reduced over a short period of time. By providing the medication on a fixed schedule, receiving it becomes independent of requests for it and as a result, reinforcing effects are eliminated. Over a couple of weeks, the dosage of medication can be reduced by mixing it with a flavoured syrup to mask the taste and then gradually reducing the amount of the analgesic in the mixture.

Pain experiences such as headache pain and chronic back pain are caused by changes in physiological processes, which are frequently triggered by stress. Consequently, relaxation and biofeedback techniques are used to help patients manage stress. Typically progressive muscle relaxation is used in which patients learn to relax and tighten different muscle groups in a quiet, comfortable environment for approximately 20 to 40 minutes in weekly sessions over a number of months. Once trained, patients are encouraged to use this technique whenever they feel a painful or stressful episode is developing.

Biofeedback is a technique in which a patient learns to exert control over basic autonomic bodily processes such as blood pressure, heart rate and blood flow as well as learning to gain increased control over voluntary processes such as muscle tension. Feedback is achieved by placing electrodes and transducers on the skin that can detect and convert bodily signals such as temperature, galvanic skin response and blood flow into electrical signals, which are then typically transmitted as a tone. Through training and hearing the tone change when a specific muscle group is relaxed, patients can learn to exert control over muscles previously not under their voluntary control. Progressive muscle relaxation and biofeedback have both been found to be effective (e.g. Andrasik and Schwartz, 2006). However, these techniques may have limited impact in patients suffering from severe chronic pain and therefore are often used in combination with other techniques (e.g. Holroyd *et al.*, 2001).

ACTIVITY 10.1

Psychological contributions to patient care

Imagine you joined a multidisciplinary clinic for people with LTIs and were asked to draw up a brief report on how application of psychological theory and research could help improve the care the clinic was offering. Make notes for your report.

KEY CONCEPTS AND TERMS

- Acupuncture
- Adaptation
- Adherence
- Anxiety reduction
- Asthma
- Biofeedback
- Calgary-Cambridge consultation model
- Cause
- Chronic obstructive pulmonary disease (COPD)
- Chronic pain
- Classical conditioning
- Cognitive care
- Complementary or alternative medicine (CAM)
- Compliance
- Concordance
- Consultation duration
- Continuity of care
- Diabetes

- Direct and positive consultation style
- Doctor-centred
- Emotional care
- Endogenous opioids
- Event-based recall
- Extinction
- Gate-control theory
- Homeopathy
- Hypnosis
- Identity
- Long-term illness (LTI)
- Multidisciplinary
- Non-painful imagery
- Operant conditioning
- Pain redefinition
- Patient-centredness
- Patient empowerment
- Patient expectations
- Patient satisfaction
- Pendleton et al.'s seven tasks

- Perceived effectiveness of treatment
- Perceived symptom seriousness
- Perspective taking
- Placebo effect
- Positive affect
- Progressive muscle relaxation
- Quality of life
- Recall
- Reinforcement
- Selective serotonin reuptake inhibitors (SSRIs)
- Self image
- Symptom detection
- Time-based recall
- Timeline and control
- Visual-analogue scale

SUMMARY

Patients are often unable to reliably assess their symptoms. Consequently, beliefs about what symptoms mean and emotional responses to their detection are crucial to the effect they have on health behaviour including consulting health care professionals. Beliefs about symptoms such as perceived seriousness and perceived effectiveness of available treatment mediate the effects of personality (e.g. neuroticism and conscientiousness) on health behaviour including adherence. Most medical interventions rely on patient adherence. Yet non-adherence is high. Patients are non-adherent for different reasons but patients' understanding, recall and satisfaction with health care all predict adherence. Key aspects of relating to patients determine patient satisfaction. Doctors' own satisfaction with their work and patient social support (especially practical support) predict adherence. In general, studies suggest that we can improve adherence although it may be challenging to do so for longer-term treatments to an extent that enhanced health outcomes follow.

Patient satisfaction, adherence and health outcomes are related to consultation management. Reaching an agreed plan with patients is important and has been referred to as 'concordance'. The Calgary-Cambridge consultation model identifies six key stages, while Pendleton *et al.* (1984) specify seven key tasks to be completed in consultations with patients. Patient-centredness and especially listening to patients' concerns is crucial to patient satisfaction. A positive, direct style, communicating expertise, is also important, especially for patients with a physical problem that can be treated with medication. For chronically ill patients perspective taking needs to be combined with empowering strategies, which help patients take more control of the consultation and their health. Evidence suggests that interventions can be successful in empowering patients' involvement in consultations.

Use of complementary or alternative medicine (CAM) is widespread but doubts remain about the effectiveness of such therapies, especially when placebo effects are controlled for and clinical outcomes are used. Large placebo effects have been observed but the impact of placebo responding on clinical outcomes may be limited to certain health problems including pain relief. A variety of processes underpin observed placebo effects including classical conditioning of drug responses. Patient expectations and stress reduction are likely to play an important role in the psychological and physiological benefits observed in placebo conditions. Adhering to treatment can bolster such expectations, which may account for the beneficial effects of adherence to placebo treatments.

People with long-term physical illness tend to be older and to be more intensive users of health care services. The challenge for people with LTIs is to adapt to their illness, adopt the most effective coping strategies and to maintain high self-efficacy and a good quality of life. Emotional responses to the illness are likely to affect quality of life and in some cases longevity. Consequently, cognitive and emotional care is critical to efficacious and cost-effective services. Psychological interventions have much to offer. For example, cognitive interventions focusing on cognition and emotion and behavioural interventions focusing on behaviour change and enhanced quality of life have been found to be effective in pain management.

SAMPLE ESSAY TITLES

- What are placebo effects and can they be used to improve health?
- How can the effectiveness of doctor–patient consultations be maximized? Discuss with reference to relevant research.
- Poor adherence to health promotion and medical advice reduces the effectiveness of health services. How can we improve adherence?
- What is meant by patient-centred consultations and are they effective?
- How can psychologists help people with long-term illnesses?

FURTHER READING

Journal articles

Eccleston, C., Morley, S.J. and Williams, A.C. (2013). Psychological approaches to chronic pain management: Evidence and challenges. *British Journal of Anaesthesia*, 111, 59–63.

Harrington, J., Noble, L.M. and Newman, S.P. (2004). Improving patients' communication with doctors: A systematic review of intervention studies. *Patient Education and Counselling*, 52, 7–16.

Kaplan, R.M. (1990). Behavior as the central outcome in health care. *American Psychologist*, 45, 1211–1220.

Little, P., Everitt, H., Williamson, I., Warner, G., Moore, M., Gould, C., Ferrier, K. and Payne, S. (2001). Observational study of effect of patient centredness and positive approach on outcomes of general practice consultations. *British Medical Journal*, 323, 908–911.

Stewart-Williams, S. (2004). The placebo puzzle: Putting together the pieces. *Health Psychology*, 23, 198–206.

11 Future directions, roles and competencies

CHAPTER PLAN

We have seen how health psychology research can reveal psychological processes underpinning health and illness and thereby suggest changes in health care practice designed to optimize effectiveness. In this chapter we anticipate future directions in health psychology research and consider the contributions that health psychologists can make to health care systems. The chapter consists of two sections: (1) future research directions in health psychology; and (2) roles and competencies for health psychologists.

LEARNING OUTCOMES

When you have completed this chapter you should be able to:

1 Discuss possible future directions in health psychology research.
2 Identify key contexts in which professional health psychologists practise and discuss the competencies they apply.

FUTURE RESEARCH DIRECTIONS IN HEALTH PSYCHOLOGY

We began by examining the main pathways through which psychological factors impact on physiological functioning and health. In particular, links between the hypothalamic–pituitary–adrenal axis and the sympathetic adrenal medullary system and the cardiovascular system (including effects on blood pressure) and how stress can affect the immune system (e.g. wound healing) and exacerbate pain. Recent research in this area has also considered how stress can result in premature ageing. It appears that stress can literally get under our skin, at a cellular level! For example, Verhoeven et al. (2015) found that psychological stress was associated with increased ageing of our DNA. They found that recent life stress shortened the length of important components of our DNA known as telomeres. In fact, these findings were similar to an earlier study by Epel and colleagues (2004a, 2004b), which showed that compared to low stress individuals, the telomeres of individuals with the highest levels of stress were shorter by the equivalent of at least 10 years of additional ageing! It will be interesting to see how such effects relate to differences in health behaviours (see e.g. the observations of Khaw et al., 2008 discussed in Chapter 1) and whether the stress–telomere relationship is moderated by social support or personality (see Chapters 5 and 6).

As the populations of many developed countries age, the promotion of healthy ageing has become a public health priority (see e.g. the findings of Yates et al., 2008 in Chapter 1). In this context, understanding the relationship between psychological factors and endocrine functioning has become important. Recent research, exploring daily cortisol profiles across the lifespan found that older age was associated with increased daily cortisol secretion throughout the day, which may act as a marker for psychological and biological vulnerability to adverse health outcomes (Nater, Hoppmann and Scott, 2013). Similarly, further research is needed to clarify the impact of other hormones such as testosterone and estrogen, whose production is known to decline with age, on quality of life outcomes including depression, cognition and sexual health (e.g. O'Connor et al., 2011b). Further research into physiological functioning is likely to focus on 'metabolic syndrome', a condition that remains somewhat controversial, characterized by obesity, insulin resistance (or type II diabetes), high blood pressure, high blood triglyceride levels and low levels of high-density lipoprotein cholesterol. Limited research has thus far indicated that stress-related changes in food intake, if maintained over time, may play a role in increasing risk of developing metabolic syndrome (Epel et al., 2004b; Newman et al., 2007).

In Chapter 3 we examined stress using psychological measures (e.g. life events and daily hassles). Research into stress and individual differences is needed to further clarify why stressors lead to poor health for some but not for others. Scientific advances in genetics offer new opportunities to study the role of specific genes in vulnerability to environmental stressors such as life events (e.g. Power et al., 2013). Diary studies of daily hassles have recently been used to help elucidate how stressors influence health behaviours (Bolger and Laurenceau, 2013; Gartland et al., 2014b; Verkuil et al., 2012). Multi-level statistical techniques have resulted in new opportunities for data analysis opening up avenues for further research in this area. The Conservation of Resources theory is a promising theoretical framework focusing on protective resources, which may help people to be more resistant to stressors while research into stress recovery may help answer the long-standing question of why some people get ill in response to stressors and others do not (Adler and Matthews, 1994). Studies have examined blood pressure and heart rate responses following stressful encounters. Future research could extend this work by examining whether hormonal and immunological parameters take longer to return to normal after stress in vulnerable individuals.

As outlined earlier, recent developments in stress theory have confirmed the significance of worry, rumination and repetitive thought as important to understanding the stress–disease relationships. Brosschot et al.'s (2006) perseverative cognition hypothesis (PCH) has suggested that worry or repetitive thinking may lead to disease by prolonging stress-related physiological activation, amplifying short-term responses, delaying recovery or reactivating responses after a stressor has been experienced. Recent evidence has demonstrated that perseverative cognition is associated with physical health outcomes using different methods including surveys, prospective studies and daily diary designs (see O'Connor et al., 2013; Verkuil et al., 2012; Verkuil et al., 2010 for a review). Therefore, these findings underline the need for future stress research to include indices of rumination as well as stress appraisal processes. This further highlights the need to assess and consider traits and unconscious processes and to embrace innovative methods and technologies in stress research (e.g. utilizing electronic data capture methods together with daily and momentary assessment techniques).

We noted in Chapters 4 and 5 how important context was to the stress–health relationship and how lack of control over work has especially negative impacts on health (e.g. Hausser et al., 2010). Awareness of workplace stress has increased greatly and requirements on employers to prevent harmful conditions at work are now legally enforceable. Consequently, there is a new impetus for research into stress reduction at work. Most interventions have focused on moderating stress impact through counselling and stress-management techniques. Further work on stress prevention, including theoretically based job redesign interventions are needed. Moreover, research into work–life balance is in its relative infancy and researchers have only just begun to study in detail positive as well as negative impacts of work on home life (e.g. Song et al., 2011).

Health inequalities are a central concern for the UK government and other first-world countries. There is evidence indicating that those with higher socio-economic status may better able to enact their intentions to engage in health protecting behaviour and to avoid health risk behaviours (Conner et al., 2013a) and also respond more positively to health promotion, thereby widening the health inequalities gap (NICE, 2007). However, there is little good evidence of the moderating effect of social inequalities on health promoting interventions. Further studies, especially those focusing on how we can empower those from disadvantaged backgrounds to take advantage of and engage with health promotion efforts are needed.

Researchers examining coping have identified many strategies and consistent styles and identified circumstances in which particular approaches are likely to lead to satisfactory outcomes (see Chapter 5). However, further work is needed on how people can proactively cope to avoid future stressors and minimize their impact. There is also a need to identify effective coping with specific stressors (e.g. in medical situations) with a view to developing practice-relevant interventions. Social support is related to health and mortality and has been found to buffer stress–health relationships. New research into the role of web-based social support networks (Coulson, 2013) may help clarify how these can be used to optimize positive and minimize negative effects.

Studies have found that people with particular personality traits (e.g. high conscientiousness) not only experience better health but also live longer (see Chapter 6). Work in this area is especially impressive because it has often employed objective health measures such as longevity. Further research could clarify the mechanisms by which personality impacts on health (see Hampson, 2012). Such understanding is crucial if we are to apply the findings to improve health. For example, work on conscientiousness suggests that its effects are partially mediated by increased health protective behaviours and decreased health risking behaviour. Given that personality traits are difficult to change, interventions might need to be targeted at individuals with particular traits (e.g. a focus on improving health behaviours among those low in conscientiousness) and at family dynamics (e.g. Matthews *et al.*, 1996). There is also a need to consider the effects of multiple personality traits simultaneously. For example, little research has attempted to examine the simultaneous influence of the 'Big Five' traits even though they show some degree of intercorrelation.

Several other personality traits have been linked to health outcomes (see Ferguson, 2013 for detailed discussion). For example, type D and alexithymia are associated with increased risk of developing cardiovascular disease (e.g. Denollet *et al.*, 1996; Waldstein *et al.*, 2002). However, the precise pathways and importance of these variables have been criticized by other researchers (e.g. see Grande *et al.*, 2012). Other personality traits may have important implications for health-related communication but have been less thoroughly investigated. Consideration of future consequences (CFC) has been identified as being important to people's understanding of health promotion interventions. People high in CFC tend to sacrifice immediate benefits in order to achieve desirable future outcomes, whereas people low in CFC place less value on long-term outcomes and are more concerned with maximizing immediate benefits. It is generally found that low CFC individuals prefer options where gains are immediate and losses occur in the future, while high CFC individuals prefer the opposite, where losses are immediate and gains occur in the future. Earlier research has indicated that CFC moderates the persuasive impact of communication messages (Orbell, Perugini and Rakow, 2004; Orbell and Hagger, 2006). Orbell *et al.* (2004) manipulated the time frame in which the costs and benefits of colorectal cancer screening occurred and found that participants low in CFC had greater intentions to participate when the positive consequences were short term and negative consequences long term. The opposite was true for high CFC individuals. Nevertheless, surprisingly little recent research has examined the role of CFC within the context of conventional health psychological interventions (e.g. see Covey, 2014). Therefore, there remains an urgent need to tailor health behaviour interventions to different personality traits and dispositional factors. Modern technologies such as the Internet and email could be used to achieve this. For example, future research should focus on developing brief, theory-driven, inexpensive, web-based interventions. These should be tailored to individual characteristics, to change health behaviours and to raise awareness of serious health problems (e.g. high blood pressure).

Research into behaviour change has begun to distinguish between initiation and maintenance of health behaviours (see Conner and Norman, 2005, 2015). Considerable research with social cognition models has focused on the initiation of health behaviour (see Chapter 7). When health benefits are associated with one-off performance (e.g. immunization) this research is immediately relevant to intervention. However, for many health behaviour patterns (e.g. healthy eating, exercise) there is little or no health benefit unless the behaviour is performed and maintained over a prolonged period of time (Conner and Norman, 2005, 2015). In such cases initiation is necessary, but not sufficient for health benefits to accrue. Further research on behaviour change maintenance and habit formation is needed (see Chapter 9). For example, are the psychological processes that prompt initiation continuous with or distinct from those sustaining maintenance? The evidence is mixed. In a meta-analytic review of the protection motivation theory, Floyd *et al.* (2000) reported that response efficacy and self-efficacy showed similar sized effects for both initiation and maintenance, although the number of studies on maintenance was modest. Sheeran, Conner and Norman

(2001) showed the theory of planned behaviour (TPB) to predict attendance at individual screening appointments, but not to predict repeated attendance. In contrast, Conner *et al.* (2002) reported the TPB to be predictive of long-term healthy eating over a period of six years.

Recent theories have focused on the factors that might be different for initiation and maintenance of health behaviours. For example, satisfaction with the outcome of the behaviour (e.g. quitting smoking) may be important in the decision to maintain, but not initiate a behaviour (Rothman, 2000). In contrast, self-efficacy may be an important determinant of both initiation and maintenance behaviours but may act in different ways (Bandura, 2000). For example, while high expectations may facilitate initiation, these expectations must become more realistic in order that dissatisfaction with outcomes during repeated performance does not inhibit maintenance (King, Rothman and Jeffery, 2002).

There is a need to identify which change techniques are likely to enhance the effectiveness of behaviour change interventions targeting particular behaviours among specified groups (see Chapters 8 and 9). The meta-analytic approach utilized by Albarracín *et al.* (2005) combined data from various studies of condom use interventions, which set new standards in exploring technique effectiveness and the extent effectiveness was moderated by audience (e.g. young versus older people). Future research will need to extend use of meta-analysis to other behaviours and to extend the range of change techniques considered (see Abraham and Michie, 2008; Webb and Sheeran, 2006). This includes use of meta-analyses to synthesize effect sizes observed in experimental studies targeting particular change processes or determinants (Sheeran, 2012). Future trial design could also involve simultaneous tests of interventions with and without particular technique combinations to establish whether the addition of these techniques enhances effectiveness. For example, would the effectiveness of interventions targeting attitudes towards increased exercise (e.g. by focusing on the consequences of exercise behaviours) be enhanced by the addition of incentives and behavioural contracts? By testing two or more versions of interventions (with and without the additional techniques) such questions can be answered experimentally.

Another important area is the development and testing of behaviour change techniques that are cost-effective when used with large populations. Although a large number of change techniques have been identified some of these techniques can be expensive to implement and may be challenging to sustain in practice because of the range of competencies required to deliver them (e.g. motivational interviewing). Other techniques may be simpler, easier to roll out to large segments of the population and so cost-effective, even if they are associated with only small to medium effect sizes on behaviour. We have considered a range of such change techniques including, for example, self-monitoring, implementation intentions, changes in choice architecture, regulation to introduce default opt-in systems and if-then planning techniques (see Chapter 9). There is growing evidence that if-then planning can be used in large-scale studies to encourage behaviour patterns such as blood donation (Godin *et al.*, 2014) and ongoing studies to suggest they might also be cost-effective in reducing smoking intiation (Conner and Higgins, 2010; Conner *et al.*, 2013a).

Similarly, a recent meta-analysis (Harkin *et al.*, 2016) suggests that simple interventions can prompt large changes in self-monitoring ($d_+ = 1.98$) that are associated with small to medium changes in behaviour ($d_+ = 0.40$). Interestingly, self-monitoring of behaviour (e.g. amount of physical activity) helps with changing that behaviour but has little effect on goal achievement (e.g. weight loss). While, in contrast, monitoring progress towards a goal like weight loss helps with achieving this goal but has no effect on behaviour change. The development of various electronic devices (such as smart-phones) that help such monitoring may considerably aid self-monitoring-based interventions. We have also seen how questionnaires can be used to deliver change techniques, including if-then planning (Godin *et al.*, 2008; van Dongen *et al.*, 2013). A recent meta-analysis (Wood *et al.*, 2015) suggests that self-prediction questions may result in small changes in behaviour including health behaviour patterns. This is a potentially low-cost delivery method. Application of such techniques and new delivery methods has the potential to produce changes in health behaviour patterns as diverse as smoking, physical activity and healthy eating that could enhance public health and be both effective and cost-effective.

Interventions to change the participation of patients in consultations have shown some promising results (Harrington *et al.*, 2004; Chapter 10). Further work on the pre-paration of patients for consultations (e.g. through web-based interventions) has the potential to enhance the health promotion impact of consultations and thereby increase their cost-effectiveness. Similarly, noting the potential effects of placebo treatments (Stewart-Wiliams, 2004) and evidence that cognitive and emotional care may maximize health benefits (Di Blasi *et al.*, 2000), further work is needed on what type of consultation is most effective for which groups of patients. If health care practitioners can be trained to maximize anxiety reduction and self-efficacy enhancement this could improve patient satisfaction, adherence and, thereby, consultation effectiveness. Such benefits may be especially important for patients with long-term illnesses and those for whom there is no obvious pharmacological intervention. For these patients, longer appointments and a greater focus on quality of life outcomes may be crucial to effectiveness. Behaviour change interventions have been successful in promoting greater self-care (e.g. Glazier *et al.*, 2006) and in prevention of long-term illnesses (Knowler *et al.*, 2002). Extensions of this work to other areas could be of great benefit to patients, while simultaneously enhancing the cost-effectiveness of health services.

There is also a need to evaluate policy interventions aimed at change. For example, how effective is the traffic-light, food-labelling system introduced by the Food Standards Agency (www.eatwell.gov.uk/foodlabels/trafficlights) in shaping consumer choice? How does it compare to other labelling systems? Similarly, the web-based NHS Direct service has been found to elicit 90 per cent satisfaction in public surveys and it is estimated that it recoups half of its running costs by encouraging more appropriate use of NHS services (National Audit Office, 2002). It would be interesting to know, however, whether services like this reduce consultation rates and/or promote health behaviours and whether we can improve their capacity to do so.

ROLES AND REQUIRED COMPETENCIES FOR HEALTH PSYCHOLOGISTS

We have seen how health psychologists (HPs) have developed and tested theories explaining motivation and behaviour change and applied such theory to the design of interventions to maintain health and prevent illness (e.g. in promoting preventive health behaviours). HPs also study psychological processes involved in causing and sustaining illness (e.g. responses to stress that undermine psychological and physical well-being). Again this work has direct relevance for interventions both at individual (e.g. stress management) and organizational (e.g. job redesign) levels. In addition, HPs examine processes relevant to the improvement of health-care systems, including understanding the effects of interactions between health care professionals and their patients. This work can have direct implications for the training of health professionals.

Research in health psychology tests basic psychological hypotheses in an applied domain as well as addressing applied questions arising from health care practice. Yet in both cases the results often have direct implications for policy and practice at individual, group (e.g. peer and family), organizational, community and national levels. Consequently, health psychology is not only a sub-discipline of the science of psychology, it is also a profession that combines a rich research background of theories and findings with a wide range of research-based practices. Postgraduate professional training courses in HP are offered worldwide (see Michie and Abraham, 2004 for comparisons between UK training and training offered in a range of other countries) and professional HPs fulfil a variety of practice roles in the UK and elsewhere.

In the UK, National Occupational Standards have been developed for a variety of professional roles including psychology. These standards identify the knowledge, skills and levels of competent performance expected after qualification from training programmes and so allow professionals and employers to match acquired skills or competencies against job demands. The 'key purpose statement' from the National Standards for Psychology is as follows:

> [T]o develop, apply and evaluate psychological principles, knowledge, theories and methods in an ethical and appropriate way (i.e. systematic, evidence-based and reflective) in order to promote work-related issues. This includes the development, well-being and effectiveness of organizations, groups and individuals for the benefit of society.
>
> (www.bps.org.uk/professional-development/nos/nos_home.cfm)

This overarching definition of professional practice in psychology is subdivided into six 'key roles'. Professional psychologists are expected to:

1 develop, implement and maintain personal and professional standards and ethical practice;
2 apply psychological and related methods, concepts, models, theories and knowledge derived from reproducible research findings;
3 research and develop new and existing psychological methods, concepts, models, theories and instruments in psychology;
4 communicate psychological knowledge, principles, methods, needs and policy requirement;
5 develop and train the application of psychological skills, knowledge, practices and procedures; and
6 manage the provision of psychological systems, services and resources.

All professional psychologists are expected to attain key roles 1–4 on qualification, while it is acknowledged that key roles 5 and 6 may only be attained though experience in practice. Each of these key roles is, in turn, subdivided into many standards of performance. These standards were derived from a series of workshops and consultations that involved a range of applied psychologists across different sub-disciplines. They provide detailed description of the functions and competencies that professional psychologists are required to perform and demonstrate once qualified. These standards have been adopted by the British Psychological Society (BPS) in accrediting psychology training courses in the UK and, in broad terms, by the European Federation of Professional Psychologists Associations (EFPA) in developing common standards across European psychology training courses (EuroPsy, 2011). EFPA represents 32 European national psychological associations, including all European Union Member States and has declared that independent practice as a psychologist requires university training equivalent to at least 5 years of full-time study and at least one year of supervised practice (EuroPsy, 2011).

The BPS Division of Health Psychology in the UK developed a competence-based qualification in professional health psychology, which maps onto the UK National Standards (BPS, 2007). This analysis and definition of health psychology competencies includes 19 core units of competence relating to generic professional competence (which would apply to all psychologists and that corresponds to key role 1 above); consultancy competence (which would map mainly onto key roles 2 and 4); research competencies (which maps mainly onto key role 3); and teaching and training competencies (which map mainly onto key role 5). Michie, Johnston and Abraham (2004) provide a useful introduction to this model.

A number of key areas of competence that characterize health psychology practice internationally can be identified (see Abraham and Michie, 2005) and mapped onto the core areas of health psychology theory and research discussed in this book. Professional HPs are able to do the following:

1   *Assess, that is, understand, describe and explain psychological and behavioural processes that result in individual differences, including individual strengths and vulnerabilities.* This may involve applying measures to characterize personality, stress levels, attitudes, patient satisfaction, adherence or health behaviours.

2   *Conduct research including developing theory and methods relevant to health-related behaviour.* This could involve applying for research funding, conducting an interpretative analysis of interview data, a systematic review, a meta-analysis, a prospective survey or randomized controlled trial.

3   *Intervene, that is, generate changes in psychological and behavioural processes that result in improved health care and health outcomes.* This could involve applying learning theory or social cognition theories to design an intervention for an individual in a health care setting, in a school class or group of workers in a private company. In Chapter 9 we listed five core competencies, which the UK National Institute for Health and Clinical Excellence recommended for all professional working in behaviour change, including HPs.

4   *Train and supervise other health professionals, that is, impart skills of psychological theorizing, assessment and intervention to others.* For example, many HPs teach

nursing and medical students (e.g. in communication skills) and may also train colleagues in psychological practices – e.g. by running training workshops for teachers or social workers. This will involve designing, delivering and evaluating training using materials appropriate to the audience.

5   *Consult both with individuals and organizations.* This would include being able to manage effective one-to-one consultations as described in Chapter 10 and at the same time being able to accept a commission for a larger piece of work such as evaluating an in-house stress management programme within a company or assisting a local authority with the reduction of unplanned teenage pregnancies. It requires highly developed communication and negotiation skills.

6   *Supervise and manage, that is guide others with less psychological training or experience in psychological practice.* Assessing, training and management are overlapping and complementary skills. Even a newly qualified professional psychologist will be able to monitor, train and report on the design and implementation of psychological research by colleagues with less training in this area. More experienced HPs will be able to manage and supervise teams of fellow HPs.

In the UK, practising health psychologists must be registered with the Health and Care Professionals Council. 'Health psychologist' is one of nine 'protected titles', which only registered professionals can use. Registration involves continuing professional development and psychologists may be audited by the council to ensure that their competencies are up to date.

HPs work in a variety of multidisciplinary settings. Hallas (2004) describes the varied work of HPs in health care demonstrating how the work draws on the full range of competencies outlined above. Hallas notes that HPs may be involved in direct patient care, assessing and enhancing individuals' psychological adjustment to illness and treatment, minimizing distress associated with medical procedures, delivering health education, facilitating patient decision-making and implementing psychological interventions to promote healthy behaviours. As well as training health care professionals, running stress management courses and advising on job redesign HPs may investigate whether an attitude change intervention could enhance patient adherence and whether this would have any effects on clinical outcomes. HPs may also work in public health services (e.g. including work on screening and/or shaping environments to facilitate health behaviour uptake at a population level). In addition HPs may work on health service policy by working in government and policy development units such as the UK National Institute for Health and Care Excellence. Interestingly a position paper from the UK Prime Minister's Strategy Unit, (Knott, Muers and Aldridge, 2007) outlined a behaviour change framework that draws explicitly on theory and research discussed in this book. The paper emphasizes from the outset the importance of understanding attitudes, values, self-efficacy, intentions and social influence in shaping social change and so emphasizes what a key role HPs have in shaping population behaviour change.

KEY CONCEPTS AND TERMS

- Blunted cortisol profile
- Competencies
- DNA
- European Federation of Professional Psychologists Associations

- Health and Care Professionals Council
- Initiation and maintenance of behaviour
- Key roles

- Metabolic syndrome
- National Occupational Standards
- Telomeres
- Traffic-light labelling

SUMMARY

Each area of research we have considered in previous chapters not only provides insights into processes underlying health and illness and effective health-care but also raises interesting new questions, which only new research can answer. These range from questions concerning fundamental biological processes to questions about coping and personality through to questions about the content and impact of behaviour change interventions and the most effective way in which to manage patient consultations.

Professional health psychologists work in a variety of multidisciplinary settings, including health care settings, organizational settings and government departments. They are trained in a number of key roles and develop a range of competencies through training involving a minimum of five years full-time-equivalent university training and one year full-time supervised practice. These competencies include research, assessment, intervention training, consultation and management skills.

SAMPLE ESSAY TITLES

- How can health psychologists contribute to the improvement of health care services?

FURTHER READING

Books

The British Psychological Society (2007). *Qualification in Health Psychology (Stage 2): Candidate Handbook.* Leicester: The British Psychological Society.

Michie, S. and Abraham, C. (eds) (2004). *Health Psychology in Practice.* Oxford: Blackwell.

Journal articles

Hampson, S.E. (2012). Personality processes: Mechanisms by which personality traits 'get outside the skin'. *Annual Review of Psychology*, 63, 315–339.

Harkin, B., Webb, T., Chang, B., Benn, Y., Prestwich, A., Conner, M., Kellar, I. and Sheeran, P. (2016). Does monitoring goal progress promote goal attainment? A meta-analysis of the experimental evidence. *Psychological Bulletin*, 42(2), 198–220.

Turk, D.C. and Burwinkle, T.M. (2000). Clinical outcomes, cost-effectiveness and the role of psychology in treatments for chronic pain sufferers. *Professional Psychology: Research and Practice*, 36, 602–610.

References

Abhyankar, P., O'Connor, D.B. and Lawton, R. (2008). The role of message framing in promoting MMR vaccination: Evidence of a loss frame advantage. *Psychology, Health and Medicine*, 13, 1–16.

Aboa-Éboulé, C., Brisson, C., Maunsell, E., Bourbonnais, R., Vézina, M., Milot, A. and Dagenais, G.R. (2011). Effort–reward imbalance at work and recurrent coronary heart disease events: A prospective study of post-myocardial infarction patients. *Psychosomatic Medicine*, 73, 436–447.

Abraham, C. (2004). Theory in health psychology research. In S. Michie and C. Abraham (eds) *Health Psychology in Practice*. Oxford: Blackwell, 65–82.

Abraham, C. (2008). Beyond stages of change: Multi-determinant continuum models of action readiness and menu-based interventions. *Applied Psychology: An International Review*, 57, 30–41.

Abraham, C. (2012). Designing and evaluating interventions to change health-related behaviour patterns. In I. Boutron, P. Ravaud and D. Moher (eds) *Randomized Clinical Trials of Nonpharmacologic Treatments*. London: Chapman & Hall, 357–368.

Abraham, C. and Michie, S. (2005). Contributing to public health policy and practice. *The Psychologist*, 12, 676–679.

Abraham, C. and Sheeran, P. (2005). The health belief model. In M. Conner and P. Norman (eds) *Predicting Health Behaviour: Research and Practice with Social Cognition Models* (2nd edn). Maidenhead: Open University Press, 28–80.

Abraham, C. and Michie, S. (2008). A taxonomy of behaviour change techniques used in interventions. *Health Psychology*, 27, 379–387.

Abraham, C. and Graham-Rowe, E. (2009). Are worksite interventions effective in increasing physical activity? A systematic review and meta-analysis. *Health Psychology Review*, 3, 108–144.

Abraham, C. and Sheeran, P. (2015). Health belief model. In M. Conner and P. Norman (eds) *Predicting and Changing Health Behaviour: Research and Practice with Social Cognition Models* (3rd edn). Maidenhead: Open University Press, 30–69.

Abraham, C., Sheeran, P. and Orbell, S. (1998). Can social cognitive models contribute to the effectiveness of HIV-preventive behavioural interventions? A brief review of the literature and a reply to Joffe (1996; 1997) and Fife-Schaw (1997). *British Journal of Medical Psychology*, 71, 297–310.

Abraham, C., Costa-Pereira, A., du Florey, C. and Ogston, S. (1999). Cognitions associated with initial medical consultations concerning recurrent breathing difficulties: A community-based study. *Psychology and Health*, 14, 913–925.

Abraham, C., Krahé, B., Dominic, R. and Fritsche, I. (2002). Does research into the social cognitive antecedents of action contribute to health promotion? A content analysis of safer-sex promotion leaflets. *British Journal of Health Psychology*, 7, 227–246.

Abraham, C., Johnson, B.T., de Bruin, M. and Luszczynska, A. (2014). Enhancing reporting of behaviour change intervention evaluations. *Journal of Acquired Immune Deficiency Syndromes*, 15, Suppl. 3: S293–S299.

Abraham, C., Southby, L., Quandte, S., Krahé, B. and van der Sluijs, W. (2007). What's in a leaflet? Identifying research-based persuasive messages in European alcohol leaflets. *Psychology and Health*, 22, 31–60.

Abraham, C., Good, A., Huedo-Medina, T.B., Warren, M.R. and Johnson, B.T. (2012). Reliability and utility of the SHARP taxonomy of behaviour change techniques. *Psychology and Health*, 27, 1–2.

Abraham, C., Wood, C.E., Johnston, M., Francis, J., Hardeman, W., Richardson, M. and Michie, M. (2015). Reliability of identification of behavior change techniques (BCTs) defined by the 'BCT Taxonomy version 1' (BCTTv1) in intervention descriptions. *Annals of Behavioral Medicine*, 49, 885–900.

Ader, R. and Cohen, N. (1975). Behaviorally conditioned immunosuppression. *Psychosomatic Medicine*, 37, 333–340.

Adler, N.E. and Matthews, K. (1994). Health psychology: Why do some people get sick and some stay well? *Annual Review of Psychology*, 45, 229–259.

Adler, N.E., Boyce, T., Chesney, M.A., Cohen, S., Folkman, S., Kahn, R.L. and Syme, S.L. (1994). Socio-economic status and health: The challenge of the gradient. *American Psychologist*, 49, 15–24.

Affleck, G., Tennen, H., Croog, S. and Levine, S. (1987). Causal attribution, perceived benefits and morbidity following a heart attack: An 8-year study. *Journal of Consulting and Clinical Psychology*, 55, 29–35.

Affleck, G., Tennen, H., Uroows, S. and Higgins, P. (1992). Neuroticism and the pain–mood relation in rheumatoid arthritis: Insights from a prospective daily study. *Journal of Consulting and Clinical Psychology*, 60, 119–126.

Affleck, G., Zautra, A., Tennen, H. and Armeli, S. (1999). Multi-level daily process designs for consulting and clinical psychology: A preface for the perplexed. *Journal of Consulting and Clinical Psychology*, 67, 746–754.

Ajzen, I. (1991). The theory of planned behaviour. *Organizational Behavior and Human Decision Processes*, 50, 179–211.

Ajzen, I. (2001). Nature and operation of attitudes. *Annual Review of Psychology*, 52, 27–58.

Ajzen, I. and Fishbein, M. (1980). *Understanding Attitudes and Predicting Social Behaviour*. Englewood Cliffs, NJ: Prentice Hall.

Ajzen, I. and Fishbein, M. (2004). Questions raised by a reasoned action approach: Reply on Ogden (2003). *Health Psychology*, 23, 431–434.

Alarcon, G.M., Edwards, J.M. and Clark, P.C. (2013). Coping strategies and first year performance in postsecondary education. *Journal of Applied Social Psychology*, 43, 1676–1685.

Albarracín, D., Johnson, B.T., Fishbein, M. and Muellerleile, P.A. (2001). Theories of reasoned action and planned behaviour as models of condom use: A meta-analysis. *Psychological Bulletin*, 127, 142–161.

Albarracín, D., Gillete, J.C., Earl, A.N., Glasman, L.R. and Durantini, M.R. (2005). A test of major assumptions about behaviour change: A comprehensive look at the effects of passive and active HIV-prevention interventions since the beginning of the epidemic. *Psychological Bulletin*, 131, 856–897.

Albrecht, L., Archibald, M., Arseneau, D. and Scott, S.D. (2013). Development of a checklist to assess the quality of reporting of knowledge translation interventions using the Workgroup for Intervention Development and Evaluation Research (WIDER) recommendations. *Implementation Science*, 8, 52.

Allender, S., Peto, V., Scarborough, P., Boxer, A. and Rayner, M. (2006). *Coronary Heart Disease Statistics*. British Heart Foundation: London.

Allom, V., Mullen, B. and Hagger, M. (2015). Does inhibitory control training improve health behaviour? A meta-analysis. *Health Psychology Review*, doi: 10.1080/17437199.2015. 1051078.

Alloy, L.B., Abrahamson, L.Y. and Francis, E.L. (1999). Do negative cognitive styles confer vulnerability to depression? *Current Directions in Psychological Science*, 8, 128–132.

Allport, F.H. (1924). *Social Psychology*. Boston, MA: Houghton Mifflin.

Almeida, D.M. (2005). Resilience and vulnerability to daily stressors assessed via diary methods. *Current Directions in Psychological Science*, 14, 64–68.

Ambady, N., LaPlante, D., Nguyen, T., Rosenthal, R., Chaumeton, N. and Levinson, W. (2002). Surgeons' tone of voice: A clue to malpractice history. *Surgery*, 132, 5–9.

American Psychological Association (2012). Stress in America survey. Retrieved 25 March 2014 from www.apa.org/news/press/releases/stress/2012/impact.aspx

American Psychological Association (2014) The road to resilience: Ten ways to build resilience. Retrieved 14 April 2014 from www.apa.org/helpcenter/road-resilience.aspx

Andrasik, F. and Schwartz, M.S. (2006). Behavioural assessment and treatment of paediatric headache. *Behavioural Modification*, 30, 93–113.

Apanovitch, A.M., McCarthy, D. and Salovey, P. (2003). Using message framing to motivate HIV testing among low-income, ethnic minority women. *Health Psychology*, 22, 60–67.

Arbuthnott, A. and Sharpe, D. (2009). The effect of physician–patient collaboration on patient adherence in non-psychiatric medicine. *Patient Education and Counselling*, 77(1), 60–67.

Armitage, C.J. and Conner, M. (2001). Efficacy of the theory of planned behaviour: A meta-analytic review. *British Journal of Social Psychology*, 40, 471–499.

Armitage, C.J., Harris, P.R., Napper, L. and Hepton, G. (2008). Efficacy of a brief intervention to increase acceptance of health risk information among adult smokers with low socioeconomic status. *The Psychology of Addictive Behaviors*, 22, 88–95.

Asch, S. (1952). *Social Psychology*. Englewood Cliffs, NJ: Prentice Hall.

Austin, J.T. and Vancouver, J.B. (1996). Goal constructs in psychology: Structure, process and content. *Psychological Review*, 120, 338–375.

Bagby, M.R., Taylor, G.J. and Parker, J.D.A. (1994). The 20-item Toronto Alexithymia Scale–II. Convergent, discriminant and concurrent validity. *Journal of Psychosomatic Research*, 38, 33–40.

Bagozzi, R.P. (1993). On the neglect of volition in consumer research: A critique and proposal. *Psychology and Marketing*, 10, 215–237.

Baird, G., Pickles, A., Simonoff, E., Charman, T., Sullivan, P., Chandler, S., Loucas, T., Meldrum, D., Afzal, M., Thomas, B., Jin, L. and Brown, D. (2008). Measles vaccination and antibody response in autism spectrum disorders. *Archives of Disease in Childhood*, published online, doi: 10.1136/adc.2007.122937.

Bakker, A.B. and Demerouti, E. (2007). The job demands–resources model: State of the art. *Journal of Managerial Psychology*, 22, 309–328.

Bakker, A.B., Westman, M. and van Emmerik, I.J.H. (2009). Advancements in crossover theory. *Journal of Managerial Psychology*, 24, 206–219.

Bakker, A.B., ten Brummelhuis, L.L., Prins, J.T. and van der Heijden, F.M.M.A. (2011). Applying the job demands–resources model to the work–home interface: A study among medical residents and their partners. *Journal of Vocational Behavior*, 79, 170–180.

Bambra, C., Egan, M., Thomas, S., Petticrew, M. and Whitehead, M. (2007). The psychosocial and health effects of workplace reorganisation: A systematic review of task restructuring interventions. *Journal of Epidemiology and Community Health*, 61, 1028–1037.

Bandura, A. (1982). Self-efficacy mechanism in human agency. *American Psychologist*, 37, 122–147.

Bandura, A. (1997). *Self-Efficacy: The Exercise of Control*. New York: Freeman.

Bandura, A. (1999). Health promotion from the perspective of social cognitive theory. *Psychology and Health*, 13, 623–650.

Bandura, A. (2000). Health promotion from the perspective of social cognitive theory. In P. Norman, C. Abraham and M. Conner (eds) *Understanding and Changing Health Behaviour: From Health Beliefs to Self-Regulation*. Switzerland: Harwood Academic, 229–242.

Bardone-Cone, A.M. and Cass, K.M. (2007). What does viewing a pro-anorexia website do? An experimental examination of website exposure and moderating effects. *International Journal of Eating Disorders*, 40, 537–548.

Barlow, J.H., Wright, C., Sheasby, J., Turner, A. and Hainsworth, J. (2002). Self-management approaches for people with chronic conditions: A review. *Patient Education and Counseling*, 48, 177–187.

Barlow, J.H., Wright, C.C., Turner, A.P. and Bancroft, G.V. (2005). A 12-month follow-up study of self-management training for people with chronic disease: Are changes maintained over time? *British Journal of Health Psychology*, 10, 589–599.

Bartholomew, L.K., Parcel, G.S., Kok, G., Gottlieb, N.H. and Fernandez, M.E. (2011). *Planning Health Promotion Programs: An Intervention Mapping Approach* (3rd edn.) San Francisco, CA: Jossey-Bass.

Bartley, M., Martikainen, P., Shipley, M. and Marmot, M. (2004). Gender differences in the relationship of partner's social class to behavioural risk factors and social support in the Whitehall II study. *Social Science and Medicine*, 59, 1925–1936.

Bartram, D., Hermann, E., Wilpert, B., Roe, R., Dopping, J., Georgas, J., Jern, S., Job, R., Lecuyer, R., Newstead, S., Nieminen, P., Odland, T., Peiro, J.M., Poortinga, Y. and Lunt, I. (2001). *EuroPsyT: A Framework for Education and Training for Psychologists in Europe*. London: Institute of Education, University of London.

Bassman, L.E. and Uellendahl, G. (2003). Complementary/alternative medicine: Ethical, professional and practical challenges for psychologists. *Professional Psychology; Research and Practice*, 34, 264–270.

Baum, A. and Posluszny, D.M. (1999). Health psychology: Mapping biobehavioural contributions to health and illness. *Annual Review of Psychology*, 50, 137–163.

Baumeister, R. (2002). Ego depletion and self-control failure: An energy model of the self's executive function. *Self and Identity*, 1, 129–136.

Beatty, D.L., Kamarck, T.W., Matthews, K.A. and Shiffman, S. (2011). Childhood socioeconomic status is associated with psychosocial resources in African Americans: The Pittsburgh Healthy Heart Project. *Health Psychology*, 30(4), 472–480.

Beecher, H.K. (1955). The powerful placebo. *Journal of the American Medical Association*, 159, 1602–1606.

Beecher, H.K. (1956). Relationship of significance of wound to pain experienced. *Journal of the American Medical Association*, 161, 1609–1613.

Beehr, T.A. and Newman, J.E. (1978). Job stress, employee health and organizational effectiveness: A facet analysis, model and literature review. *Personnel Psychology*, 31, 665–699.

Belloc, N.B. and Breslow, L. (1972). Relationship of physical health status and health practices. *Preventive Medicine*, 9, 469–421.

Benedetti, F., Pollo, A. and Colloca, L. (2007). Opioid-mediated placebo responses boost pain endurance and physical performance: Is it doping in sport competitions? *Journal of Neuroscience*, 27, 11934–11939.

Berkanovic, E., Telesky, C. and Reeder, S. (1981). Structural and social psychological factors in the decision to seek medical care for symptoms. *Medical Care*, 19, 693–709.

Berkman, L.F. and Syme, S.L. (1979). Social networks, host resistance and mortality: A 9-year follow-up study of Alameda County residents. *American Journal of Epidemiology*, 109, 186–204.

Bissell, P., May, C.T. and Noyce, P.R. (2004). From compliance to concordance: Barriers to accomplishing a re-framed model of health care interactions. *Social Science and Medicine*, 58, 851–862.

Blaschke, T.F., Osterberg, L., Vrijens, B. and Urquhart, J. (2012) Adherence to medications: Insights arising from studies on the unreliable link between prescribed and actual drug dosing histories. *Annual Review of Pharmacology and Toxicology*, 52, 275–301.

Blaxter, M. (1990). *Health and Lifestyles*. London: Tavistock.

Bogg, T. and Roberts, B.W. (2004). Conscientiousness and health-related behaviours: A meta-analysis of the leading behavioural contributors to mortality. *Psychological Bulletin*, 130, 887–919.

Bogg, T. and Roberts, B. W. (2013). The case for conscientiousness: Evidence and implications for a personality trait marker of health and longevity. *Annals of Behavioral Medicine*, 45, 278–288.

Bolger, N. (1990). Coping as a personality process: A prospective study. *Journal of Personality and Social Psychology*, 59, 525–537.

Bolger, N. and Laurenceau, J-P. (2013). *Intensive Longitudinal Methods: An Introduction to Diary and Experience Sampling Research*. New York: Guilford.

Bolger, N., Davis, A. and Rafaeli, E. (2003). Diary methods: Capturing life as it is lived. *Annual Review of Psychology*, 54, 579–616.

Bonanno, G.A. (2012). Uses and abuses of the resilience construct: Loss, trauma and health related constructs. *Social Science and Medicine*, 74, 753–756.

Bonanno, G.A., Galea, S., Bucciarelli, A. and Vlahov, D. (2007). What predicts psychological resilience after disaster? The role of demographics, resources and life stress. *Journal of Consulting and Clinical Psychology*, 75, 671–682.

Bonanno, G.A., Kennedy, P., Galatzer-Levy, I.R., Lude, P. and Elfström, M.L. (2012). Trajectories of resilience, depression and anxiety following spinal cord injury. *Rehabilitation Psychology*, 57, 236–247.

Bond, F.W. and Bunce, D. (2001). Job control mediates change in a work reorganization intervention for stress reduction. *Journal of Occupational Health Psychology*, 6, 290–302.

Bond, F.W., Flaxman, P.E. and Bunce, D. (2008). The influence of psychological flexibility on work redesign: Mediated moderation of a work reorganization intervention. *Journal of Applied Psychology*, 93, 645–654,

Boneva, B., Kraut, R. and Frohlich, D. (2001). Using e-mail for personal relationships: The difference gender makes. *American Behavioral Scientist*, 45, 530–549.

Booth, T., Mottus, R., Corley, J., Gow, A.J., Henderson, R.D., Maniega, S.M., Murray, C., Royle, N.A., Sprooten, E., Hernández, M.V., Bastin, M.E., Penke, L., Starr, J. M. Wardlaw, J.M., Deary, I.J. and Ian, J. (2014). Personality, health and brain integrity: The Lothian birth cohort study 1936. *Health Psychology*, 33, 1477–1486.

Booth-Kewley, S. and Friedman, H. (1987). Psychological predictors of heart disease: A quantitative review. *Psychological Bulletin*, 101, 343–362.

Booth-Kewley, S. and Vickers, R.R. (1994). Associations between major domains of personality and health behaviour. *Journal of Personality*, 62, 281–298.

Borek, A., Abraham, C., Smith, J., Greaves, C. and Tarrant, M. (2015). A checklist to improve reporting of group-based behaviour-change interventions. *BMC Public Health*, 15, 963.

Borland, R. (2014). *Understanding Hard to Maintain Behaviour Change: A Dual Process Approach.* Chichester, UK: Wiley & Sons.

Bosma, H., Peter, R., Siegrist, J. and Marmot, M. (1998). Two alternative job stress models and the risk of coronary heart disease. *American Journal of Public Health*, 88, 68–74.

Bower, J.E. and Segerstrom, S.C. (2004). Stress management, finding benefit and immune function: Positive mechanisms for intervention effects on physiology. *Journal of Psychosomatic Research*, 56, 9–11.

Bower, J.E., Moskowitz, J.T. and Epel, E. (2009). Is benefit finding good for your health? *Current Directions in Psychological Science*, 18, 337–341.

Boyle, C.M. (1970). Difference between patients and doctors interpretation of some common medical terms. *British Medical Journal*, 71, 286–289.

BPS (2007). *Qualification in Health Psychology (Stage 2): Candidate Handbook.* Leicester, UK: The British Psychological Society.

Brehm, J. (1966). *A Theory of Psychological Reactance.* New York: Academic Press.

Breslow, L. and Enstrom, J.E. (1980). Persistence of health habits and their relationship to mortality. *Preventive Medicine*, 9, 469–483.

Briñol, P. and Petty, R.E. (2005). Individual differences in attitude change. In D. Albarracín, B.T. Johnson and M. Zanna (eds) *The Handbook of Attitudes*. Mahwah, NJ: Lawrence Erlbaum, 575–616.

Brosschot, J.F. and Van Der Doef, M. (2006). Daily worrying and somatic health complaints: Testing the effectiveness of a simple worry reduction intervention. *Psychology and Health*, 21, 19–31.

Brosschot, J.F., Gerin, W. and Thayer, J.F. (2006). The perserverative cognition hypothesis: A review of worry, prolonged stress-related physiological activation and health. *Journal of Psychosomatic Research*, 60, 113–124.

Brough, P. and Kelling, A. (2002). Women, work and well-being family–work conflict. *New Zealand Journal of Psychology*, 31, 29–38.

Brough, P., Timms, C., Siu, O., Kalliath, T., O'Driscoll, M., Sit, C.H.P., Lo, D. and Lu, C. (2013). Validation of the job demands–resources model in cross-national samples: Cross sectional and longitudinal predictions of psychological strain and work engagement. *Human Relations*, 66, 1312–1315.

Brown, G.W. (1974). Meaning, measurement and stress of life events. In B.S. Dohrenwend and B.P. Dohrenwend (eds) *Stressful Life Events: Their Nature and Effects*. London: Wiley, 217–243.

Brown, G.W. and Harris, T.O. (1978). *Social Origins of Depression: A Study of Psychiatric Disorder in Women*. London: Tavistock.

Burke, R.J., Weir, T. and DuWors, R.E. (1980). Perceived type A behaviour of husbands and wives' satisfaction and well-being. *Journal of Occupational Behavior*, 1, 139–150.

Burman, M.A. and Gewirtz, J.C. (2004). Timing of fear expression in trace and delay conditioning measured by fear-potentiated startle in rats. *Learning and Memory*, 11, 205–212.

Butland, B., Jebb, S., Kopelman, P., McPherson, K., Thomas, S., Mardell, J. and Parry, V. (2007). *Foresight: Tackling Obesities – Future Choices Project Report* (2nd edn). London: Government Office for Science.

Butler, A.B., Grzywacz, J., Ettner, S.L., Liu, B. (2009). Work flexibility, self-reported health and health care utilization. *Work and Stress*, 23, 45–59.

Butler, C. and Steptoe, A. (1986). Placebo responses: An experimental study of psychophysiological processes in asthmatic volunteers. *British Journal of Clinical Psychology*, 25, 173–183.

Byrne, D. (1961). The repression-sensitization scale: Rationale, reliability and validity. *Journal of Personality*, 29, 334–349.

Byrne, P.S. and Long, B.E.L. (1976). *Doctors Talking to Patients*. London: HMSO.

Cacioppo, J.T. and Cacioppo, S. (2014). Social relationships and health: The toxic effects of perceived social isolation. *Social and Personality Psychology Compass*, 8, 58–72.

Cacioppo, J.T., Petty, R.E. and Morris, K.J. (1983). Effects of need for cognition on message evaluation, recall and persuasion. *Personality and Social Psychology*, 45, 805–818.

Campbell, M., Fitzpatrick, R., Haines, A., Kinmonth, A.L., Sandercock, P., Spiegelhalter, D. and Tyrer, P. (2000). Framework for design and evaluation of complex interventions to improve health. *British Medical Journal*, 321, 694–696.

Canals, J., Bladé, J. and Domènech, E. (1997). Smoking and personality predictors in young Spanish people. *Personality and Individual Differences*, 23, 905–908.

Cannon, W. (1932). *The Wisdom of the Body*. New York: Norton.

Cantillon, P., Morgan, M., Dundas, R., Simpson, J., Bartholomew, J. and Shaw, A. (1997). Patients' perceptions of changes in their blood pressure. *Journal of Human Hypertension*, 11, 221–225.

Carlson, D.S., Kacmar, K., Wayne, J.H. and Grzywacz, J.G. (2006). Measuring the positive side of the work–family interface: Development and validation of a work–family enrichment scale. *Journal of Vocational Behavior*, 68, 131–164.

Carmody, T.P., Crossen, J.R. and Wiens, A.N. (1989). Hostility as a health risk factor: Relationships with neuroticism, type A behaviour, attentional focus and interpersonal style. *Journal of Clinical Psychology*, 45, 754–762.

Carroll, D., Bennett, P. and Davey Smith, G. (1993). Socio-economic health inequalities: Their origins and implications. *Psychology and Health*, 8, 295–316.

Carroll, D., Ebrahim, S., Tilling, K., Macleod, J. and Davey Smith, G. (2002). Admissions for myocardial infarction and World Cup football: Database survey. *British Medical Journal*, 325, 1439–1442.

Carver, C.S. and Scheier, M.F. (1982). Control theory: A useful conceptual framework for personality–social, clinical and health psychology. *Psychological Bulletin*, 92, 111–135.

Carver, C.S. and Scheier, M.F. (1994). Situational coping and coping dispositions in a stressful transaction. *Journal of Personality and Social Psychology*, 66, 184–195.

Carver, C.S., Scheier, M.F. and Weintraub, J.K. (1989). Assessing coping strategies: A theoretically based approach. *Journal of Personality and Social Psychology*, 56, 267–283.

Carver, C.S., Scheier, M.F. and Segerstrom, S.C. (2010). Optimism. *Clinical Psychology Review*, 30, 879–889.

Carver, C.S., Pozo, C., Harris, S.D., Noriega, V., Scheier, M.F. Robinson, D.S., Ketcham, A.S., Moffat F.L. Jr and Clark, K.C. (1993). How coping mediates the effects of optimism on distress: A study of women with early stage breast cancer. *Journal of Personality and Social Psychology*, 65, 375–390.

Carver, C.S., Smith, R.G., Antoni, M.H., Petronis, V.M., Weiss, S. and Derhagopian, R.P. (2005). Optimistic personality and psychosocial well-being during treatment predict psychosocial well-being among long-term survivors of breast cancer. *Health Psychology*, 24, 508–516.

Caspi, A., Roberts, B.W. and Shiner, R.L. (2005). Personality development: Stability and change. *Annual Review of Psychology*, 56, 453–484.

Caspi, A., Begg, D., Dickson, N., Harrington, H., Langley, J., Moffitt, T.E. and Silva, P.A. (1997). Personality differences predict health-risk behaviour in young adulthood: Evidence from a longitudinal study. *Journal of Personality and Social Psychology*, 73, 1052–1062.

Cassidy, T., Giles, M. and McLaughlin, M. (2014). Benefit finding and resilience in child caregivers. *British Journal of Health Psychology*, 19, 606–618.

Cegala, D.J., McClure, L., Marinelli, T.M. and Post, D.M. (2000). The effects of communication skills training on patients' participation during medical interviews. *Patient Education and Counselling*, 41, 209–222.

Centre for Disease Control and Prevention (2012). *A Framework for Program Evaluation*. Centers for Disease Control and Prevention. Retrieved on 16 September 2015 from www.cdc.gov/eval/framework/index.htm

Chaiken, S. (1980). Heuristic versus systematic information processing and the use of source versus message cues in persuasion. *Journal of Personality and Social Psychology*, 39, 752–766.

Chen, C.C., David, A.S., Nunnerley, H., Mitchell, M., Dawson, J.L., Berry, H., Dobbs, J. and Fahy. T. (1995). Adverse life events and breast cancer: Case-control study. *British Medical Journal*, 311, 1527–1530.

Chesney, M.A., Eagleston, J.R. and Rosenman, R.H. (1980). The type A structured interview: A behavioral assessment in the rough. *Journal of Behavioral Assessment*, 2, 255–272.

Chida, Y. and Steptoe, A. (2008). Positive psychological well-being and mortality: A quantitative review of prospective observational studies. *Psychosomatic Medicine*, 70, 741–756.

Chida, Y. and Steptoe, A. (2009). The association of anger and hostility with future coronary heart disease. *Journal of the American College of Cardiology*, 53, 936–946.

Chida, Y. and Steptoe, A. (2010). Greater cardiovascular responses to laboratory mental stress are associated with poor subsequent cardiovascular risk status: A meta-analysis of prospective evidence. *Hypertension*. 55, 1026–1032.

Choosing Health (2004). *Choosing Health: A Consultation to Improve People's Health*. London: HMSO.

Christensen, A.J., Moran, P.J. and Wiebe, J.S. (1999). Assessment of irrational health beliefs: Relation to health practices and medical regimen adherence. *Health Psychology*, 18, 169–176.

Christiansen, A.J. and Smith, T.W. (1995). Personality and patient adherence: Correlates of the five-factor model in renal dialysis. *Journal of Behavioral Medicine*, 18, 305–313.

Christodoulou, M. (2012). Pro-anorexia websites pose public health challenge. *The Lancet*, 379, 9811, 93–192.

Cialdini, R.B. (1995). Principles and techniques of social influence. In A. Tesser (ed.) *Advanced Social Psychology*. New York: McGraw-Hill, 257–281.

Cialdini, R.B. and Trost, M.R. (1998). Social influence: Social norms, conformity and compliance. In D.T. Gilbert, S.T. Fiske and G. Lindzey (eds) *The Handbook of Social Psychology* (4th edn). New York: McGraw-Hill, vol. 2, 151–192.

Cioffi, D. (1991). Beyond attentional strategies: A cognitive-perceptual model of somatic interpretation. *Psychological Bulletin*, 109(1), 25–41.

Clow, A. (2001). The physiology of stress. In F. Jones and J. Bright (eds) *Stress: Myth, Theory and Research*. London: Pearson Education, 47–61.

Cohen, J. (1992). A power primer. *Psychological Bulletin*, 112, 155–159.

Cohen, S. (2005). The Pittsburgh common cold studies: Psychosocial predictors of susceptibility to respiratory infectious illness. *International Journal of Behavioral Medicine*, 12, 123–131.

Cohen, S. and Wills, T.A. (1985). Stress, social support and the buffering hypothesis. *Psychological Bulletin*, 98, 310–357.

Cohen, S., Kamarck, T. and Mermelstein, R. (1983). A global measure of perceived stress. *Journal of Health and Social Behavior*, 24, 386–396.

Cohen, S., Tyrrell, D.A.J. and Smith, A.P. (1991). Psychological stress and susceptibility to the common cold. *New England Journal of Medicine*, 325, 606–612.

Cohen, S., Doyle, W.J. and Skoner, D.P. (1999). Psychological stress, cytokine production and severity of upper respiratory illness. *Psychological Medicine*, 61, 175–180.

Cohen, S., Miller, G.E. and Rabin, B.S. (2001). Psychological stress and antibody response to immunization: A critical review of the human literature. *Psychosomatic Medicine*, 63, 7–18.

Cohen, S., Doyle, W.J. and Baum, A. (2006). Socio-economic status is associated with stress hormones. *Psychosomatic Medicine*, 68, 414–420.

Cohen, S., Frank, E., Doyle, W.J., Skoner, D.P., Rabin, B.S. and Gwaltney, J.M., Jr. (1998). Types of stressors that increase susceptibility to the common cold in adults. *Health Psychology*, 17, 214–223.

Cohen, S., Janicki-Deverts, D., Turner, R.B., Casselbrant, M.L., Li-Korotky, H., Epel, E.S. and Doyle, W.J. (2013a). Association between telomere length and experimentally induced upper respiratory viral infection in healthy adults. *Journal of the American Medical Association*, 309, 699–705.

Cohen, S., Janicki-Deverts, D., Turner, R.B., Marsland, A.L., Casselbrant, M.L., Li-Korotky, H-S., Epel, E.S. and Doyle, W.J. (2013b). Childhood socioeconomic status, telomere length and susceptibility to upper respiratory infection. *Brain Behavior and Immunity*, 34, 31–38.

Conn, V.S., Hafdahl, A.R., Cooper, P.S., Brown, L.M. and Lusk, S.L. (2009). Meta-analysis of workplace physical activity interventions. *American Journal of Preventive Medicine*, 37, 330–339.

Conner, M. and Abraham, C. (2001). Conscientiousness and the theory of planned behavior: Towards a more complete model of the antecedents of intentions and behaviour. *Personality and Social Psychology Bulletin*, 27, 1547–1561.

Conner, M. and Norman, P. (eds) (2005). *Predicting Health Behaviour: Research and Practice with Social Cognition Models* (2nd edn). Maidenhead: Open University Press.

Conner, M. and Sparks, P. (2005). The theory of planned behaviour and health behaviours. In M. Conner and P. Norman (eds) *Predicting Health Behaviour: Research and Practice with Social Cognition Models* (2nd edn). Maidenhead: Open University Press, 170–222.

Conner, M. and Higgins, A. (2010). Long-term effects of implementation intentions on prevention of smoking uptake among adolescents: A cluster randomized controlled trial. *Health Psychology*, 29, 529–538.

Conner, M. and Norman, P. (eds) (2015). *Predicting and Changing Health Behaviour: Research and Practice with Social Cognition Models* (3rd edn). Maidenhead: Open University Press.

Conner, M. and Sparks, P. (2015). The theory of planned behaviour and the reasoned action approach. In M. Conner and P. Norman (eds) *Predicting and Changing Health Behaviour: Research and Practice with Social Cognition Models* (3rd edn). Maidenhead: Open University Press, 142–188.

Conner, M., Fitter, M. and Fletcher, W. (1999). Stress and snacking: A diary study of daily hassles and between meal snacking. *Psychology and Health*, 14, 51–63.

Conner, M., Norman, P. and Bell, R. (2002). The theory of planned behaviour and healthy eating. *Health Psychology*, 21, 194–201.

Conner, M., Rodgers, W. and Murray, T. (2007). Conscientiousness and the intention–behaviour relationship: Predicting exercise behaviour. *Journal of Sports and Exercise Psychology*, 29, 518–533.

Conner, M., Godin, G., Norman, P. and Sheeran, P. (2011). Using the question-behaviour effect to promote disease prevention behaviours: Two randomized controlled trials. *Health Psychology*, 30, 300–309.

Conner, M., McEachan, R., Jackson, C., McMillan, B., Woolridge, M. and Lawton, R. (2013a). Moderating effect of socioeconomic status on the relationship between health cognitions and behaviors. *Annals of Behavioral Medicine*, 46, 19–30.

Conner, M., Grogan, S., Lawton, R., Armitage, C., West, R., Siddiqi, K., Gannon, B., Torgerson, C., Flett, K. and Simms-Ellis, R. (2013b). Study protocol: A cluster randomized controlled trial of implementation intentions to reduce smoking initiation in adolescents. *BMC Public Health*, 13, 54.

Conrad, P. (1985). The meaning of medications: Another look at compliance. *Social Science and Medicine*, 20, 29–37.

Contrada, R.J. and Baum, A. (2011). *Handbook of Stress Science: Psychology, Biology and Health*. New York: Springer.

Cook, W.W. and Medley, D.M. (1954). Proposed hostility and pharisaic-virtue scores for the MMPI. *Journal of Applied Psychology*, 38, 414–418.

Cooke, R. and Sheeran, P. (2004). Moderation of cognition–intention and cognition–behaviour relations: A meta-analysis of properties of variables from the theory of planned behaviour. *British Journal of Social Psychology*, 43, 159–186.

Cooper, C.L. and Dewe, P. (2004). *Stress: A Brief History*. Oxford: Blackwell.

Cooper, C.L., Sloan, S.J. and Williams, S. (1988). *The Occupational Stress Indicator*. Windsor: NFER-Nelson.

Cooper, M.L., Wood, P.K., Orcutt, H.K. and Albino, A.W. (2003). Personality and the predisposition to engage in risky or problem behaviours during adolescence. *Journal of Personality and Social Psychology*, 84, 390–410.

Cornwell, E.Y. and Waite, L.J. (2009). Social disconnectedness, perceived isolation and health among older adults. *Journal of Health and Social Behavior*, 50, 31–48.

Costa, P.T., Jr. and McCrae, R.R. (1980). Influence of extraversion and neuroticism on subjective well-being: Happy and unhappy people. *Journal of Personality and Social Psychology*, 40, 19–28.

Costa, P.T., Jr. and McCrae, R.R. (1987). Neuroticism, somatic complaints and disease: Is the bark worse than the bite? *Journal of Personality*, 55, 299–316.

Costa, P.T., Jr. and McCrae, R.R. (1990). Personality: Another 'hidden factor' in stress research. *Psychological Inquiry*, 1, 22–24.

Costa, P.T., Jr. and McCrae, R.R. (1992). Four ways five factors are basic. *Personality and Individual Differences*, 13, 653–665.

Coulson, N.S. (2013). How do online patient support communities affect the experience of inflammatory bowel disease? An online survey. *Journal of the Royal Society of Social Medicine Short Reports*, 4, 1–8.

Coulson, N.S., Buchanan, H. and Aubeeluck, A. (2007). Social support in cyberspace: A content analysis of communication within a Huntington's disease online support group. *Patient Education and Counseling*, 68, 173–178.

Coulter, A., Entwistle, V. and Gilbert, D. (1999). Sharing decisions with patients: Is the information good enough? *British Medical Journal*, 318, 318–322.

Courneya, K.S. and Hellsten, L.M. (1998). Personality correlates of exercise behaviour, motives, barriers and preferences: An application of the five-factor model. *Personality and Individual Differences*, 24, 625–633.

Covey, J. (2014). The role of dispositional factors in moderating message framing effects. *Health Psychology*, 33, 52–65.

Cox, T. (1978). *Stress*. London: Macmillan.

Cox, T. and Mackay, C. (1985). The measurement of self-reported stress and arousal. *British Journal of Psychology*, 76, 183–186.

Coyne, J.C. and Gottlieb, B.H. (1996). The mismeasure of coping by checklist. *Journal of Personality*, 64, 959–991.

Craig, P., Dieppe, P., Macintyre, S., Michie, S., Nazareth, I. and Petticrew, M. (2008). Developing and evaluating complex interventions: the new Medical Research Council guidance. *British Medical Journal*, 337, a1655–a1655.

Creswell, J.D., Lam, S., Stanton, A.L., Taylor, S.E., Bower, J.E. and Sherman, D.K. (2007). Does self-affirmation, cognitive processing, or discovery of meaning explain cancer-related health benefits of expressive writing? *Personality and Social Psychology Bulletin*, 33, 238–250.

Crowley, A.E. and Hoyer, W.D. (1994). An integrative framework for understanding two-sided persuasion. *Journal of Consumer Research*, 20, 561–574.

Crowley, M.J., Zullig, L.L., Shah, B.R., Shaw, R.J., Lindquist, J.H., Peterson, E.D. and Bosworth, H.D. (2015). Medication non-adherence after myocardial infarction: An exploration of modifying factors. *Journal of General Internal Medicine*, 30, 83–90.

Crowne, D.P. and Marlowe, D. (1960). A new scale of social desirability independent of psychopathology. *Journal of Consulting Psychology*, 24, 349–354.

Csiernik, R. (2011). The glass is filling: An examination of employee assistance program evaluations in the first decade of the new millennium. *Journal of Workplace Behavioral Health*, 26, 334–335.

Cummings, M.K., Becker, M.H. and Maile, M.C. (1980). Bringing the models together: An empirical approach to combining variables used to explain health actions. *Journal of Behavioral Medicine*, 3, 123–145.

Cunningham, A.J. (1985). The influence of mind on cancer. *Canadian Psychology*, 26, 13–29.

Dahlgren, A., Kecklund, G., Theorell, T. and Akerstedt, T. (2009). Day-to-day variation in saliva cortisol–relation with sleep, stress and self-rated health. *Biological Psychology*, 82, 149–155.

Dakof, G.S. and Taylor, S.E. (1990). Victims perceptions of social support: What is helpful and from whom? *Journal of Personality and Social Psychology*, 58, 80–89.

Daly, J., Willis, K., Small, R., Green, J., Welch, N., Kealy, M. and Hughes, E. (2007). A hierarchy of evidence for assessing qualitative health research. *Journal of Clinical Epidemiology*, 60, 43–49.

Dancey, C.P., Taghavi, M. and Fox, R.J. (1998). The relationship between daily stress and symptoms of irritable bowel: A time-series approach. *Journal of Psychosomatic Research*, 44, 537–545.

Danner, D.D., Snowdon, D.A. and Friesen, W.V. (2001). Positive emotions in early life and longevity: Findings from the Nun Study. *Journal of Personality and Social Psychology*, 80, 804–813.

Das, E.H., de Wit, J.B.F. and Stroebe, W. (2003). Fear appeals motivate acceptance of action recommendations: Evidence for a positive bias in the processing of persuasive messages. *Personality and Social Psychology Bulletin*, 29, 650–664.

Davidson, K.W., Goldstein, M., Kaplan, R.M., Kaufmann, P.G., Knatterund, G.L., Orleans, C.T., Spring, B., Trudeau, K.J. and Whitlock, E. P. (2003). Evidence-based behavioral medicine: What is it and how do we achieve it? *Annals of Behavioral Medicine*, 26, 161–171.

Davidson, K.W., Gidron, Y., Mostofsky, E. and Trudeau, K.J. (2007). Hospitalization cost offset of a hostility intervention for coronary heart disease patients. *Journal of Consulting and Clinical Psychology*, 75, 657–662.

de Bruin, M., Viechtbauer, W., Schaalma, H.P., Kok, H., Abraham, C. and Hospers, H.J. (2010). Standard care impact on effects of highly active antiretroviral therapy adherence interventions: A meta-analysis of randomized controlled trials. *JAMA Internal Medicine*, 170, 240–250.

de Lange, A.H., Taris, T.W., Kompier, M.A.J., Houtman, I.L.D. and Bongers, P.M. (2003). The very best of the millennium: Longitudinal research and the demand-control-(support) model. *Journal of Occupational Health Psychology*, 8, 282–305.

de Rijk, A.E., Le Blance, P.M., Schaufeli, W.B. and de Jonge, J. (1998). Active coping and need for control as moderators of the job demand–control model: Effects on burnout. *Journal of Occupational and Organizational Psychology*, 71, 1–18.

Dean, J. (2013). *Making Habits, Breaking Habits*. Boston, MA: De Capo Press.

Deci, E.L., Koestner, R. and Ryan, R.M. (1999). A meta-analytic review of experiments examining the effects of extrinsic rewards on intrinsic motivation. *Psychological Bulletin*, 125, 627–668.

Deelstra, J.T., Peeters, M.C.W., Zijlstra, F.R.H. and van Doornen, L.P. (2003). Receiving instrumental support at work: When help is not welcome. *Journal of Applied Psychology*, 88, 324–331.

Delgado, M.R., Jou, R.L., LeDoux, J.E. and Phelps, E.A. (2009). Tracking the mechanisms of avoidance learning in humans during fear conditioning. *Frontiers in Behavioral Neuroscience*, 3, 1–9.

DeLongis, A., Coyne, J.C., Dakof, G., Folkman, S. and Lazarus, R.S. (1982). Relationships of daily hassles, uplifts and major life events to health status. *Health Psychology*, 1, 119–136.

Demerouti, E., Bakker, A.B., Nachreiner, F. and Schaufeli, W.B. (2001). The job demand–resources model of burnout. *Journal of Applied Psychology*, 86, 499–512.

Demers, R.R., Altamore, H., Mustin, A., Kleinman, A. and Leonardi, D. (1980). An exploration of the depth and dimensions of illness behaviour. *Journal of Family Practice*, 11, 1085–1092.

Denollet, J., Sys, S.U., Stroobant, N., Rombouts, H., Gillebert, T.C. and Brutsaert, D.L. (1996). Personality as independent predictors of long-term mortality in patients with coronary heart disease. *The Lancet*, 34, 417–421.

Department of Health (2001). *The Expert Patient: A New Approach to Chronic Disease Management for the 21st Century.* London: Department of Health, HMSO.

Department of Health (2008). *Raising the Profile of Long-Term Conditions Care: A Compendium of Information.* Leeds: Department of Health.

Department of Health (2013, March 25). Reducing obesity and improving diet. Retrieved 27 August 2013, from www.gov.uk/government/policies/reducing-obesity-and-improving-diet

Department of Work and Pensions (2015). *Helping People to Find and Stay in Work.* London: Crown Copyright.

Derakshan, N. and Eysenck, M.W. (1997). Repression and repressors: Theoretical and experimental approaches. *European Psychologist,* 2, 235–246.

DeRubeis, R.J. and Crits-Christoph, P. (1998). Empirically supported individual and group psychological treatments for adult mental disorders. *Journal of Consulting and Clinical Psychology,* 66, 37–52.

Detweiler, J.B., Bedell, B.T., Salovey, P., Pronin, E. and Rothman, A.J. (1999). Message framing and sunscreen use: Gain-framed messages motivate beach-goers. *Health Psychology,* 18, 189–196.

Deutsch, M. and Gerard, H.G. (1955). A study of normative and informational social influence upon individual judgment. *Journal of Abnormal and Social Psychology,* 51, 629–636.

Di Blasi, Z., Harkness, E., Ernst, E., Georgiou, A. and Kleijnen, J. (2000) Influence of context effects on health outcomes: A systematic review. *The Lancet,* 357, 757–762.

DiClemente, C.C. (1986). Self-efficacy and smoking cessation maintenance: A preliminary report. *Journal of Social and Clinical Psychology,* 4, 302–315.

DiClemente, C.C., Prochaska, J.O., Fairhurst, S.K., Velicer, W.F., Velasquez, M.M. and Rossi, J.S. (1991). The process of smoking cessation: An analysis of precontemplation, contemplation and preparation stages of change. *Journal of Consulting and Clinical Psychology,* 59, 295–304.

Dienstbier, R.A. (1989). Arousal and physiological toughness: Implications for mental and physical health. *Psychological Review,* 96, 84–100.

Digman, J.M. (1990). Personality structure: Emergence of the five-factor model. *Annual Review of Psychology,* 41, 417–440.

DiMatteo, M.R. (2004). Social support and patient adherence to medical treatment: A meta-analysis. *Health Psychology,* 23, 207–218.

DiMatteo, M.R., Sherbourne, C.D., Hays, Ordway, L., Kravitz, R.L., McGlynn, E.A., Kaplan, S. and Rogers, W.H. (1993). Physicians' characteristics influence patients' adherence to medical treatment: Results from the medical outcomes study. *Health Psychology,* 12, 93–102.

Dohrenwend, B.P. (2000). The role of adversity and stress in psychopathology: Some evidence and its implications for theory and research. *Journal of Health and Social Behaviour,* 41, 1–19.

Dohrenwend, B.P. (2006). Inventorying stressful life events as risk factors for psychopathology: Towards resolution of the problem of intracategory variability. *Psychological Bulletin,* 132, 477–495.

Dohrenwend, B.P. and Shrout, P.E. (1985). 'Hassles' in the conceptualization and measurement of life stress variables. *American Psychologist*, 40, 780–785.

Dohrenwend, B.P., Link, B.G., Kern, R., Shrout, P.E. and Markowitz, J. (1990). Measuring life events: The problem of variability within categories. *Stress Medicine*, 6, 179–187.

Dohrenwend, B.S., Dohrenwend, B.P., Dodson, M. and Shrout, P.E. (1984). Symptoms, hassles, social supports and life events: The problem of confounded measures. *Journal of Abnormal Psychology*, 93, 222–230.

Doidge, N. (2007). *The Brain that Changes Itself*. New York: Penguin Books.

Doll, R., Peto, R., Wheatley, K., Gray, R. and Sutherland, I. (1994). Mortality in relation to smoking: Forty years' observations on male British doctors. *British Medical Journal*, 309, 901–911.

Donovan, J.L. and Blake, D.R. (1992). Patient non-compliance: Deviance or reasoned decision-making. *Social Science and Medicine*, 34, 507–513.

Doran, G.T. (1981). There's a SMART way to write management's goals and objectives. *Management Review*, 70, 35–36.

Dovey-Pearce, G., Doherty, Y. and May, C. (2007). The influence of diabetes upon adolescent and young adult development: A qualitative study. *British Journal of Health Psychology*, 12, 75–91.

Durantini, M.R., Albarracin, D., Mitchell, A.L., Earl, A.N. and Gillette, J.C. (2006). Conceptualizing the influence of social agents of behaviour change: A meta-analysis of the effectiveness of HIV-prevention interventionists for different groups. *Psychological Bulletin*, 132, 212–248.

Durie, R. and Wyatt, K. (2007). New communities, new relations: The impact of community organization on health outcomes. *Social Science and Medicine*, 65, 1928–1948.

Dwamena, F., Holmes-Rovner, M., Gaulden, C.M., Jorgenson, S., Sadigh, G., Sikorskii, A., Lewin, S., Smith, R.C., Coffey, J. and Olomu, A. (2012) Interventions for providers to promote a patient-centred approach in clinical consultations (Review). *The Cochrane Library Systematic Review*.

Eccleston, C., Morley, S.J. and Williams, A.C. (2013). Psychological approaches to chronic pain management: Evidence and challenges. *British Journal of Anaesthesia*, 111, 59–63.

Eisend, M. (2006). Two-sided advertising: A meta-analysis. *International Journal of Research in Marketing*, 23, 187–198.

Eisend, M. (2007). Understanding two-sided persuasion: An empirical assessment of theoretical approaches. *Psychology and Marketing*, 24, 615–640.

Ellis, J. (1998). Prospective memory and medicine-taking. In L.B. Myers and K. Midence (eds) *Adherence to Treatment in Medical Conditions*. Amsterdam: Harwood Academic, 1113–1132.

Elwyn, G., Edwards, A., Gwyn, R. and Grol, R. (1999). Towards a feasible model of shared decision making: Focus group study with general practice registrars. *British Medical Journal*, 319, 753–756.

Engbers, L.H., van Poppel, M.N.R., Chin, A., Paw, M.J.M. and van Mechelen, V. (2005). Worksite health promotion programs with environmental changes: A systematic review. *American Journal of Preventive Medicine*, 29, 61–70.

Ennis, N.E., Hobfoll, S.E. and Schröder, K.E.E. (2000). Money doesn't talk, it swears: How economic stress and resistance resources impact inner-city women's depressive mood. *American Journal of Community Psychology*, 28, 149–173.

Epel, E.S., Blackburn, E.H., Lin, J., Dhabhar, F.S., Adler, N.E., Morrow, J.D. and Cawthon, R.M. (2004a). Accelerated telomere shortening in response to life stress. *Proceedings of the National Academy of Sciences*, 101, 17312–17315.

Epel, E., Jimenez, S.Y., Brownell, K., Stroud, L., Stoney, C. and Niaura, R. (2004b). Are stress eaters at risk for the metabolic syndrome? *Annals of the New York Academy of Sciences*, 1032: 208–210.

Epstein, L.H. (1984). The direct effects of compliance on health outcome. *Health Psychology*, 3, 385–393.

Epton, T., Harris, P.R., Kane, R., van Koningsbruggen, G.M. and Sheeran, P. (2015). The impact of self-affirmation on health-behaviour change: A meta-analysis. *Health Psychology*, 34, 187–196.

Ernst, E. and Resch, K.L. (1995). Concept of true and perceived placebo. *British Medical Journal*, 311, 551–553.

Erskine, J.A.K., Georgiou, G.J. and Kvavilashvili, L. (2010). I suppress therefore I smoke. *Psychological Science*, 21, 1225–1230.

Esterling, B.A., Antoni, M.H., Kumar, M. and Schneiderman, N. (1993). Defensiveness, trait anxiety and Epstein–Barr viral capsid antigen antibody titers in healthy college students. *Health Psychology*, 12, 132–139.

EuroPsy (2009). EuroPsy – the European certificate in psychology. Retrieved 18 March 2016 from www.europsy-efpa.eu/sites/default/files/uploads/EuroPsy%20Regulations%20July%202011.pdf

Everson, S.A., Kaplan, G.A., Goldberg, D.E. and Salonen, J.T. (1996a). Anticipatory blood pressure response to exercise predicts future high blood pressure in middle-aged men. *Hypertension*, 27, 1059–1064.

Everson, S.A., Kaplan, G.A., Goldberg, D.E. and Cohen, R.D. (1996b). Hopelessness and risk of mortality and incidence of myocardial infarction and cancer. *Psychosomatic Medicine*, 58, 103–121.

Everson, S.A., Lynch, J.W., Kaplan, G.A., Lakka, T.A., Sivenius, J. and Salonen, J.T. (2001). Stress-induced blood pressure reactivity and incident stroke in middle-aged men. *Stroke*, 32, 1263–1270.

Eysenck, H.J. (1967). *The Biological Basis of Personality*. Springfield, IL: Charles Thomas.

Eysenck, H.J. and Eysenck, S.B.G. (1964). *Eysenck Personality Inventory*. San Diego, CA: Education and Industry Testing Service.

Eysenck, M.W. and Matthews, A. (1987). Trait anxiety and cognition. In H.J. Eysenck and M. Martin (eds) *Theoretical Foundations of Behavior Therapy*. Dordrecht: Kluwer Academic/Plenum, 197–216.

Fagundes, C.P., Glaser, R. and Kiecolt-Glaser, J.K. (2013). Stressful early life experiences and immune dysregulation across the lifespan. *Brain, Behavior and Immunity*, 27, 8–12.

Feldman, P.J., Cohen, S., Doyle, W.J., Skoner, D.P. and Gwaltney, J.M., Jr. (1999). The impact of personality on the reporting of unfounded symptoms and illness. *Journal of Personality and Social Psychology*, 77, 370–378.

Ferguson, E. (2013). Personality is of central concern to understand health: Towards a theoretical model for health psychology. *Health Psychology Review*, 7, S32-S70.

Ferguson, E., Matthews, G. and Cox, T. (1999). The appraisal of life events (ALE) scale: Reliability and validity. *British Journal of Health Psychology*, 4, 97–11.

Ferguson, E., Williams, L., O'Connor, R.C., Howard, S., Hughes, B., Johnston, D.W., Hay, J., O'Connor, D.B., Lewis, C.A., Grealy, M.A., O'Carroll, R.E. (2009). A taxometric analysis of Type D personality. *Psychosomatic Medicine*, 71, 981–986.

Fernandez, E. and Turk, D.C. (1989). The utility of cognitive coping strategies for altering pain perception: A meta-analysis. *Pain*, 38, 123–135.

Ferrer, R.A., Shmueli, D., Bergman, H.E., Harris, P.R. and Klein, W.M.P. (2012). Effects of self-affirmation on implementation intentions and the moderating role of affect. *Social Psychological and Personality Science*, 3, 300–307.

Festinger, L. (1957). *A Theory of Cognitive Dissonance*. Palo Alto, CA: Stanford University Press.

Fifield, J., McQuillan, J., Armeli, S., Tennen, H., Reisine, S. and Affleck, G. (2004). Chronic strain, daily work stress and pain among workers with rheumatoid arthritis: Does job stress make a bad day worse? *Work and Stress*, 18, 275–291.

Finniss, D., Kaptchuk, T.J., Miller, F. and Benedetti, F. (2010). Biological, clinical and ethical advances of placebo effects. *The Lancet*, 375(9715), 686–695.

Fishbein, M. and Ajzen, I. (1975). *Belief, Attitude, Intention Theory and Research*. Reading, MA: Addison-Wesley.

Fishbein, M. and Ajzen, I. (2010). *Predicting and Changing Behaviour: The Reasoned Action Approach*. New York: Psychology Press.

Fishbein, M., Triandis, H.C., Kanfer, F.H., Becker, M., Middlestadt, S.E. and Eichler, A. (2001). Factors influencing behavior and behaviour change. In A. Baum, T.A. Revenson and J.E. Singer (eds) *Handbook of Health Psychology*. Mahwah, NJ: Lawrence Erlbaum, 3–17.

Fisher, J.D. and Fisher, W.A. (1992). Changing AIDS-risk behaviour. *Psychological Bulletin*, 111, 455–471.

Fisher, J.D., Fisher, W.A., Williams, S.S. and Malloy, T.E. (1994). Empirical tests of an information-motivation-behavioural skills model of AIDS preventive behaviour. *Health Psychology*, 13, 238–250.

Fisher, J.D., Fisher, W.A., Bryan, A.D. and Misovich, S.J. (2002). Information-motivation-behavioural skills model-based HIV risk behaviour change intervention for inner-city high school youth. *Health Psychology*, 21, 177–186.

Fiske, S.T. and Taylor, S.E. (1991). *Social Cognition* (2nd edn). New York: McGraw-Hill.

Flaxman, P.E. and Bond, F.W. (2010). Worksite stress management training: Moderated effects and clinical significance. *Journal of Occupational Health Psychology*, 14, 347–358.

Flesch, R. (1948). A new readability yardstick. *Journal of Applied Psychology*, 32, 221–233.

Flor, H. and Turk, D.C. (2011). *Chronic Pain: An Integrated Biobehavioral Perspective*. Seattle, WA: IASP Press.

Floyd, D.L., Prentice-Dunn, S. and Rogers, R.W. (2000). A meta-analysis of research on protection motivation theory. *Journal of Applied Social Psychology*, 30, 407–429.

Fogel, J., Albert, S.M., Schnabel, F., Ditkoff, B.A. and Neugut, A.I. (2002). Internet use and social support in women with breast cancer. *Health Psychology*, 21, 398–404.

Folkman, S. (1997). Positive psychological states and coping with severe stress. *Social Science and Medicine*, 45, 1207–1221.

Folkman, S. and Lazarus, R.S. (1985). If it changes it must be a process: Study of emotion and coping during three stages of a college examination. *Journal of Personality and Social Psychology*, 48, 150–170.

Folkman, S. and Lazarus, R.S. (1988). *Ways of Coping Questionnaire Sampler Set: Manual, Test Booklet, Scoring Key*. Palo Alto, CA: Consulting Psychologists Press.

Folkman, S. and Moskowitz, J.T. (2000). Positive affect and the other side of coping. *American Psychologist*, 55, 647–654.

Folkman, S. and Moskowitz, J.T. (2004). Coping: Pitfalls and promise. *Annual Review of Psychology*, 55, 745–774.

Fordyce, W.E. (1976). *Behavioural Methods for Chronic Pain and Illness*. St Louis, IL: Mosby.

Foster, N.E., Thomas, E., Barlas, P., Hill, J.C., Young, J., Mason, E. and Hay, E.H. (2007). Acupuncture as an adjunct to exercise-based physiotherapy for osteoarthritis of the knee: Randomized controlled trial. *British Medical Journal*, 335, 436.

Fransson, E.I., Heikkila, K., Nyberg, S.T., Zins, M., Westerlund, H., Westerholm, P., Väänänen, A., Virtanen, M., Vahtera, J., Theorell, T., Suominen, S., Singh-Manoux, A., Siegrist, J., Sabia, S., Rugulies, R., Pentti, J., Oksanen, T., Nordin, M., Nielsen, M.L., Marmot, M.G., Magnusson, L.L., Hanson, I.E., Madsen, E.H., Lunau, T., Leineweber, C., Kumari, M., Kouvonen, A., Koskinen, A., Koskenvuo, M., Knutsson, A., Kittel, F., Jöckel, K-H., Joensuu, M., Houtman, I.L., Hooftman, W.E., Goldberg, M., Geuskens, G.A., Ferrie, J., Erbel, R., Dragano, N., De Bacquer, D., Clays, E., Casini, A., Burr, H., Borritz, M., Bonenfant, S., Bjorner, J.B., Alfredsson, L., Hamer, M., Batty, G.D. and Kivimäki, M. (2012). Job strain as a risk factor for leisure-time physical inactivity: An individual participant meta-analysis of up to 170,000 men and women. *American Journal of Epidemiology*, 176, 1078–1089.

Frattaroli, J. (2006). Experimental disclosure and its moderators: A meta-analysis. *Psychological Bulletin*, 132, 823–865.

Freeman, G.K., Horder, J.P., Shah, N.C. *et al.* (2002). Evolving general practice consultation in Britain: Issues of length and context. *British Medical Journal*, 324, 880–882.

Freijy, T. and Kothe, E.J. (2013). Dissonance-based interventions for health behaviour change: A systematic review. *British Journal of Health Psychology*, 18, 310–337.

French, J.P.R., Jr. and Raven, B. (1960). The bases of social power. In D. Cartwright and A. Zander (eds) *Group Dynamics*. New York: Harper & Row, 607–623.

Friedman, H.S. (2000). Long-term relations of personality and health: Dynamisms, mechanisms, tropisms. *Journal of Personality*, 68, 1089–1108.

Friedman, H.S. and Booth-Kewley, S. (1987). The disease-prone personality. *American Psychologist*, 42, 539–555.

Friedman, H.S., Tucker, J.S., Tomlinson-Keasay, C., Schwartz, J.E., Wingard, D.L. and Criqui, M.H. (1993). Does childhood personality predict longevity? *Journal of Personality and Social Psychology*, 65, 176–185.

Friedman, H.S., Tucker, J.S., Schwartz, J.E., Wingard, D.L. and Criqui, M.H. (1995). Childhood conscientiousness and longevity: Health behaviours and cause of death. *Journal of Personality and Social Psychology*, 68, 696–703.

Friedman, M. and Rosenman, R.H. (1974). *Type A Behavior and Your Heart*. New York: Knopf.

Friedman, R., Sobel, D., Myers, P., Caudill, M. and Benson, H. (1995). Behavioural medicine, clinical health psychology and cost offset. *Health Psychology*, 14, 509–518.

Frisina, P.G., Borod, J.C. and Lepore, S.J. (2004). A meta-analysis of the effects of written emotional disclosure on the health outcomes of clinical populations. *Journal of Nervous and Mental Disease*, 192, 629–634.

Fuertus, J.N., Mislowack, A., Bennett, J., Gilbert, T.C., Fontan, G. and Boylan, L.S. (2007). The physician–patient working alliance. *Patient Education and Counselling*, 66(1), 29–36.

Gallagher, E.J., Viscoli, C.M. and Horwitz, R.I. (1993). The relationship of treatment adherence to the risk of death after myocardial infarction in women. *Journal of the American Medical Association*, 270, 742–744.

Gallagher, K. and Updegraff, J.A. (2012). Health message framing effects on attitudes, intentions and behaviour: A meta-analytic review. *Annals of Behavioral Medicine*, 43, 101–116.

Gallo, L.C. and Matthews, K.A. (2003). Understanding the association between socioeconomic status and physical health: Do negative emotions play a role? *Psychological Bulletin*, 129, 10–51.

Ganster, D.C., Mayes, B.T., Sime, W.E. and Tharp, G.D. (1982). Managing organizational stress: A field experiment. *Journal of Applied Psychology*, 67, 533–542.

Gartland, N., O'Connor, D.B. and Lawton, R. (2012). Effects of conscientiousness on the appraisals of daily stressors. *Stress and Health*, 28, 80–86.

Gartland, N., O'Connor, D.B., Lawton, R. and Bristow, M. (2014a). Exploring day-to-day dynamics of daily stressor appraisals, physical symptoms and the cortisol awakening response. *Psychoneuroendocrinology*, 50, 130–138.

Gartland, N., O'Connor, D.B., Lawton, R. and Ferguson, E. (2014b). Investigating the effects of conscientiousness on daily stress, affect and physical symptom processes: A daily diary study. *British Journal of Health Psychology*, 19, 311–328.

Gatchel, R.J., Bo Peng, Y., Peters, M.L., Fuchs, P.H. and Turk, D.C. (2007) The biopsychosocial approach to chronic pain: Scientific advances and future directions. *Psychological Bulletin*, 133, 581–624.

Geyer, S. (1991). Life events prior to the manifestation of breast cancer: A limited prospective study covering eight years before diagnosis. *Journal of Psychosomatic Research*, 35, 355–363.

Gidron, Y., Davidson, K. and Bata, I. (1999). The short-term effects of a hostility-reduction intervention on male coronary heart disease patients. *Health Psychology*, 18, 416–420.

Giummarra, M.J., Gibson, S.J., Georgiou-Karistianis, N. and Bradshaw, J.L. (2007). Central mechanisms in phantom limb perception: The past, present and future. *Brain Research Reviews*, 54, 219–232.

Glasgow, R.E., Bull, S.S., Gillette, C., Klesges, L.M. and Dzewaltowski, D.M. (2002). Behavior change intervention research in healthcare settings: A review of recent reports with emphasis on external validity. *American Journal of Preventive Medicine*, 23, 62–69.

Glazier, R.H., Bajcar, J., Kennie, N.R. and Willson, K. (2006). A systematic review of interventions to improve diabetes care in socially disadvantaged populations. *Diabetes Care*, 29, 1675–1688.

Godin, G. and Conner, M. (2008). Intention–behaviour relationship based on epidemiological indices: An application to physical activity. *American Journal of Health Promotion*, 22, 180–182.

Godin, G., Conner, M. and Sheeran, P. (2005). Bridging the intention–behaviour 'gap': The role of moral norm. *British Journal of Social Psychology*, 44, 497–512.

Godin, G., Sheeran, P., Conner, M. and Germain, M. (2008). Asking questions changes behaviour: Mere measurement effects on frequency of blood donation. *Health Psychology*, 27, 179–184.

Godin, G., Germain, M., Conner, M., Delage, G. and Sheeran, P. (2014). Promoting the return of lapsed blood donors: A 7-arm randomized controlled trial of the question-behaviour effect. *Health Psychology*, 33, 646–655.

Golden, J., Conroy, R.M., Bruce, I., Denihan, A., Greene, E., Kirby, M. and Lawlor, B.A. (2009). Loneliness, social support networks, mood and well-being in community-dwelling elderly. *International Journal of Geriatric Psychiatry*, 24, 657–781.

Goldschmidt, A.B., Wonderlich, S.A., Crosby, R.D., Engel, S.G., Lavender, J.M., Peterson, C.B., Crow, S.J., Cao, L. and Mitchell, J. (2014). Ecological momentary assessment of stressful events and negative affect in bulimia. *Journal of Consulting and Clinical Psychology*, 82, 30–39.

Gollwitzer, P.M. (1990). Action phases and mind-sets. In E.T. Higgins and R.M. Sorrentino (eds) *Handbook of Motivation and Cognition: Foundations of Social Behavior*. New York: Guilford Press, vol. 2, 53–92.

Gollwitzer, P.M. (1993). Goal achievement: The role of intentions. *European Review of Social Psychology*, 4, 142–185.

Gollwitzer, P.M. (1999). Implementation intentions: Strong effects of simple plans. *American Psychologist*, 54, 493–503.

Gollwitzer, P.M. and Sheeran, P. (2006). Implementation intentions and goal achievement: A meta-analysis of effects and processes. *Advances in Experimental Social Psychology*, 38, 69–121.

Grande, G., Romppel, M. and Barth, J. (2012). Association between type D personality and prognosis in patients with cardiovascular diseases: a systematic review and meta-analysis. *Annals of Behavioral Medicine*, 43, 299–310.

Grandey, A.A. and Cropanzano, R. (1999). The conservation of resources model applied to work–family conflict and strain. *Journal of Vocational Behavior*, 54, 350–370.

Grant, K.E., Compas, B.E., Thurm, A.E., McMahon, S.D. and Gipson, P.Y. (2004). Stressors and child and adolescent psychopathology: Measurement issues and prospective effects. *Journal of Clinical Child and Adolescent Psychology*, 33, 412–425.

Greaves, C.J., Sheppard, K.E., Abraham, C., Hardeman, W., Roden, M., Evans, P.H. and the IMAGE Study Group. (2011). Systematic review of reviews of intervention components associated with increased effectiveness in dietary and physical activity interventions. *BMC Public Health*, 11(119), 1–12.

Green, A.S., Rafaeli, E., Bolger, N., Shrout, P.E. and Reis, H.T. (2006). Paper or plastic? Data equivalence in paper and electronic diaries. *Psychological Methods*, 11, 87–105.

Green, L.W. and Glasgow, R.E. (2006). Evaluating the relevance, generalization and applicability of research: Issues in external validation and translation methodology. *Evaluation and the Health Professions*, 29, 126–153.

Greenhaus, J.H. and Beutell, N.J. (1985). Sources of conflict between work and family roles. *Academy of Management Review*, 10, 76–80.

Greer, S. and Morris, T. (1975). Psychological attributes of women who develop breast cancer: A controlled study. *Journal of Psychosomatic Research*, 19, 147–153.

Greve, W. (2001). Traps and gaps in action explanation: Theoretical problems of a psychology of human action. *Psychological Bulletin*, 108, 435–451.

Grzywacz, J.G. and Bass, B.L. (2003). Work, family and mental health: Testing different models of work–family fit. *Journal of Marriage and Family*, 65, 248–262.

Grzywacz, J.G., Casey, P.R. and Jones, F. (2007). The effects of workplace flexibility on health behaviours: A cross-sectional and longitudinal analysis. *Journal of Occupational and Environmental Medicine*, 49, 1302–1309.

Guh, D.P., Zhang, W., Bansback, N., Amarsi, Z., Birmingham, C.L. and Anis, A.H. (2009). The incidence of co-morbidities related to obesity and overweight: A systematic review and meta-analysis. *BMC Public Health*, 9(1), 88.

Hadlow, J. and Pitts, M. (1991). The understanding of common terms by doctors, nurses and patients. *Social Science and Medicine*, 32, 193–196.

Haefner, D.P. and Kirscht, J.P. (1970). Motivational and behavioural effects of modifying health beliefs. *Public Health Reports*, 85, 478–484.

Hagger-Johnson, G., Berwick, B., Conner, M., O'Connor, D.B. and Shickle, D. (2012). School-related conscientiousness, alcohol drinking and cigarette smoking in a representative sample of English school pupils. *British Journal of Health Psychology*, 17, 644–665.

Hahn, V.C. and Dormann, C. (2013). The role of partners and children for employees' psychological detachment from work and well-being. *Journal of Applied Psychology*, 98, 26–36.

Hahn, V.C., Binneweis, C., Sonnentag, S. and Mojza, E.J. (2011). Learning how to recover from job stress: Effects of a recovery training program on recovery, recovery-related self-efficacy and well-being. *Journal of Applied Psychology*, 16, 202–216.

Haines, V.Y., III, Marchand, A. and Harvey, S. (2006). Crossover of workplace aggression experiences in dual-earner couples. *Journal of Occupational Health Psychology*, 11, 305–314.

Hakanen, J.J., Schaufeli, W.B. and Ahola, K. (2008). A 3-year cross-lagged study of burnout, depression, commitment and work engagement. *Work and Stress*, 22, 224–241.

Hall, K., Staiger, P.K., Simpson, A., Best, D. and Lubman, D. (2015). After 30 years of dissemination, have we achieved sustained practice change in motivational interviewing? *Addiction*, online preprint.

Hallas, C.N. (2004). Health psychology within health service settings. In S. Michie and C. Abraham (eds) *Health Psychology in Practice*. Oxford: Blackwell, 353–371.

Hamilton, B.E., Martin, J.A. and Ventura, S.J. (2014). Births: Preliminary data for 2009. *National Vital Statistics Reports*, 59.

Hampson, S.E. (2012). Personality processes: Mechanisms by which personality traits 'get outside the skin'. *Annual Review of Psychology*, 63, 315–339.

Hampson, S.E., Andrews, J.A., Barckley, M., Lichenstein, E. and Lee, M.E. (2000). Conscientiousness, perceived risk and risk reduction behaviours: A preliminary study. *Health Psychology*, 19, 496–500.

Hampson, S.E, Goldberg, L.R., Vogt, T.M. and Dubanoski, J.P. (2006). Forty years on: Teachers' assessment of children's personality traits predict self-reported health behaviours and outcomes at mid-life health. *Psychology*, 25, 57–64.

Hampson, S.E., Edmonds, G.W., Goldberg, L.R., Dubanoski, J.P. and Hillier, T.A. (2013). Childhood conscientiousness relates to objectively measured adult physical health four decades later. *Health Psychology*, 32, 925–928.

Hanson, E.K., Maas, C.J., Meijman, T.F. and Godaert, G.L. (2000). Cortisol secretion throughout the day, perceptions of the work environment and negative affect. *Annals of Behavioral Medicine*, 22, 316–324.

Hanusch, B.C., O'Connor, D.B., Scott, A., Ions, P., Ions, K. and Gregg, P.J. (2014). Effects of psychological distress and illness perceptions on recovery from total knee replacement. *Bone and Joint Journal*, 96-B, 210–216.

Harkin, B., Webb, T., Chang, B., Benn, Y., Prestwich, A., Conner, M., Kellar, I. and Sheeran, P. (2016). Does monitoring goal progress promote goal attainment? A meta-analysis of the experimental evidence. *Psychological Bulletin*, 42(2), 198–220.

Harrington, J., Noble, L.M. and Newman, S.P. (2004). Improving patients' communication with doctors: a systematic review of intervention studies. *Patient Education and Counselling*, 52, 7–16.

Harris, P.R. and Napper, L. (2005). Self-affirmation and the biased processing of threatening health-risk information. *Personality and Social Psychology Bulletin*, 31, 1250–1263.

Hart, S.L., Vella, L. and Mohr, D.C. (2008). Relationships among depressive symptoms, benefit finding, optimism and positive affect in multiple sclerosis patients after psychotherapy for depression. *Health Psychology*, 27, 230–238.

Haskard Zolnierek, K.B. and DiMatteo, M.R. (2009). Physician communication and patient adherence to treatment: A meta-analysis. *Medical Care*, 47(8), 826–834.

Haslam, C., Haslam, S.H., Knight, C., Gleibs, I., Ysseldyk, R. and McCloskey, L. (2014). We can work it out: Group decision-making builds social identity and enhances the cognitive performance of care residents. *British Journal of Psychology*, 105, 17–34.

Hausser, J.A., Mojzisch, A., Niesel, M. and Schulz-Hardt, S. (2010). Ten years on: A review of recent research on the job demand control (support) model and psychological well-being. *Work and Stress*, 24, 1–35.

Hawkley, L.C. and Cacioppo, J.T. (2010). Loneliness matters: A theoretical and empirical review of consequences and mechanisms. *Annals of Behavioral Medicine*, 40, 218–227.

Hay, J.L., Ford, J.S., Klein, D., Primavera, L.H., Buckley, T.R., Stein, T.R., Shike, M. and Ostroff, J.S. (2003). Adherence to colorectal cancer screening in mammography-adherent older women. *Journal of Behavioral Medicine*, 26, 553–576.

Haynes, R.B., Yao, X., Degani, A., Kripalani, S., Garg, A. and McDonald, H.P. (2005). Interventions for enhancing medication adherence. *Cochrane Database of Systematic Reviews 2005*, 4, CD000011.

Health and Safety at Work Act (1974). London: HMSO.

Health and Safety Executive (2015). *Work Related Stress, Anxiety and Depression Statistics in Great Britain 2015*. London: Crown Copyright.

Heatherton, T.F., Herman, C.P. and Polivy, J. (1991). Effects of physical threat and ego threat on eating behaviour. *Journal of Personality and Social Psychology*, 60, 138–143.

Heatherton, T.F., Herman, C.P. and Polivy, J. (1992). Effects of distress on eating: The importance of ego-involvement. *Journal of Personality and Social Psychology*, 62, 801–803.

Hedges, L.V. and Olkin, I. (1985). *Statistical Methods for Meta-Analysis*. New York: Academic Press.

Hegel, M.T., Ayllon, T., Thiel, G. and Oulton, B. (1992). Improving adherence to fluid restrictions in male hemodialysis patients: A comparison of cognitive and behavioural approaches. *Health Psychology*, 11, 324–330.

Heil, S.H., Higgins, S.T., Bernstein, I.M., Solomon, L.J., Rogers, R.E., Thomas, C.S., Badger. G.J. and Lynch, M.E. (2008). Effects of voucher-based incentives on abstinence from cigarette smoking and fetal growth among pregnant women. *Addiction*, 103, 1009–18.

Heikkila, K., Fransson, E.I., Nyberg, S.T., Zins, M., Westerlund, H., Westerholm, P., Virtanen, M., Vahtera, J., Suominen, S., Steptoe, A., Salo, P., Pentti, J., Oksanen, T., Nordin, M., Marmot, M.G., Lunau, T., Ladwig, K-H, Koskenvuo, M., Knutson, A., Kittel, F., Jockel, K-H., Goldberg, M., Erbel, R., Dragano, N., DeBacquer, D., Clays, E., Casini, A., Alfredsdon, L., Ferrie, J.E., Singh-Manoux, A., Batty, G.D. and Kivimaki, M. (2013). Job strain and health-related lifestyle: Findings from an individual-participant meta-analysis of 118,000 working adults. *American Journal of Public Health*, 103, 2090–2097.

Helgeson, V.S., Reynolds, K.A. and Tomich, P.L. (2006). A meta-analytic review of benefit finding and growth. *Journal of Consulting and Clinical Psychology*, 74, 797–816.

Herbert, T.B. and Cohen, S. (1993). Depression and immunity: A meta-analytic review. *Psychological Bulletin*, 113, 472–486.

Herculano-Houzel, S. (2009). The human brain in numbers: A linearly scaled-up primate brain. *Frontiers in Human Neuroscience*, 3, 31.

Hewitt, P.L. and Flett, G.L. (1996). Personality traits and the coping process. In M. Zeidner and N.S. Endler (eds) *Handbook of Coping: Theory, Research, Applications*. New York: Wiley, 410–433.

Hill, C. and Abraham, C. (2008). School-based, randomized controlled trial of an evidence-based condom promotion leaflet. *Psychology and Health*, 23, 41–56.

Hill, C., Abraham, C. and Wright, D. (2007). Can theory-based messages in combination with cognitive prompts promote exercise in classroom settings? *Social Science and Medicine*, 65, 1049–1058.

Hingson, R.W. and Howland, J. (2002). Comprehensive community interventions to promote health: Implications for college-age drinking problems. *Journal of Alcohol Studies*, 14, 226–240.

Hobfoll, S.E. (1989). Conservation of resources: A new attempt at conceptualizing stress. *American Psychologist*, 44, 513–524.

Hobfoll, S.E. (2001). The influence of culture, community and the nested-self in the stress process: Advancing conservation of resources theory. *Applied Psychology: An International Review*, 50, 337–421.

Hobfoll, S.E. (2007). General resource evaluation. Retrieved October 2007 from www.personal. kent.edu/~shobfoll/COR-E.pdf

Hobfoll, S.E. (2011). Conservation of resources theory: Its implications for stress, health and resilience. In S. Folkman (ed.) *Oxford Handbook of Stress Health and Coping*. Oxford: Oxford University Press, 127–147.

Hochbaum, G.M. (1958). *Public Participation in Medical Screening Programs: A Socio-Psychological Study. Public Health Service Publication No. 572*. Washington, DC: United States Government Printing Office.

Hoffmann, T.C., Glasziou, P.P., Boutron, I., Milne, R., Perera, R., Moher, D., Altman, D.G., Barbour, V., Macdonald, H., Johnston, M., Lamb, S.E., Dixon-Woods, M., McCulloch, P., Wyatt, J.C., Chan, A.W. and Michie, S. (2014). Better reporting of interventions: Template for intervention description and replication (TIDieR) checklist and guide. *British Medical Journal*, 348, g1687–g1687.

Holmes, T.H. and Rahe, R.H. (1967). The social readjustment rating scale. *Journal of Psychosomatic Research*, 11, 213–218.

Holmes, T.H. and Masuda, M. (1974). Life change and illness susceptibility. In B.S. Dohrenwend and B.P. Dohrenwend (eds) *Stressful Life Events: Their Nature and Effects*. London: Wiley, 45–72.

Holroyd, K., Nash, J., Pingel, J., Cordingley, G. and Jerome, A. (1991). A comparison of pharmacological (amitriptyline HCl) and nonpharmacological (cognitive-behavioural) therapies for chronic tension headaches. *Journal of Consulting and Clinical Psychology*, 59, 387–393.

Holroyd, K.A., O'Donnell, F.J., Stensland, M., Lipchik, G.L., Cordingley, G.E. and Carlson, B.W. (2001). Management of chronic tension-type headache with tricyclic antidepressant medication, stress management therapy and their combination. *Journal of the American Medical Association*, 285, 2208–2215.

Holsti, O.R. (1969). *Content Analysis for the Social Sciences and Humanities*. Reading, MA: Addison-Wesley.

Honeycutt, A.A., Clayton, L., Khavjou, O., Finkelstein, E.A., Prabhu, A., Blitstein, J.L., Evans, W.D. and Renaud, J.M. (2006). *Guide to Analysing the Cost-Effectiveness of Community Public Health Prevention Approaches*. Retrieved 23 February 2016 from http://aspe.hhs.gov/ health/reports/06/cphpa/report.pdf

House, J.S., Landis, K.R. and Umberson, D. (1988). Social relationships and health. *Science*, 241, 540–545.

House of Lords (2000). *Select Committee on Technology and Science, Sixth Report*. London: HMSO.

Hovland, C.I., Janis, I.L. and Kelley, H.H. (1953). *Communications and Persuasion: Psychological Studies in Opinion Change*. New Haven, CT: Yale University Press.

Howell, R.T., Kern, M.L. and Lyubomirsky, S. (2007). Health benefits: Meta-analytically determining the impact of well-being on objective health outcomes. *Health Psychology Review*, 1, 83–136.

Howie, J.R.G., Heaney, D.J., Maxwell, M., Walker, J.J., Freeman, G.K. and Rai, H. (1999). Quality at general practice consultations: Cross sectional survey. *British Medical Journal*, 319, 738–743.

Hróbjartsson, A. and Gøtzsche, P.C. (2001). Is the placebo powerless? An analysis of clinical trials comparing placebo with no treatment. *New England Journal of Medicine*, 344, 1594–1602.

HSE (1995). *Stress at Work: A Guide for Employers.* Suffolk: HSE Books.

HSE (2007). *The Management Standards.* Retrieved 12 March 2014 from www.hse.gov.uk/stress/standards

Hu, Q., Schaufeli, W.B. and Toon, T.W. (2011). The job demands–resources model: An analysis of additive and joint effects of demands and resources. *Journal of Vocational Behavior*, 79, 181–190.

Hughes, D. (1983). Consultation length and outcome in two group general practices. *Journal of the Royal College of General Practitioners*, 33, 143–147.

Hwang, A., Peng, L., Wen, Y., Tsai, Y., Chang, L., Chiou, S. and Chen, L. (2014). Predicting all-cause and cause specific mortality by static and dynamic measurements of allostatic load: A 10-year population-based cohort study in Taiwan. *Journal of the American Medical Directors Association*, 15, 490–496

Jacobs, N., Myin-Germeys, I., Derom, C., Delespaul, P., van Os, J. and Nicolson, N.A. (2007). A momentary assessment study of the relationship between affective and adrenocortical stress responses in daily life. *Biological Psychology*, 74, 60–66.

Janz, N.K. and Becker, M.H. (1984). The health belief model: A decade later. *Health Education Quarterly*, 11, 1–47.

Jenkins, C.D., Zyzanski, S.J. and Rosenman, R.H. (1971). Progress toward validation of a computer-scored test for the type a coronary-prone behaviour pattern. *Psychosomatic Medicine*, 33, 193–202.

Jenkins, V., Fallowfield, L. and Saul, J. (2001). Information needs of patients with cancer: Results from a large study in UK cancer centres. *British Journal of Cancer*, 84, 48–51.

Jensen, M.D., Ryan, D.H., Apovian, C.M., Ard, J.D., Comuzzie, A.G., Donato, K.A. for the Obesity Society. (2014). 2013 AHA/ACC/TOS guideline for the management of overweight and obesity in adults: A report of the American College of Cardiology/American Heart Association Task Force on Practice Guidelines and The Obesity Society. *Journal of the American College of Cardiology*, 63(25, Pt B), 2985–3023.

Jensen, M.P. and Turk, D.C. (2014). Contributions of psychology to the understanding and treatment of people with chronic pain: Why it matters to ALL psychologists. *American Psychologist*, 69, 105–118.

John, O.P. and Srivastava, S. (1999). The Big Five trait taxonomy: History, measurement and theoretical perspectives. In L.A. Pervin and O.P. John (eds) *Handbook of Personality: Theory and Research* (2nd edn). New York: Guilford Press, 102–138.

Johnson, E.J. and Goldstein, D. (2003). Do defaults save lives? *Science*, 302, 1338–1339.

Johnson, J.V. and Hall, E.M. (1988). Job strain, work place social support and cardiovascular disease: A cross-sectional study of a random sample of the working population. *American Journal of Public Health*, 78, 1336–1342.

Jokela, M., Hintsanen, M., Hakulinen, C., Batty, G.D., Nabi, H., Singh-Manoux, A. and Kivimaki, M. (2013a). Association of personality with the development and persistence of obesity: A meta-analysis based on individual-participant data. *Obesity Reviews*, 14, 315–323.

Jokela, M., Batty, G.D., Nyberg, S.T., Virtanen, M., Nabi, H., Singh-Manoux, A. and Kivimaki, M. (2013b). Personality and all-cause mortality: Individual-participant meta-analysis of 3,947 deaths in 76,150 adults. *American Journal of Epidemiology*, 178, 667–675.

Jones, F. and Kinman, G. (2001). Approaches to studying stress. In F. Jones and J. Bright (eds) *Stress: Myth, Theory and Research*. London: Prentice Hall, 17–45.

Jones, S.L., Jones, P.K. and Katz, J. (1988b). Health belief model intervention to increase compliance with emergency department patients. *Medical Care*, 26, 1172–1184.

Jones, F., Kinman, G. and Payne, N. (2006). Work stress and health behaviours: A work–life balance issue. In F. Jones, R.J. Burke and M. Westman (eds) *Work–Life Balance: A Psychological Perspective*. Hove: Psychology Press, 185–215.

Jones, F., Bright, J.E.H., Searle, B. and Cooper, L. (1998). Modelling occupational stress and health: The impact of the demand-control model on academic research and on workplace practice. *Stress Medicine*, 14, 231–236.

Jones, F., O'Connor, D.B., Conner, M., McMillan, B. and Ferguson, E. (2007). Effects of daily hassles and eating style on eating behaviour. *Journal of Applied Psychology*, 92, 1731–1740.

Kabat-Zinn, J. (1990). *Full Catastrophe Living: Using the Wisdom of Your Body and Mind to Face Stress, Pain and Illness*. New York: Delacorte.

Kabat-Zinn, J. (2003). Mindfulness based interventions in Context: Past, present and future. *Clinical Psychology: Science and Practice*, 10(2), 144–156.

Kahneman, D. (2011). *Thinking, Fast and Slow*. St Ives, UK: Clays.

Kalat, J.W. (2009). *Biological Psychology*. New York: Thomson Wadsworth.

Kalichman, S.C., Benotsch, E.G., Weinhardt, L., Austin, J., Luke, W. and Cherry, C. (2003). Health-related internet use, coping, social support and health indicators in people living with HIV/AIDS: Preliminary results from a community survey. *Health Psychology*, 22, 111–116.

Kamarck, T.W. and Lovallo, W.R. (2003). Cardiovascular reactivity to psychological challenge: Conceptual and measurement considerations. *Psychosomatic Medicine*, 65, 9–21.

Kanner, A.D., Coyne, J.C., Schaefer, C. and Lazarus, R.S. (1981). Comparison of two modes of stress measurement: Daily hassles and uplifts versus major life events. *Journal of Behavioral Medicine*, 4, 1–39.

Kaplan, R.M. (1990). Behavior as the central outcome in health care. *American Psychologist*, 45, 1211–1220.

Kaplan, R.M. and Stone, A.A. (2013). Bringing the laboratory and clinic to the community: Mobile technologies for health promotion and disease prevention. *Annual Review of Psychology*, 64, 471–498.

Kaptchuk T.J. (2009). Placebo controls, exorcisms and the devil. *The Lancet*, 374, 1234–1235.

Karasek, R.A. (1979). Job demands, job decision latitude and mental strain: Implications for job design. *Administrative Science Quarterly*, 24, 285–308.

Karasek, R.A. (1985). *Job Content Questionnaire and User's Guide*. Lowell, MA: Department of Work Environment, University of Massachusetts.

Karasek, R.A. (1989). Control in the workplace and its health related aspects. In S.L. Sauter, J.J. Hurrell and C.L. Cooper (eds) *Job Control and Worker Health*. Chichester: Wiley, 129–160.

Karasek, R.A. and Theorell, T. (1990). *Healthy Work: Stress, Productivity and the Reconstruction of Working Life*. New York: Basic Books.

Kasl, S.V. and Cobb, S. (1966). Health behaviour, illness behavior and sick role behavior. *Archives of Environmental Health*, 12, 246–266.

Kellogg Foundation (2004) *Logic Model Development Guide: Using Logic Models to Bring Together Planning, Evaluation and Action* (2nd edn). Battle Creek, MI: Kellogg Foundation.

Kendler, K.S., Kessler, R.C., Walters, E.E., Maclean, C., Neale, M.C., Heath, A.C. and Eaves, L.J. (1995). Stressful life events, genetic liability and onset of an episode of major depression in women. *American Journal of Psychiatry*, 152, 833–842.

Kendrick, A.H., Higgs, C.M., Whitfield, M.J. and Laszlo, G. (1993). Accuracy of perception of severity of asthma: Patients treated in general practice. *British Medical Journal*, 14, 422–424.

Kennedy, A., Reeves, D. and Bower, P. (2007) The effectiveness and cost–effectiveness of a national lay-led self care support programme for patients with long-term conditions: A pragmatic randomized controlled trial. *Journal of Epidemiology and Community Health*, 61, 254–261.

Kennedy, H., Landor, M. and Todd. L. (eds) (2011). *Video Interaction Guidance: A Relationship-Based Intervention to Promote Attunement, Empathy and Well-being*. London: Jessica Kingsley.

Kern, M.L. and Friedman, H.S. (2008). Do conscientious individuals live longer? A quantitative review. *Health Psychology*, 27, 505–512.

Kessler, D.A. (2009). *The End of Overeating: Taking Control of the Insatiable American Appetite*. Emmaus, PA: Rodale.

Kessler, R.C. (1997). The effects of stressful life events on depression. *Annual Review of Psychology*, 48, 191–214.

Khaw, K.T., Wareham, N., Bingham, S., Welch, A., Luben, R. and Day, N. (2008). Combined impact of health behaviours and mortality in men and women: The EPIC-Norfolk prospective population study. *PLOS Medicine*, 5.

Kidd, J., Marteau, T.M., Robinson, S., Ukoumunne, O.C. and Tydeman, C. (2004). Promoting patient participation in consultations: A randomized controlled trial to evaluate the effectiveness of three patient-focused interventions. *Patient Education and Counseling*, 52, 107–112.

Kiecolt-Glaser, J.K., Marucha, P.T., Malarkey, W.B., Mercado, A.M. and Glaser, R. (1995). Slowing of wound healing by psychological stress. *The Lancet*, 346, 1194–1196.

Kiecolt-Glaser, J.K., Page, G.G., Marucha, P.T., MacCallum, R.C. and Glaser, R. (1998). Psychological influences on surgical recovery: Perspectives from psychoneuroimmunology. *American Psychologist*, 53, 1209–1218.

Kiecolt-Glaser, J.K., McGuire, L., Robles, T. and Glaser, R. (2002). Emotions, morbidity and mortality: New perspectives from psychoneuroimmunology. *Annual Review of Psychology*, 53, 83–107.

Kiesler, S. and Kraut, R. (1999). Internet use and ties that bind. *American Psychologist*, 54, 783–784.

King, C.M., Rothman, A.J. and Jeffery, R.W. (2002). The challenge study: Theory-based interventions for smoking and weight-loss. *Health Education Research*, 17, 522–530.

King, J.B. (1982). The impact of patients' perceptions of high blood pressure on attendance at screening: An extension of the health belief model. *Social Science and Medicine*, 16, 1079–1091.

Kirsch, I. and Sapirstein, G. (1998). Listening to prozac but hearing placebo: A meta-analysis of antidepressant medication. *Prevention and Treatment*, 1, 0002a.

Kirschbaum, C., Pirke, K.M. and Hellhammer, D.H. (1993). The 'Trier Social Stress Test': A tool for investigating psychobiology stress responses in a laboratory setting. *Neuro-psychobiology*, 28, 76–81.

Kivimaki, M., Leino-Arjas, P., Luukonen, R., Riihimaki, H., Vahtera, J. and Kirjonen, J. (2002). Work stress and risk of cardiovascular mortality: Prospective cohort study of industrial employees. *British Medical Journal*, 325, 1386.

Kivimaki, M., Nyberg, S.T., Batty, G.D., Fransson, E.I., Alfredsson, L., Bjorner, J.B., Borritz, M., Burr, H., Casini, A., Clays, E., De Bacquer, D., Dragano, N., Ferrie, J.E., Geuskens, G.A., Goldberg, M., Hamer, M., Hooftman, W.E., Houtman, I.L. and Joensuu, M. (2012). Job strain as a risk factor for coronary heart disease: A collaborative meta-analysis of individual participant data. *The Lancet*, 380, 1491–1497.

Knott, D., Muers, S. and Aldridge, S. (2007). *Achieving Culture Change: A Policy Framework*. London: Cabinet Office, Prime Minister's Strategy Unit.

Knowler, W.C., Barrett-Connor, P.H.E. and Fowler, S.E. (2002). Reduction in the incidence of type 2 diabetes with lifestyle intervention or metformin. *New England Journal of Medicine*, 346, 393–403.

Knowles, E.S. and Rinner, D.D. (2007). Omega approaches to persuasion: Overcoming resistance. In A.R. Pratkanis (ed.) *The Science of Social Influence: Advances and Future Progress*. New York: Psychology Press, 83–114.

Kok, G., Gottlieb, N.H., Peters, G.J.Y., Mullen, P.D., Parcel, G.S., Ruiter, R.A.C., Fernández, M.E., Markham, C. and Bartholomew, L.K. (2015). A taxonomy of behaviour change methods: An intervention mapping approach. *Health Psychology Review*. doi: 10.1080/17437199.2015.1077155.

Kola, S., Walsh, J.C., Hughes, B.M. and Howard, S. (2013). Matching intra-procedural information with coping style reduces psychophysiological arousal in women undergoing colposcopy. *Journal of Behavioural Medicine*, 36, 401–412.

Kolk, A., Hanewald, G.J.F.P., Schagen, S. and Gijsbers van Wijk, C.M.T. (2003). A symptom perception approach to common physical symptoms. *Social Science and Medicine*, 57, 2343–2354.

Kools, M. (2012). Making written materials easy to understand. In C. Abraham and M. Kools (eds) *Writing Health Communication: An Evidence-Based Guide for Professionals*. London: Sage.

Kools, M., Van de Wiel, M.W.J., Ruiter, R.A.C., Crüts, A. and Kok, G. (2006). The effect of graphic organizers on subjective and objective comprehension of a health education text. *Health Education and Behavior*, 33, 760–772.

Korsch, B.M., Gozzi, E.K. and Francis, V. (1968). Gaps in doctor–patient communication: Doctor–patient interaction and patient satisfaction. *Pediatrics*, 42, 855–871.

Kouvonen, A., Kivimaki, M., Väänänen, A., Heponiemi, T., Elovainio, M., Ala-Mursula, L., Virtanen, M., Pentti, J., Linna, A. and Vahtera, J. (2007). Job strain and adverse health behaviours: The Finnish public sector study. *Journal of Occupational and Environmental Medicine*, 49, 68–74.

Kraft, T.L. and Pressman, S.D. (2012). Grin and bear it: The influence of manipulated positive facial expression on the stress response. *Psychological Science*, 23, 1372–1378.

Kraut, R., Patterson, M., Lundmark, V., Kiesler, S., Mukopadhyay, T. and Scherlis, W. (1998). Internet paradox: A social technology that reduces social involvement and psychological well-being. *American Psychologist*, 53, 1017–1031.

Kraut, R., Kiesler, S., Boneva, B., Cummings, J.N., Helgeson, V. and Crawford, A.M. (2002). Internet paradox revisited. *Journal of Social Issues*, 58, 49–74.

Kunz, A.H. and Pfaff, D. (2002). Agency theory, performance evaluation and the hypothetical construct of intrinsic motivation. *Accounting, Organizations and Society*, 27, 275–295.

Kunz-Ebrecht, S.R., Mohamed-Ali, V., Feldman, P.J., Kirschbaum, C. and Steptoe, A. (2003). Cortisol responses to mild psychological stress are inversely associated with proinflammatory cytokines. *Brain, Behavior and Immunity*, 17, 373–383.

Kushner, R.F. and Foster, G.D. (2000). Obesity and quality of life. *Nutrition*, 16, 947–952.

Lake. A., Browne, J., Ress, G., Abraham, C. and Speight, J. (2015). *Developing Tailored Messages to Reduce the Risk of Vision Loss and Blindness in Adults with Young-Onset Type 2 Diabetes: A Mixed Methods Study*. Vancouver: World Diabetes Congress.

Lawrence, N.S., Verbruggen, F., Morrison, S., Adams, R.C. and Chambers, C.D. (2015). Stopping to food can reduce intake: Effects of stimulus-specificity and individual differences in dietary restraint. *Appetite*, 85, 91–103.

Lazarus, R.S. (1966). *Psychological Stress and the Coping Process*. New York: McGraw-Hill.

Lazarus, R.S. (1990). Theory-based stress measurement. *Psychological Inquiry*, 1, 3–13.

Lazarus, R.S. (1993). Coping theory and research: Past, present and future. *Psychosomatic Medicine*, 55, 234–247.

Lazarus, R.S. (1999). *Stress and Emotion: A New Synthesis*. London: Springer.

Lazarus, R.S. (2001). Conservation of resources theory (COR): Little more than words masquerading as a new theory. *Applied Psychology: An International Review*, 50, 381–391.

Lazarus, R.S. and Folkman, S. (1984). *Stress, Appraisal and Coping*. New York: Springer.

Lazarus, R.S., Kanner, A.D. and Folkman, S. (1980). Emotions: A cognitive-phenomenological analysis. In R. Plutchik and H. Kellerman (eds) *Theories of Emotion*. New York: Academic Press, 189–217.

LeShan, L. (1959). Psychological states as factors in the development of malignant disease. *Journal of the National Cancer Institute*, 22, 1–18.

Lessard, J. and Holman, E.A. (2014). FKBP5 and CRHRi polymorphisms moderate the stress–physical health association in a national sample. *Health Psychology*, 33, 1046–1056.

Leventhal, H., Nerenz, D.R. and Steele, D.J. (1984). Illness representation and coping with health threats. In A. Baum, S.E. Taylor and J.E. Singer (eds) *Handbook of Psychology and Health*. Hillsdale, NJ: Lawrence Erlbaum, 219–252.

Leventhal, H., Benyamini, Y., Brownlee, S., Diefenbach, M., Leventhal, E.A., Parker-Miller, L. and Le Robitail, C. (1997). Illness representations: Theoretical foundations. In K.J. Petrie and J. Weinman (eds) *Perceptions of Health and Illness: Current Research and Applications*. Amsterdam: Harwood Academic, 19–45.

Levine, J.D., Gordon, N. and Fields, H.L. (1978). The mechanism of placebo analgesia. *The Lancet*, 23, 654–657.

Levy, B.R., Slade, M.D., Kunkel, S.R. and Kasl, S.V. (2002). Longevity increased by positive self-perceptions of aging. *Journal of Personality and Social Psychology*, 83, 261–270.

Ley, P. (1973). Communication in the clinical setting. *British Journal of Orthodontics*, 1, 173–177.

Ley, P. (1988) *Communicating with the Patient*. London: Croom Helm.

Ley, P., Whitworth, M., Skilbeck, C., Woodward, R., Pinsent, R. and Pike, L. (1976). Improving doctor–patient communications in general practice. *Journal of the Royal College of General Practitioners*, 26, 720–724.

Liang, J., Krause, N.M. and Bennett, J.M. (2001). Social exchange and well-being: Is giving better than receiving? *Psychology and Aging*, 16, 511–523.

Linden, W., Rutledge, T. and Con, A. (1998). A case for the usefulness of laboratory social stressors. *Annals of Behavioral Medicine*, 20, 310–316.

Litt, M.D., Tennen, H., Affleck, G. and Klock, S. (1992). Coping and cognitive factors in adaptation to in vitro fertilization failure. *Journal of Behavioral Medicine*, 15, 171–188.

Littell, J.H. and Girvin, H. (2002). Stages of change: A critique. *Behavior Modification*, 26, 223–273.

Little, P., Everitt, H., Williamson, I., Warner, G., Moore, M., Gould, C., Ferrier, K. and Payne, S. (2001). Observational study of effect of patient centredness and positive approach on outcomes of general practice consultations. *British Medical Journal*, 323, 908–911.

Locke, E.A (1991). Goal theory vs. control theory: Contrasting approaches to understanding work motivation. *Motivation and Emotion*, 15, 9–28.

Locke, E.A. and Latham, G.P. (2002). Building a practically useful theory of goal setting and task motivation. A 35-year odyssey. *American Psychologist*, 57, 705–717.

Lockwood, P., Wong, C., McShane, K. and Dolderman, D. (2005). The impact of positive and negative fitness exemplars on motivation. *Basic and Applied Social Psychology*, 27, 1–13.

Long, B.C. and Flood, K.R. (1993). Coping with work stress: Psychological benefits of exercise. *Work and Stress*, 1, 108–119.

Lorig, K., Mazonson, P.D. and Holman, H.R. (1993). Evidence suggesting that health education for self-management in patients with chronic arthritis has sustained health benefits while reducing health care costs. *Arthritis and Rheumatism*, 36, 439–446.

Lorig, K., Gonzalez, V.M. and Laurent, D. (1999b). *The Chronic Disease Self-Management Workshop Leaders' Manual*. Stanford, CA: Stanford Patient Education Research Center, Stanford University.

Lorig, K., Sobel, D., Stewart, S., Brown, B., Bandura, A., Ritter, P., Gonzalez, V., Laurent, D. and Holman, H.R. (1999a). Evidence suggesting that a chronic disease self-management program can improve health status while reducing hospitalization: A randomized trial. *Medical Care*, 37, 5–14.

Lumley, M.A., Tojek, T.M. and MacKlem, D.J. (1999). The effects of written emotional disclosure among repressive and alexithymic people. In S.L. LePore and J.M. Smyth (eds) *The Writing Cure*. Washington, DC: American Psychological Association, 75–117.

Luszczynska, A. and Schwarzer, R. (2005). Social cognitive theory. In M. Conner and P. Norman (eds) *Predicting Health Behaviour: Research and Practice with Social Cognition Models* (2nd edn). Maidenhead: Open University Press, 127–169.

Luszczynska, A. and Schwarzer, R. (2015). Social cognitive theory and the health action approach. In M. Conner and P. Norman (eds) *Predicting and Changing Health Behaviour: Research and Practice with Social Cognition Models* (3rd edn). Maidenhead: Open University Press, 225–251.

Luszczynska, A., Sobczyk, A. and Abraham, C. (2007). Planning to lose weight: RCT of an implementation intention prompt to enhance weight reduction among overweight and obese women. *Health Psychology*, 26, 507–512.

McCabe, P.M., Schneiderman, N., Field, T. and Wellens, A.R. (eds) (2000). *Stress, Coping and Cardiovascular Disease*. Mahwah, NJ: Lawrence Erlbaum.

McCrae, R.R. and Costa, P.T. (1987). Validation of the five-factor model of personality across instruments and observers. *Journal of Personality and Social Psychology*, 54, 81–90.

McCabe, R.R. and Priebe, S. (2004). The therapeutic relationship in the treatment of severe mental illness: A review of methods and findings. *International Journal of Social Psychiatry*, 50(2), 115–128.

McEachan, R.R.C., Conner, M., Taylor, N.J. and Lawton, R.J. (2011). Prospective prediction of health-related behaviours with the theory of planned behaviour: A meta-analysis. *Health Psychology Review*, 5, 97–144.

McEwen, B.S. (1998). Protective and damaging effects of stress mediators. *New England Journal of Medicine*, 338, 171–179.

McEwen, B.S. (2007). Physiology and neurobiology of stress and adaptation: Central role of the brain. *Physiological Reviews*, 87, 873–904.

McEwen, B.S. and Stellar, E. (1993). Stress and the individual: Mechanisms leading to disease. *Archives of Internal Medicine*, 153, 2093–2101.

McGowan, L., Luker, K., Creed, F. and Chew-Graham, C.A. (2007). How do you explain a pain that can't be seen?: The narratives of women with chronic pelvic pain and their disengagement with the diagnostic cycle. *British Journal of Health Psychology*, 12, 261–274.

McGuire, J.F., Piacentini, J., Brennan, E.A., Lewin, A.B., Murphy, T.K., Small, B.J. and Storch, E.A. (2014). A meta-analysis of behaviour therapy for Tourette Syndrome. *Journal of Psychiatric Research*, 50, 106–112.

Mackenbach, J.P. (2006). *Health Inequalities: Europe in Profile*. Report commissioned by UK Presidency of the EU. London: Department of Health.

McLeod, J. and McLeod, J. (2001). How effective is workplace counselling? A review of the research literature. *Counselling and Psychotherapy Research*, 1, 184–190.

McNeil, A.D., Jarvis, M.J., Stapleton, J.A., Russell, M.A.H., Eiser, J.R., Gammage, P. and Gray, E.M. (1988). Prospective study of factors predicting uptake of smoking in adolescents. *Journal of Epidemiology and Community Health*, 43, 72–78.

McWilliam, C.L. (2009). Patients, persons or partners? Involving those with chronic disease in their care. *Chronic Illness*, 5(4), 277–292.

Maddux, J.E. and Rogers, R.W. (1983). Protection motivation and self-efficacy: A revised theory of fear appeals and attitude change. *Journal of Experimental Social Psychology*, 19, 469–479.

Maio, G.R. and Haddock, G. (2015). *The Psychology of Attitudes and Attitude Change*. London: Sage.

Major, D.A. and Germano, L.M. (2006). The changing nature of work and its impact on the work–family interface. In F. Jones, R.J. Burke and M. Westman (eds) *Work–Life Balance: A Psychological Perspective*. Hove: Psychology Press, 13–38.

Major, V.S., Klein, K.J. and Ehrhart, M.G. (2002). Work time, work interference with family and psychological distress. *Journal of Applied Psychology*, 87, 427–436.

Manuck, S.B., Kaplan, J.R. and Clarkson, T.B. (1983). Behaviourally induced heart rate reactivity and atherosclerosis in cynomolgus monkeys. *Psychosomatic Medicine*, 45, 95–108.

Marlatt, G.A. and Donovan, D.M. (eds) (2005). *Relapse Prevention: Maintenance Strategies in the Treatment of Addictive Behaviors*. New York: The Guilford Press.

Marmot, M.G., Davey-Smith, G.M., Stansfield, S., Patel, C., North, F., Head, J., White, I., Brunner, E. and Feeney, A. (1991). Health inequalities among British civil servants: The Whitehall II study. *The Lancet*, 337, 1387–1393.

Marteau, T.M., Ogilvie, D., Martin, R., Suhrcke, M. and Kelly, M.P. (2011). Judging nudging: Can nudging improve population health? *British Medical Journal*, 342, d228.

Martin, R., Hewstone, M. and Martin, P.Y. (2007). Majority versus minority influence: The role of message processing in determining resistance to counter-persuasion. *European Journal of Social Psychology*, 38, 16–34.

Marucha, P.T., Kiecolt-Glaser, J.K. and Favagehi, M. (1998). Mucosal wound healing is impaired by examination stress. *Psychosomatic Medicine*, 60, 362–365.

Maslach, C. (1982). Understanding burnout: Definitional issues in analyzing a complex phenomenon. In W.S. Paine (ed.) *Job Stress and Burnout*. Beverley Hills, CA: Sage, 29–40.

Maslin, M.A. and Christensen, B. (2007). Tectonics, orbital forcing, global climate change and human evolution in Africa: Introduction to the African paleoclimate special volume. *Journal of Human Evolution*, 53, 443–464.

Mason, J.W. (1971). A re-evaluation of the concept of 'non-specificity' in stress theory. *Journal of Psychiatric Research*, 8, 323–353.

Matarazzo, J.D. (1980) Behavioral health and behavioural medicine: Frontiers for a new health psychology. *American Psychologist*, 35, 807–817.

Matthews, K.A. (1988). Coronary heart disease and type A behaviour: Update on and alternative to the Booth-Kewley and Friedman (1987) quantitative review. *Psychological Bulletin*, 104, 373–380.

Matthews, K.A. and Gump, B.B. (2002). Chronic work stress and marital dissolution increase risk of post-trial mortality in men from the multiple risk factor intervention trial. *Archives of Internal Medicine*, 162, 309–315.

Matthews, K.A., Woodall, K.L., Kenyon, K. and Jacob, T. (1996). Negative family environment as a predictor of boys' future status on measures of hostile attitudes, interview behaviour and anger expression. *Health Psychology*, 15, 30–37.

Matthews, K.A., Katholi, C.R., McCreath, H., Whooley, M.A., Williams, D.R., Zhu, S. and Markovitz, J.H. (2004). Blood pressure reactivity to psychological stress predicts hypertension in the CARDIA Study. *Circulation*, 110, 74–78.

Mazure, C.M. (1998). Life stressors as risk factors in depression. *Clinical Psychology: Science and Practice*, 5, 291–313.

Meissner, M. (1971). The long arm of the job: A study of work and leisure. *Industrial Relations*, 10, 239–423.

Melzack, R. (1999). From the gate to the neuromatrix. *Pain*, Suppl. 6, 121–126.

Melzack, R. and Wall, P.D. (1965). Pain mechanisms: A new theory. *Science*, 50, 971–979.

Merz, E.L., Fox, R.S. and Malcarne, V.L. (2014). Expressive writing interventions in cancer patients: A systematic review. *Health Psychology Review*, 8, 339–361.

Michel, A., Bosch, C. and Rexroth, M. (2014). Mindfulness as a cognitive-emotional segmentation strategy: An intervention promoting work–life balance. *Journal of Occupational Psychology*, 87, 733–754.

Michie, S. and Abraham, C. (eds) (2004). *Health Psychology in Practice*. Oxford: Blackwell.

Michie, S., Mills, J. and Weinman, J. (2003). Patient-centredness in chronic illness: What is it and does it matter? *Patient Education and Counselling*, 51, 197–206.

Michie, S., Johnston, M. and Abraham, C. (2004). Health psychology training: The UK model. In S. Michie and C. Abraham (eds) *Health Psychology in Practice*. Oxford: Blackwell, 9–45.

Michie, S., Abraham, C., Whittington, C., McAteer, J. and Gupta, S. (2009). Effective techniques in healthy eating and physical activity interventions: A meta-regression. *Health Psychology*, 28, 690–701.

Michie, S., Ashford, S., Sniehotta, F.F., Dombrowski, S.U., Bishop, A. and French, D.P. (2011). A refined taxonomy of behaviour change techniques to help people change their physical activity and healthy eating behaviours: The CALO-RE taxonomy. *Psychology and Health*, 26, 1479–1498.

Michie, S., Richardson, M., Johnston, M., Abraham, C., Francis, J., Hardeman, W., Eccles, M.P., Cane, J. and Wood, C.E. (2013). The behavior change technique taxonomy (v1) of 93 hierarchically clustered techniques: Building an international consensus for the reporting of behavior change interventions. *Annals of Behavioral Medicine*, 46, 81–86.

Mielewczyk, F. and Willig, C. (2007). Old clothes and an older look: The case for a radical makeover in health behaviour research. *Theory Psychology*, 17, 811–837.

Milgram, S. (1974). *Obedience to Authority: An Experimental View*. New York: Harper & Row.

Miller, G.A. Galanter, E. and Pribam, K.H. (1960). *Plans and the Structure of Behavior*. New York: Holt, Rinehart & Winston.

Miller, G.E., Cohen, S. and Ritchey, A.K. (2002). Chronic psychological stress and the regulation of pro-inflammatory cytokines: A glucocorticoid resistance model. *Health Psychology*, 21, 531–541.

Miller, G.E., Chen, E. and Parker, K.J. (2011). Psychological stress in childhood and susceptibility to the chronic diseases of aging: Moving towards a model of behavioural and biological mechanisms. *Psychological Bulletin*, 137, 959–997.

Miller, S.M. and Mangan, C.E. (1983). Interacting effects of information and coping style in adapting to gynecologic stress: Should the doctor tell all. *Journal of Personality and Social Psychology*, 45, 223–236.

Miller, S.M., Summerton, J. and Brody, D.S. (1988). Styles of coping with threat: Implications for health. *Journal of Personality and Social Psychology*, 54, 142–148.

Miller, T.Q., Turner, C.W., Tindale, R.S., Posavac, E.J. and Dugoni, B.L. (1991). Reasons for the trend towards null findings in research on type A behaviour. *Psychological Bulletin*, 110, 469–485.

Miller, T.Q., Smith, T.W., Turner, C.W., Guijarro, M.L. and Hallet, A.J. (1996). A meta-analytic review of research on hostility and physical health. *Psychological Bulletin*, 119, 322–348.

Milne, S., Orbell, S. and Sheeran, P. (2002). Combining motivational and volitional interventions to promote exercise participation: Protection motivation theory and implementation intentions. *British Journal of Health Psychology*, 7, 163–184.

Mo, P.K.H. and Coulson, N.S. (2012). Developing a model for online support group use, empowering processes and psychosocial outcomes for individuals living with HIV/AIDS. *Psychology and Health*, 27, 445–449.

Mokdad, A.H., Marks, J.S., Stroup, D.F. and Gerberding, J.L. (2004). Actual causes of death in the United States, 2000. *Journal of the American Medical Association*, 291, 1238–1245.

Moncrieff, J. and Kirsch, I. (2005). Efficacy of antidepressants in adults. *British Medical Journal*, 331, 155–157.

Montgomery, P., Grant, S., Hopewell, S., Macdonald, G., Moher, D., Michie, S. and Mayo-Wilson, E. (2013). Protocol for CONSORT-SPI: An extension for social and psychological interventions. *Implementation Science*, 8, 99.

Moore, G., Audrey, S., Barker, M., Bond, L., Bonell, C., Hardeman, W., Moore, L., O'Cathain, A., Tinati, T., Wight, D. and Baird, J. (2014). *Process Evaluation of Complex Interventions: Medical Research Council Guidance*. London: MRC Population Health Science Research Network.

Morisky, D.E., Green, L.W. and Levine, D.M. (1986). Concurrent and predictive validity of a self-report measure of medication adherence. *Medical Care*, 24, 67–74.

Morledge, T.J., Allexandre, D., Fox, E., Fu, A.Z., Higashi, M.K., Kruzikas, D.T., Pham, S.V. and Reese, P.R. (2013). Feasibility of an online mindfulness program for stress management: A randomized control trial. *Annals of Behavioral Medicine*, 46, 137–148.

Morley, S., Eccleston, C. and Williams, A. (1999). Systematic review and meta-analysis of randomized controlled trials of cognitive behaviour therapy and behaviour therapy for chronic pain in adults, excluding headache. *Pain*, 80, 1–13.

Moscovici, S. (1976). *Social Influence and Social Change*. London: Academic Press.

Moscovici, S. and Lage, E. (1976). Studies in social influence III: Majority versus minority influence in a group. *European Journal of Social Psychology*, 6, 149–174.

Moskowitz, J.T., Epel, E.S. and Acree, M. (2008). Positive affect uniquely predicts lower risk of mortality in people with diabetes. *Health Psychology*, 27, S73–S82.

Mostofsky, E., Maclure, M., Sherwood, J.B., Tofler, G.H., Muller, J.E. and Mittleman, M.A. (2012). Risk of acute myocardial infarction after the death of a significant person in one's life: The determinants of myocardial infarction onset study. *Circulation*, 125, 491–496.

Mullen, P.D. (1997). Compliance becomes concordance. *British Medical Journal*, 314, 691–692.

Mund, M. and Mitte, K. (2012). The costs of repression: A meta-analysis on the relations between repressive coping and somatic diseases. *Health Psychology*, 31(5), 640–649.

Murcott, T. (2005). The *Whole Story; Alternative Medicine on Trial?* (2nd edn). Basingstoke: Macmillan.

Murphy, L.R. (2003). Stress management at work: Secondary prevention of stress. In M.J. Schabracq, J.A.M. Winnubst and C.L. Cooper (eds) *The Handbook of Work and Health Psychology* (2nd edn). Chichester: Wiley, 533–548.

Murray, M. and Chamberlain, K. (eds) (1999). *Qualitative Health Psychology: Theories and Methods.* London: Sage.

Myers, L.B. and Midence, K. (1998). Concepts and issues in adherence. In L.B. Myers and K. Midence (eds) *Adherence to Treatment in Medical Conditions.* Amsterdam: Harwood Academic, 1–24.

Myers, L.B., Vetere, A. and Derakshan, N. (2004). Are suppression and repressive coping related? *Personality and Individual Differences*, 36, 1009–1013.

Myrtek, M. (2001). Meta-analyses of prospective studies on coronary heart disease, type A personality and hostility. *International Journal of Cardiology*, 79, 245–251.

Nater, U.M., Hoppmann, C.A. and Scott, S.B. (2013). Diurnal profiles of salivary cortisol and alpha-amylase change across the adult lifespan: Evidence from repeated daily life assessments. *Psychoneuroendocrinology*, 38, 3167–3171.

National Audit Office (2002). *NHS Direct in England: Report by the Comptroller and Auditor General.* London: The Stationery Office.

National Institute for Clinical Excellence (2004). *Depression: Management of Depression in Primary and Secondary Care. Clinical Practice Guideline No. 23.* London: NICE.

National Institute for Health and Clinical Excellence (NICE) (2007). *Behaviour Change at Population, Community and Individual Levels. Public Health Guidance No. 6.* London: NICE.

National Institute for Health and Clinical Excellence (NICE) (2014). *Behaviour Change: Individual Approaches. Public Health Guidance No. 49.* London: NICE.

Nazarian, D. and Smyth, J. (2013). An experimental test of instructional manipulations in expressive writing interventions: Examining processes of change. *Journal of Social and Clinical Psychology*, 32, 71–96.

Nebel, L.E., Howell, R.H., Krantz, D.S., Falconer, J.J., Gottdiener, J.S. and Gabbay, F.H. (1996). The circadian variation of cardiovascular stress levels and reactivity: Relationship to individual differences in morningness/eveningness. *Psychophysiology*, 33, 273–281.

Neisser, U. (1967). *Cognitive Psychology.* New York: Appleton-Century-Crofts.

Netterstrom, B., Friebel, L. and Ladegaard, Y. (2013) Effects of a multidisciplinary stress treatment programme on patient return to work and symptom reduction: Results from a randomized, wait-list controlled trial. *Psychotherapy and Psychosomatics*, 82, 177–186.

Newman, E., O'Connor, D.B. and Conner, M. (2007). Daily hassles and eating behaviour: The role of cortisol reactivity status. *Psychoneuroendocrinology*, 32, 125–132.

Newton, T.L. and Contrada, R.J. (1992). Repressive coping and verbal–autonomic response dissociation: The influence of social context. *Journal of Personality and Social Psychology*, 62, 159–167.

Nezlek, J.B. (2001). Multilevel random coefficient analyses of event- and interval-contingent data in social and personality psychology research. *Personality and Social Psychology Bulletin*, 27, 771–785.

Niaura, R., Herbert, P.N., McMahon, N. and Sommerville, L. (1992). Repressive coping and blood lipids in men and women. *Psychosomatic Medicine*, 54, 698–706.

Nielsen, M.B., Mearns, K., Matthiesen, S.B. and Eid, J. (2011).Using the job demands–resources model to investigate risk perception, safety climate and job satisfaction in safety critical organizations. *Scandinavian Journal of Psychology*, 52, 465–475.

Nielsen, N.R. and Brøenbæk, M. (2006). Stress and breast cancer: A systematic update on current knowledge. *Nature Clinical Practice Oncology*, 3, 612–620.

NIOSH (2010). What is OHP? Retrieved 14 February 2016 from www.cdc.gov/niosh/topics/ohp/#what

Noar, S.M., Hall, M.G., Francis, D.B., Ribisl, K.M., Pepper, K.J. and Brewer, N. (2015). Pictorial cigarette pack warnings: A meta-analysis of experimental studies. *Tobacco Control*, Online First. 6 May 2015, doi: 10.1136/tobaccocontrol-2014–051978

Norman, P. and Parker, S. (1996). The interpretation of change in verbal reports: Implications for health psychology. *Psychology and Health*, 11, 301–314.

Norman, P. and Conner, M. (2015). Predicting and changing health behaviour: Future directions. In M. Conner and P. Norman (eds) *Predicting and Changing Health Behaviour: Research and Practice with Social Cognition Models* (3rd edn). Maidenhead: Open University Press, 390–430.

Norman, P., Boer, H. and Seydel, E.R. (2005). Protection motivation theory. In M. Conner and P. Norman (eds) *Predicting Health Behaviour: Research and Practice with Social Cognition Models* (2nd edn). Maidenhead: Open University Press, 81–126.

Norman, P., Boer, H., Seydel, R. and Mullan, B. (2015). Protection motivation theory. In M. Conner and P. Norman (eds) *Predicting and Changing Health Behaviour: Research and Practice with Social Cognition Models* (3rd edn). Maidenhead: Open University Press, 70–105.

O'Brien, T.B. and Delongis, A. (1996). The interactional context of problem-, emotion-and relationship-focused coping: The role of the big five personality factors. *Journal of Personality*, 64, 775–811.

O'Connor, D.B. and O'Connor, R.C. (2004). Perceived changes in food intake in response to stress: The role of conscientiousness. *Stress and Health*, 20, 279–291.

O'Connor, D.B. and Ashley, L. (2008). Are alexithymia and emotional characteristics of disclosure associated with blood pressure reactivity and psychological distress following written emotional disclosure? *British Journal of Health Psychology*, 13, 495–512.

O'Connor, D.B., Ferguson, E. and O'Connor, R.C. (2005). Intentions to use hormonal male contraception: The role of message framing, attitudes and stress appraisals. *British Journal of Psychology*, 96, 351–369.

O'Connor, D.B., O'Connor, R.C. and Marshall, R. (2007). Perfectionism and psychological distress: Evidence of the mediating effects of rumination. *European Journal of Personality*, 21, 429–452.

O'Connor, D.B., Armitage, C.J. and Ferguson, E. (2015). Randomized test of an implementation intention-based tool to reduce stress-induced eating. *Annals of Behavioral Medicine*, 49, 331–343.

O'Connor, D.B., O'Connor, R.C., White, B.L. and Bundred, P.E. (2000a). Job strain and ambulatory blood pressure in British general practitioners: A preliminary study. *Psychology, Health and Medicine*, 5, 241–250.

O'Connor, D.B., O'Connor, R.C., White, B.L. and Bundred, P.E. (2000b). The effect of job strain on British general practitioners' mental health. *Journal of Mental Health*, 9, 637–654.

O'Connor, D.B., Jones, F., Conner, M., McMillan, B. and Ferguson, E. (2008a). Effects of daily hassles and eating style on eating behaviour. *Health Psychology*, 27, S20–S31.

O'Connor, D.B., Corona, G., Forti, G. and the EMAS study group (2008b). Assessment of sexual health in ageing men in Europe: Development and validation of the European male ageing study (EMAS) sexual function questionnaire (EMAS-SFQ). *Journal of Sexual Medicine*, 5, 1374–1385.

O'Connor, D.B., Conner, M., Jones, F., McMillan, B. and Ferguson, E. (2009). Exploring the benefits of conscientiousness: An investigation of the role of daily stressors and health behaviors. *Annals of Behavioral Medicine*, 37, 184–196.

O'Connor, D.B., Walker, S., Hendrickx, H., Talbot, D. and Schaefer, A. (2013). Stress-related thinking predicts the cortisol awakening response and somatic symptoms in healthy adults. *Psychoneuroendocrinology*, 38, 438–446.

O'Connor, D.B., Hurling, R., Hendrickx, H., Osborne, G., Hall, J., Walklet, E., Whaley, A. and Wood, H. (2011a). Effects of written emotional disclosure on implicit self-esteem and body image. *British Journal of Health Psychology*, 16, 488–501.

O'Connor, D.B., Lee, D.M., Corona, G., Forti, G., Tajar, A., O'Neill, T.W., Pendleton, N., Bartfai, G., Boonen, S., Casanueva, F.F., Finn, J.D., Giwercman, A., Han, T.S., Huhtaniemi, I.T., Kula, K., Labrie, F., Lean, M.E.J., Punab, M., Silman, A.J., Vanderschueren, D., Wu, F.C.W. and the EMAS study group. (2011b). The relationships between sex hormones and sexual function in middle-aged and elderly European men. *Journal of Clinical Endocrinology and Metabolism*, 96, E1577–1587.

O'Connor, R.C. and O'Connor, D.B. (2003). Predicting hopelessness and psychological distress: The role of perfectionism and coping. *Journal of Counseling Psychology*, 50, 362–372.

O'Driscoll, M. Brough, P. and Kalliath, T. (2006). Work–family conflict and facilitation. In F. Jones, R.J. Burke and M. Westman (eds) *Work–Life Balance: A Psychological Perspective*. Hove: Psychology Press, 117–142.

Oettingen, G. (1996). Positive fantasy and motivation. In P.M. Gollwitzer and J.A. Bargh (eds) *The Psychology of Action: Linking Cognition and Motivation to Behavior*. New York: Guilford Press, 236–259.

The Office for National Statistics (2014). *Conceptions in England and Wales, 2012: Statistical Bulletin*. Retrieved 23 March 2016 from www.ons.gov.uk/ons/rel/vsob1/conception-statistics--england-and-wales/2012/2012-conceptions-statistical-bulletin.html

Ogden, J. (2003). Some problems with social cognition models: A pragmatic and conceptual analysis. *Health Psychology*, 22, 424–428.

O'Keefe, D.J. and Jensen, J.D. (2009). The relative persuasiveness of gain-framed and loss-framed messages for encouraging disease detection behaviors: A meta-analytic review. *Journal of Communication*, 59, 296–316.

O'Keefe, D.J. and Nan, X. (2012). The relative persuasiveness of gain- and loss-framed messages for promoting vaccination: A meta-analytic review. *Health Communication*, 27, 776–777.

Ong, A.D., Bergeman, C.S., Bisconti, T.L. and Wallace, K.A. (2006). Psychological resilience, positive emotions and successful adaptation to stress in later life. *Journal of Personality and Social Psychology*, 91, 730–749.

Orbell, S. and Hagger, M.S. (2006). Temporal framing and the decision to take part in type 2 diabetes screening: Effects of individual differences in consideration of future consequences on persuasion. *Health Psychology*, 25, 537–548.

Orbell, S., Crombie, I. and Johnston, G. (1995). Social cognition and social structure in the prediction of cervical screening uptake. *British Journal of Health Psychology*, 1, 35–50.

Orbell, S., Perugini, M. and Rakow, T. (2004). Individual differences in sensitivity to health communications: Consideration of future consequences. *Health Psychology*, 23, 388–396.

Ormell, J. and Wohlfarth, T. (1991). How neuroticism, long-term difficulties and life situation change influence psychological distress: A longitudinal model. *Journal of Personality and Social Psychology*, 60, 744–755.

Ozer, D.J. and Benet-Martinez, V. (2006). Personality and the prediction of consequential outcomes. *Annual Review of Psychology*, 57, 401–421.

Parkes, K.R. (1991). Locus of control as a moderator: An explanation for additive versus interactive findings in the demand-discretion model of work stress? *British Journal of Psychology*, 82, 291–312.

Paulussen, T., Kok, G. and Schaalma, H. (1994). Antecedents of adoption of classroom-based HIV-education in secondary schools. *Health Education Research*, 9, 485–496.

Pavlov, I.P. (1927). *Conditional Reflexes*. Oxford: Oxford University Press.

Payne, S. (2004). Designing and conducting qualitative studies. In S. Michie and C. Abraham (eds) *Health Psychology in Practice*. Oxford: Blackwell, 126–149.

Payne, S., Large, S., Jarrett, N. and Turner, P. (2000). Written information given to patients and families by palliative care units: A national survey. *The Lancet*, 355, 1792.

Pendleton, D., Schofield, T., Tate, P. and Havelock, P. (1984). *The Consultation: An Approach to Learning and Teaching*. Oxford: Oxford University Press.

Penley, J.A. and Tomaka, J. (2002). Associations among the Big Five: Emotional responses and coping with acute stress. *Personality and Individual Differences*, 32, 1215–1228.

Pennebaker, J.W. (1997). Writing about emotional experiences as a therapeutic process. *Psychological Science*, 8, 162–166.

Peterson, C. (2000). The future of optimism. *American Psychologist*, 55, 44–55.

Peterson, C. and Seligman, M.E.P. (1987). Explanatory style and illness. *Journal of Personality*, 55, 237–265.

Peterson, C., Vaillant, G.E. and Seligman, M.E.P. (1988) Pessimistic explanatory style is a risk factor for physical illness: A 35-year longitudinal study. *Journal of Personality and Social Psychology*, 55, 23–27.

Petrie, K.J., Booth, R.J., Pennebaker, J.W., Davison, K.P. and Thomas, M.G. (1995). Disclosure of trauma and immune response to a hepatitis B vaccination program. *Journal of Consulting and Clinical Psychology*, 63, 787–792.

Petrie, K.J., Fontanilla, I., Thomas, M.G., Booth, R.J. and Pennebaker, J.W. (2004). Effect of written emotional expression on immune function in patients with human immunodeficiency virus infection: A randomized trial. *Psychosomatic Medicine*, 66, 272–275.

Petticrew, M.P., Lee, K. and McKee, M. (2012). Type A behaviour pattern and coronary heart disease: Philip Morris's 'Crown Jewel'. *Public Health Ethics*, 102, 2019–2025.

Petty, R.E. and Cacioppo, J.T. (1986). The elaboration likelihood model of persuasion. In L. Berkowitz (ed.) *Advances in Experimental Social Psychology*. New York: Academic Press, 19, 123–205.

Phillips, A.C., Ginty, A.T. and Hughes, B.M. (2013). The other side of the coin: Blunted cardiovascular and cortisol reactivity are associated with negative health outcomes. *International Journal of Psychophysiology*, 90, 1–7.

Piacentini, J., Woods, D.W., Scahill, L., Wilhelm, S., Peterson, A.L., Chang, S., Ginsburg, G.S., Deckersbach, T., Dziura, J., Levi-Pearl, S. and Walkup, J.T. (2010). Behavior therapy for children with Tourette disorder: A randomized controlled trial. *Journal of the American Medical Association*, 303, 1929–1937.

Piet, J., Wurtzen, H. and Zachariae, R. (2012). The effect of mindfulness-based training on symptoms of anxiety in adult cancer patients and survivors: A systematic review and meta-analysis. *Journal of Consulting and Clinical Psychology*, 6, 1007–1020.

Pittet, D.S. (2002). Promotion of hand hygiene: Magic, hype, or scientific challenge? *Infection Control and Hospital Epidemiology*, 23, 118–119.

Pittet, D.S., Hugonnet, S., Harbarth, S., Mourouga, P., Sauvan, V., Touveneau, S. and Perneger, T.V. (2000). Effectiveness of a hospital-wide programme to improve compliance with hand hygiene. *The Lancet*, 356, 1307–1312.

Pollock, K. (1988). On the nature of social stress: Production of a modern mythology. *Social Science and Medicine*, 26, 381–392.

Popper, K. (1963). *Conjecture and Refutation*. London: Routledge & Kegan Paul.

Porcelli, P., Tulipani, C., Maiello, E., Cilenti, G. and Todarello, O. (2007). Alexithymia, coping and illness behaviour correlates of pain experience in cancer patients. *Psycho-oncology*, 16, 644–650.

Porter, M. (2004). Deciding to consult. In B. Alder, M. Porter, C. Abraham and E. van Teijlingen (eds) *Psychology and Sociology: Applied to Medicine* (2nd edn). Edinburgh: Churchill Livingstone, 86–87.

Power, R.A., Wingenbach, T., Cohen-Woods, S., Uher, R., Ng, M.Y., Butler, A.W., Ising, M., Craddock, N., Owen, M.J., Korszun, A., Jones, L., Jones, I., Gill, M., Rice, J.P., Maier, W., Zobel, A., Mors, O., Placentino, A., Rietschel, M., Lucae, S., Holsboer, F., Binder, E.B., Keers, R., Tozzi, F., Muglia, P., Breen, G., Craig, I.W., Müller-Myhsok, B., Kennedy, J.L., Strauss, J., Vincent, J.B., Lewis, C.M., Farmer, A.E. and McGuffin, P. (2013). Estimating the heritability of reporting stressful life events captured by common genetic variants. *Psychological Medicine*, 43, 1965–1971.

Pratkanis, A.R. (2007). Social influence analysis: An index of tactics. In A.R. Pratkanis (ed.) *The Science of Social Influence: Advances and Future Progress*. New York: Psychology Press, 17–82.

Pressman, S.D. and Cohen, S. (2005). Does positive affect influence health? *Psychological Bulletin*, 131, 925–971.

Prestwich, A., Conner, M., Lawton, R., Ward, J., McEachan, R. and Ayres, K. (2012). Randomized controlled trial of collaborative implementation intentions targeting working adults' physical activity. *Health Psychology*, 31, 486–495.

Prestwich, A., Sheeran, P., Webb, T. and Gollwitzer, P. (2015). Implementation intentions. In M. Conner and P. Norman (eds) *Predicting and Changing Health Behaviour: Research and Practice with Social Cognition Models* (3rd edn). Maidenhead: Open University Press, 321–357.

Prime Minister's Strategy Unit (2004). *Personal Responsibility and Changing Behaviour: The State of Knowledge and its Implications for Public Policy.* London: HMSO.

Prochaska, J.O. and DiClemente, C.C. (1984). *The Transtheoretical Approach: Crossing Traditional Boundaries of Therapy.* Homewood, IL: Dow Jones Irwin.

Prochaska, J.O., DiClemente, C.C. and Norcross, J.C. (1992). In search of how people change: Applications to addictive behaviors. *American Psychologist,* 47, 1102–1114.

Prochaska, J.O., Velicer, W.F., Guadagnoli, E., Rossi, J.S. and DiClemente, C.C. (1991). Patterns of change: Dynamic topology applied to smoking cessation. *Multivariate Behavioral Research,* 26, 83–107.

Proper, K.I., Koning, M., van der Beck, A.J., Hildebrandt, V.H., Bosscher, R.J. and van Mechelen, W. (2003). The effectiveness of worksite psychical activity programs on physical activity, fitness and health. *Clinical Journal of Sport Medicine,* 13, 106–117.

Protheroe, D., Turvey, K., Horgan, K., Benson, E., Bowers, D. and House, A. (1999). Stressful life events and difficulties and onset of breast cancer: Case control study. *British Medical Journal,* 319, 1027–1030.

Quitkin, F.M., Rabkin, J.G., Gerald, J., Davis, J.M. and Klein, D.F. (2000). Validity of clinical trials of antidepressants. *American Journal of Psychiatry,* 157, 327–337.

Rabin, B.S. (1999). *Stress, Immune Function and Health: The Connection.* New York: Wiley.

Ragland, D.R. and Brand, R.J. (1985). Coronary heart disease mortality in the western collaborative group study: Follow-up experience of 22 years. *American Journal of Epidemiology,* 127, 462–475.

Rahe, R.H. and Paasikivi, J. (1971). Psychosocial factors and myocardial infarction: An outpatient study in Sweden. *Journal of Psychosomatic Research,* 8, 35–44.

Randall, R., Griffiths, A. and Cox, T. (2005). Evaluating organizational stress-management interventions using adapted study designs. *European Journal of Work and Organizational Psychology,* 14, 23–41.

Rank, S.G. and Jacobson, C.K. (1977). Hospital nurses' compliance with medication over-dose orders: A failure to replicate. *Journal of Health and Social Behavior,* 18, 188–193.

Reed, G.M., Kemeny, M.E., Taylor, S.E., Wang, H.Y.J. and Vissher, B.R. (1994). Realistic acceptance as a predictor of decreased survival time in gay men with AIDS. *Health Psychology,* 13, 299–307.

Reid, L.D. and Christensen, D.B. (1988). A psychosocial perspective in the explanation of patients' drug-taking behaviour. *Social Science and Medicine,* 27, 277–285.

Repetti, R.L. and Wood, J. (1997). Effects of daily stress at work on mothers' interactions with preschoolers. *Journal of Family Psychology,* 11, 90–108.

Reynolds, J.S. and Perrin, N.A. (2004). Mismatches in social support and psychosocial adjustment to breast cancer. *Health Psychology,* 23, 425–430.

Reynolds, K.J and Branscombe, N.R. (2015). *Psychology of Change.* New York: Psychology Press.

Rhodes, R.E., Courneya, K.S. and Hayduk, L.A. (2002). Does personality moderate the theory of planned behaviour in the exercise domain? *Journal of Sport and Exercise Psychology,* 24, 120–132.

Riazi, A., Pickup, J. and Bradley, C. (2004). Daily stress and glycaemic control in Type 1 diabetes: Individual differences in magnitude, direction and timing of stress-reactivity. *Diabetes Research and Clinical Practice*, 66, 237–244.

Richardson, K.M. and Rothstein, H.R. (2008). Effects of occupational stress management intervention programs: A meta-analysis. *Journal of Occupational Health Psychology*, 13, 69–93.

Rietveld, S. and Prins, P.J.M. (1998). The relationship between negative emotions and acute subjective and objective symptoms of childhood asthma. *Psychological Medicine*, 28, 407–415.

Rivis, A. and Sheeran, P. (2003). Descriptive norms as an additional predictor in the theory of planned behaviour: A meta-analysis. *Current Psychology: Developmental, Learning, Personality, Social*, 22, 218–233.

Robinson, E.J. and Whitfield, M.J. (1985). Improving the efficacy of patients' comprehension monitoring: A way of increasing patients' participation in general practice consultations. *Social Science Medicine*, 21, 915–919.

Rodgers, W., Conner, M. and Murray, T. (2008). Distinguishing among perceived control, perceived difficulty and self-efficacy as determinants of intentions and behaviours. *British Journal of Social Psychology*, 47, 607–630.

Rodrigues, A.M., O'Brien, N., French, D.P., Glidewell, L., Sniehotta, F.F. (2015). The question–behavior effect: genuine effect or spurious phenomenon? A systematic review of randomized controlled trials with meta-analyses. *Health Psychology*, 34, 61–78.

Roediger, H.L. III and Karpicke, J.D. (2006). The power of testing memory: Basic research and implication for educational practice. *Perspectives on Psychological Science*, 1, 181–210.

Rogers, E.M. (2003). *Diffusion of Innovations* (5th edn). New York: Free Press.

Rollnick, S. and Miller, W.R. (1995). What is motivational interviewing? *Behavioural and Cognitive Psychotherapy*, 23, 325–334.

Rook, J.W. and Zijlstra, F.R.H. (2006). The contribution of various types of activities to recovery. *European Journal of Work and Organizational Psychology*, 15, 218–240.

Rook, K.S. (1984). The negative side of social interaction: Impact on psychological well-being. *Journal of Personality and Social Psychology*, 46, 1097–1108.

Rosen, M.I., Rigsby, M.O., Salahi, J.T., Ryan, E. and Cramer, J.A. (2004). Electronic monitoring and counseling to improve medication adherence. *Behaviour Research and Therapy*, 42, 409–422.

Rosenman, R.H., Friedman, M., Straus, R., Wurm, M., Kositchek, R., Hahn, W. and Werthessen, N.T. (1964). A predictive study of coronary heart disease. *Journal of the American Medical Association*, 189, 15–22.

Rosenman, R.H., Brand, R.J., Sholtz, R.I. and Friedman, M. (1976). Multivariate prediction of coronary heart disease during 8.5-year follow-up in the western collaborative group study. *American Journal of Cardiology*, 37, 903–910.

Rosenstock, I.M., Strecher, V.J. and Becker, M.H. (1988). Social learning theory and the health belief model. *Health Education Quarterly*, 15, 175–183.

Rosenthal, R. and Rubin, D.B. (1982). A simple general purpose display of magnitude of experimental effect. *Journal of Educational Psychology*, 74, 166–169.

Roter, D.L., Hall, J.A., Merisca, R., Nordstrom, B., Cretin, D. and Svarstad, B. (1998). Effectiveness of interventions to improve patient compliance: A meta-analysis. *Medical Care*, 36, 1138–1161.

Rothman, A.J. (2000). Toward a theory-based analysis of behavioral maintenance. *Health Psychology*, 19, 64–69.

Rothman, A.J. and Salovey, P. (1997). Shaping perceptions to motivate healthy behavior: The role of message framing. *Psychological Bulletin*, 121, 3–19.

Rothman, A., Salovey, P., Antone, C., Keough, K. and Martin, C. (1993). The influence of message framing on intentions to perform health behaviors. *Journal of Experimental Social Psychology*, 29, 408–433.

Rovelli, M., Palmeri, D., Vossler, E., Bartus, S., Hull, D. and Schweizer, R. (1989). Compliance in organ transplant recipients. *Transplantation Proceedings*, 21, 833–844.

Ruiter, R.A.C., Abraham, C. and Kok, G. (2001). Scary warnings and rational precautions: A review of the psychology of fear appeals. *Psychology and Health*, 16, 613–630.

Rutledge, T. and Hogan, B.E. (2002). A quantitative review of prospective evidence linking psychological factors with hypertension development. *Psychosomatic Medicine*, 64, 758–766.

Rutledge, T., Linke, S.E., Olson, M.B., Francis, J., Johnson, B.D., Bittner, V., York, K., McClure, C., Kelsey, S.F., Reis, S.E., Cornell, C.E., Vaccarino, V., Sheps, D.S., Shaw, L.J., Krantz, D.S., Parashar, S. and Merz, C.N. (2008). Social networks and incident stroke among women with suspected myocardial ischemia. *Psychosomatic Medicine*, 70, 282–287.

Sackett, D.L. and Snow, J.C. (1979). The magnitude of compliance and non-compliance. In R.B. Haynes, D.W. Taylor and D.L. Sackett (eds) *Compliance in Health Care*. Baltimore, MD: Johns Hopkins University Press, 11–22.

Sapolsky, R.M. (1993). Endocrinology alfresco: Psychoendocrine studies of wild baboons. *Recent Progress in Hormone Research*, 48, 437–468.

Sarafino, E. (2008). *Health Psychology: Biopsychosocial Interaction* (6th edn). New York: Wiley.

Sargent, R.P., Shepard, R.M. and Glantz, S.A. (2004). Reduced incidence of admissions for myocardial infarction associated with public smoking ban: Before and after study. *British Medical Journal*, 328, 977–980.

Savage, R. and Armstrong, D. (1990). Effects of a general practitioner's consulting style on patients' satisfaction: A controlled study. *British Medical Journal*, 301, 968–970.

Schaalma, H.P., Abraham, C., Gillmore, M.R. and Kok, G. (2004). Sex education as health promotion: What does it take? *Archives of Sexual Behaviour*, 33, 259–269.

Scharloo, M., Kaptein, A.A., Weinman, J.A., Willems, L.N.A. and Rooijmans, H.G.M. (2000). Physical and psychological correlates of functioning in patients with chronic obstructive pulmonary disease. *Journal of Asthma*, 37, 17–29.

Schaufeli, W.B., Leiter, M.P. and Maslach, C. (2009). Burnout: 35 years of research and practice. *Career Development International*, 14, 204–220.

Scheier, M.F. and Carver, C.S. (1987). Dispositional optimism and physical well-being: The influence of generalized outcome expectations on health. *Journal of Personality*, 55, 169–210.

Scheier, M.F. and Carver, C.S. (1992). Effects of optimism on psychological and physical well-being: Theoretical overview and empirical update. *Cognitive Therapy and Research*, 16, 201–228.

Scheier, M.F., Weintraub, J.K. and Carver, C.S. (1986). Coping with stress: Divergent strategies of optimists and pessimists. *Journal of Personality and Social Psychology*, 51, 1257–1264.

Scheier, M.F., Matthews, K.A., Owens, J., Magovern, G.J., Sr., Lefebvre, R.C., Abbott, R.A. and Carver, C.S. (1989). Dispositional optimism and recovery from coronary artery bypass surgery: The beneficial effects of physical and psychological well-being. *Journal of Personality and Social Psychology*, 57, 1024–1040.

Scheier, M.F., Matthews, K.A., Owens, J.Schulz, R., Bridges, M.W., Magovern, G.J. and Carver, C.S. (1999). Optimism and rehospitalization after coronary artery bypass graft surgery. *Archives of Internal Medicine*, 159, 829–835.

Schinke, S.P. and Gordon, A.N. (1992). Innovative approaches to interpersonal skills training for minority adolescents. In R.J. DiClemente (ed.) *Adolescents and AIDS: A Generation in Jeopardy*. Newbury Park, CA: Sage, 181–193.

Schneider, G.M., Jacobs, D.W., Gevirtz, R.N. and O'Connor, D.T. (2003). Cardiovascular haemodynamic response to repeated mental stress in normotensive subjects at genetic risk of hypertension: Evidence of enhanced reactivity, blunted adaptation and delayed recovery. *Journal of Human Hypertension*, 17, 829–840.

Schuler, J.L. and O'Brien, W.H. (1997). Cardiovascular recovery from stress and hypertension risk factors: A meta-analytic review. *Psychophysiology*, 34, 649–665.

Schulz, K.F., Altman, D.G., Moher, D. and the CONSORT Group. (2010). CONSORT 2010 statement: Updated guidelines for reporting parallel group randomized trials. *British Medical Journal*, 340, c332.

Schulz, P., Schlotz, W. and Becker, P. (2011) [2004]. *The Trier Inventory of Chronic Stress (TICS): Manual* (Trans. W. Schlotz, supported by Google Translate). Göttingen, Germany: Hogrefe.

Schulz, R., Czaja, S.J., McKay, J.R., Ory, M.G. and Belle, S.H. (2010). Intervention taxonomy (ITAX): Describing essential features of interventions (HMC). *American Journal of Health Behavior*, 34, 811–821.

Schwartz, G.E. (1980). Testing the biopsychosocial model: The ultimate challenge facing behavioural medicine? *Journal of Consulting and Clinical Psychology*, 50, 1040–1053.

Schwartz, J.E., Neale, J., Marco, C., Shiffman, S.S. and Stone, A.A. (1999). Does trait coping exist? A momentary assessment approach to the evaluation of traits. *Journal of Personality and Social Psychology*, 77, 360–369.

Schwartz, M.D., Taylor, K.L., Willard, K.S., Siegel, J.E., Lamdan, R.M. and Moran, K. (1999). Distress, personality and mammography utilization among women with a family history of breast cancer. *Health Psychology*, 18, 327–332.

Schwarzer, R. (2001). Stress, resources and proactive coping. *Applied Psychology: An International Review*, 50, 400–407.

Schwarzer, R. (2008). Modeling health behaviour change: How to predict and modify the adoption and maintenance of health behaviours. *Applied Psychology: An International Review*, 57, 1–29.

Sears, S.R., Stanton, A.L. and Danoff-Burg, S. (2003). The yellow brick road and the emerald city: Benefit finding, positive reappraisal coping and post-traumatic growth in women with early-stage breast cancer. *Health Psychology*, 22, 487–497.

Seelig, D., Wang A-L., Jaganathan, K., Loughead, J.W., Blady, S.J., Childress, A.R., Romer, D. and Langleben, D.D. (2014). Low message sensation health promotion videos are better remembered and activate areas of the brain associated with memory encoding. *PLoS ONE,* 9(11), e113256.

Segerstrom, S.C. and O'Connor, D.B. (2012). Stress, health and illness: Four challenges for the future. *Psychology and Health,* 27, 128–140.

Segerstrom, S.C., Taylor, S.E., Kemeny, M.E. and Fahey, J.L. (1998). Causal attributions predict rate of immune decline in HIV-seropositive gay men. *Health Psychology,* 15, 485–493.

Seligman, M.E.P. and Csikszentmihalyi, M. (2000). Positive psychology: An introduction. *American Psychologist,* 55, 5–14.

Selye, H. (1950). Stress and the general adaptation syndrome. *British Medical Journal,* 1, 1383–1392.

Selye, H. (1956). *The Stress of Life.* New York: McGraw-Hill.

Shankar, A., McMunn, A., Banks, J. and Steptoe, A. (2011). Loneliness, social isolation and behavioral and biological health indicators in older adults. *Health Psychology,* 30, 377–385.

Shankar, A., Hamer, M., McMunn, A. and Steptoe, A. (2013). Social isolation and loneliness: Relationships with cognitive function during 4 years of follow-up in the English longitudinal study of ageing. *Psychosomatic Medicine,* 75, 161–170.

Sheeran, P. (2012). *The Impact of Changing Attitudes, Norms and Self-Efficacy on Health-Related Intentions and Behavior: A Meta-Analysis,* 29th European Health Psychology Society Conference, Limassol, Cyprus.

Sheeran, P. and Orbell, S. (2000). Using implementation intentions to increase attendance for cervical cancer screening. *Health Psychology,* 19, 283–289.

Sheeran, P. and Abraham, C. (2003). Mediator of moderators: Temporal stability of intention and the intention–behaviour relationship. *Personality and Social Psychology Bulletin,* 29, 205–215.

Sheeran, P., Abraham, C. and Orbell, S. (1999). Psychosocial correlates of heterosexual condom use: A meta-analysis. *Psychological Bulletin,* 125, 90–132.

Sheeran, P., Conner, M. and Norman, P. (2001). Can the theory of planned behaviour explain patterns of behaviour change? *Health Psychology,* 20, 12–19.

Sheeran, P., Aubrey, R. and Kellett, S. (2007). Increasing attendance for psychotherapy: Implementation intentions and the self-regulation of attendance-related negative affect. *Journal of Consulting and Clinical Psychology,* 75, 853–863.

Sheeran, P., Milne, S., Webb, T.L. and Gollwitzer, P.M. (2005). Implementation intentions and health behaviours. In M. Conner and P. Norman (eds) *Predicting Health Behaviour: Research and Practice with Social Cognition Models* (2nd edn). Maidenhead: Open University Press, 276–323.

Sher, L. (2004). Daily hassles, cortisol and the pathogenesis of depression. *Medical Hypotheses,* 62, 198–202.

Sherif, M. (1936). *The Psychology of Social Norms.* New York: Harper.

Sherman, D.A.K., Nelson, L.D. and Steele, C.M. (2000). Do messages about health risks threaten the self? Increasing the acceptance of threatening health messages via self-affirmation. *Personality and Social Psychology Bulletin,* 26, 1046–1058.

Sherman, S.J. (1980). On the self-erasing nature of errors of prediction. *Journal of Personality and Social Psychology,* 39, 211–221.

Shipley, B.A., Weiss, A., Der, G., Taylor, M.D. and Deary, I.J. (2007). Neuroticism, extraversion and mortality in the UK health and lifestyle survey: A 21-year prospective cohort study. *Psychosomatic Medicine*, 69, 923–931.

Shultz, S. and Maslin, M. (2013). Early human speciation, brain expansion and dispersal influenced by African climate pulses. *PLoS ONE*, 8(10), e76750.

Siegel, P.A., Post, C., Brockner, J., Fishman, A.Y. and Garden, C. (2005). The moderating influence of procedural fairness on the relationship between work–life conflict and organizational commitment. *Journal of Applied Psychology*, 90, 13–24.

Siegler, I.C., Feaganes, J.R. and Rimer, K. (1995). Predictors of adoption of mammography in women under age 50. *Health Psychology*, 14, 274–278.

Siegrist, J. (1996). Adverse health effects of high-effort/low-reward conditions. *Journal of Occupational Health Psychology*, 1, 27–41.

Siegrist, J. (2002). Effort–reward imbalance at work and health. *Historical and Current Perspectives on Stress and Health*, 2, 261–291.

Siegrist, J. (2005). Effort reward imbalance at work. Institut für Medizinische Soziologie der Heinrich Heine Universität Düsseldorf. Retrieved 14 February 2016 from www.uniklinik-duesseldorf.de/unternehmen/institute/institut-fuer-medizinische-soziologie/forschung-research/the-eri-model-stress-and-health/theoretical-background-of-the-effort-reward-imbalance-model

Silverman, J., Kurtz, S. and Draper, J. (2005). *Skills for Communicating with Patients* (2nd edn). Oxford: Radcliffe Medical Press.

Simera, I., Moher, D., Hoey, J., Schulz, K.F. and Altman, D.G. (2013). A catalogue of reporting guidelines for health research. *European Journal of Clinical Investigation*, 40, 35–53.

Simpson, M., Buckman, R., Stewart, M., Maguire, P., Lipkin, M., Novack, D. and Till, J. (1991). Doctor–patient communication: The Toronto consensus statement. *British Medical Journal*, 303, 1385–1387.

Skinner, B.F. (1938). *The Behavior of Organisms*. New York: Appleton-Century-Crofts.

Skinner, B.F. (1974). *About Behaviorism*. New York: Knopf.

Skinner, E.A., Edge, K., Altman, J. and Sherwood, H. (2003). Searching for the structure of coping: A review and critique of category systems for classifying ways of coping. *Psychological Bulletin*, 129, 216–269.

Skinner, T.C., Hampson, S.E. and Fife-Schaw, C. (2002). Personality, personal model beliefs and self-care in adolescents and young adults with type 1 diabetes. *Health Psychology*, 21, 61–70.

Sloan, D.M. and Marx, B.P. (2004). Taking pen to hand: Evaluating theories underlying the written disclosure paradigm. *Clinical Psychology: Science and Practice*, 11, 121–137.

Smith, A., Johal, S., Wadsworth, E. and Britain, G. (2000). *The Scale of Occupational Stress: The Bristol Stress and Health and Work Study*. London: HSE Books.

Smith, J.A. (ed.) (2003). *Qualitative Psychology: A Practical Guide to Research Methods* (2nd edn). London: Sage.

Smith, J.A. and Osborne, M. (2007). Pain as an assault on the self: An interpretative phenomenological analysis. *Psychology and Health*, 22, 517–531.

Smith, T.W. (1994). Concepts and methods in the study of anger, hostility and health. In A.G. Seigman and T.W. Smith (eds) *Anger, Hostility and the Heart*. Hillsdale, NJ: Lawrence Erlbaum, 23–42.

Smith, T.W., Glazer, K., Ruiz, J.M. and Gallo, L.C. (2004). Hostility, anger, aggressiveness and coronary heart disease: An interpersonal perspective on personality, emotion and health. *Journal of Personality*, 72, 1217–1270.

Smyth, J.M. (1998). Written emotional expression: Effect sizes, outcome types and moderating variables. *Journal of Consulting and Clinical Psychology*, 66, 174–184.

Smyth, J.M., Stone, A.A., Hurewitz, A. and Kaell, A. (1999). Effects of writing about stressful experiences on symptom reduction in patients with asthma or rheumatoid arthritis: A randomized trial. *Journal of the American Medical Association*, 281, 1304–1309.

Smyth, J.M., Ockenfels, M.C., Porter, L., Kirschbaum, C., Hellhammer, D.H. and Stone, A.A. (1998). Stressors and mood measured on a momentary basis are associated with salivary cortisol secretion. *Psychoneuroendocrinology*, 23, 353–370.

Sniehotta, F.F., Presseau, J. and Araujo-Soares, V. (2014). Time to retire the theory of planned behaviour. *Health Psychology Review*, 8, 1–7.

Snow, H. (1893). *Cancer and the Cancer Process*. London: J. & A. Churchill.

Snyder, C.R., Sympson, S.C., Ybasco, F.C., Borders, T.F., Babyak, M.A. and Higgins, R.L. (1996). Development and evaluation of the State Hope Scale. *Journal of Personality and Social Psychology*, 70, 321–335.

Solberg Nes, L. and Segerstrom, S.C. (2006). Dispositional optimism and coping: A meta-analytic review. *Personality and Social Psychology Review*, 10, 235–251.

Somerfield, M.R. (1997). The utility of systems models of stress and coping for applied research. *Journal of Health Psychology*, 2, 133–151.

Song, Z., Foo, M.D., Uy, M.A. and Sun, S. (2011). Unraveling the daily stress crossover between unemployed individuals and their employed spouses. *Journal of Applied Psychology*, 96, 151–68.

Sonnentag, S. and Zijlstra, F.R.H. (2006). Job characteristics and off-job activities as predictors of need for recovery, well-being and fatigue. *Journal of Applied Psychology*, 91, 330–350.

Sonnentag, S., Binnewies, C. and Mojza, E.J. (2008). 'Did you have a nice evening?' A day-level study on recovery experiences, sleep and affect. *Journal of Applied Psychology*, 93, 674–684.

Staines, G.L. (1980). Spillover versus compensation: A review of the literature on the relationship between work and non-work. *Human Relations*, 33, 111–129.

Stajkovic, A.D. and Luthans, D. (1998). Self-efficacy and work-related performance: A meta-analysis. *Psychological Bulletin*, 124, 240–261.

Steele, C.M. (1988). The psychology of self-affirmation: Sustaining the integrity of the self. In L. Berkowitz (ed.) *Advances in Experimental Social Psychology*. San Diego, CA: Academic Press, 261–302.

Steele, G.P., Henderson, S. and Duncan-Jones, P. (1980). The reliability of reporting adverse experiences. *Psychological Medicine*, 10, 301–306.

Steptoe, A. and Marmot, M. (2005). Impaired cardiovascular recovery following stress predicts 3-year increases in blood pressure. *Journal of Hypertension*, 23, 529–536.

Steptoe, A. and Wardle, J. (2005). Positive affect and biological function in everyday life. *Neurobiology of Aging*, 26, S108–S112.

Steptoe, A. and Kivimaki, M. (2013). Stress and cardiovascular disease: An update on current knowledge. *Annual Review of Public Health*, 34, 337–354.

Steptoe, A., Hamer, M. and Chida, Y. (2007). The effects of acute psychological stress on circulating inflammatory factors in humans: A review and meta-analysis. *Brain Behavior and Immunity*, 21, 901–912.

Steptoe, A., Dockray, S. and Wardle, J. (2009). Positive affect and psychobiological processes relevant to health. *Journal of Personality*, 77, 1747–1776.

Steptoe, A., Shankar, A., Demakakos, P. and Wardle, J. (2013). Social isolation, loneliness and the all-cause mortality in older men and women. *Proceedings of the National Academy of Sciences*, 110, 5797–5801.

Stewart, M.A. (1995). Effective physician–patient communication and health outcomes: A review. *Canadian Medical Association Journal*, 152, 1423–1433.

Stewart-Williams, S. (2004). The placebo puzzle: Putting together the pieces. *Health Psychology*, 23, 198–206.

Stone, A.A., Shiffman, S., Schwartz, J.E., Broderick, J.E. and Hufford, M.R. (2002). Patient non-compliance with paper diaries. *British Medical Journal*, 324, 1193–1194.

Stone, J., Aronson, E., Crain, A.L., Winslow, M.P. and Fried, C.B. (1994). Inducing hypocrisy as a means of encouraging young adults to use condoms. *Personality and Social Psychology Bulletin*, 20, 116–128.

Strack, F. and Deutsch, R. (2004). Reflective and impulsive determinants of social behavior. *Personality and Social Psychology Review*, 8, 220–247.

Stronks, K., van de Mheen, H., Looman, C.W.N. and Mackenbach, J.P. (1998). The importance of psychosocial stressors for socioeconomic inequalities in perceived health. *Social Science and Medicine*, 46, 611–623.

Sultan, S., Epel, E., Sachon, C., Vaillant, G. and Hartemann-Heurtier, A. (2008). A longitudinal study of coping, anxiety and glycemic control in adults with type 1 diabetes. *Psychology and Health*, 23, 73–89.

Sutton, S. (1997). Predicting and explaining intentions and behaviour: How well are we doing? *Journal of Applied Social Psychology*, 28, 1317–1338.

Sutton, S. (2000). A critical review of the transtheoretical model applied to smoking cessation. In P. Norman, C. Abraham and M. Conner (eds) *Understanding and Changing Health Behaviour: From Health Beliefs to Self-regulation*. Reading: Harwood Academic Press, 207–225.

Sutton, S. (2005). Stage models of health behaviour. In M. Conner and P. Norman (eds) *Predicting Health Behaviour: Research and Practice with Social Cognition Models* (2nd edn). Maidenhead: Open University Press, 223–275.

Sutton, S. (2015). Stage theories. In M. Conner and P. Norman (eds) *Predicting and Changing Health Behaviour: Research and Practice with Social Cognition Models* (3rd edn). Maidenhead: Open University Press, 279–320.

Sweeney, A.M. and Moyer, A. (2015). Self-affirmation and responses to health messages: A meta-analysis on intentions and behaviour. *Health Psychology*, 34, 149–159.

Swientek, B. (2001). Let them eat cake: Mad cow disease prevention in Europe. Retrieved 7 June 2007 from http://findarticles.com/p/articles/mi_m3289/is_1_170/ai_70204304.

Symmons, D., Turner, G., Webb, R., Barrett, E., Lunt, M., Scott, D. and Silman, A. (2002). The prevalence of rheumatoid arthritis in the United Kingdom: New estimates for a new century. *Rheumatology*, 41, 793–800.

Tarrant, M., Hagger, M.S. and Farrow, C.V. (2011). Social categorization, social consensus and the promotion of health behaviour. In J. Jetten, S.A. Haslam and C. Haslam (eds) *The Social Cure: Identity, Health and Well-Being*. New York: Psychology Press, 39–54.

Taylor, N., Conner, M. and Lawton, R. (2012). The impact of theory on the effectiveness of worksite physical activity interventions: A meta-analysis and meta-regression. *Health Psychology Review*, 6, 33–73.

Temoshok, L., Heller, B.W., Sagabiel, R., Blois, M.S., Sweet, D.M., DiClemente, R.J. and Gold, M.L. (1985). The relationship of psychosocial factors to prognostic indicators in cutaneous malignant melanoma. *Journal of Psychosomatic Research*, 29, 139–154.

Tennen, H., Affleck, G., Coyne, J.C., Larsen, R.J. and DeLongis, A. (2006). Paper and plastic in daily diary research: Comment on Green, Rafaeli, Bolger, Shrout and Reis. *Psychological Methods*, 11, 112–118.

Thaler, R.H. and Sunstein, C. (2008). *Nudge: Improving Decisions About Health, Wealth and Happiness*. New Haven, CT: Yale University Press.

Theorell, T. and Rahe, R.H. (1971). Psychosocial factors and myocardial infarction. *Journal of Psychosomatic Research*, 15, 25–31.

Tolman, E.C. (1948). Cognitive maps in rats and men. *Psychological Review*, 55, 189–208.

Tolmunen, T., Lehto, S.M., Heliste, M., Kurl, S. and Kauhanen, J. (2010). Alexithymia is associated with increased cardiovascular mortality in middle-aged Finnish men. *Psychosomatic Medicine*, 72, 187–191.

Tortolero, S.R., Markham, C.M., Parcel, G.S., Peters, R.J. Jr, Escobar-Chaves, S.L., Basen-Engquist, K. and Lewis, H.L. (2005). Using intervention mapping to adapt an effective HIV, sexually transmitted disease and pregnancy prevention program for high-risk minority youth. *Health Promotion Practice*, 6, 286–298.

Triplett, N. (1898). The dynamogenic factors in pacemaking and competition. *American Journal of Psychology*, 9, 507–533.

Turk, D.C. and Salovey, P. (1986). Clinical information processing: Bias inoculation. In R.E. Ingham (ed.) *Information Processing Approaches to Clinical Psychology*. New York: Academic Press, 305–323.

Turk, D.C. and Burwinkle, T.M. (2000). Clinical outcomes, cost-effectiveness and the role of psychology in treatments for chronic pain sufferers. *Professional Psychology: Research and Practice*, 36, 602–610.

Turk, D.C., Meichenbaum, D. and Genest, M. (1983). *Pain and Behavioural Medicine: A Cognitive-Behavioral Perspective*. New York: Guilford.

Turner, J.C. (1991). *Social Influence*. Buckingham: Open University Press.

Tversky, A. and Kahneman, D. (1981). The framing of decisions and the psychology of choice. *Science*, 211, 453–458.

Twisk, J.W.R., Snel, J., Kemper, H.C.G. and van Mechelen, W. (1999). Changes in daily hassles and life events and the relationship with coronary heart disease risk factors: A 2-year longitudinal study in 27–29-year-old males and females. *Journal of Psychosomatic Research*, 46, 229–240.

Tyler, R. (2001). BSE/'mad cow disease' crisis spreads throughout Europe. Retrieved 7 June 2007 from www.wsws.org/articles/2001/jan2001/bse-j23.shtml

Uchino, B.N. (2009). Understanding the links between social support and physical health: A life-span perspective with emphasis on the separability of perceived and received support. *Perspectives on Psychological Science*, 4, 236–255.

Uchino, B.N., Cacioppo, J.T. and Kiecolt-Glaser, J.K. (1996). The relationship between social support and physiological processes: A review with emphasis on underlying mechanisms and implications for health. *Psychological Bulletin*, 119, 488–531.

Vaananen, A., Buunk, B.P., Kivimaki, M., Pentti, J. and Vahtera, J. (2005). When it is better to give than to receive: Long-term health effects of perceived reciprocity in support exchange. *Journal of Personality and Social Psychology*, 89, 176–193.

van Beurden, S. B., Greaves, C.J., Smith, J.R. and Abraham C. (2016 in press). Techniques for modifying impulsive processes associated with unhealthy eating: A systematic review. *Health Psychology*.

van dem Knesebeck, O. and Siegrist, J. (2003). Reported nonreciprocity of social exchange and depressive symptoms: Extending the model of effort–reward imbalance beyond work. *Journal of Psychosomatic Research*, 55, 209–214.

Van der Doef, M. and Maes, S. (1998). The job demand-control (-support) model and physical outcomes: A review of the strain and buffer hypotheses. *Psychology and Health*, 13, 909–936.

Van der Doef, M. and Maes, S. (1999). The job demand-control (-support) model and psychological well-being: A review of 20 years of empirical research. *Work and Stress*, 13, 87–114.

van der Klink, J.L., Blonk, R.W.B., Schene, A.H. and van Dijk, F.J.H. (2001). The benefits of interventions for work-related stress. *American Journal of Public Health*, 91, 270–276.

van Dongen, A., Abraham, C., Ruiter, R. and Veldhuizen, I. (2013). Does questionnaire distribution promote blood donation? An investigation of question-behavior effects. *Annals of Behavioral Medicine*, 45, 163–172.

van Dulmen, S., Sluijs, E., van Dijk, L., de Ridder, D., Heerdink, R. and Bensing, J. (2007). Patient adherence to medical treatment: A review of reviews. *BMC Health Services Research*, 7, 55.

Van Hooff, M.L.M., Guerts, S.A.E., Beckers, D.G.J. and Kompier, M.A.J. (2011). Daily recovery from work: The role of activities, effort and pleasure. *Work and Stress*, 25, 55–74.

Van Vegchel, N.V., De Jonge, J. and Landsbergis, P.A. (2005). Occupational stress in (inter)action: The interplay between job demands and job resources. *Journal of Organizational Behavior*, 26, 535–560.

Van Vegchel, N.V., De Jonge, J., Meijer, T. and Hamers, J.P.H. (2001). Different effort constructs and effort–reward imbalance: Effects on employee well-being in ancillary health care workers. *Journal of Advanced Nursing*, 34, 128–136.

Vartiainen, E., Paavola, M., McAlister, A. and Puska, P. (1998). Fifteen-year follow-up of smoking prevention effects in the North Karelia Youth Project. *American Journal of Public Health*, 88, 81–85.

Vas, J., Méndez, C., Perea-Milla, E., Vega, E., Panadero, M.D., León, J.M., Borge, M.A., Gaspar, O., Sánchez-Rodríguez, F., Aguilar, I. and Jurado, R. (2004). Acupuncture as a complementary therapy to the pharmacological treatment of osteoarthritis of the knee: Randomized controlled trial. *British Medical Journal*, 329, 1216.

Vedhara, K. and Irwin, M. (2005). *Human Psychoneuroimmunology*. Oxford: Oxford University Press.

Veling, H., Aarts, H. and Stroebe, W. (2013). Using stop signals to reduce impulsive choices for palatable unhealthy foods. *British Journal of Health Psychology*, 18, 354–368.

Verhoeven, J.E., van Oppen, P., Puterman, E., Elzinga, B. and Pennix, B.W. (2015). The association of early and recent psychosocial life stress with leukocyte telomere length. *Psychosomatic Medicine*, 77, 882–891.

Verkuil, B., Brosschot, J.F., Gebhardt, W. and Thayer, J.F. (2010). When worries make you sick: A review of perseverative cognition, the default stress response and somatic health. *Journal of Experimental Psychopathology*, 1, 87–118.

Verkuil, B., Brosschot, J.F., Meerman, E.E. and Thayer, J.F. (2012). Effects of momentary assessed stressful events and worry episodes on somatic health complaints. *Psychology and Health*, 27, 141–158.

Vickers, A. and Zollman, C. (1999). ABC of complementary medicine: The manipulative therapies: Osteopathy and chiropractic. *British Medical Journal*, 319, 1176–1179.

Victor, C.R. and Yang, K. (2012). The prevalence of loneliness among adults: A case study of the United Kingdom. *Journal of Psychology*, 146, 85–104.

Victor, C.R., Scambler, S.J., Bowling, A. and Bond, J. (2005) The prevalence of and risk factors for, loneliness in later life: A survey of older people in Great Britain. *Ageing and Society*, 25, 357–375.

Vollrath, M.E. (ed.) (2006). *Handbook of Personality and Health*. Chichester, UK: Wiley.

Vollrath, M.E, Knoch, D. and Cassano, L. (1999). Personality, risky behaviour and perceived susceptibility to health risks. *European Journal of Personality*, 13, 39–50.

Volpp, K.G., John, L.K., Troxel, A.B., Norton, L., Fassbender, J. and Loewenstein, G. (2008). Financial incentive-based approaches for weight loss: A randomized trial. *Journal of the American Medical Association*, 3000, 2631–2637.

Von Elm, E., Altman, D.G., Egger, M., Pocock, S.J., Gøtzsche, P.C. and Vandenbroucke, J.P. for the STROBE Initiative (2007). The strengthening of the reporting of observational studies in epidemiology (STROBE) statement: Guidelines for reporting observational studies. *PLoS Medicine*, 4, e296.

Waldron, I. (1988). Why do women live longer than men? *Journal of Human Stress*, 2, 2–13.

Waldstein, S.R., Kauhanen, J., Neumann, S.A. and Katzel, L.I. (2002). Alexithymia and cardiovascular risk in older adults: Psychosocial, psychophysiological and biomedical correlates. *Psychology and Health*, 17, 597–610.

Wang, S., Repetti, R.L. and Campos, B. (2011). Job stress and family social behaviour: The moderating role of neuroticism. *Journal of Occupational Health Psychology*, 16, 441–456.

Wanless, D. (2002). *Securing Our Future Health: Taking a Long-Term View.* London: HMSO.

Wardle, J. and Steptoe, A. (1991). The European health and behaviour survey: Rationale, methods and initial results from the United Kingdom. *Social Science and Medicine*, 33, 925–936.

Ware, J.E., Kosinski, M. and Keller, S.D. (1996). A 12-item short-form health survey: Construction of scales and preliminary tests of reliability and validity. *Medical Care*, 34, 220–233.

Warr, P. (1987). *Work, Unemployment and Mental Health.* Oxford: Oxford University Press.

Watson, D. (1988). Intraindividual and interindividual analyses of positive and negative affect: Their relation to health complaints, perceived stress and daily activities. *Journal of Personality and Social Psychology*, 54, 1020–1030.

Watson, D. and Clark, L.A. (1984). Negative affectivity: The disposition to experience aversive emotional states. *Psychological Bulletin*, 96, 465–490.

Watson, D. and Pennebaker, J.W. (1989). Health complaints, stress and distress: Exploring the central role of negative affectivity. *Psychological Review*, 96, 234–254.

Watson, D. and Hubbard, B. (1996). Adaptational style and dispositional structure: coping in the context of the five-factor model. *Journal of Personality*, 64, 737–774.

Webb, T.L. and Sheeran, P. (2006). Does changing behavioural intentions engender behaviour change? A meta-analysis of the experimental evidence. *Psychological Bulletin*, 132, 249–268.

Weber, R.P. (1990). *Basic Content Analysis* (2nd edn). Newbury Park, CA: Sage.

Wegner, D.M. (1994). Ironic processes of mental control. *Psychological Review*, 101, 34–52.

Weinberger, D.A., Schwartz, G.E. and Davidson, R.J. (1979). Low-anxious, high-anxious and repressive coping styles: Psychometric patterns and behavioural and physiological responses to stress. *Journal of Abnormal Psychology*, 88, 369–380.

Wenzlaff, R.M. and Wegner, D.M. (2000). Thought suppression. In S.T. Fiske (ed.) *Annual Review of Psychology*. Palo Alto, CA: Annual Reviews, vol. 51, 59–91.

West, R. (2005). Time for a change: Putting the transtheoretical (stages of change) model to rest. *Addiction*, 100, 1036–1039.

West, R., McNeill, A. and Raw, M. (2000). Smoking cessation guidelines for health professionals: An update. *Thorax*, 55, 987–999.

Whelan, J. (2002). WHO calls for countries to shift from acute to chronic care. *British Medical Journal*, 324, 1237.

White, K. (2000). Psychology and complementary and alternative medicine. *Professional Psychology: Research and Practice*, 31, 671–681.

Whitehead, M. and Dahlgren, G. (1991). What can be done about inequalities in health? *The Lancet*, 338, 1059–1063.

Whitlock, G., Lewington, S., Sherliker, P., Clarke, R., Emberson, J., Halsey, J. (2009). Body-mass-index and cause-specific mortality in 900000 adults: Collaborative analyses of 57 prospective studies. *The Lancet*, 373, 1083–1096.

Whitlock, J.L., Powers, J.L. and Eckenrode, J. (2006). The virtual cutting edge: The internet and adolescent self-injury. *Developmental Psychology*, 42, 407–417.

WHOQOL Group (1995). The World Health Organization Quality of Life Assessment (The WHOQOL): Position paper from the World Health Organization. *Social Science and Medicine*, 41, 1403–1409.

Wiedenfeld, S.A., O'Leary, A., Bandura, A., Brown, S., Levine, S. and Raska, K. (1990). The impact of perceived self-efficacy in coping with stressors on components of the immune system. *Journal of Personality and Social Psychology*, 59, 1082–1094.

Wight, D., Raab, G.M., Henderson, M., Abraham, C., Buston, K., Hart, G. and Scott, S. (2002). Limits of teacher-delivered sex education: Interim behavioural outcomes from randomized trial. *British Medical Journal*, 320, 1243–1244.

Wilkinson, R.G. (1992). National mortality rates: The impact of inequality? *American Journal of Public Health*, 82, 1082–1084.

Wilkinson, R.G. (1996). *Unhealthy Societies: The Afflictions of Inequality*. London: Routledge.

Wilkinson, R.G. (1997). Health inequalities: Relative or absolute material standards? *British Medical Journal*, 314, 591–595.

Williams, K.J. and Alliger, G.M. (1994). Role stressors, mood spillover and perceptions of work–family conflict in employed parents. *Academy of Management Journal*, 37, 837–868.

Williams, L., O'Connor, R.C., Howard, S., Hughes, B.M., Johnston, D.W., Hay, J.L., O'Connor, D.B., Lewis, C.A., Ferguson, E., Sheehy, N., Grealy, M.A. and O'Carroll, R.E. (2008). Type D personality mechanisms of effect: The role of health-related behaviour and social support. *Journal of Psychosomatic Research*, 64, 63–69.

Williams-Piehota, P., Pizarro, J., Schneider, T.R., Mowad, L. and Salovey, P. (2005). Matching health messages to monitor-blunter coping styles to motivate screening mammography. *Health Psychology*, 24, 58–67.

Williams-Piehota, P., Latimer, A.E., Katulak, N.A., Cox, A., Silvera, S.A.N., Nowad, L. and Salovey, P. (2009). Tailoring messages to individual differences in monitoring-blunting styles to increase fruit and vegetable intake. *Journal of Nutrition Education and Behavior*, 41, 398–405.

Willis, T.A., O'Connor, D.B. and Smith, L. (2005). The influence of morningness–eveningness on anxiety and cardiovascular responses to stress. *Physiology and Behavior*, 85, 125–133.

Witte, K. (1992). Putting the fear back into fear appeals: The extended parallel process model. *Communication Monographs*, 59, 329–349.

Witte, K. and Allen, M. (2000). A meta-analysis of fear appeals: Implications for effective public health campaigns. *Health Education and Behavior*, 27, 591–615.

Wittrock, M.C. and Alesandrini, K. (1990). Generation of summaries and analogies and analytic-holistic abilities. *American Educational Research Journal*, 27, 489–502.

Wood, C., Conner, M., Sandberg, T., Taylor, N., Godin, G. and Sheeran, P. (2015). The impact of asking intention or self-prediction questions on subsequent behaviour: A meta-analysis. *Personality and Social Psychology Bulletin*, doi: 10.1177/1088868315592334

Wood, R.E. and Bandura, A. (1989). Impact of conceptions of ability on self-regulatory mechanisms and complex decision making. *Journal of Personality and Social Psychology*, 56, 407–415.

Wood, W., Kallgren, C.A. and Mueller Preisler, R. (1985). Access to attitude-relevant information in memory as a determinant of persuasion: The role of message attributes. *Journal of Experimental Social Psychology*, 21, 73–85.

World Health Organization (1948). Preamble to the Constitution of the World Health Organization as adopted by the International Health Conference, New York, 19–22 June, 1946; signed on 22 July 1946 by the representatives of 61 States (Official Records of the World Health Organization, 2, 100) and entered into force on 7 April 1948.

World Health Organization (2013, March). Obesity and overweight. Fact sheet No. 311. Retrieved 27 August 2013 from www.who.int/mediacentre/factsheets/fs311/en/index.html

Wright, C.C., Barlow, J.H., Turner, A.P. and Bancroft, G.V. (2003). Self-management training for people with chronic disease: An exploratory study. *British Journal of Health Psychology*, 8, 465–476.

Wyatt, K., Lloyd, J., Abraham, C., Creanor, S., Dean, S. and Densham, E. (2013). The Healthy Lifestyles Programme (HeLP), a novel school-based intervention to prevent obesity in school children: Study protocol for a randomized controlled trial. *Trials*, 14, 95.

Xanthopoulou, D., Bakker, A.B., Demerouti, E. and Schaufeli, W.B. (2007). The role of personal resources in the job demand–resources model. *International Journal of Stress Management*, 14, 121–141.

Yates, L.B., Djousse, L., Kurth, T., Buring, J.E. and Gaziano, J.M. (2008). Exceptional longevity in men: Modifiable factors associated with survival and function to age 90 years. *Archives of Internal Medicine*, 168, 284–290.

Zautra, A.J. (2003). *Emotions, Stress and Health*. New York: Oxford University Press.

Zautra, A.J. and Reich, J.W. (2011). Resilience: The meanings, methods and measures of a fundamental characteristic of human adaptation. In S. Folkman (ed.) *The Oxford Handbook of Stress, Health and Coping*. Oxford: Oxford University Press, 173–185.

Zola, I.K. (1973). Pathways to the doctor: From person to patient. *Social Science and Medicine*, 7, 677–689.

Index